The Photographic History of The Civil War

Armies & Leaders

GENERAL JAMES CONNOR   GENERAL JOHN W. GEARY   GENERAL JOHN B. MAGRUDER   GENERAL ROBERT D. LILLEY   GENERAL P. G. T. BEAUREGARD   GENERAL LEWIS WALLACE   GENERAL HENRY A. WISE   GENERAL JOSEPH L. BRENT

BLACQUE BEY   GENERAL R. E. LEE   GEORGE PEABODY   W. W. CORCORAN   JAMES LYONS

"SOLDIERS AND CITIZENS"

ROBERT E. LEE WITH FORMER UNION AND CONFEDERATE LEADERS AFTER THE ARMIES' WORK WAS DONE

By great good fortune this unique photograph, taken at White Sulphur Springs, Virginia, in August, 1869, was preserved more than forty years by a Confederate veteran of Richmond, Mr. James Blair, through whose courtesy it appears here—to sound the key-note of this volume as no preface could. Such a fraternal gathering could have been paralleled after no other great war in history. For in this neighborly group, side by side, are bitter foemen of not five years past. Near the unmistakable figure of Lee stands Lew Wallace, the commander who in 1864 had opposed Lee's lieutenant—Early—at the Monocacy; the division leader who at Shiloh, first grand battle of the war, had fired on the lines in gray commanded by the dashing Confederate general who now touches him on the right—Beauregard. To the left stand Connor and Geary, formerly generals of opposing forces in the Carolinas. There is the tall "Prince John" Magruder, the venerable Henry A. Wise, and other one-time leaders of the Gray. And for a further touch of good citizenship, there is added the distinguished presence of George Peabody of Massachusetts, and W. W. Corcoran of Washington—philanthropists of the noblest type, but not alone in this group "as having helped their fellow men."

The Photographic History of The Civil War
Armies & Leaders

Contributors

ROBERT S. LANIER
Managing Editor

WILLIAM CONANT CHURCH
Brevet Lieutenant-Colonel, U. S. V.; Editor of "The Army and Navy Journal"; Author of "Life of Ulysses S. Grant," "Life of John Ericsson," etc.

WILLIAM PETERFIELD TRENT, LL.D.
Professor of English Literature in Columbia University; Author of "Robert E. Lee," "Southern Statesmen of the Old Regime," etc.

WALTER LYNWOOD FLEMING, PH.D.
Professor of History, Louisiana State University; Author of "Secession and Reconstruction of Alabama," etc.

JOHN E. GILMAN
Commander-in-Chief, Grand Army of the Republic, 1910–1911

ALLEN C. REDWOOD
Artist and Author; Late Army of Northern Virginia; Author of "Johnny Reb Papers," etc.

HILARY A. HERBERT
Late Colonel, Eighth Alabama Infantry; Late Secretary of Navy of the United States

MARCUS J. WRIGHT
Late Brigadier-General, Confederate States Army; Agent for the Collection of War Records, United States War Department

SAMUEL A. CUNNINGHAM
Late Sergeant-Major, Confederate States Army; Founder and Editor of "The Confederate Veteran"

THE FAIRFAX PRESS
New York

This 1983 edition is published by The Fairfax Press,
distributed by Crown Publishers, Inc.

Manufactured in the United States of America

Library of Congress Cataloging in Publication Data
Main entry under title:

The Photographic History of the Civil War. Armies and Leaders.

Reprint. Originally published as v. 10 of: The photographic history of the
Civil War / Francis Trevelyan Miller, editor-in-chief; Robert S. Lanier,
managing editor. 1912, c1911.
1. United States. Army—History—Civil War, 1861–1865.   2. Confederate States
of America. Army—History.   3. Generals—United States—Biography.
4. United States. Army—Biography.   5. Confederate States of America. Army—
Biography.   I. Lanier, Robert S. (Robert Sampson), 1880–
E491.P56   1983   973.7′42   83-1686

ISBN: 0-517-411458

h g f e d c b

CONTENTS

PHOTOGRAPHIC DESCRIPTIONS THROUGHOUT THIS BOOK
  Roy Mason
  George L. Kilmer, Late U. S. V.

FOREWORD

ON April 14, 1861, Fort Sumter underwent a thirty-four-hour bombardment by the Confederate Army. As the fighting drew to a close, Union officer Major Robert Anderson lowered the flag and turned the fort over to the Confederacy. The American Civil War had begun. It would be four long, hard-fought years before the guns would finally be silenced.

The Photographic History of the Civil War: Armies and Leaders captures the images of both intense drama and horror created by this internal national conflict. This unique collection of black-and-white photographs takes the reader into the campsites and onto the battlefields where victories were won and lives were lost. The superb text and photograph descriptions present an authoritative yet sensitive portrayal of the War Between the States.

This volume profiles the leaders from both sides of the Civil War and analyzes the makeup of the armies which comprised the fighting ranks. The military leaders discussed here include Ulysses S. Grant, Robert E. Lee, William T. Sherman and "Stonewall" Jackson. While each of these men came from different backgrounds, they all shared an unwavering determination and strong belief in the causes they fought for. The individual armies are descibed here in great detail also. How each troop was formed, its involvement in the war, and the officers who led the soldiers into battle are all carefully described.

An analytical look is taken at the losses suffered by many of these armies throughout the war. Every successful battle was at the expense of many lives. For instance, it appears that almost all of the heavy losses of the Confederate regiments were suffered when they were either winning victories or stubbornly holding on to the field of battle. Several tables included here break down the number of men killed, wounded, or missing during the major battles, and list the number of deaths resulting from all causes in the Union armies, deaths in Confederate armies and the casualties from individual regiments from both armies.

By the 1860s the camera was on its way to becoming an important medium for communication. The method used during this period was known as daguereotype, named after its inventor Frenchman Louis Jacques Mandé Daguerre. By using this wet-plate process, however, the Civil War photographer was unable to capture action shots. Yet this disadvantage did not prevent him from capturing on film the human and material wreckage created by the war—the wistful face of the dying young soldier or the sabotaged railroad. The Battle of Bull Run marked the beginning of American military photography.

The Civil War photographers risked constant danger of battle and worked under the most difficult conditions—the bitter cold during the winters of 1862 and 1863 and the blistering heat in the summer. Important Civil War photographers—including Mathew B. Brady, Timothy O'Sullivan and Alexander Gardner as well as other combat photographers—provided the American people with an inside look at this war through their work.

The photographs gathered here are truly remarkable. The camera lens not only has captured the soldier in uniform, but also the soulful expressions worn by each face weathered by the war. These poignant photographs stirred the hearts of Americans on both sides of the Mason-Dixon line then and will continue to do so today.

K.M.B.

INTRODUCTION

SOLDIERS
AND
CITIZENS

VETERANS AFTER ONE YEAR

SELF-RELIANCE, COURAGE AND DIGNITY ARE IMPRINTED ON THE FACES OF THESE "VETERANS"—MEN OF McCLERNAND'S CORPS IN THEIR QUARTERS AT MEMPHIS, TENNESSEE, AFTER THE COSTLY ATTEMPT ON VICKSBURG BY WAY OF CHICKASAW BLUFFS. YET THEY HAVE BEEN SOLDIERS HARDLY A YEAR—THE BOY ON THE RIGHT, SO SLIGHT AND YOUNG, MIGHT ALMOST BE MASQUERADING IN AN OFFICER'S UNIFORM. OF SUCH WERE THE SOLDIERS WHO EARLY IN THE WAR FOUGHT THE SOUTH IN THE FLUSH OF HER STRENGTH AND ENTHUSIASM

EDWIN M. STANTON
Secretary of War.

MONTGOMERY BLAIR
Postmaster-General.

GIDEON WELLES
Secretary of the Navy.

SALMON P. CHASE
Secretary of the Treasury.

HANNIBAL HAMLIN
Vice-President.

WILLIAM H. SEWARD
Secretary of State.

CALEB B. SMITH
Secretary of the Interior.

MEMBERS OF PRESIDENT LINCOLN'S OFFICIAL FAMILY

Other members were: War, Simon Cameron (1861); Treasury, W. P. Fessenden, July 1, 1864, and Hugh McCulloch, March 4, 1865; Interior, John P. Usher, January 8, 1863; Attorney-General, James Speed, December 2, 1864; Postmaster-General, William Dennison, September 24, 1864.

EDWARD BATES
Attorney-General.

JAMES A. SEDDON
Secretary of War.

CHRISTOPHER G. MEMMINGER
Secretary of the Treasury.

STEPHEN R. MALLORY
Secretary of the Navy.

JOHN H. REAGAN
Postmaster-General.

ALEXANDER H. STEPHENS
Vice-President.

JUDAH P. BENJAMIN
Secretary of State.

MEN WHO HELPED PRESI–DENT DAVIS GUIDE THE SHIP OF STATE

The members of the Cabinet were chosen not from intimate friends of the President, but from the men preferred by the States they represented. There was no Secretary of the Interior in the Confederate Cabinet.

GEORGE DAVIS
Attorney-General.

VICE–PRESIDENT STEPHENS AND MEMBERS OF THE CONFEDERATE CABINET

Judah P. Benjamin, Secretary of State, has been called the brain of the Confederacy. President Davis wished to appoint the Honorable Robert Barnwell, Secretary of State, but Mr. Barnwell declined the honor.

AFTER THE GREAT MASS MEETING IN UNION SQUARE, NEW YORK, APRIL 20, 1861

Knots of citizens still linger around the stands where Anderson, who had abandoned Sumter only six days before, had just roused the multitude to wild enthusiasm. Of this gathering in support of the Government the *New York Herald* said at the time: "Such a mighty uprising of the people has never before been witnessed in New York, nor throughout the whole length and breadth of the Union. Five stands were erected, from which some of the most able speakers of the city and state addressed the multitude on the necessity of rallying around the flag of the Republic in this hour of its danger. A series of resolutions was proposed and unanimously adopted, pledging the meeting to use every means to preserve the Union intact and inviolate. Great unanimity prevailed throughout the whole proceedings; party politics were ignored, and the entire meeting—speakers and listeners—were a unit in maintaining the national honor unsullied. Major Anderson, the hero of Fort Sumter, was present, and showed himself at the various stands, at each of which he was most enthusiastically received. An impressive feature of the occasion was the flag of Sumter, hoisted on the stump of the staff that had been shot away, placed in the hand of the equestrian statue of Washington."
[14]

RECRUITING ON BROADWAY, 1861

Looking north on Broadway from "The Park" (later City Hall Park) in war time, one sees the Stars and Stripes waving above the recruiting station, p a s t which the soldiers stroll. There is a convenient booth with liquid refreshments. To the right of the picture the rear end of a street car is visible, but passenger travel on Broadway itself is by stage. On the left is the Astor House, then one of the foremost hostelries of the city. In the lower photograph the view is from the

balcony of the Metropolitan looking north on Broadway. The twin towers on the left are those of St. Thomas's Church. The lumbering stages, with the deafening noise of their rattling windows as they drive over the cobblestones, are here in force. More hoop-skirts are retreating in the distance, and a gentleman in the tall hat of the period is on his way down town. Few of the buildings seen here remained half a century later. The time is summer, as the awnings attest.

THE WAR'S GREAT "CITIZEN" AT HIS MOMENT OF TRIUMPH

Just behind the round table to the right, rising head and shoulders above the distinguished bystanders, grasping his manuscript in both hands, stands Abraham Lincoln. Of all the occasions on which he talked to his countrymen, this was most significant. The time and place marked the final and lasting approval of his political and military policies. Despite the bitter opposition of a majority of the Northern political and social leaders, the people of the Northern States had renominated Lincoln in June, 1864. In November, encouraged by the victories of Farragut at Mobile, Sherman in Georgia, and Sheridan in the Shenandoah Valley, they had reëlected him President of the United States by an electoral vote of 212 to 21. Since the election, continued Northern victories had made certain the

LINCOLN READING HIS SECOND INAUGURAL ADDRESS ON MARCH 4, 1865

speedy termination of the war. Not long since, his opponents had been so numerous and so powerful that they fully expected to prevent his renomination. Lincoln himself, shortly after his renomination, had come to believe that reelection was improbable, and had expressed himself as ready "to cooperate with the President-elect to save the Union." Yet neither in Lincoln's demeanor nor in his inaugural address is there the slighest note of personal exultation. For political and military enemies alike he has " malice toward none; charity for all." Indeed the dominant feeling in his speech is one of sorrow and sympathy for the cruel sufferings of both North and South. Not only in the United States, but throughout the civilized world, the address made a profound and immediate impression.

INTRODUCTION

SOLDIERS AND CITIZENS

"GRANT at Appomattox—Lee at Gettysburg—those are the men for me!" Thus exclaimed a long-time writer on military matters, after the contemplation of certain portraits that follow these pages. His criticism halted before the colossal moral qualities of the two war leaders—the generosity that considered the feelings of the conquered general as well as the private soldiers' need of horses "for the spring plowing"—the nobility that, after Pickett's charge at Gettysburg, promptly shouldered all the responsibility.

Those heights of character, as chronicled in the pages that follow and in other volumes of this History, are heroic, universal. They surpass the bounds of any period or nation; they link America with the greatness of the ages. If they, together with the sacrifice and fortitude of thousands more among the "Armies and Leaders," are made to live more vividly for those who study the narrative and portraits of this volume, and the nine volumes preceding it, their publication will indeed have been justified.

The personal inspiration of the war pictures centers, naturally, in the portraits and groups. Several hundred of them are presented in the pages following. Study of them soon reveals a difference between soldier and non-combatant, as expressed in bearing and cast of countenance. It is astonishing how accurately, after examining a number of the war photographs of every description, one may distinguish in

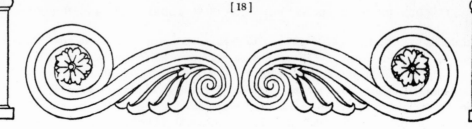

**FROM
THE ARMY
TO THE
WHITE HOUSE**

War-time portraits of
six soldiers whose
military records
assisted them
to the Pres-
idential
Chair.

Garfield in '63—(left to right) Thomas, Wiles, Tyler, Simmons, Drillard, Ducat, Barnett, Goddard,
Rosecrans, Garfield, Porter, Bond, Thompson, Sheridan.

Brig.-Gen. Andrew Johnson
President, 1865–69.

General Ulysses S. Grant
President, 1869–77.

Bvt. Maj.-Gen. Rutherford B. Hayes
President, 1877–81.

Maj.-Gen. James A. Garfield
President, March to September, 1881.

Bvt. Brig.-Gen. Benjamin Harrison
President, 1889–93.

Brevet Major William McKinley
President, 1897–1901.

many cases between fighters and non-combatants. This is true, even when the latter are represented in full army over-coats, with swords and the like, as was customary to some extent with postmasters, quartermasters, commissariat and hospital attendants.

The features are distinctive of the men who have stood up under fire, and undergone the even severer ordeal of submission to a will working for the common good, involving the sacrifice of personal independence. Their dignity and quiet self-confidence are obscured neither by the extreme growth of facial hair fashionable in the sixties, nor by the stains of marching and camping. Where the photograph " caught " the real soldiers under any circumstances of dress or undress, health or disease, camp-ease, or wounds that had laid the subjects low, the stamp of discipline stands revealed.

The young officers' portraits afford particularly interesting study. The habit of quick decision, the weighing of responsibilities involving thousands of human lives which has become a daily matter, like the morning and evening train-catching of the modern business commuter—these swift and tremendous affairs are borne with surprising calmness upon the young shoulders.

To represent in some coherent form the men of Civil War time, this volume has been set aside. It becomes highly desirable to the fundamental plan of this history.

The editors have devoted an entire volume to the consideration of the personnel of the Union and Confederate armies. But in this field, vaster than most of the present generation have imagined, even a book as extensive as this can be no more than suggestive.

Brevet Major George Haven Putnam,
176th New York, Prisoner at
Libby and Danville in the
Winter of 1864-65.

Brevet Lieut.-Colonel Harrison Gray Otis:
Twice Wounded; Brig.-Gen. in Spanish
War, Maj.-Gen. in Philippines.

Chief of Scouts Henry Watterson, C. S. A.,
Aide-de-Camp to General Forrest,
Chief of Scouts under General
Jos. E. Johnston.

REPRESENTATIVE CIVIL WAR OFFICERS—SUCCESSFUL ALSO IN LATER LIFE

George Haven Putnam, publisher and author, led in the move for international copyright. Harrison Gray Otis served as an editor in California more than 30 years, and fought again in the Spanish War. Henry Watterson, as editor of the Louisville *Courier-Journal*, did much to reconcile North and South. Andrew Carnegie's millions, made from iron and steel, went largely to philanthropy and the advancement of peace. Nathan B. Forrest, the daring Confederate cavalryman, later developed two vast plantations. Thomas T. Eckert became President of the Western Union Telegraph Company. Grenville M. Dodge, Chief Engineer of the Union Pacific, built thousands of miles of railroads, opening up the Western empire.

Andrew Carnegie Superintended Military Railways and Government
Telegraph Lines in 1861.

Lieut.-General Nathan B. Forrest, C. S. A.,
Entered as Private; Lieut.-Col.,
1861, Maj.-Gen., 1864.

Brevet Brig.-General Thomas T. Eckert,
Superintendent of Military Telegraph;
Asst. Sec. of War, 1864-66.

Maj.-General Grenville M. Dodge, Wounded
Before Atlanta; Succeeded Rosecrans
in the Department of Missouri.

Soldiers and Citizens ✦ ✦ ◇

Consider the typical fighting man on the Union side alone—the brevet brigadier-general, or the colonel, often deserving of promotion to that rank. When it is reflected that the rank of brevet brigadier-general was conferred upon eleven hundred and seventy Federal officers who never attained the full rank, and that the colonels who displayed conspicuous gallantry numbered as many, perhaps twice as many, more, it is evident that the editors of this volume in presenting portraits of more than three hundred of the generals, by brevet, have made this feature of the work as comprehensive as possible. To exhaust the list of such officers would require a separate volume.

Consistency, likewise, would demand at least another volume for colonels. But who would undertake to decide what particular thousand among the upward of ten thousand claimants among this rank should have a place in the gallery of fame? And if gallant colonels, why not the equally gallant lieutenant-colonels, majors, and captains, who at times commanded regiments?

That there are limitations is evident. The nature of the work decides its scope to a large degree. The war-time camera has been the arbiter. Here and there it caught the colonel as well as the general, the captain as well as the colonel, and the private as well as the captain. On the whole, its work was well balanced, marvelously so, and the results are before the readers of *The Photographic History of the Civil War: Armies and Leaders*.

Merely to suggest the function of the Civil War as a school of citizenship, portraits are presented with this introduction of six soldiers who became President; of a group like Grenville M. Dodge, Harrison Gray Otis, and Thomas T. Eckert, who helped to develop American material resources; together with

Brevet Brigadier-General Stewart L. Woodford, Lieut.-Gov. of New York, 1866–68; President Electoral College, 1872; M. C., 1873–75; U. S. Dist. Atty., 1877–83; U. S. Minister to Spain, 1879–98.

Brevet Brigadier-General James Grant Wilson, Author of Addresses on Lincoln, Grant, Hull, Farragut, etc.; President New York Gen. and Biog. Soc. and of Am. Ethnological Society.

Brevet Major-General William B. Hazen, Chief Signal Officer, Raised 41st Ohio Volunteers; Marched with Sherman to the Sea; Commanded 15th Army Corps; U. S Military Attaché to France.

WAR–TIME PORTRAITS OF TYPICAL SOLDIERS WHO TURNED TO PUBLIC LIFE AND EDUCATION

Notable as lawyers, writers and statesmen are General Carl Schurz (on the left), who became Minister to Spain, Secretary of the Interior, and editor of the New York *Evening Post;* and General Lewis Wallace (to the right), Governor of New Mexico, Minister to Turkey, and author of "Ben Hur" and other historical novels.

Major-General Carl Schurz.

Major-General Lewis Wallace.

Colonel George E. Waring, Jr., Led a Brigade of Cavalry; Reorganized Street Cleaning System of New York City; Died in Havana, Cuba, Fighting Yellow Fever.

Brevet Brigadier-General Francis W. Palfrey, Register in Bankruptcy in 1872; Author of "Antietam and Fredericksburg" in 1882; Author of Many Scholarly and Important Papers.

Lieutenant E. Benjamin Andrews: Wounded at Petersburg, 1864; Professor of History and Political Economy, Brown University, 1882–88; President thereof, 1889–98.

Brevet Brigadier-General Francis A. Walker, Superintendent Ninth and Tenth Censuses; Commissioner of Indian Affairs in 1872; President Mass. Inst. of Technology, 1881.

several, such as Henry Watterson, Carl Schurz, George E. Waring, Jr., and Francis A. Walker, whose influence has put much of our journalism and public life on a higher plane.

As these lines are penned, no less than four Civil War soldiers—two Union, two Confederate—are serving as members of the highest American tribunal—the Supreme Court:—Chief Justice White and Justice Lurton (Confederate); Justices Harlan and Holmes (Union). Ex-Confederates again have been found in the cabinets of both Republican and Democratic Presidents, as well as in the National Congress.

But immense indeed would be the literary enterprise undertaking to cover all the results in American civic life of Civil War training. There have been State governors by the hundreds who could look back upon service with the armies. There have been members of legislatures by the tens of thousands. And the private soldiers—hundreds of thousands of them, mere boys when they enlisted to fight through the four years, expanded into important citizens of their communities, as a direct result of their service in the Blue and the Gray.

The youths of eighteen or nineteen, who rushed to the defense of their flag in 1861, lacked, as most boys do, some notable phenomenon, blow, catastrophe to fire their imaginations and give them confidence in themselves. Without such inspiration their highest destiny would have fallen far short of fulfilment.

But those same youths who survived to the summer of 1865—how differently they stood!—erect, with arms well hung, with quiet dignity, with the self-assurance learned from years of quick decision and unhesitating following of duty through

WAR-TIME POR-
TRAITS OF FEDERAL
SOLDIERS WHO CON-
TRIBUTED TO THE
PHOTOGRAPHIC
HISTORY HALF A
CENTURY LATER

Captain A. W. Greely, 1863; Later Maj.-
Gen., U. S. A.; Chief Signal Service
("Signals"; "Telegraph").

Private Geo. L. Kilmer in '64, Wearing
the "Veteran Stripe" at 18
(Military Editor).

Private J. E. Gilman, Lost an Arm at Gettysburg; Commander-in-Chief G. A. R. 1910–11
("Grand Army of the Republic").

Bvt. Brig.-Gen. T. F. Roden-
bough, U. S. A., in 1865;
Wounded at Trevilian and
Winchester; Later Sec-
retary U. S. Military
Service Institution
("Cavalry" Editor).

Capt. F. Y. Hedley in '64, Age 20; Later Editor
and Author of "Marching Through Georgia"
("School of the Soldier," "Marching
and Foraging").

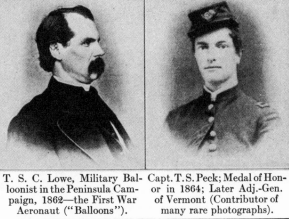

Col. W. C. Church; Later Edi-
tor of the *Army and Navy
Journal* and Author of Life of
Ulysses S. Grant ("Grant").

T. S. C. Lowe, Military Bal-
loonist in the Peninsula Campaign, 1862—the First War
Aeronaut ("Balloons").

Capt. T. S. Peck; Medal of Hon-
or in 1864; Later Adj.-Gen.
of Vermont (Contributor of
many rare photographs).

Col. L. R. Stegman, Wounded
at Cedar Creek, Gettysburg,
Ringgold and Pine Moun-
tain (Consulting Editor).

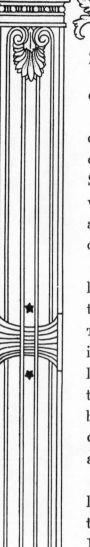

Soldiers and Citizens ✦ ✦ ✦ ✦ ✦

danger.

If, for instance, one should study the careers of those countless thousands of fearless sheriffs who have kept order in communities throughout the country, after service under the Stars and Stripes or the Stars and Bars, it would become overwhelmingly apparent that without such training in resolution and resourcefulness, most of the men who were young in 1861 could possibly have become village constables—no more.

The leading biographies in this volume have naturally been left free from the editorial scrutiny that has aimed to render the test throughout the largest part of the PHOTOGRAPHIC HISTORY as detached and impersonal as possible. The value, for instance, of the chapter on Grant, by Colonel W. C. Church, lies not only in the trained military criticism of technical operations by the veteran editor of the *Army and Navy Journal*, but also in the author's personal acquaintance with the Union commander, extending through many years, and the graphic and sure touch conveyable only by such personal intimacy.

Nor was it to be expected or desired that Professor William P. Trent, a writer and scholar Southern born, should fail to emphasize the lofty personal traits of his hero, Lee; or that Mr. Allen C. Redwood, whose rare privilege it was to " fight with ' Stonewall,' " should not portray his honest and frank admiration for the most surprising military genius developed by the Civil War.

Particularly gratifying to the humanist is the sketch of Sherman, written from the standpoint of the most sympathetic discrimination by a Southern historical student—Professor Walter L. Fleming, of the Louisiana State University.

Two groups of portraits accompanying this introduction show

WAR–TIME
PHOTOGRAPHS OF
CONFEDERATE SOLDIERS

CONTRIBUTORS TO THE
PHOTOGRAPHIC
HISTORY

Col. Hilary A. Herbert; Later Member
of Congress and Secretary of the
Navy ("The Meaning of
Losses in Battle").

Lieut.-Col. J. W. Mallet; Later Professor
of Chemistry, University of Virginia
("Confederate Ordnance").

Private John A. Wyeth in '61, at 16;
Later Organizer of the New
York "Polyclinic" ("Con-
federate Raids").

Lieut. R. H. McKim in '62; Later Rector
Church of the Epiphany, Washington,
and Military and Religious Writer
("The Confederate Army").

Captain F. M. Colston, Artillery Officer
with Alexander ("Memoirs of
Gettysburg" and Many
Rare Photographs).

Allen C. Redwood, of the 55th Virginia,
with "Stonewall" Jackson; Later
Artist and Author (Confederate
Reminiscences; "Jackson").

Brig.-Gen. M. J. Wright;
Later U. S. War Dept.
Agent ("Records of
the War" and
Statistics).

Col. D. G. McIntosh;
Later Attorney-at-
Law ("Artillery
of the Confed-
eracy").

Col. T. M. R. Talcott;
Later Civil Engineer
("Reminiscences of
the Confederate
Engineers").

S. A. Cunningham;
Later Editor *Confed-
erate Veteran* ("Uni-
ted Confederate
Veterans").

Deering J. Roberts, Sur-
geon; Later Editor
Southern Practitioner
("Confederate Med-
ical Service").

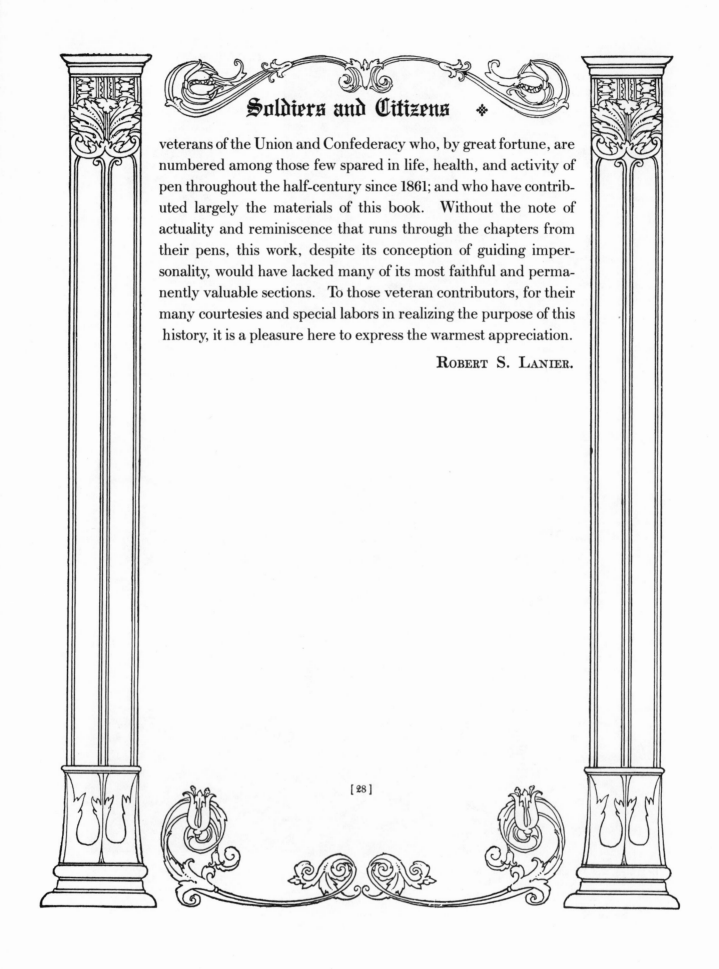

Soldiers and Citizens ❖

veterans of the Union and Confederacy who, by great fortune, are numbered among those few spared in life, health, and activity of pen throughout the half-century since 1861; and who have contributed largely the materials of this book. Without the note of actuality and reminiscence that runs through the chapters from their pens, this work, despite its conception of guiding impersonality, would have lacked many of its most faithful and permanently valuable sections. To those veteran contributors, for their many courtesies and special labors in realizing the purpose of this history, it is a pleasure here to express the warmest appreciation.

ROBERT S. LANIER.

I

GRANT

DURING THE WILDERNESS CAMPAIGN, 1864

WHEN GRANT LOST AN ARMY BUT SAVED A NATION

GRANT ON LOOKOUT MOUNTAIN—1863

Wearing epaulets and a sword—quite unusual for him—but calm and imperturbable as of old, with his crumpled army hat, plain blouse, his trousers tucked into his boot-tops, and the inevitable cigar, Ulysses S. Grant stands at a historic spot.   Less than a week before, when the Union soldiers under Thomas, still smarting from their experience at Chickamauga, stood gazing at the Confederate works behind which rose the crest of Missionary Ridge, the Stars and Stripes were thrown to the breeze on the crest of Lookout Mountain. Eager hands pointed, and a great cheer went up from the Army of the Cumberland.   They knew that the Union troops with Hooker had carried the day in their "battle above the clouds."   That was the 25th of November, 1863; and that same afternoon the soldiers

AT THE SPOT WHERE HOOKER SIGNALED VICTORY THE WEEK BEFORE

of Thomas swarmed over the crest of Missionary Ridge while Grant himself looked on and wondered. When a few days later Grant visited the spot whence the flag was waved, an enterprising photographer, already on the spot, preserved the striking scene. Seated with his back against a tree, General J. A. Rawlins gazes at his leader. Behind him stands General Webster, and leaning against the tree in Colonel Clark B. Lagow. The figure in the right foreground is Colonel William S. Hillyer. Seated by the path is an orderly. They have evidently come to survey the site of Hooker's battle from above. Colonel Lagow is carrying a pair of field glasses. Less than four months later Grant was commissioned lieutenant-general and placed in general command of the Union armies.

ULYSSES SIMPSON GRANT

By William Conant Church
Brevet Lieutenant-Colonel, United States Volunteers

THE man of all men who knew General Grant best, his friend and chief ally, General W. T. Sherman, declared that Grant more nearly than any other man impersonated the American character of 1861–65, and was the typical hero of our great Civil War.

It is an anomaly of history that a man so distinguished in war should be so unwarlike in personal characteristics as was Ulysses Simpson Grant, and so singularly free from the ambitions supposed to dominate the soldier. He sickened at the sight of blood, was so averse to inflicting pain that, as a lad, he never enjoyed the boyish sport of killing small animals, and at no time in his life was he fond of hunting. Indeed, no more gentle-hearted and kindly man is known to American history, not excepting Abraham Lincoln.

Numerous circumstances in the life of Grant illustrate his consideration for others. At Vicksburg, Mississippi, where over thirty thousand Confederates surrendered to him, July 4, 1863, he directed his exulting troops "to be orderly and quiet as the paroled prisoners passed" and to make no offensive remarks. The only cheers heard there were for the defenders of Vicksburg, and the music sounded was the tune of "Old Hundred," in which victor and vanquished could join. The surrender at Appomattox, Virginia, April 9, 1865, was characterized by almost feminine tenderness and tact, and a sympathetic courtesy toward the conquered so marked that an observer was moved to ask, "Who's surrendering here, anyway?"

A simple-hearted country lad disposed to bucolic life, so

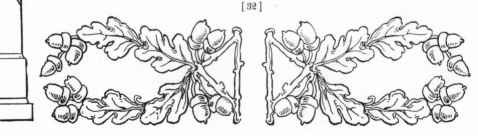

GRANT IN 1863—BEFORE THE FIRST OF HIS GREAT VICTORIES

Grant was described in 1861 as a man "who knows how to do things."   In February, 1862, he captured Forts Henry and Donelson, thus opening the way for a Federal advance up the Tennessee River, and was promptly commissioned major-general.   His experience at Shiloh in April, coupled with failures in official routine during the Donelson campaign which were not approved by his superiors, left him under a cloud which was not removed until the capture of Vicksburg, July 4, 1863, revealed capacity of a high order.   The government's plan of conducting the war was then entrusted to him to work out with practically unlimited power.

unbelligerent that he never had even a " spat " at West Point, displaying no martial qualities except, perhaps, in his love of horses and in their fearless handling, there was in him no suggestion of the vocation of the soldier. He entered the Military Academy simply because his father desired that he should do so, and while there he secretly rejoiced because of the report that Congress was proposing to abolish the academy. The thought of the girl he left behind was constantly with him during his cadet course, though this youthful romance ended in the disillusion which often attends such experiences.

And it was this man, whose personal characteristics were all so unlike those distinguishing the remorseless conqueror, " slaughtering men for glory's sake," who was selected from among the heroes of our great domestic strife for the appellation of " butcher." No one of them less deserved this title, for none of them accomplished as great results with a less proportionate loss of life. The repulse of Lee at Gettysburg, in 1863, was obtained at a cost of 23,000 casualties—3155 killed, 14,529 wounded, 5365 missing—and at the end Lee marched with his army from the field of battle. The more complete victory at Vicksburg, with the surrender of Pemberton's entire army of 30,000 men, was obtained by Grant with a casualty list of only 9362, including about 450 missing.

Heavy as were the losses during the year which preceded the surrender of the Army of Northern Virginia, they were less than the aggregate loss, including " missing," of previous commanders of the Army of the Potomac in unsuccessful attempts to accomplish the same result in the same field. Grant's total of killed and wounded was 19,597 less than the average number killed and injured annually by the railroads of the United States during the four years ending 1910.

Those who " control the destiny of to-morrow " are those who are the most apt in learning that, in great matters, it is

BEFORE VICKSBURG

AFTER VICKSBURG

The close-set mouth, squared shoulders and lowering brow in this photograph of Grant, taken in December, 1862, tell the story of the intensity of his purpose while he was advancing upon Vicksburg—only to be foiled by Van Dorn's raid on his line of communications at Holly Springs. His grim expression and determined jaw betokened no respite for the Confederates, however. Six months later he marched into the coveted stronghold. This photograph was taken by James Mullen at Oxford, Mississippi, in December, 1862, just before Van Dorn's raid balked the general's plans.

This photograph was taken in the fall of 1863, after the capture of the Confederacy's Gibraltar had raised Grant to secure and everlasting fame. His attitude is relaxed and his eyebrows no longer mark a straight line across the grim visage. The right brow is slightly arched with an almost jovial expression. But the jaw is no less vigorous and determined, and the steadfast eyes seem to be peering into that future which holds more victories. He still has Chattanooga and his great campaigns in the East to fight and the final magnificent struggle in the trenches at Petersburg.

necessary to disregard personal considerations and to keep the mind open to the suggestions from within; who are not blinded by what has been well described as "the pride of self-derived intelligence." Grant succeeded because his specially trained faculties and especially adapted experiences were obedient to larger suggestions than those of personal ambition and self-glorification. This explains Grant, as it explains Lincoln and Washington.

"Sam" Grant, as his colleagues at the Military Academy were accustomed to call him, because of the " U. S.," Uncle Sam, in his name; "'Sam' Grant," as one of those same colleagues once said, "was as honest a man as God ever made." Honest, not merely in a pecuniary sense but in all of his mental processes, and in this simple honesty of his nature we find the explanation not only of his greatness but of the errors into which he fell in the attempt to deal with the subtleties of human selfishness and intrigue.

It was characteristic of Grant's mental processes that he always thought on straight lines, and his action was equally direct and positive. He was not so much concerned with the subtleties of strategy as with a study of the most direct road to the opponent's center. One of the chief perplexities on the field of battle is "the fog of war," the difficulty of divining the movements of the foe, by which your own are to be determined. Grant was less confused by this than most commanders, keeping his adversary so occupied with his own aggressive movements that he had little opportunity to study combinations against him. He was fertile in expedients; his mind was always open to the suggestions of opportunity, and it was his habit to postpone decision until the necessity for decision arose.

Grant recognized earlier than others the fact that, if his own troops were lacking in the military knowledge and training required to make them a facile instrument in his hands, his antagonists were no better equipped in this respect. He saw that the best training for the high-spirited and independent

On this page are three photographs of General Grant, taken in the most critical year of his career, the year when he took Vicksburg in July, then in November gazed in wonder at his own soldiers as they swarmed up the heights of Missionary Ridge. The following March he was made general-in-chief of the armies of the United States. Congress passed a vote of thanks to General Grant and his army, and ordered a gold medal to be struck in his honor. But as we see him here, none of these honors had come to him; and the deeds themselves

GRANT IN 1863

were only in process of accomplishment. Even Sherman, the staunch friend and supporter of Grant, had doubts which were only dispelled by the master stroke at Vicksburg, as to the outcome of Grant's extraordinary methods and plans. He was himself conscious of the heavy responsibility resting upon him and of the fact that he stood on trial before the country. Other faithful generals had been condemned at the bar of public opinion before their projects matured. The eyes in these portraits are stern, and the expressions intense.

PORTRAITS OF 1863—SHOWING GRANT IN REPOSE

volunteers he commanded was that of the battlefield. If action involved risk, inaction was certain to produce discontent and even demoralization, while the fatalities of the camp were those chiefly to be dreaded, for microbes were more deadly than bullets. His early successes were due to the application of his methods to conditions as he found them, without waiting for their improvement. When he met the battalions of Lee, then trained and seasoned by three years of war, the struggle was protracted, but in the end he triumphed through his policy of vigorous and persistent attack, bringing a contest which had then extended over three years of inconclusive fighting to a final conclusion in one year.

General Grant was born, April 27, 1822, in a little one-story cottage on the banks of the Ohio River, at Point Pleasant, Clermont County, Ohio. His grandfather, Captain Noah Grant, was a Connecticut soldier of the army of the Revolution who, in 1800, settled on the Connecticut Reservation of Ohio. His mother, Hannah Simpson, was of a sterling American family of pioneers, noted for integrity, truthfulness, and sturdy independence of character. She was a noble woman of strong character, and it was from her that the son inherited his remarkable capacity for reticence, tempered in him by an occasional relapse into the garrulity of his father. If he was incapable of indirection in thought or speech, he could be silent when speech might betray what he did not wish to have known.

Among his friends, when occasion served, he was a fluent and interesting talker. He never gossiped, never used profane or vulgar language, was charitable and generous to a fault, and considerate in his treatment of all. He was good-natured and fond of his joke. Uncomplaining self-control was characteristic of both mother and son, as was also equability of temper and "saving common sense."

To estimate Grant correctly, it is necessary to consider him apart from the personal influences by which he was swayed,

IN THE AUTUMN OF 1863—GRANT'S CHANGING EXPRESSIONS

Although secure in his fame as the conqueror of Vicksburg, Grant still has the greater part of his destiny to fulfil as he faces the camera. Before him lie the Wilderness, Spotsylvania, Cold Harbor, and the slow investment of Petersburg. This series forms a particularly interesting study in expression. At the left hand, the face looks almost amused. In the next the expression is graver, the mouth close set. The third picture looks plainly obstinate, and in the last the stern fighter might have been declaring, as in the following spring: "I propose to fight it out on this line if it takes all summer." The eyes, first unveiled fully in this fourth view, are the unmistakable index to Grant's stern inflexibility, once his decision was made.

IN THE AUTUMN OF 1864—AFTER THE STRAIN OF THE WILDERNESS CAMPAIGN

Here is a furrowed brow above eyes worn by pain. In the pictures of the previous year the forehead is more smooth, the expression grave yet confident. Here the expression is that of a man who has won, but won at a bitter cost. It is the memory of the 50,000 men whom he left in the Wilderness campaign and at Cold Harbor that has lined this brow, and closed still tighter this inflexible mouth. Again, as in the series above, the eyes are not revealed until the last picture. Then again flashes the determination of a hero. The great general's biographers say that Grant was a man of sympathy and infinite pity. It was the more difficult for him, spurred on to the duty by grim necessity, to order forward the lines in blue that withered, again and again, before the Confederate fire, but each time weakened the attenuated line which confronted them.

for he was a man of unusual domesticity, and tenacity of friendship not always distinguished by perspicacity in discerning character.

To the sincere but unobtrusive piety of his mother, Grant owed a reverence for religion which he displayed throughout life and which supported him during that last desperate struggle with death, ending at Mount MacGregor, New York, on July 23, 1885. His belief in the invisible powers was the hidden current of the great soldier's life. It explains alike his calmness in victory and his unfaltering courage in defeat. There was no shock of battle so fierce, no episode of the combat so exciting that could disturb his impassible demeanor. "I have had many hard experiences in my life," he once said to the writer, when chatting in front of his camp-fire at Petersburg, "but I never saw the moment when I was not confident that I should win in the end."

If he was not blinded by a sense of his individual importance, there was no lack of self-confidence in Grant. He had a just estimate of his own abilities and a correct understanding, as a soldier, of the work for which his abilities and experiences had fitted him. If he did not possess what is usually regarded as the temperament of the soldier, there was no lack of the training or experience of the soldier. If not a brilliant student, according to the standards of West Point, he made a faithful use of the opportunity which that institution gave him for a military training. In his class-standing he held a middle place with others of the graduates most distinguished in our Civil War; a relatively higher place than Jefferson Davis, James Longstreet, William J. Hardee, and others of the South; and than Sheridan, Hooker, Buell, and other leaders of the Northern armies.

No soldier of like rank was more distinguished in the war with Mexico than Grant, then a lieutenant. It is no small achievement for a subaltern to be brought into the lime-light

GRANT

IN JUNE, 1864—

A SUMMER DAY AT CITY POINT

WHILE

GREAT EVENTS

WERE HANGING IN THE BALANCE

Third from the left sits General Grant at his headquarters at City Point, on a high bluff at the junction of the James and the Appomattox rivers. At this moment his reputation hangs in the balance. In the three successive battles of the Wilderness, Spotsylvania, and Cold Harbor, he has lost 49,000 men, but the still-trusting North hurries fresh men and vast supplies to the front. Always unassuming in appearance, General Grant had changed in this photograph to his summer garb. The general's blouse, like the others, was of plain material, single-breasted, and had four regulation brass buttons in front. It was substantially the coat of a private soldier, with nothing to indicate the rank of an officer except the three gold stars of a lieutenant-general on the shoulder-straps. Judging from the experience of the past few weeks, the outlook for the future was far from bright. Yet here Grant sits serene, undaunted, confident that no army with ever lessening resources can stand the weight of metal and men which he has been hurling for many weeks against Lee.

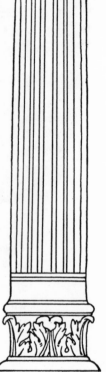

of publicity, as Grant was by mention in general orders commending him for acts of special distinction in battle, showing both intelligence and daring.

Meeting General Grant not long after his return to military life, Henry Villard reported that "there was certainly nothing in his outward appearance or in his personal ways or conversation to indicate the great military qualities he possessed. Firmness seemed to me about the only characteristic expressed in his features. Otherwise, he was a very plain, unpretentious, unimposing person, easily approached, reticent as a rule, and yet showing at times a fondness for a chat about all sorts of things. This ordinary exterior, however, made it as difficult for me, as in the case of Abraham Lincoln, to persuade myself that he was destined to be one of the greatest arbiters of human fortunes." Yet Fremont, who saw him at this time, discovered in him "the soldierly qualities of self-poise, modesty, decision, attention to detail."

Grant had never been brought into contact with men of public reputation and had no influential friends to push his fortunes when the Civil War opened to him an opportunity. His skill as a drill-master was discovered by accident, and this secured an opportunity for him to go to the Illinois capital with the Galena company he had been drilling. He attracted the attention of Governor Yates and was given a clerical position in the adjutant-general's office in filling out army forms. When his appointment as colonel to an unruly volunteer regiment followed, he at once gave proof of the education he had acquired at West Point and his experience of fifteen years' service in the regular army.

In executing his first orders to take the field, he astonished his superiors by marching his regiment across country instead of moving it comfortably by rail. And when the laggards of the regiment were compelled to march in their stocking feet

GRANT—ON HIS FIRST TRIP NORTH

The war is over. Grant has received in a magnanimous spirit, rarely paralleled in history, the surrender of Lee. Here he appears in Philadelphia on his first trip North after the war. His bearing is that of a man relieved of a vast responsibility, but with the marks of it still upon him. He is thinner than the full-chested soldier in the photograph taken in 1863, after the fall of Vicksburg. His dress is careless, as always, but shows more attention than when he was in the field. He looks out of the picture with the unflinching eyes that had been able to penetrate the future and see the wisdom of the plan that proved the final undoing of the Confederacy.

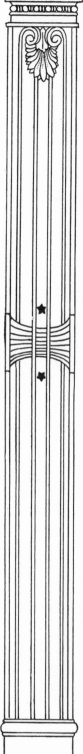

at the hour designated, they learned that " 6 A.M. " with their new colonel meant six o'clock in the morning. Another revelation came when they first faced him on parade, and their vociferous demands for a speech were met by the terse reply, " Men, go to your quarters." Thus, in various ways, they learned from day to day that they were in the hands of a man who understood the trade of war.

It was precisely because he was a master-workman at his trade that Grant was able to make his personal qualities effective when opportunity was given him. He was limited by the imperfections of the instruments he had at hand and was subjected to criticism accordingly, as at Shiloh, April 6, 1862, where his failure to protect his camp is explained by a fear lest a display of apprehension might demoralize troops misled by the ignorant cry of " spades to the rear," which then filled the air. They would have regarded defensive measures as an evidence of weakness and cowardice, and confidence is an essential factor in the management of raw troops, of which both the armies were then composed. They had at that time advanced but one stage beyond the condition of an armed mob, only partially responsive to the skilled handling of the educated and trained soldier.

Previous to the battle of Pittsburg Landing, as Shiloh is also called, Grant had given proof of his energy and his promptness in taking the initiative in the occupation of Paducah, Kentucky, September 6, 1861; in the comparatively trifling affair at Belmont, Missouri, November 7, 1861; and in his important success in the capture of Fort Donelson on the Cumberland River, Tennessee, in February, 1862, where he had the efficient assistance of the gunboats, under Flag-Officer Foote. These successes increased his confidence in himself, as back came the echo of exultant popular approval when the country saw how capable this man was of accomplishing great results with troops lacking in arms, equipment, transportation, and supplies, as well as in organization, but who

GRANT IN 1865—THE ZENITH OF HIS CAREER

Behind Grant in 1865 lay all his victories on the field of battle; before him the highest gift within the power of the American people—the presidency.   He says in his memoirs that after Vicksburg he had a presentment that he was to bring the war to a successful end and become the head of the nation.   Grant's sturdy, persistent Scottish ancestry stood him in good stead.   He was a descendant of Matthew Grant, one of the settlers of Windsor, Connecticut, in 1635, and a man of much importance in the infant colony.   His American ancestors were fighting stock.   His great-grandfather, Noah Grant, held a military commission in the French and Indian War, and his grandfather, also named Noah, fought in the Revolution.   Henry Ward Beecher summed up the causes of Grant's meteoric rise from store clerk in 1861, to president in 1869, as follows: "Grant was available and lucky."   His dominant trait was determination.

comprehended the significance of his foe's weakness in the same respects.

Grant had learned that if he did not run away his antagonists were likely to do so, and he had ascertained the potency of the formulas with which his name was associated: "No terms except unconditional and immediate surrender," and "I propose to move immediately upon your works." This met the temper of the time, impatient of strategy and paper plans and demanding tangible results.

The circumstances which led to Grant's resignation from the army, July 31, 1854, however they might have been explained by those who knew him best, had created a distrust of him in the minds of his military superiors, Halleck and McClellan, so that he was left wholly dependent upon works accomplished for his recognition by the North and at Washington. He neither sought nor obtained favor from his superiors; he made no complaint of insufficient support, as so many did, but doggedly pursued a consistent course of doing the best he could with what the War Department placed at his disposal, learning from his successes and profiting by his mistakes as well as by those of the foe.

There was one who was superior to this professional distrust of Grant, and that was Abraham Lincoln. He had found a man who could accomplish, and the fortune of that man was thenceforth secure in the hands of the chief executive. After Shiloh, Grant fully realized that the country had entered upon a long and desperate struggle, and he shaped his course accordingly. He drew the line of distinction between friend and foe more sharply, and, where he found it necessary, directed his warfare against the property as well as the persons of those in arms against him, and their abettors. Thus he passed another landmark in his progress to final success.

Another essential lesson was to be learned. That came when a colonel, December 20, 1862, surrendered his depot of

GRANT IN CHARACTERISTIC POSE, WITH HIS STAFF IN 1864

The indifferent attitude of the general-in-chief is most characteristic. Grant had begun the investment of Petersburg when this photograph was taken. Around him are the men who had followed him faithfully through the faith-shaking campaigns of the Wilderness. He never made known his plans for an advance to anyone, but his calm confidence communicated itself to all who listened to him. In the most critical moments he manifested no perceptible anxiety, but gave his orders with coolness and deliberation. At the left of the photograph sits General John A. Rawlins, who has foresworn his customary mustache and beard which the next picture shows him as wearing. He was first aide-de-camp to Grant, then assistant adjutant-general and chief of staff. Behind Grant, who stands in the center with one hand thrust carelessly into his pocket, sits Lieutenant Frederick Grant, later major-general in the United States Army. In front of Grant stands Colonel M. B. Ryan, and on the extreme right sits Colonel Ely S. Parker, military secretary, who was a full-blooded Indian, a grandnephew of the famous Red Jacket, and chief of the tribes known as the Six Nations.

supplies at Holly Springs and compelled General Grant to sub-sist his army of thirty thousand men upon the country for two weeks, his communications with his rear being severed at the same time by Forrest's enterprising Confederate cavalry. Grant was preparing to move against Vicksburg at the time, and the surrender of that place, July 4, 1863, followed a march overland to its rear from Bruinsburg, April 30, 1863, without supplies for his troops, other than those obtained from the country as he advanced, Grant carrying no personal bag-gage himself but a toothbrush. Sherman, who protested most vigorously against this hazardous movement, nevertheless later on applied the lesson it taught him when on his march to the sea, in 1864, he broke through the hollow shell of the Confed-eracy and closed it in from the south, while Grant advanced from the north, and crushed the armies of Lee and Johnston.

The surrender of the Southern armies in April and May, 1865, put an end to military activities, to be succeeded by the contests in the forum of political discussion; the death of Lincoln and the succession of Johnson following so immediately upon the surrender of Lee threw the whole question of the readjust-ment of political relations between the North and the South into chaos. In spite of his desire and his effort to keep within the limitations of his military function, General Grant found him-self involved in the embittered contests of the reconstruction period, with which he was not fitted to deal either by tempera-ment or training.

The politicians and the political activities of the North had, during the four years of war, been a constant source of embarrassment to our soldiers striving to conduct war with sole reference to success in the field. This had intensified the soldier's natural distrust of politicians and political methods, and Grant had never learned the art of which Lincoln was the supreme master—that of utilizing the selfish ambitions of men to accomplish great patriotic and public purposes.

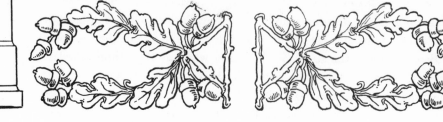

MEN ABOUT TO WITNESS APPOMATTOX

No photographer was present at Appomattox, that supreme moment in our national history, when Americans met for the last time as foes on the field. Nothing but fanciful sketches exist of the scene inside the McLean home. But here is a photograph that shows most of the Union officers present at the conference. Nine of the twelve men standing above stood also at the signing of Lee's surrender, a few days later. The scene is City Point, in March, 1865. Grant is surrounded by a group of the officers who had served him so faithfully. At the surrender, it was Colonel T. S. Bowers (third from left) upon whom Grant called to make a copy of the terms of surrender in ink. Colonel E. S. Parker, the full-blooded Indian on Grant's staff, an excellent penman, wrote

GRANT BETWEEN RAWLINS AND BOWERS

out the final copy. Nineteen years later, General Horace Porter recorded with pride that he loaned General Lee a pencil to make a correction in the terms. Colonels William Duff and J. D. Webster, and General M. R. Patrick, are the three men who were not present at the interview. All of the remaining officers were formally presented to Lee. General Seth Williams had been Lee's adjutant when the latter was superintendent at West Point some years before the war. In the lower photograph General Grant stands between General Rawlins and Colonel Bowers. The veins standing out on the back of his hand are plainly visible. No one but he could have told how calmly the blood coursed through them during the four tremendous years.

Ulysses S. Grant ✦ ✦ ✦ ✦

During his stormy period of civil administration, Grant was like a landsman tossing upon an angry sea who makes his port by virtue of the natural drift of the winds and tides rather than through his skill in navigation. The policies President Grant advocated during his two terms of office were sound, and if he did not show the politician's skill in availing himself of the varying winds of popular sentiment, he did exhibit a statesmanlike comprehension of the measures promotive of the best interests of the country. Refusing to be misled by the financial heresies of his time, in spite of the fact that they were advocated by a powerful faction in his own party, he took an uncompromising stand in his first inaugural in favor of paying the public debt in the currency of the world, and vetoed the bill to increase the issues of the simulacrum of coin, of merely local value. He reduced taxation and promoted economy in Government expenditures and reform in the civil service. He improved the condition of our Indian wards; he was a sincere friend of Mexico, against which he had fought in his youth; he strove to cultivate good relations with the Orientals, and he established our intercourse with England upon the firm foundations of the treaty of Washington.

How strange, how eventful, how checkered a career was this of the chief soldier of the Republic! Thirty-two years of unconscious preparation for a great career in the bucolic experiences of his youth, in his training at the Military Academy and in war, followed by seven years of a life which taught the bitterest lessons of humility and self-abnegation. Next, a rapid advance to a position which made him during more than twenty years a chief among those upon whom the attention of the world was focused; then a further descent into the valley of misfortune, until the final heroic struggle with the conqueror of us all once more centered upon him the affectionate interest of his countrymen and the sympathetic attention of the world.

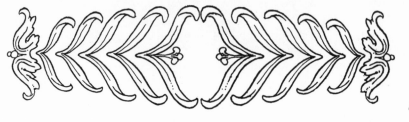

II

LEE

RESIDENCE OF ROBERT E. LEE, ON FRANKLIN STREET, RICHMOND, OCCUPIED BY HIS FAMILY DURING THE WAR— THREE OF THE PORTRAITS OF GENERAL LEE THAT FOLLOW WERE TAKEN IN THE BASEMENT OF THIS HOUSE—IT LATER BECAME THE HOME OF THE VIRGINIA HISTORICAL SOCIETY

ROBERT E. LEE

By William P. Trent
Professor of English Literature in Columbia University

"GENERAL LEE has been the only great man with whom I have been thrown who has not dwindled upon a near approach." This is the significant remark of one of his personal friends, Major A. R. H. Ranson of the Confederate artillery. The present writer, who never had the privilege of seeing General Lee, finds himself, in a sense, completely in accord with the veteran staff-officer, since he, too, can say that of all the great figures in history and literature whom he has had occasion to study through books, no one has stood out freer from human imperfections, of whatever sort, than the man and soldier upon whom were centered the affections, the admiration, and the hopes of the Southern people during the great crisis of their history. General Lee is the hero of his surviving veterans, of his fellow Virginians and Southerners, of many of those Americans of the North and West against whom he fought, and of his biographers. He is the Hector of a still-unwritten Iliad—a fact which the sketch that follows cannot prove, any more than it can set forth his claims to military fame in an adequately expert fashion, but to the truth of which it may perhaps bring a small bit of not valueless testimony—the testimony of personal conviction.*

Robert Edward Lee, the third son of the cavalry leader "Light Horse Harry" Lee by his second wife, Anne Hill Carter, was born at the family mansion, "Stratford," in Westmoreland County, Virginia, on January 19, 1807. On

*For a fuller, though necessarily limited treatment of Lee's character and career reference may be made to the writer's volume in the "Beacon Biographies," which has guided him in the present sketch.

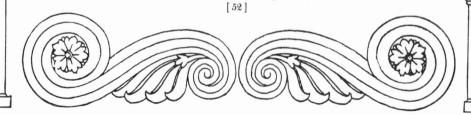

"LEE WAS ESSENTIALLY A VIRGINIAN"

Old Christ Church at Alexandria, Virginia. The church attended by both Washington and Lee calls up associations that explain the reference of General Adams. In 1811, at the age of four, Robert E. Lee removed from Westmoreland County to Alexandria, which remained his home until he entered West Point, in 1825. During these years he was gaining his education from private tutors and devoting himself to the care of his invalid mother. Many a Sunday he passed through the trees around this church, of which Washington had been one of the first vestrymen, to occupy the pew that is still pointed out to visitors. The town serves to intensify love of Virginia; here Braddock made his headquarters before marching against the French, in 1755, with young George Washington as an aide on his staff; and here on April 13th of that year the Governors of New York, Massachusetts, Pennsylvania, Maryland, and Virginia had met, in order to determine upon plans for the expedition. In the vicinity were Mount Vernon, the estate of Washington, and Arlington, which remained in the family of Washington's wife. The whole region was therefore full of inspiration for the youthful Lee.

both sides he came of the best stock of his native State. When he was four years old, his father removed to Alexandria in order to secure better schooling for the eight children. Later, the old soldier was compelled to go to the West Indies and the South in search of health, and it came to pass that Robert, though a mere boy, was obliged to constitute himself the nurse and protector of his invalid mother. The beautiful relation thus established accounts in part for the blended dignity and charm of his character. It does not account for his choice of a profession, but perhaps that is sufficiently explained by the genius for the soldier's calling which he must have inherited from his father. As with Milton before him, the piety and purity of his youth were inseparably combined with grace and strength.

He entered West Point in 1825 on an appointment secured by Andrew Jackson, and he graduated four years later with the second highest honors of the class and an extraordinarily perfect record. Appointed second lieutenant of engineers, he hastened home to receive the blessing of his dying mother. Two years later (June, 1831), after work on the fortifications at Hampton Roads, he was married, at the beautiful estate of Arlington on the Potomac, to Mary Randolph Custis, granddaughter of Washington's wife, a lovely and accomplished young woman destined to be a fitting helpmeet. As his father-in-law was wealthy, Lee, who loved country life, must have been tempted to settle down at Arlington to manage the estate that would one day pass to his wife, but his genuine devotion to his profession prevailed, and he went on building coast defenses.

In 1834, he was transferred to Washington as first lieutenant assisting the chief engineer of the army. He was thus enabled to live at Arlington, but, while in no sense of the term a society man, he also saw something of life at the capital. Three years later he was sent West to superintend work on the upper Mississippi. His plans were approved and well carried

LEE IN 1850
FROM THE ORIGINAL DAGUERREOTYPE—WITHOUT THE UNIFORM
PAINTED ON LATER

Through the courtesy of General G. W. C. Lee—who furnished information of much value concerning several portraits in this chapter—there is reproduced above the actual appearance of his distinguished father in 1850. This portrait was copied, embellished with a uniform painted on by hand, and widely circulated. To study the unretouched original is particularly interesting. Lee at this period was in Baltimore, in charge of defenses then being constructed. Three years before, in the Mexican War, he had posted batteries before Vera Cruz so that the town was reduced in a week. After each of the battles of Cerro Gordo, Churubusco, and Chapultepec, he received promotion, and for his services in the last he was breveted colonel. A born soldier, the son of a soldier, this handsome young man is not as handsome by far as the superb general who later lent grace and dignity to the Confederate gray. He little realized the startling future when this photograph was taken.

out; he was made captain in 1838, and, meanwhile, leading a somewhat uneventful life, he slowly acquired a reputation as a reliable officer. In 1841, he was put in charge of the defenses of New York, and in this position he remained until the outbreak of the Mexican War.

The part he played at this crisis throws much light upon his character and his after career. He distinguished himself in Mexico more brilliantly, perhaps, than any other officer of his years, and thus he gave proof of his native military bent and of the thoroughness with which he had studied the art of war. He was not in sympathy with the political "Jingoes" of the time, a fact which affords a measure of his mental rectitude. But he was modestly indisposed to speak out upon political matters, being, as he conceived, a soldier charged with executing the will of his country as expressed by its statesmen.

It might have been predicted that, in the event of a civil war, such a man would side with that part of the nation in which he was born and bred, that his services would be strictly military in character, that the thought of making himself a dictator or even of interfering with the civil administration would never cross his mind. He would exhibit the highest virtues of the soldier and the private citizen; he would not, like Washington, go farther and exhibit the highest virtues of the statesman. It is probably best for his own fame and for the Nation that this should have been so. The Republic is fortunate in possessing three men, each consummate in private character, two illustrious in the separate spheres of military and civil command, Lee the soldier, and Lincoln the statesman, and one unique in combining the two high orders of genius, the greatest of Americans, the "Father of his Country."

At the beginning of the Mexican War, Lee was attached to General Wool's command in the Northern departments. He attracted notice chiefly by his brilliant scouting. Early in 1847, at the request of General Winfield Scott, he joined the

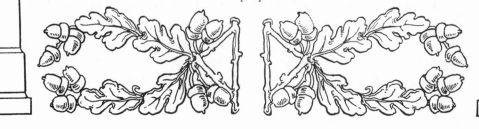

ARLINGTON, THE HOME OF LEE, FROM THE GREAT OAK

The beautiful estate by the Potomac came to General Lee from the family of George Washington. While Lee, as a boy and youth, lived in Alexandria he was a frequent caller at the Arlington estate, where Mary Lee Custis, the only daughter of George Washington Parke Custis, was his companion and playfellow. Before he had completed his course at West Point the friendship had ripened into love and the two became engaged. Her father is said to have considered her entitled to a more wealthy match than young Lee, who looked forward to a career in the army. But in 1831, two years after his graduation, the ceremony was performed and on the death of Custis in 1857, the estate passed into the possession of Robert E. Lee as trustee for his children. The management had already been in his hands for many years, and though constantly absent on duty, he had ordered it so skilfully that its value steadily increased. On the outbreak of the Civil War and his decision to cast in his lot with Virginia, he was obliged to leave the mansion that overlooked the national capital. It at once fell into the hands of Federal troops. Nevermore was he to dwell in the majestic home that had sheltered his family for thirty years. When the war was over, he gave the Pamunkey estate to his son Robert and himself retired to the quiet, simple life of Lexington, Virginia, as president of the institution that is now known, in his honor, as Washington and Lee University.

staff of that commander before Vera Cruz. In the fighting that ensued he displayed a skill and bravery, not unmixed with rashness, that won him high praise from his superior. In the reconnaissances before the victory of Contreras, he specially distinguished himself, and this was also the case at the battle of Chapultepec, where he was wounded. Having already been brevetted major and lieutenant-colonel, he was now brevetted colonel, and he took his share in the triumphant entry of the city of Mexico on September 14, 1847.

He was soon busy once more, employing his talents as engineer in the surveys made of the captured city, and showing his character in endeavoring to reconcile the testy Scott with his subordinates. Later, he was put in charge of the defenses of Baltimore, and later still, in 1852, he was made superintendent of the Military Academy at West Point. During his administration the discipline was improved and the course of study lengthened. In 1855, he was promoted lieutenant-colonel of the Second Cavalry, and in the spring of the next year he joined his regiment in western Texas. Pursuit of marauding Indians and study of animals and plants employed his hours, but he suffered from his separation from his wife and children, domestic affection being as characteristic a trait as his genius for battle. In July, 1857, the command of his regiment devolved upon him, and three months later he was called to Arlington on account of the death of his father-in-law, Mr. Custis. Despite the change in his circumstances, he returned to his command in Texas and remained until the autumn of 1859, when he was given leave to visit his family. It was during this visit that he was ordered with a company of marines to Harper's Ferry to dislodge John Brown. Then, after giving the legislature of Virginia some advice with regard to the organization of the militia, he took command of the Department of Texas. From afar he watched sadly the

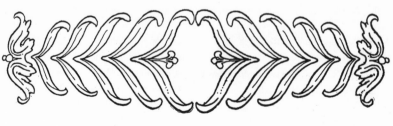

LEE'S BOYHOOD PLAYGROUND

When Robert E. Lee came over from Alexandria as a boy, to play soldier in the gardens and grounds around this beautiful mansion overlooking the Potomac, he could hardly have thought of its occupation during his life-time by a hostile force determined to bend his native State to its will.   When he was graduated from West Point in 1829 and proudly donned the army blue, he little imagined that thirty-two years later, after he had paced his room all night in terrible perplexity, he would doff the blue for another color sworn to oppose it.   The estate about Arlington house was a fair and spacious domain.   Every part of it had rung in his early youth and young manhood with the voice of her who later became his wife.   He had whispered his love in its shaded alleys, and here his children had come into the world.   Yet here stand men with swords and muskets ready to take his life if they should meet him on the field of battle.   Arlington, once famous for its hospitality, has since extended a silent welcome to 20,000 dead.   Lee's body is not here, but reposes in a splendid marble tomb at Washington and Lee University, where he ruled with simple dignity after the finish of the war.

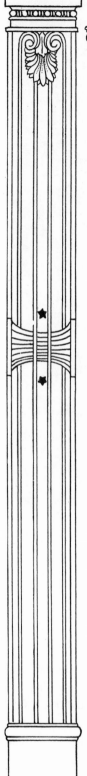

drift of the two sections toward war, and in February, 1861, upon the secession of Texas, he was recalled to Washington.

It is needless to discuss exhaustively Lee's attitude on the questions that were dividing the country. He did not believe in slavery or secession, but, on the other hand, he did not admit that the general Government had the right to invade and coerce sovereign States, and he shared the conviction of his fellow Southerners that their section had been aggrieved and was threatened with grave losses. He sided with those whom he regarded as his "people," and they have continued to honor his decision, which, as we have seen, was inevitable, given his training and character.

It was equally inevitable, in view of the oaths he had taken, and of the existence of theories of government to which he did not subscribe, that his entering the service of the Confederacy should seem to many Americans a wilful act of treason. His conduct will probably continue to furnish occasion for censure to those who judge actions in the light of rigid political, social, and ecclesiastical theories instead of in the light of circumstances and of the phases of character. To his admirers, on the other hand, who will increase rather than diminish, Lee will remain a hero without fear and without reproach.

Lee spent the weeks immediately following the inauguration of Lincoln in a state of great nervous tension. There seems to be little reason to doubt that, had he listened to the overtures made him, he could have had charge of the Union forces to be put in the field. On April 20, 1861, he resigned the colonelcy of the First Cavalry, and on the 23d he accepted the command of the military forces of Virginia in a brief speech worthy of the career upon which he was entering. A little less than a month later he became a brigadier of the Confederacy, that being then the highest grade in the Southern service.

For some time he chafed at not being allowed to take the field, but he could not be spared as an organizer of troops and

WHERE LEE STOOD SUPREME—THE WILDERNESS IN 1864

From the point of view of the military student Lee's consummate feats of generalship were performed in the gloom of the Wilderness. On this ground he presented an always unbroken front against which Grant dashed his battalions in vain. Never were Lee's lines here broken; the assailants must always shift their ground to seek a fresh opportunity for assault. At this spot on the battlefield of the Wilderness the opposing forces lay within twenty-four feet of each other all night. The soldiers, too, had learned by this 1864 campaign to carry out orders with judgment of their own. The rank and file grew to be excellent connoisseurs of the merits of a position. "If they only save a finger it will do some good," was General Longstreet's reply, when his engineer officers complained that their work on Marye's Hill was being spoiled by being built higher by the gunners of the Washington artillery—who had to fight

LEE IN THE FIELD
THE BEST KNOWN PORTRAIT

behind them. For this reason the significance of the lines as shown in many war maps is often very puzzling to the students of to-day, who have never seen the actual field of operations and have no other guide. Much of the ground disputed by the contending forces in our Civil War was quite unlike the popular conception of a battlefield, derived from descriptions of European campaigns, or from portrayals of the same, usually fanciful. For at this variety of warfare, Lee was a master, as well as on the rolling open plains of the Virginia farm. The portrait of Lee opposite was taken during the campaign preceding this test of the Wilderness. The reproduction here is directly from the photograph—taken at Lee's first sitting in war-time, and his only one "in the field." Reproductions of this picture painted, engraved, and lithographed were widely circulated after the war. The likeness was much impaired.

an adviser to President Davis. While others were winning laurels at First Manassas (Bull Run) he was trying to direct from a distance the Confederate attempts to hold what is now West Virginia, and in August he took personal charge of the difficult campaign. There is no denying the fact that he was not successful. His subordinates were not in accord, his men were ill supplied, the season was inclement, and the country was unfavorable to military operations. Perhaps a less kindly commander might have accomplished something; it is more certain that Lee did not deserve the harsh criticism to which for the moment he was subjected.

He was next assigned to command the Department of South Carolina, Georgia, and Florida, and he showed remarkable skill in laying down plans of coast defenses which long held the Union fleet at bay. In March, 1862, he was recalled to Richmond to direct the military operations of the Confederacy under President Davis, who was not a merely nominal commander-in-chief. Lee's self-control and balance of character enabled him to fill the post without friction, and for a time he was permitted to be with his wife and children, who were exiles from the confiscated estate of Arlington. He prepared men and supplies to oppose McClellan's advance toward Richmond, and successfully resisted "Joe" Johnston's plan to withdraw troops from the South and risk all on a pitched battle with McClellan near the capital. When, later, Johnston was wounded at Seven Pines, the command of the Confederate army on the Chickahominy devolved upon Lee (June, 1862) and he was at last in a position to make a full display of his genius as a strategist and an offensive fighter.

He at once decided, against the opinions of most of his officers, not to fall back nearer Richmond, and, after sending J. E. B. Stuart on a scouting circuit of the Union army, he prepared for the offensive. The attack made on June 26th failed because " Stonewall " Jackson's fatigued soldiers, who

ALL

THE ORIGINAL

WAR-TIME PHOTOGRAPHS

OF

ROBERT E. LEE

AS

PRESENTED

IN THIS CHAPTER

AND IN

OTHER VOLUMES

LEE
AT THE HEIGHT OF
HIS FAME
1863

"I believe there were none of the little things of life so irksome to him as having his picture taken in any way," writes Captain Robert E. Lee of his illustrious father. Lee was photographed in war-time on three occasions only: one was in the field, about '62-'63; the second in Richmond in 1863; and the third immediately after the surrender, at his Richmond home. Several of the portraits resulting have appeared in other volumes of this history; all the rest are presented with this chapter. Lee's first sitting produced the full-length on page 235, Volume II, and the full-face on the page preceding this—the popular portrait, much lithographed and engraved, but rarely shown, as here, from an original photograph, with the expression not distorted into a false amiability, but calm and dignified as in nature. Lee's second sitting was before Vannerson's camera in Richmond, 1863. Richmond ladies had made for their hero a set of shirts, and had begged him to sit for a portrait. Lee, yielding, courteously wore one of the gifts. The amateur shirtmaking is revealed in the set of the collar, very high in the neck, as seen in the photographs on this page. Another negative of this second oc-

casion, a full-length, is reproduced in Volume IX, page 123. The third photographing of Lee was done by Brady. It was the first opportunity of the camera wizard since the war began to preserve for posterity the fine features of the Southern hero. The position selected by Brady was under the back porch of Lee's home in Richmond, near the basement door, on account of the better light. The results were excellent. Three appear with this chapter: a magnificent three-quarter view, enlarged on page 63; a full-length, on page 69; and a group with Custis Lee and Colonel Taylor, on page 67. Another view of this group will be found on page 83 of Volume I; and the fifth of these Brady pictures, a seated profile of Lee alone, on page 23 of Volume III. An early daguerreotypist had portrayed Lee in 1850 as a young engineer-colonel—see page 55. The general's later life is covered by his celebrated photograph on "Traveler" in September, 1866, on page 121 of Volume IX; by the two portraits of '67 and '69 on page 73; by the photograph with Johnston, taken in 1869, on page 341 of Volume I, and by the striking group photograph that forms the frontispiece to this volume.

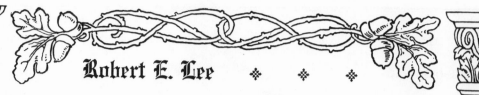

had just performed brilliant feats in the Valley of Virginia were not brought up in time. The next day's struggle resulted in a Pyrrhic victory for Lee, who was left, however, in complete control of the north bank of the Chickahominy.

The remainder of the great Seven Days' fighting around Richmond need not be described. Lee himself did not escape criticism; he was often badly supported; the Federals, as at Malvern Hill, showed themselves to be gallant foes, but the net result was the retreat of McClellan to the shelter of his gunboats, the relief of Richmond, and the recognition of Lee as the chief defender of the South. The Confederate commander was not fully satisfied, believing that with proper support he ought to have crushed his adversary. Perhaps he was oversanguine, but it is clear that aspiring aggressiveness is a necessary element in the character of a general who is to impress the imagination of the world.

His next procedure, McClellan having again begun to retreat, was to join Jackson against Pope, who had been threatening the Piedmont region. After complicated operations, in which the Federal general showed much bewilderment, and after daringly dividing his army in order to enable Jackson to move on Pope's rear, Lee won the complete victory of Second Manassas on August 30, 1862. Despite his inferior numbers, his aggressiveness and his ability to gage his opponents had enabled him to rid Virginia of Federal forces, and he resolved to invade Maryland. Davis acquiesced in his farsighted plan, and the march began on September 5th. The detaching of Jackson to take Harper's Ferry and the loss of one of Lee's orders, which fell into McClellan's hands, soon gave a somewhat sinister turn to the campaign. Lee's boldness and extraordinary capacity on the field enabled him, however, to fight the drawn battle of Sharpsburg, or Antietam, on September 17th with remarkable skill, yet with dreadful losses to

LEE—THE GENERAL WHO SHOULDERED "ALL THE RESPONSIBILITY"

The nobility revealed by the steadfast lips, the flashing eyes in this magnificent portrait is reflected by a happening a few days before its taking. It was 1865. The forlorn hope of the Confederacy had failed. Gordon and Fitzhugh Lee had attacked the Federal lines on April 9th, but found them impregnable. Lee heard the news, and said: "Then there is nothing left me but to go and see General Grant."—"Oh, General, what will history say to the surrender of the army in the field?"—Lee's reply is among the finest of his utterances: "Yes, I know they will say hard things of us; they will not understand how we were overwhelmed by numbers; but that is not the question, Colonel; the question is, is it right to surrender this army? If it is right, then I will take all the responsibility."

both sides. In the end he was forced to withdraw into Virginia, the campaign, from at least the political point of view, having proved a failure. As a test of efficient handling of troops in battle, Antietam, however, is a crowning point in Lee's military career.

The Army of Northern Virginia repassed the Potomac in good order, and Lee took up his headquarters near Winchester, doing his best to obtain supplies and to recruit his forces. Here, as later, one sees in him a figure of blended dignity and pathos, making a deep appeal to the imagination. His bearing and attire befitted the commander of one of the most efficient armies ever brought together; yet his most impressive qualities were his poise, his considerateness for others, his forgetfulness of self. No choice morsel for him while sick and wounded soldiers were within reach of his ministrations. Bullets might be whizzing around him, but he would stoop to pick up and care for a stunned young bird. No wonder that when, on a desperate day in the Wilderness, he attempted to head a charge, his lovingly indignant soldiers forced him back. They had visions of a hapless South deprived of its chief champion. To-day their sons have visions of a South fortunate in being a contented part of a great, undivided country and in possessing that choicest of possessions, a hero in whom power and charm are mingled in equal measure.

But we must take up once more our thin thread of narrative. Burnside superseded McClellan, and Lee, with the support of Longstreet and "Stonewall" Jackson, encountered him at Fredericksburg, where, on December 13, 1862, the Federals suffered one of the most disastrous defeats of the war. Hooker succeeded Burnside and began operations well by obtaining at Chancellorsville a position in Lee's rear. Then came the tremendous fighting of May 2 and 3, 1863, followed by Hooker's retreat across the Rappahannock on the 6th. The Confed-

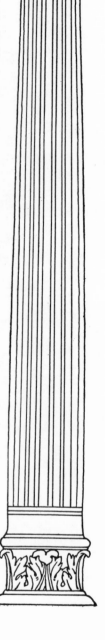

LEE IN RICHMOND AFTER THE WAR

The quiet distinction and dignity of the Confederate leader appears particularly in this group portrait—always a trying ordeal for the central figure.   Superbly calm he sits, the general who laid down arms totally unembittered, and set a magnificent example to his followers in peace as he had in war.   Lee strove after the fall of the Confederacy, with all his far-reaching influence, to allay the feeling aroused by four years of the fiercest fighting in history.   This photograph was taken by Brady in 1865, in the basement below the back porch of Lee's Franklin Street house in Richmond.   On his right stands General G. W. C. Lee, on his left, Colonel Walter Taylor.   This is one of five photographs taken by Brady at this time.   A second and third are shown on pages 65 and 69, a fourth on page 83 of Volume I, and a fifth on page 23 of Volume III.

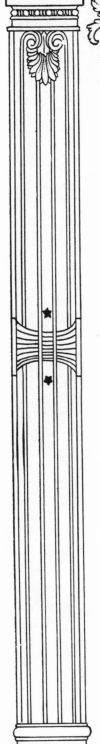

erate victory was dearly paid for, not only in common soldiers but in the death of " Stonewall " Jackson.

Weakened though Lee was, he determined upon another invasion of the North—his glorious, but ill-fated, Gettysburg campaign. Was it justifiable before those three days of fierce fighting that ended in Pickett's charge? Was Lee merely candid, not magnanimous, when he took upon himself the responsibility for the failure of his brilliant plans; or are his biographers in the right when they seek to relieve him at the expense of erring and recalcitrant subordinates? In his confidence in himself and his army, did he underrate the troops and the commander opposing him? Could Meade, after July 3d, have crushed Lee and materially shortened the war?

However these military questions may be finally answered, if final answers are ever obtained, Lee's admirers need feel little apprehension for his fame. The genius to dare greatly and the character to suffer calmly have always been and will always be the chief attributes of the world's supreme men of action. These, in splendid measure, are the attributes of Lee, and they were never more conspicuously displayed than in the Gettysburg campaign. Success is not always a true measure of greatness, but insistence upon success as a standard is a very good measure for a certain kind of smallness.

Meade not acting on the offensive, Lee began to retreat and at last got his army across the Potomac. Meade followed him into Virginia, but no important fighting was done in that State during the remainder of 1863, a year in which the Confederacy fared badly elsewhere. Lee suggested that he should be relieved by a younger man, but President Davis was too wise to accede, and the Southern cause was assured of its champion, even though the gaunt forms of famine and defeat kept drawing nearer and nearer.

Lee's army suffered severely during the winter of 1863–64 in the defenses behind the Rapidan, but its chief bore all privations with a simple Christian fortitude that renders super-

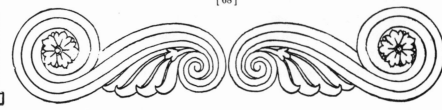

LEE IN 1865

The gray-haired man who wears his uniform with such high distinction is the general who had shown every kind of bravery known to the soldier, including the supreme courage to surrender his army in the field when he saw that further fighting would be a useless sacrifice of lives. This was a photograph taken by Brady, shortly before Lee left his home to become president of Washington University.

fluous any reference to Roman stoicism. With the spring he girded himself to meet his future conqueror, Grant, in campaigns which proved that, although he himself could be finally crushed by weight of numbers, he was nevertheless the greater master of the art of war. Grant's army was nearly twice as large as that of Lee, but this superiority was almost neutralized by the fact that he was taking the offensive in the tangled region known as the Wilderness. The fighting throughout May and June, 1864, literally defies description. Grant at last had to cease maneuvering and to fight his way out to a junction with Butler on the James. He would attack time and again with superb energy, only to be thrown back with heavy losses. Lee used his advantage of fighting on interior lines and his greater knowledge of the country, and so prevented any effective advance on Richmond. Finally, after the terrible slaughter at Cold Harbor, he forced Grant to cease hammering. Yet, after all, the Federal commander was not outfought. He had to submit to the delay involved in taking Petersburg before he could take Richmond, but the fall cf the Confederate capital was inevitable, since his own losses could be made up and Lee's could not.

On June 18, 1864, Lee's forces joined in the defense of Petersburg, and Grant was soon entrenching himself for the siege of the town. The war had entered upon its final stage, as Lee clearly perceived. The siege lasted until the end of March, 1865, Grant's ample supplies rendering his victory certain, despite the fact that when he tested the fighting quality of his adversaries he found it unimpaired. In one sense it was sheer irony to give Lee, in February, 1865, the commandership-in-chief of the Confederate armies; yet the act was the outward sign of a spiritual fact, since, after all, he was and had long been the true Southern commander, and never more so than when he bore privation with his troops in the wintry trenches around Petersburg.

LEE

AND HIS STAFF

AS THE WAR ENDED

MEN

WHO STAYED

THROUGH APPOMATTOX

These twelve members of General Robert E. Lee's staff surrendered with him at Appomattox Court House, and with him signed a parole drawn up by Grant, to the effect that they would not take up arms against the United States until or unless they were exchanged. This military medallion was devised by the photographer Rockwell during General Lee's stay in Richmond in April, 1865. These facts are furnished by Major Giles B. Cooke (No. 12, above), who had verified them by writing General Lee himself after the surrender.

Robert E. Lee ✦ ✦ ✦

Late in March and early in April, the Federals made Lee's position untenable, and he pressed on to Amelia Court House, where the expected supplies failed him, Richmond having meanwhile surrendered on April 3, 1865. Grant, drawing near, sent Lee on April 7th a courteous call to surrender. Lee, still hoping against hope for supplies, asked Grant's terms. Before the final surrender he took his chance of breaking through the opposing lines, but found them too strong. Then he sent a flag of truce to Grant, and a little before noon on April 9th held a meeting with him in a house at Appomattox Court House. It is superfluous to say that in his bearing at the interview and in the terms he offered his exhausted foes, Grant illustrated as completely the virtue of magnanimity as Lee did that of dignified resignation.

With tears in his eyes, Lee told his ragged but still undaunted veterans that their cause was lost. Then he issued a noble address to the survivors of his army, received visits from old friends among his opponents, and rode away on "Traveller" toward Richmond. In the fallen capital, even the Federal troops greeted him with enthusiasm, and he was at last once more in the bosom of his family. In June, he went to the country for rest, and later in the summer he accepted the presidency of Washington College at Lexington, now Washington and Lee University. He had previously refused many gifts and offers of positions which seemed tainted by mercenary considerations.

As a college president, General Lee both in character and in poise of intellect ranks with the first. During the five years of his administration the institution prospered financially, and the course of studies was liberally enlarged, no narrow military conceptions being allowed to prevail. He was as beloved by his students as he had been by his soldiers, and he was content with his small sphere of influence, declining most wisely to accept the governorship of the State and a political career

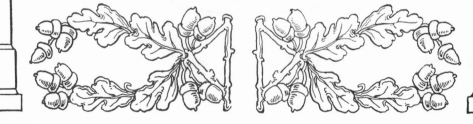

LEE IN 1867

PRESIDENT OF WASHINGTON COLLEGE, LATER
WASHINGTON AND LEE UNIVERSITY

LEE IN 1869

THE YEAR BEFORE HIS DEATH AT THE AGE
OF SIXTY-THREE

THE DECLINING YEARS

In these portraits the bright eyes of the daring leader have lost none of their fire; the handsome head still remains erect. In October, 1865, Lee had been installed as president of Washington College at Lexington, Virginia, later named in his honor Washington and Lee University. Under his management new chairs were founded, the scheme of study enlarged, and from the moral side it would have been impossible to secure finer results. Lee's greatness of soul was shown in the way in which he urged the Southern people loyally to accept the result of the war. On the morning of October 12, 1870, at the age of sixty-three, he died—mourned throughout the Union which he had helped to reunite, and throughout the civilized world, which had watched with admiration his gallant fight and nobility of soul. "To those who saw his composure under the greater and lesser trials of life," wrote Colonel William Preston Johnson, his intimate friend, "and his justice and forbearance with the most unjust and uncharitable, it seemed scarcely credible that his serene soul was shaken by the evil that raged around him." On his dying bed he fought over the great battles of the war. How strongly he felt his responsibility is shown by nearly his last words: "Tell Hill he must come up."

for which neither his years nor his temperament fitted him.

His health, which had begun to be impaired in 1863, gradually failed him, and in 1869 grew somewhat alarming. In the spring of 1870, he took a trip South with little result, and then he went to some springs for the summer. He resumed his duties at the college, but soon was taken ill in consequence of an accidental exposure, and after a short illness he died on October 12, 1870. His last words were of the war and his often dilatory subordinates: " Tell Hill he *must* come up."

Tributes came from friend and foe, and now, after forty years have passed, they continue to come. Lee is to the Southern people and to many military experts in foreign countries the greatest commander of armies that America has ever produced. He is to all who have studied his character, and to many who have merely heard or read of him in a general way, one of the noblest of men. He is the ideal gentleman, not merely of Nature's making, but of race and breeding; in other words, a true aristocrat. Yet to his aristocratic virtues, he added the essentially democratic virtues, and he was an ideal Christian as well as an ideal gentleman and man.

Lee's rank among the great men of the world is not so easy to determine, yet it seems clear that he must be named with the greatest of all time, with soldiers like Marlborough, for example, and that an additional luster attaches to his fame which few other great captains enjoy, since he attracts sympathy and love almost more than he does admiration. More completely perhaps than any other modern man of Anglo-Saxon stock he is qualified to be at once a hero of history and a hero of romance. He is the representative of a people that has suffered; hence his character and career possess a unique spiritual value not fully to be estimated by those who apply to him the normal tests of historical greatness.

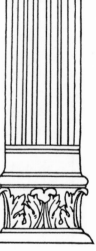

III

SHERMAN

A LEADER WHO FOUGHT, BUT WHO WON MORE
BY MARCHES THAN OTHERS WON BY FIGHTING

MAJOR–GENERAL WILLIAM T. SHERMAN AND HIS GENERALS

This photograph shows Sherman with seven major-generals who "went through" with him —fighting their way to Atlanta, and marching on the famous expedition from Atlanta to the sea and north through the Carolinas to the battle of Bentonville and Johnston's surrender.

From left to right they are:

MAJOR-GENERAL
O. O. HOWARD
Commanding the Army of the Tennessee

MAJOR-GENERAL
J. A. LOGAN
Formerly Commanding the Army of the Tennessee

MAJOR-GENERAL
W. B. HAZEN
Commanding a Division in the Fifteenth Army Corps

MAJOR-GENERAL
W. T. SHERMAN
Commanding the Military Division of the Mississippi

MAJOR-GENERAL
JEFF C. DAVIS
Commanding the Fourteenth Army Corps

MAJOR-GENERAL
H. W. SLOCUM
Commanding the Army of Georgia

MAJOR-GENERAL
J. A. MOWER
Commanding the Twentieth Army Corps

WILLIAM TECUMSEH SHERMAN

By WALTER L. FLEMING, PH.D.
Professor of History, Louisiana State University

THE armies of the United States were led in 1864–65 by two generals, to whom, more than to any other military leaders, was due the final victory of the Northern forces. Both Grant and Sherman were Western men; both were somewhat unsuccessful in the early years of the war and attained success rather late; to both of them the great opportunity finally came, in 1863, in the successful movement which opened the Mississippi, and their rewards were the two highest commands in the Federal army and the personal direction of the two great masses of men which were to crush the life out of the weakening Confederacy. Grant was the chief and Sherman his lieutenant, but some military critics hold that the latter did more than his chief to bring the war to an end. They were friends and were closely associated in military matters after 1862; in temperament and in military methods each supplemented the other, and each enabled the other to push his plans to success.

William Tecumseh Sherman was born in Lancaster, Ohio, February 8, 1820. The family was of New England origin, and had come to America from England in the seventeenth century. About two hundred years later, Sherman's father and mother migrated to what was then the unsettled West and made their home in Ohio. His father, a lawyer and in his later years a justice of the Ohio Supreme Court, died in 1829, leaving a large family of children without adequate support. The subject of this sketch was adopted into the family of Thomas Ewing, who was later United States senator, and Secretary of the Interior in the cabinets of Harrison and Tyler. The boy

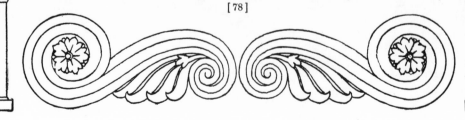

BEFORE THE MARCH TO THE SEA

These two photographs of General Sherman were taken in 1864—the year that made him an international figure, before his march to the sea which electrified the civilized world, and exposed once for all the crippled condition of the Confederacy. After that autumn expedition, the problem of the Union generals was merely to contend with detached armies, no longer with the combined States of the Confederacy. The latter had no means of extending further support to the dwindling troops in the field. Sherman was the chief Union exponent of the tactical gift that makes marches count as much as fighting. In the early part of 1864 he made his famous raid across Mississippi from Jackson to Meridian and back again, destroying the railroads, Confederate stores, and other property, and desolating the country along the line of march. In May he set out from Chattanooga for the invasion of Georgia. For his success in this campaign he was appointed, on August 12th, a major-general in the regular army. On November 12th, he started with the pick of his men on his march to the sea. After the capture of Savannah, December 21st, Sherman's fame was secure; yet he was one of the most heartily execrated leaders of the war. There is a hint of a smile in the right-hand picture. The left-hand portrait reveals all the sternness and determination of a leader surrounded by dangers, about to penetrate an enemy's country against the advice of accepted military authorities.

grew up with the Western country in which he lived, among energetic, brainy farmers, lawyers, and politicians, the state-makers of the West.

When sixteen years of age, Sherman secured an appointment to West Point, where he tells us " I was not considered a good soldier." But he was at least a good student, for he graduated as number six in a class of forty-two, the survivors of one hundred and forty-one who had entered four years before.

After graduation, in 1840, he was assigned to the Third Artillery, with which he served for six years in the Southern States, mainly in Florida and South Carolina. In South Carolina, he made the acquaintance of the political and social leaders of the South. At this time, in fact up to the Civil War, Sherman was probably better acquainted with Southern life and Southern conditions than with Northern. He spent some of his leisure time in the study of his profession and finally attacked the study of law.

Most of the next ten years was spent in California, where he was sent, in 1846, at the outbreak of the Mexican War. As aide to Generals S. W. Kearny, Mason, and Smith, in turn, Sherman was busy for four years in assisting to untangle the problems of the American occupation.

In 1850, he returned to Ohio and was married to Senator Ewing's daughter, Ellen Boyle Ewing, a woman of strong character and fine intellect, who for thirty-six years was to him a genuine helpmeet. About the same time, he was made captain in the Commissary Department and served for a short time in St. Louis and New Orleans, resigning early in 1853 that he might return to California to take charge of a banking establishment, a branch house of Lucas, Turner and Company, of St. Louis.

During this second period of life in California, we see Sherman as a business man—a banker. He was cautious and

SHERMAN IN 1865

If Sherman was deemed merciless in war, he was superbly generous when the fighting was over. To Joseph E. Johnston he offered most liberal terms of surrender for the Southern armies. Their acceptance would have gone far to prevent the worst of the reconstruction enormities. Unfortunately his first convention with Johnston was disapproved. The death of Lincoln had removed the guiding hand that would have meant so much to the nation. To those who have read his published correspondence and his memoirs Sherman appears in a very human light. He was fluent and frequently reckless in speech and writing, but his kindly humanity is seen in both.

successful, and soon his bank was considered one of the best on the Pacific coast. This was due mainly to the prudent management by which the institution was enabled to weather the storm that destroyed nearly all the Californian banks in 1856–57. But Sherman had always reported to his headquarters in St. Louis that the bank could not make profits under the existing conditions, and in 1857 his advice was accepted and the business closed.

From 1853 to 1857, Sherman appears in but one conspicuous instance in another rôle than that of banker. In 1856, he accepted the appointment of general of militia in order to put down the Vigilantes, an organization formed in San Francisco to crush the lawlessness which had come as a natural result of the weakness and corruption of the local government. He sympathized with the members of the organization in their desire to put down disorder, but maintained that the proper authorities should be forced to remedy matters, and that illegal methods of repressing crime should not be tolerated. For a time it seemed that he would succeed, but the local authorities were much disliked and distrusted by the people, and the promised support was not given him by the United States military authorities, with the result that his plans failed.

During the next two years, Sherman decided that as a business man he was a failure. In his letters, he vigorously asserts it as a fact; and in truth his business career must have been extremely unsatisfactory to him. In spite of good management, the San Francisco venture had failed. For a few months afterward he was in charge of another branch of the same business in New York, and, during the great panic of 1857, this also was discontinued on account of the failure of the main house in St. Louis. Then he went to Kansas, decided to practise law and was admitted to the bar, "on general intelligence," he said, and with his brother-in-law formed the law firm of Ewing, Sherman and McCook.

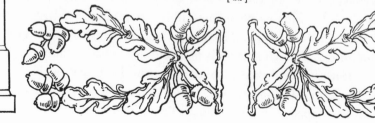

SHERMAN IN 1876

A SOLDIER TO THE END

The tall figure of "Old Tecumseh" in 1876, though crowned with gray, still stood erect and commanding. Upon the appointment of Grant as full general, in July, 1866, Sherman had been promoted to the lieutenant-generalship. When Grant became President of the United States, March 4, 1869, Sherman succeeded him as general. An attempt was made to run him against Grant in 1872, but he emphatically refused to allow his name to be used. He retired from the army on full pay in February, 1884. Although he was practically assured of the Republican nomination for President that year, he telegraphed that he would not accept the nomination if given, and would not serve if elected. He spent his later years among his old army associates, attending reunions, making speeches at soldiers' celebrations, and putting his papers in order for future historians. He resolutely refused all inducements to enter the political arena, and to the end he remained a soldier.

W. T. Sherman ✦ ✦ ✦ ✦

Sherman's law career, as he described it, was rather humorous. He lost his only case, a dispute over the possession of a shanty, but joined with his client to defeat the judgment by removing the house at night. Afterward, he undertook army contracts for constructing military roads and opened a large tract of Kansas wild land for Senator Ewing. Disgusted with business life, Sherman decided to reenter the army, and applied for a paymastership. But his friends of the War Department recommended him instead for the superintendency of the Louisiana State Seminary (now the Louisiana State University), then being organized. He was elected to that position in August, 1859, and for a third time he made his home in the South.

He was an efficient college executive; the seminary was soon organized and running like clockwork, students and instructors all under the careful direction of the superintendent, who very soon became a general favorite, not only with "his boys" but with the faculty of young Virginian professors. He had no regular classes, but gave episodical instruction in American history and geography, and on Fridays conducted the "speaking." He was a good story-teller, and frequently his room would be crowded with students and young professors, listening to his descriptions of army life and of the great West.

He was a firm believer in expansion and "our manifest destiny," and frequently lectured to students and visitors on those events in American history which resulted in the rounding-out of the national domain. It was due, perhaps, to his long residence in the far West that he regarded slavery as in no sense the cause of the sectional troubles of 1860–61. It was all the result, he maintained, of the machinations of unscrupulous politicians scheming for power, working upon a restless people who were suffering from an overdose of Democracy. It is clear that Sherman, while appreciating both the Northern

SHERMAN'S LEADERS IN THE ATLANTA CAMPAIGN

THE FIRST OF FIVE GROUPS OF LEADERS WHO MADE POSSIBLE SHERMAN'S LACONIC MESSAGE
OF SEPTEMBER, 1864: "ATLANTA IS OURS AND FAIRLY WON"

James D. Morgan, Leader of a Division
in Palmer's Corps.

R. M. Johnson, Leader of a Division
in the Fourteenth Corps.

John Newton Led the Second Division
of the Fourth Corps.

Alpheus S. Williams, Leader of a Division
under General Joseph Hooker.

Edward M. McCook, Dashing Leader of a
Cavalry Division in Front of Atlanta.

Wager Swayne, Originally Colonel of the
43d Ohio, Brevetted Major-General.

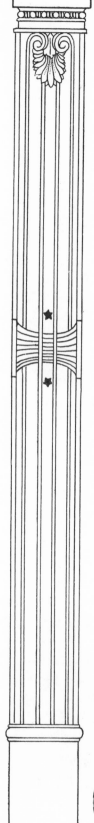
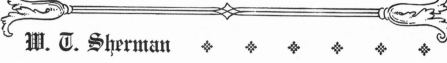

and the Southern points of view, did not fully comprehend the forces which for years had been driving the sections apart.

When Louisiana seceded, Sherman announced publicly what was already generally known—that he would not remain at the seminary; that he would take no part against the United States. It is said that he wept bitterly when he heard of the withdrawal of South Carolina. One of the strongest arguments against secession was, in his opinion, the geographic one. Familiar with all the Southern country, especially the Mississippi valley, he insisted that Nature itself had already decided the question against secession and that the South ought to struggle within the Union for redress of grievances. He believed that the South, though itself at fault, was aggrieved. He could not be prevailed upon to remain, and in February, 1861, he left the seminary and the State.

Sherman at once went to Washington where he found the politicians busy, and as they and Lincoln were " too radical " to suit him, he left, profanely declaring that " the politicians have got the country into this trouble; now let them get it out." For two months he was president of a street-railway company in St. Louis, and while here he was a witness of the division of Missouri into hostile camps. He watched the North while it gradually made up its mind to fight, and then he offered his services to the War Department, and was appointed colonel of the Thirteenth United States Infantry.

Sherman's military career falls into four rather distinct parts: The Manassas, or Bull Run, campaign, and Kentucky, in 1861; the Shiloh-Corinth campaign, in 1862; the opening of the Mississippi, in 1863; the campaigns in Georgia and the Carolinas, in 1864–65. During the first two years, he was making mistakes, getting experience, and learning his profession. In the third campaign, his military reputation was made secure, and in the last one he crushed half the Confederacy mainly by his destructive marches.

At Bull Run, or Manassas, he commanded a brigade with

Thos. H. Ruger Commanded a Brigade under General Hooker.

J. C. Veatch, Division Leader in the Sixteenth Army Corps.

Morgan L. Smith, Leader of the Second Division, Fourteenth Corps.

J. D. Cox Commanded a Division under General Schofield.

LEADERS IN THE ATLANTA CAMPAIGN— GROUP No. 2

COMMANDERS OF BRIGADES AND DIVISIONS WHICH FOUGHT UNDER McPHERSON, THOMAS AND HOOKER IN THE CAMPAIGN FOR ATLANTA, SUMMER OF '64

M. D. Manson, Brigade Leader in the Twenty-third Corps.

Charles Cruft Commanded a Brigade under General Stanley.

J. A. J. Lightburn Led a Division in the Army of the Tennessee.

W. L. Elliott, Chief of Cavalry under General Thomas

credit, and though it was routed he quickly restored its organization and *morale,* and for this he was made a brigadier-general of volunteers.

Transferred to Kentucky to assist General Robert Anderson, his former commander, in organizing the Federals of Kentucky, he came near ruining his career by the frankness of his speech to the Secretary of War and to the newspaper men. The administration evidently desired to minimize the gravity of the situation in the West, but Sherman insisted that to hold Kentucky sixty thousand men were necessary, and to open the valley to the Gulf two hundred thousand would be needed. He was better acquainted with the Southern temper than were the Northern politicians and the newspapers, some of which now declared him insane for making such a statement. He was hounded by them for several months and was almost driven from the service. The course of the war showed that he was correct.

During the next year was begun the movement to open the Mississippi valley. From the beginning of the war this had been one of Sherman's favorite projects. It was a Western feeling that the river must be opened, that the valley must belong to one people. Sherman saw service in responsible commands in the Shiloh-Corinth campaign. At Shiloh, he, like the other Federal and Confederate commanders, was hardly at his best; all of them still had much to learn. But in the rather uneventful Corinth military promenade, Sherman began to show his wonderful capacity for making marches count as much as fighting. He was now regarded as one of the best minor leaders, was no longer considered insane, and was made a major-general of volunteers as a reward for his services in the campaign.

In the Vicksburg campaign of 1863, which completed the opening of the Mississippi and cut in two the Confederacy, Sherman bore a conspicuous part, first under McClernand and

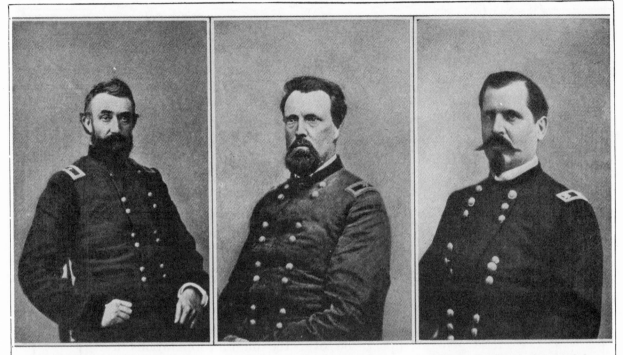

Nathan Kimball Led a Division in the Fourth Corps.

Samuel Beatty, Leader of a Brigade in the Fourth Corps.

William B. Hazen Commanded a Division under McPherson.

J. M. Corse "Held the Fort" at Alatoona Pass.

Joseph F. Knipe, Leader of a Brigade in the Twentieth Corps.

LEADERS IN THE ATLANTA
CAMPAIGN
GROUP No. 3

GENERAL OFFICERS WHO LED BRIGADES OR DIVISIONS IN THE HUNDRED DAYS' MARCHING AND FIGHTING FROM RESACA TO ATLANTA

Charles Candy Led a Brigade in Geary's Division of the Twentieth Corps.

later under Grant. It was the successful termination of the Vicksburg campaign which made secure the military reputations of both Grant and Sherman. Their good fame was enhanced by the subsidiary campaigns into the interior of Mississippi, and by the battle on Missionary Ridge, in Tennessee. Henceforth, "political" generals were less in evidence and the professional soldiers came to the front. Grant was called to exercise the chief command over all the armies of the Union. To Sherman, who was now made a brigadier-general of regulars, was given the supervision of the entire Southwest, embracing practically all of the military frontier not under Grant's immediate control. He was to direct the chief army which was to strike at the vitals of the lower South, and to exercise general supervision over the military operations in Tennessee, Mississippi, Alabama, and Arkansas, which were designed to make secure the hold of the Federals upon the lower Mississippi valley.

The river was held, and the army of one hundred thousand men, under the immediate command of Sherman, carried to successful conclusion, in 1864–65, three campaigns—that against Atlanta, the "store-house of the Confederacy," for which he was made major-general in the regular army, the march through Georgia to the sea, cutting the Confederacy in two a second time, and the campaign through the Carolinas, which was designed to crush the two principal armies of the South between Sherman's and Grant's forces.

For three months of the Atlanta campaign—May, June, and July—Sherman was pitted against Joseph E. Johnston, one of the Confederacy's greatest generals, the one best qualified to check Sherman's march. But Johnston, with his smaller force, fell back slowly from one strong position to another, holding each until flanked by Sherman, who could make progress in no other way. When Atlanta was reached, Johnston was superseded by John B. Hood, who at once initiated an

M. D. Leggett, Division
Leader in Blair's Corps.

William Harrow Commanded
Division in Logan's Corps,

John W. Fuller, Leader of a
Division in Dodge's Corps.

Thomas W. Sweeny Led a
Division in Dodge's Corps.

George D. Wagner Commanded a
Division under Howard.

LEADERS IN THE ATLANTA CAMPAIGN—No. 4

PROMINENT LEADERS IN THE ARMY OF
THE CUMBERLAND AND THE TENNESSEE
IN SHERMAN'S MASTERLY MOVEMENT
TO THE HEART OF GEORGIA

William F. Barry, Chief of Artillery
on Sherman's Staff.

W. W. Belknap, Promoted in
Front of Atlanta.

John B. Turchin, Leader in
the Fourteenth Corps.

William T. Ward Led a Di-
vision under Hooker.

John W. Sprague, Leader in
the Sixteenth Corps.

offensive policy but was severely defeated in several battles during the latter days of July and in August. For his success in this campaign, Sherman was made a major-general in the regular army. Finally Hood evacuated Atlanta, started on the fatal Tennessee campaign, and left the Federal commander free to move on through the almost undefended country to the Atlantic seaboard.

Sherman had provided for the defense of Tennessee and had garrisoned the important exposed posts which he considered it necessary to retain. On November 12, 1864, communications with the North were severed. He started with sixty-two thousand men on the "promenade" through Georgia, and for a month was not heard from except through Confederate sources. In December, Savannah was captured and was made a Federal base of supplies. Then began the march to the North through the Carolinas, which was much more difficult than the march to the sea, and Sherman was again confronted with his old antagonist, Joseph E. Johnston, who had been placed in command of the remnants of the Confederate forces. But the contest was more unequal than it had been in 1864, and when Lee surrendered in Virginia, Johnston in North Carolina gave up the struggle, and the war was practically at an end.

Here it is proper to add an estimate of the military qualities of the great Federal commander. Like the other successful commanders, he attained the fullness of his powers slowly. Not all military experts agree that he was a great commander on the battlefield, and in his successful campaigns he was generally pitted against weaker Confederate forces, acting (Hood excepted) uniformly on the defensive. Sherman's armies had no such experiences as did those which opposed Robert E. Lee. He was aided by such blunders of his opponents as were never made by Lee. But all agree that under the military and

Jos. A. Cooper Commanded a Brigade in the Twenty-third Corps.

M. F. Force Commanded a Brigade under Blair.

John H. King Commanded a Division in the Fourteenth Corps.

LEADERS IN THE

ATLANTA AND

NASHVILLE CAMPAIGNS

Milo S. Hascall, Leader of a Division in the Twenty-third Corps.

GENERAL OFFICERS
CONSPICUOUS IN SHERMAN'S
ADVANCE AND SOME
WHO PROTECTED THE FLANK
AND REAR OF HIS ARMY

David S. Stanley, Leader of the Fourth Corps; an All-around Soldier.

H. M. Judah Commanded a Division of the Twenty-third Corps.

Charles C. Walcutt, Leader of a Brigade in the Fifteenth Corps.

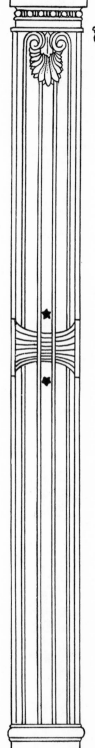

economic conditions existing in the Southwest, Sherman was preeminently fitted to undertake the task of breaking to pieces the weakening South. He was a great strategist if not so successful as a tactician; he won more by marches than others by fighting; he had a genius for large conceptions, and with his clear comprehension of Southern conditions he was able to strike with irresistible force at the weak points in the defense. Thus it was, according to Robert E. Lee, that he was enabled to give the Confederacy a mortal wound before any of its armies surrendered.

One feature of Sherman's campaigns, after leaving Atlanta, has been severely criticised. Much of the destruction of private property in Georgia and South Carolina, it is held, was not only unnecessary but amounted to cruelty in depriving the population of the necessities of life. Woodrow Wilson says of the work of the armies under Sherman's command: "They had devoted themselves to destruction and the stripping of the land they crossed with a thoroughness and a care for details hardly to be matched in the annals of modern warfare— each soldier played the marauder very heartily." Sherman himself intimated that the march would "make Georgia howl," and would "make its inhabitants feel that war and ruin are synonymous terms." The most intense feeling on the subject still exists in the communities over which Sherman marched in 1864–65, a feeling which does not exist against any other commander on either side, nor against Sherman himself in the regions over which he fought before 1864.

That Sherman himself did not intend to go beyond the limits of legitimate warfare is clear, and the unfortunate excesses were due mainly to the somewhat demoralized discipline of the troops, to the fact that they were in the midst of a hostile country, to the increasing bitterness that had developed as the war progressed, to the natural development of the permitted "foraging" into reckless plundering, and in part to certain characteristics of Sherman himself, which probably affected the

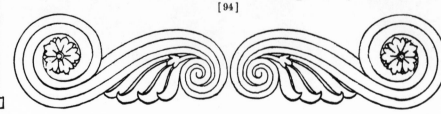

ARMY AND CORPS LEADERS WHO ENDED THE WAR IN THE NORTHWEST AND SOUTHWEST

As Sherman cut the southeastern Confederacy in two by his march to the sea, so Sheridan (center of group above) and Canby (shown below) wiped off the map the theaters of war in the northwest and southwest respectively. With Merritt and Torbert, and the dashing Custer, Sheridan swept the Shenandoah Valley. Canby, as commander of the military division of West Mississippi, directed the Mobile campaign of March-April, 1865, which resulted in the occupation by the Federals of Mobile and Montgomery. A raid by James H. Wilson (second from right) had prepared the way for this result. In May, 1865, Canby received the surrender of the Confederate forces under Generals R. Taylor and E. Kirby Smith, the largest Confederate forces which sur-

GENERAL EDWARD R. S. CANBY

rendered at the end of the war. The cavalry leaders in the upper picture are, from left to right: Generals Wesley Merritt, David McM. Gregg, Philip Henry Sheridan, Henry E. Davies, James Harrison Wilson, and Alfred T. A. Torbert. Wilson was given the cavalry corps of the military district of the Mississippi in 1865, and Torbert commanded the cavalry corps of the Army of the Shenandoah under Sheridan. These six great leaders are among the men who handled the Federal cavalry in its last days, welding it into the splendid, efficient, aggressive, fighting force that finally overwhelmed the depleted ranks of their Confederate opponents, Forrest and Wheeler in the West and Rosser, Lomax, Stuart, the two Lees and Hampton in the East.

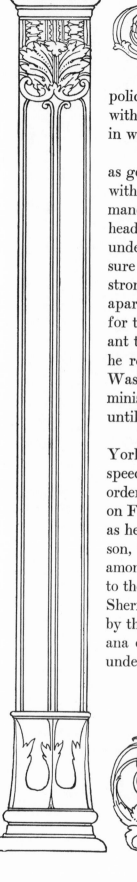

W. T. Sherman

policy of his corps commanders, who were more directly charged with the conduct of the troops. But if Sherman was merciless in war, he was superbly generous when the fighting was over.

When Grant was made President, Sherman succeeded him as general of the army, and knowing Grant's views to coincide with his own, he hoped so to reorganize the army that the commanding general, not the Secretary of War, would be the real head of the army. With Grant's assistance the reforms were undertaken, but they lasted less than a month, the political pressure upon the President in favor of the old system being too strong for him to bear. Sherman and Grant then drifted apart; the former could do little toward carrying out his plans for the betterment of the army, and finally, to escape unpleasant treatment, he removed his headquarters to St. Louis where he remained until President Hayes invited him to return to Washington and inaugurate his cherished plans of army administration. This pleasing professional situation continued until Sherman's retirement, in 1884.

During his later years, he spent most of his time in New York among old army associates, attending reunions, making speeches at soldier's celebrations, and putting his papers in order for the use of future historians. He died in New York on February 14, 1891, aged seventy-one years. He was buried, as he wished, in St. Louis, by the side of his wife and his little son, who had died nearly thirty years before. Inconspicuous among the many generals who went to New York to do honor to the dead leader was a quiet old gentleman in civilian dress— Sherman's ablest antagonist in war, Joseph E. Johnston, and by the side of the grave at St. Louis was one of his old Louisiana colleagues, proud of his unique experience, " a professor under Sherman and a soldier under 'Stonewall' Jackson."

IV

JACKSON

THOMAS J. JACKSON IN THE FORTIES

A PORTRAIT TAKEN DURING THE MEXICAN WAR,
WHERE JACKSON SERVED AS A SECOND
LIEUTENANT, THE YEAR AFTER HIS
GRADUATION FROM WEST POINT

STONEWALL JACKSON—A MEMORY

By Allen C. Redwood

Fifty-fifth Virginia Regiment, Confederate States Army

WHEN the early details of the first important collision between the contending forces in Virginia, in 1861, began to come in, some prominence was given to the item relating how a certain brigade of Virginia troops, recruited mostly from the Shenandoah valley and the region adjacent to the Blue Ridge, had contributed, largely by their steadiness under fire, almost for the first time, to the sustaining of the hard-pressed and wavering Confederate left flank, and the subsequent conversion of what had threatened to be a disastrous defeat to the Southern arms into a disorderly and utter rout of the opposing army.

War was a very new experience to most of that generation, and the capacity for absorbing sensational bulletins was commensurate with the popular expectation, if it did not exceed it. Those of us who were as yet doing the commonplace duty of detached garrisons, were consumed with envy of our more fortunate comrades who had taken part in what then seemed the great battle of the war and which our inexperience even conjectured might determine the pending issues. A man who had " been at Manassas " might quite safely draw upon his imagination to almost any extent in relating its happenings, with no fear that the drafts would not be duly honored by our credulity. As to the civilian element, its appetite was bounded only by the supply; like poor little Oliver Twist, it continually presented its porringer, eagerly demanding " more! "

Of this mass of fiction—of unthreshed grain—there remains yet one kernel of veracious history, and the incident was predestined to exercise significant and far-reaching influence

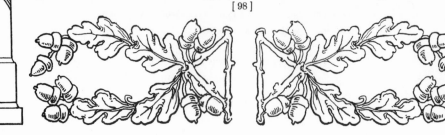

THOMAS JONATHAN JACKSON

AS FIRST LIEUTENANT, U. S. A.

Jackson's very soul impressed itself on the glass of this early negative through his striking features—more clearly read than later, when a heavy beard had covered the resolute lips, and the habit of command had veiled the deep-seeing, somber eyes. When the quiet Virginia boy with the strong religious bent graduated eighteenth in his class of seventy from West Point in 1846, his comrades little thought that he was destined to become the most suddenly famous of American generals. The year after his graduation he attracted attention by his performances as lieutenant of artillery under General Scott in Mexico, and was brevetted captain and major for bravery at Contreras, Churubusco, and Chapultepec. Fourteen years later he earned his sobriquet of "Stonewall" in the first great battle of the Civil War. Within two years more he had risen to international fame—and received his mortal wound on the field of battle. He was reserved, almost somber with his men, yet he earned the love and enthusiastic devotion of the soldiers who came to be known as "Jackson's foot cavalry," so unparalleled were the marches they made under his leadership. They came to trust his judgment as infallible, and in spite of overwhelming odds they followed no matter where he led.

upon the struggle, then in its very inception. In that fiery baptism, a man still unknown to fame was to receive, at the hands of a gallant soldier about to surrender his soul to the Maker who gave it, the name which, to the world, was to supplant that conferred by his natural sponsors, and by which he will ever be known as among the great captains of his race and of history. The supreme effort of the Federal commander was directed against the left of the army of Johnston and Beauregard and upon the open plateau surrounding the Henry house. The battle was raging furiously, and seemingly the Southern line at that point was on the verge of utter disaster, when the Carolinian, General Barnard E. Bee, rode from his shattered and wavering brigade over to where Jackson still held fast with his mountain men.

"General," he said in tones of anguish, "they are beating us back."

"No, sir," was the grim reply; "we will give them the bayonet." Bee rode back and spoke to his brigade: "Look at Jackson there, standing like a stone wall. Rally behind the Virginians!" and the front of battle was restored. The rest is history.

Thus it came to pass that popular inquiry began as to who this man Jackson might be, and what were his credentials and antecedents. The young cadets from the Virginia Military Institute, who promptly flocked to the colors of the State and of the Confederacy, could give but little satisfactory information; to their boyish minds he was just "Old Jack," instructor in natural philosophy and artillery tactics, something of a martinet and stickler for observance of regulation, and, on the whole, rather "queer" and not at all approachable. That he should be in command of a brigade seemed to them due far more to some peculiar fortune than to any inherent fitness residing in him. True, he was said to have graduated from the

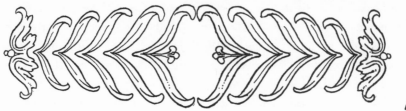

JACKSON—HIS MOST REVEALING PHOTOGRAPH

A PICTURE SECURED ONLY BY THE URGING
OF GENERAL BRADLEY T. JOHNSON

Jackson, a modest hero, nearly always shrank from being photographed. At the height of his fame he answered a publisher's letter with a refusal to write the desired magazine article or to send any picture of himself, though the offer was a very flattering one. The photograph above was made in Winchester, in February, 1862, at the Rontzohn gallery, where Jackson had been persuaded to spend a few minutes by the earnest entreaties of General Bradley T. Johnson. Some five months later Jackson was to send Banks whirling down the Shenandoah Valley, to the friendly shelter of the Potomac and Harper's Ferry, keep three armies busy in pursuit of him, and finally turn upon them and defeat two of them. This, with the profile portrait taken near Fredericksburg, shown on page 115 of Volume II, represents the only two sittings of Jackson during the war. Captain Frank P. Clark, who served three years in close association with the general, considered this the best likeness.

United States Military Academy, and was known to have been a some-time officer of the army, serving in Magruder's battery in Mexico during the campaign of Scott from Vera Cruz to the capital city.

It was even intimated that he had won certain brevets there for service at Vera Cruz, Contreras, and Chapultepec, rising from the grade of second lieutenant to that of major within a period of eighteen months, but to the youthful sense all that was very ancient history, of a piece with the Peloponnesian War, for instance, and the mists of antiquity hung about the record and made its outlines very vague. To the young, ten years seems a great while, and during that period their reticent, rigid instructor had been quite out of touch with anything military other than their cadet battalion or the gun details of the institute battery of 6-pounders, with human teams, which it was his duty to put through their evolutions on the drill-ground.

The human side of this man has almost no record during these years, apart from what comes to us through the letters to his wife; he was not a man who wore his heart on his sleeve, and life seems to have always been to him as a trust, for which he held himself strictly accountable, and which was not to be squandered in trivialities of any sort. As we know now, he had much to do, and the time for it was to be all too brief for its full accomplishment; yet he seems to have been not quite devoid of some sense of humor, in spite of his habitual reserve and aloofness.

It is related that upon one occasion, at this stage of his career, he propounded to his class this question, " Young gentlemen, can any of you explain to me the reason why it has never been possible to send a telegraphic despatch from Lexington to Staunton? " Several theories were advanced, such as that the presence of iron ore in the surrounding mountains might have had the effect of deflecting the electric current. At last, one boy—the dullard of the class, usually—suggested,

Lt. Genl. T. J. Jackson & Staff

W. J. Hawks Maj. Chf. C.S.

R. L. Dabney Maj. A.A.G.

J. Hotchkiss Capt. Top. Eng.

W. Allan Lt. Col. Chf. Ord.

Hunter McGuire Maj. & Med. Dir.

A. S. Pendleton Lt. Col. A.A.G.

COPY RIGHT SECURED

Richmond Va.

J. P. Smith Capt. A.D.C.

J. G. Morrison Capt. A.D.C.

H. K. Douglas Maj.

D. B. Bridgeford Maj. P.M.

"STONEWALL" AND THE MEN WHO BORE HIS ORDERS

Their honors came not easily to Jackson's staff officers. Tireless himself, regardless of all personal comforts, he seemed to consider others endowed with like qualities. After a day of marching and fighting it was no unusual thing for him to send a staff member on a thirty or forty mile ride. He was on terms of easy friendship and confidence with his aides off duty, but his orders were explicit and irrevocable. He had no confidants as to his military designs—quite the opposite: Before starting on his march to Harper's Ferry he called for a map of the Pennsylvania frontier, and made many inquiries as to roads and localities to the north of Frederick, whereas his route lay in the opposite direction. His staff, like his soldiers, first feared his apparent rashness, and then adored him for his success.

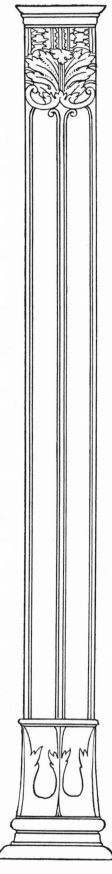

Stonewall Jackson ❖

diffidently, that it might be owing to the fact that there was no telegraph line then existing between the two points. " Yes, sir," replied Major Jackson; " that is the reason."

But, in the main, he was eminently practical and almost totally lacking in the minor graces and frivolities which render men socially possible, and, had not the great occasion arisen which was to afford scope for his ability, it seems as if he must have entirely escaped notice for the rest of his life. We are prone to look at things in that light, ignoring the fact that it is the man who has kept up his training who is ready and fit to seize opportunity when it shall present itself. Jackson had been " in training " all the while, even though no one—not even himself—may have suspected to what purpose.

This is the man who, more than any other, saved the day for the Confederacy at Manassas (First Bull Run), in 1861. Then he disappeared from view—a way he had, as his antagonists were to learn later—for a while, and at one time it seemed as if the theater of active operations was to know his presence no more, when, in response to an order from the War Department in Richmond, along with his acquiescence, he tendered his resignation from the command he then held.

Fortunately, this document went through the headquarters of his superior, General Joseph E. Johnston, who before forwarding it wrote to Jackson asking reconsideration, and so the services of the latter were retained to the Confederacy, and we were to hear much of his doings from that time until his untimely and tragic death. But in the months immediately succeeding Bull Run, he was almost lost sight of, and it was only at the opening of the campaign of 1862 that he began to loom again upon the military horizon.

The fortunes of the young Confederacy seemed then at a low ebb; from all the western portion came bulletins of disaster. In Virginia, a vast Federal host had been marshaled and was about to begin closing in upon the capital, and

John Echols, Colonel of a "Stonewall" Regiment at Bull Run; Later Led a Brigade in Lee's Army.

J. D. Imboden, at Bull Run and always with Jackson; Later Commanded a Cavalry Brigade.

W. B. Taliaferro, with Jackson throughout 1862; Last, at Fredericksburg.

Arnold Elzey, a Brigade and Division Commander under Jackson and later.

CONFEDERATE GENERALS WITH JACKSON

AT THE DAWN OF HIS BRILLIANT CAREER

Isaac R. Trimble. Where "Stonewall" was, There was Trimble also.

Stonewall Jackson ❖ ❖

all the outlying posts of the Confederate line were being severally driven in. Johnston had retired from Manassas to the line of the Rappahannock, presently to proceed to York-town, and eventually to retire thence to the Chickahominy. It was while lying there, awaiting McClellan's attack, that we began to get news of very active proceedings in the Valley region, which came to have important bearing upon our for-tunes, and in the final issue to determine the contest we were expecting and awaiting in our immediate front.

To those sultry, squalid camps, reeking with malaria and swarming with flies, came from beyond the far-away Blue Ridge stirring and encouraging tidings of rapid march and sudden swoop; of telling blows where least expected; of skilful maneuvering of a small force, resulting in the frustrating of all combinations of one numerically its superior, and paralyzing for the time being all the plans of the Federal War Depart-ment and the grand strategy of the " young Napoleon " at the head of its armies in the field.

It seemed as if the *sobriquet* conferred upon Manassas field had become the veriest of misnomers; the " Stonewall " had acquired a marvelous mobility since that July day not yet a year old and had become a catapult instead. And what, per-haps, appealed to our personal interest more forcibly was the story of the capture of the rich spoil of war, the supplies, of which we were already beginning to feel the need. Our daily diet of unrelieved bread and bacon grew fairly nauseating at the thought of the bounty so generously provided by " Commis-sary-General " Banks, and of the extra dainties inviting pillage in the tents of Israel—but we were to get our share, with ac-crued interest, later on.

We had not yet ceased to marvel over these exploits when Jackson executed one of his mysterious disappearances, puz-zling alike to friend and foe, and he next announced himself by the salvo of his guns, driving in McClellan's exposed right.

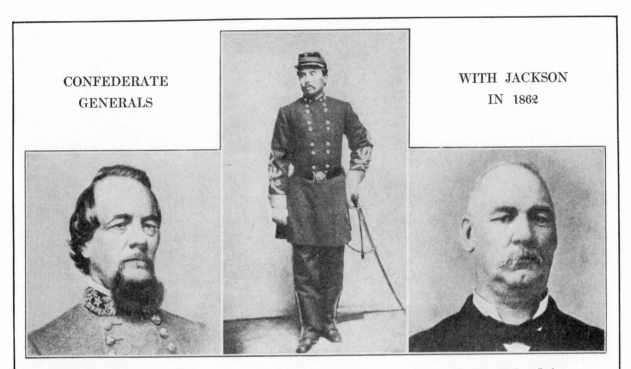

CONFEDERATE
GENERALS

WITH JACKSON
IN 1862

Edward Johnson Led an Independent Command under
Jackson in 1862.

George H. Steuart, Later
a Brigade Commander
in Lee's Army.

James A. Walker Led a
Brigade under Jackson at Antietam.

E. M. Law, Conspicuous at South Mountain
and Maryland Heights.

Charles W. Field, Later in Command of
one of Longstreet's Divisions.

This exposed condition was due to his own activity in the Valley, which had held McDowell inert upon the Rappahannock with thirty-five thousand muskets which should have been with the force north of the Chickahominy, inviting attack. Jackson rarely declined such invitations; he could scent an exposed flank with the nose of a hound and was "fast dog" following the trail when struck. Besides his habitual celerity of movement, was his promptness in delivering attack, which was an element of his success.

"The first musket upon the ground was fired," says a distinguished English authority, "without giving the opposing force time to realize that the fight was on and to make its dispositions to meet the attack or even to ascertain in what force it was being made." The quiet, retiring pedagogue of the "V. M. I." had not been wasting those ten years in which most of his leisure had been devoted to the study of the campaigns of the great strategists of history, from Cæsar to Napoleon, and his discipline in Mexico had given him some useful suggestions for their application to modern conditions. Also it had afforded the opportunity for giving that invaluable asset, the ability to gage the caliber of the men cooperating with him or opposed to him, with most of whom he had come in contact personally—a peculiarity of our Civil War, and one of important bearing upon all the operations conducted by officers of the regular establishment who, almost without exception, held high command in both armies.

But as yet we had no personal knowledge of this man who had been so rapidly coming to the fore. His work done, and well done, amid the Chickahominy lowlands, he was soon to heed the call coming to him from the hill country which gave him birth, and where his most notable service had so far been rendered. His old antagonists were reassembling there as a formidable army and under a new leader, and the line of direct

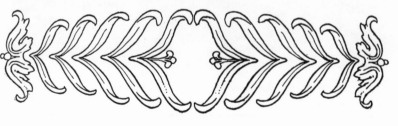

A. R. Lawton Led Ewell's Old Division at the Battle of Antietam.

Roswell S. Ripley, Wounded at Antietam in Defense of Lee's Left Flank.

R. E. Colston Commanded Trimble's Division at Chancellorsville.

Henry Heth Commanded the Light Division at Chancellorsville.

CONFEDERATE

GENERALS

WITH

JACKSON

AT ANTIETAM

AND

CHANCELLORS–

VILLE

Jas. J. Archer Commanded a Brigade at Chancellorsville.

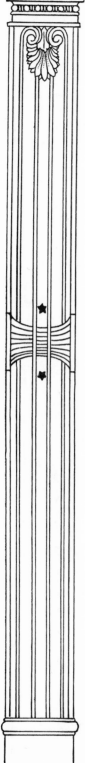

approach to the Confederate capital was to be attempted from that direction. Already he had proceeded thither with his two divisions which had made the Valley campaign—his own and Ewell's—when ours, commanded by A. P. Hill, received orders to join them, and all three were thenceforth incorporated in the Second Corps of the Army of Northern Virginia, as long as he commanded it.

We had fought the sharp engagement of Cedar Mountain on the 9th of August, 1862, and checked Pope's advance to the Rapidan. Then, after some days of rest, we again took the initiative and, crossing the little river, went after him. But the general who had heretofore " seen only the backs of his enemies " did not see fit to await our coming, but made so prompt and rapid a retrograde movement that even our expeditious " foot cavalry " could not come up with him before he passed the Rappahannock. It was on this hurried pursuit, passing through Brandy Station, that a figure came riding along the toiling foot column toward the front. He was in no wise remarkable in appearance, and it was with surprise that the writer heard that he was no other than our commander, General " Stonewall " Jackson.

He wore a rather faded gray coat and cap to match—the latter of the " cadet " pattern then in vogue and tilted so far over his eyes that they were not visible, and his mount and general appearance were not distinctive of high rank. In fact, he seemed some courier carrying a message to some general officer on ahead. Despite his West Point training, he was never a showy horseman—in which respect he had a precedent in the great Napoleon. When we took Harper's Ferry, in September of that same year, one of the surrendered garrison remarked, when Jackson was pointed out to him, " Well, he's not much to look at, but if we'd only had *him,* we'd never have been in this fix."

But within the interval we were to see much of him, and our appreciation speedily penetrated below the surface indica-

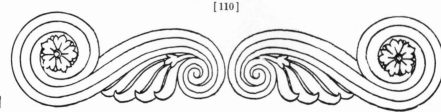

B. D. Fry, Colonel of the 13th Alabama; Later led a Brigade in Pickett's Charge.

F. T. Nichols, Wounded in the Flank Attack on Howard's Corps, May 2, 1863.

Harry T. Hays, Later Charged the Batteries at Gettysburg.

Robert F. Hoke, Later Defender of Petersburg, Richmond and Wilmington.

William Smith, Colonel of the 49th Virginia; Later at Gettysburg.

CONFEDERATE

GENERALS

WITH

JACKSON

AT THE

LAST—

CHANCEL-

LORSVILLE

J. R. Jones Commanded a Brigade of Virginians in Trimble's Division.

F. L. Thomas Commanded a Brigade in A. P. Hill's Division.

tions as we came to know and trust the man who conducted us to unfailing victory. Soldiers always forgive the means so that the end may be assured, and no man ever worked his troops harder than did Jackson, or ever awakened in them more intense enthusiasm and devotion. His appearance never failed to call forth that tumultuous cheer which was part of the battle onset. This was mostly, it must be admitted, in a spirit of mischief and for the sake of "making 'old Jack' run," for he never liked an ovation and always spurred out of the demonstration at top speed. Rigid disciplinarian that he was in all essentials, there was not the suspicion of concern with pomp and circumstance in all his make-up. War was to him much too serious an affair to be complicated by anything of the sort, nor was he at all tolerant of excuses when there was work in hand—results alone counted.

At Chantilly, our division commander sent word to him that he was not sure that he could hold his position as his ammunition was wet. "My compliments to General Hill and say that the enemy's ammunition is as wet as his, and to hold his ground," was Jackson's reply. Yet, unsparing as he was of his men when the urgency of the occasion demanded it, he was equally unsparing of himself, and, moreover, was always concerned for their well-being once the emergency was past, realizing that all warlike preparation is to the end of lavish expenditure at the supreme moment. In camp he was always solicitous that the troops should be well cared for, but when it came to take the field,

> "What matter if our shoes are worn,
> ' What matter if our feet are torn,
>   Quick step—we're with him ere the dawn."

That was "Stonewall Jackson's Way." A purposeful man, obstacles were to him but things to be overcome or ignored if they stood in the way of his plans. When one of his

A. H. Colquitt, Later Conspicuous in the Defense of Petersburg.

R. L. Walker, Commander of a Light Artillery Brigade.

CONFEDERATE
GENERALS
WITH
JACKSON

IN HIS
MASTERLY
1863
CAMPAIGN

S. McGowan, Later Commanded the South Carolina Brigade which Immortalized His Name.

Alfred Iverson, Later at Gettysburg and with Hood at Atlanta.

E. A. O'Neal Charged with His Brigade in Rodes' First Line at Chancellorsville.

subordinates, after the three days' hard fighting of the Second Manassas, preceded by a march of almost a hundred miles within a little more than a like period of time, objected that his men could not march further until they should have received rations, he was promptly put under arrest by Jackson, bent as he was upon following up his advantage and overwhelming Pope's defeated army before it could reach the protection of its entrenched lines at Alexandria, some thirty miles distant.

A master of men, Jackson infused those of his command with much of his own indomitable spirit, as expressed in the lines quoted from the old song of the corps, until they came to take pride in their hardships and privations and to profess a Spartan-like contempt for the sybaritic softness, as they considered it, of the other corps of the army. As to their confidence in his ability to meet and to dominate any situation, it simply had no bounds. In the movement on Manassas and during the engagement, with hostile forces coming from almost every direction, and while as yet we had no tidings of Longstreet, we were remote from our base and the foe was in superior force between; we were footsore and fagged nearly to the limit of human endurance, but there was no faltering in the belief that Jackson saw his way out of the toils which seemed to compass him about, as he had aforetime in the Valley campaign. Those thin lines never held their ground more tenaciously nor charged with more *élan* than during those eventful August days.

The last time my eyes were to behold him—how well it comes to mind!—was upon the morning of the fateful May 2, 1863, before the close of which day was to be ended his career as a soldier. We were moving out by the flank on a little woodland road, where we had been in bivouac the night before; it was a gloomy, overcast morning, as if giving premonition of the calamity to come to us before the next rising of the sun. Before we reached the plank road, in a small opening among

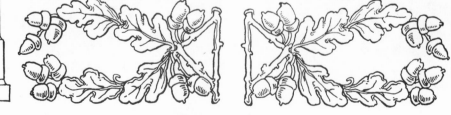

CONFEDERATE GENERALS OF LONGSTREET'S CORPS

WHO COÖPERATED WITH JACKSON IN '62 AND '63

Lafayette McLaws With His Division Supported Jackson's Attacks at Harper's Ferry and Chancellorsville; Later Conspicuous at Gettysburg and Chickamauga.

Joseph Brevard Kershaw Captured Maryland Heights, Opposite Jackson's Position at Harper's Ferry.

James L. Kemper Commanded a Brigade on Jackson's Right at the Second Battle of Manassas.

Ambrose R. Wright With His Brigade Closed the Pass Along the Canal at Harper's Ferry.

the pines were two mounted figures whom we recognized as Lee and Jackson. The former was seemingly giving some final instructions, emphasizing with the forefinger of his gantleted right hand in the palm of the left what he was saying—inaudible to us. The other, wearing a long rubber coat over his uniform (it had been raining a little, late in the night), was nodding vivaciously all the while.

After the Confederate success at Chancellorsville came Gettysburg. The question is often asked what would have happened had Jackson been present on that memorable field—Jackson, the man who was always up to time, if he brought but a fragment of his force with him, and whose " first musket on the ground was fired." As General Fitz Lee significantly related the case, " Suppose Jackson to have been four miles off the field at midnight of July 1st and been advised that General Lee wished the key-point of the enemy's position attacked next day; would the time of that attack have approximated more nearly to 4 A.M. or 4 P.M.? "—for answer, see the verse already quoted. For if the other corps commanders did not " like to go into battle with one boot off," ours would, at a pinch, go in barefoot—but he got there!

In the numerous discussions of the Gettysburg campaign which have come into notice since the event, much space has been given to the comparison of the relative forces of the two armies contending on that field. The disparity under the most liberal estimates inclines always in favor of the Federals, yet it seems to the writer that not enough account has been taken of the most significant shortage on the Confederate side of the balance. Successful battles had been waged and won more than once against greater odds, in point of mere numbers—as at Sharpsburg (Antietam) and Chancellorsville, for instance. But at Gettysburg, we were short just *one* man—who had been dead just two months—and his name was "Stonewall" Jackson.

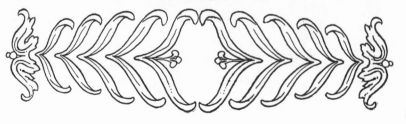

V

THE MEANING OF
LOSSES
IN WARFARE

MEN OF THE FAMOUS "VERMONT BRIGADE," ALL FROM THE ONE
STATE, WHICH SUFFERED MORE HEAVILY THAN ANY OTHER FEDERAL
BRIGADE DURING THE WAR—WITHIN A WEEK AT THE WILDERNESS
AND SPOTSYLVANIA, IT LOST 1,645 OUT OF 2,100 EFFECTIVE MEN

THE REGIMENT THAT SUSTAINED THE GREATEST LOSS OF ANY IN THE UNION ARMY

In the assault on Petersburg, June 18, 1864, these boys from Maine, serving as infantry, sustained the greatest loss of any one regiment in any one action of the war. Before the site where Fort Stedman was subsequently built 635 men were killed and wounded out of nine hundred engaged, a loss of over seventy per cent. in seven minutes. Such slaughter has never been paralleled in any warfare, ancient or modern. Of all the regiments in the Union armies this regiment lost most during the four years. Twenty-three officers and 400 enlisted men were killed and mortally wounded, and two hundred and sixty died of disease. The First Maine Heavy Artillery was organized at Bangor, and mustered in August 21, 1862. It left the State for Washington on August 24th. This section of the tremendous regimental quota—eighteen hundred men—is drilling at Fort Sumner in the winter of 1863. The men little imagine, as they go skilfully through their evo-

THE FIRST MAINE HEAVY ARTILLERY DRILLING IN FORT SUMNER,
ON A WINTER'S DAY OF '63

lutions in the snow, that the hand of death is to fall so ruthlessly on their ranks.   From the defenses of Wash-
ington they went to Belle Plain, Virginia, on May 15, 1864, as a part of Tyler's Heavy Artillery Division.
Four days later, at Harris's Farm on the Fredericksburg Road, the first of their great disasters fell upon them.
In this engagement their killed numbered eighty-two, their wounded 394, and their missing five.   Less than
a month later came the awful slaughter at Petersburg.   The remnant of the regiment served until its fall,
April 2, 1865.   After taking part in the Grand Review at Washington and remaining in its defenses till September 11th, the organization was mustered out, and ordered to Bangor, Maine.   On September 20, 1865,
the survivors of this "fighting regiment" were mustered out.   The Second Wisconsin Infantry lost a greater
percentage in killed during its whole term—19.7 per cent. as against 19.2 per cent. in the First Maine.

LOSSES IN THE BATTLES OF THE CIVIL WAR, AND WHAT THEY MEAN

By Hilary A. Herbert
Late Colonel, Eighth Alabama Infantry, Confederate States Army,
and late Secretary of the Navy of the United States

STATISTICS of losses in battles do not furnish an unfailing test of courage. Mistakes of officers, unavoidable surprises—these, now and then, occasion losses that soldiers did not knowingly face, and there are sometimes other reasons why the carnage in a particular command in this battle or that does not with accuracy indicate steadfast bravery. Such statistics, however, as all military experts agree, do tell a graphic story, when exceptional instances are not selected.

Colonel Dodge, in his "Bird's-Eye View of Our Civil War," exhibits statistics showing the percentage of losses in the most notable battles fought since 1745, and from them deduces this conclusion, "It thus appears that in ability to stand heavy pounding, since Napoleon's Waterloo campaign, the American has shown himself preeminent."

Colonel Dodge would have been justified in going much further. Waterloo itself, the most famous of the world's battles, does not show such fighting as Americans did at Sharpsburg (Antietam), Gettysburg, or Chickamauga.

In "Stonewall Jackson and the American Civil War," by Lieutenant-Colonel G. F. R. Henderson, a British military expert, is a complete list of killed and wounded in great battles from 1704 to 1882, inclusive. Since Eylau, 1807, there has been no great battle in which the losses of the victor—the punishment he withstood to gain his victory—equal the twenty-seven per cent. of the Confederates in their victory at Chickamauga.

The Henderson tables give the losses of both sides in each

MEN OF THE FIFTH GEORGIA

MORE THAN HALF THIS REGIMENT WAS KILLED AND WOUNDED AT THE BATTLE OF CHICKAMAUGA

Lounging beneath the Stars and Bars are eight members of an Augusta, Georgia, company—The "Clinch Rifles." Their new parapher-
nalia is beautifully marked "C. R." They have a negro servant. In a word, they are inexperienced Confederate volunteers of May,
1861, on the day before their company became a part of the Fifth Georgia Regiment. Pass to November, 1863; imagine six of the soldiers in the group lying dead or groaning with wounds, and but three unhurt,—and you have figured the state of the regiment after it
was torn to shreds at the battle of Chickamauga. It was mustered in for twelve months at Macon, Georgia, May 11, 1861, being the last
regiment taken for this short term. The Sixth Georgia and those following were mustered in for three years or the war. The Clinch
Rifles were sent to garrison Pensacola, Florida, where General Braxton Bragg would occasionally come from his headquarters, eight miles
away, to drill them. The ten companies were all from towns, or cities, and nicely uniformed, though each in a different style. This
led Bragg to name them his "Pound Cake Regiment." In July and August, 1862, the Fifth marched from Chattanooga, Tennessee, to
Bardstown, Kentucky, thence to the eastern part of the State, and down through Cumberland Gap to Knoxville, 800 miles in all. It
lost heavily in the battle of Murfreesboro. At bloody Chickamauga, September 19 and 20, 1863, its killed and wounded were more than
54 per cent. of the regiment—surpassed by few organizations in history. It suffered again at Missionary Ridge, and in the spring of
1864, when it stood against Sherman through the Atlanta campaign. The regiment fought on through the campaigns from Savannah,
Georgia, up to North Carolina, and in the last combat at Bentonville, North Carolina. It surrendered at Greensboro, April, 26, 1865.

battle, but indicate the percentage of those suffered by the victors only. These show fighting losses. In losses by a defeated army, those received in retreating cannot be separated from those received in fighting. If, however, a defeated army is not routed, but retires, still in fighting condition, and the foe is so crippled that he cannot make effective pursuit, as was the case at Chickamauga, or if the defeated army does not leave the field at all, until, say, twenty-four hours after the battle, as was the case with the Confederates at Sharpsburg and Gettysburg, the losses on both sides are to be counted as fighting losses, and their percentage is a fair measure of " capacity to stand pounding."

Gaged, then, by this standard, which for large armies in a great battle is absolutely fair, Waterloo is eclipsed by Gettysburg; Gettysburg is eclipsed by Sharpsburg, and Sharpsburg eclipsed by Chickamauga.

Here are some of Colonel Henderson's percentages, which tell the story, the percentage of the Federal losses at Chickamauga being calculated from Henderson's figures. At Waterloo, the victors' loss was twenty per cent. At Gettysburg, the victors lost also twenty per cent. But, at Waterloo, the French army dissolved; at Gettysburg, the Confederates held to their position nearly all the following day, and the majority of the Confederates did not know they had been defeated there until after the war.

At Sharpsburg, their victory cost the Federals not twenty, but twenty-three per cent., and the Confederates held fast to their position all the next day.

At Chickamauga, their victory cost the Confederates twenty-seven per cent., and the Federals, inflicting this loss, retreated; but General Thomas, the " Rock of Chickamauga," still held fast to prevent pursuit, and Rosecrans' army was ready to fight the next day. At Waterloo, the entire loss in killed and wounded, of the French, was thirty-one per cent.

OFFICERS OF A WESTERN FIGHTING REGIMENT—THE 36TH ILLINOIS

Of the Illinois regiments the Thirty-sixth fought in every important battle of the entire war in Western territory, and suffered in killed alone a loss of no less than 14.8 per cent., a figure exceeded among Illinois organizations only by the 14.9 per cent. of the Ninety-third. No Federal regiment lost as much as 20 per cent. killed and only 200 out of the 3,559 organizations as much as ten per cent. The Thirty-sixth Illinois lost 204 men out of a total enrollment of 1,376. These figures refer to deaths alone, excluding wounded and missing. At the battle of Stone's River, Tennessee, the regiment lost forty-six killed, 151 wounded, and fifteen missing, a total of 212. This was its heaviest blow in any one battle. It fought at Pea Ridge, an early engagement in the West, at Chaplin Hills, at the bloody battle of Chickamauga, and on the corpse-strewn slopes of Missionary Ridge. It fought under Sherman from Resaca to Atlanta, and when that general marched away on his expedition to the coast, the Thirty-sixth turned back to suffer its fourth largest loss in killed at the battle of Franklin, and to help Thomas crush Hood at the battle of Nashville. Such were the Western fighting regiments.

A REGIMENT
THAT LOST
14.8% IN
KILLED ALONE

ILLINOIS
INFANTRY
IN THE
WEST

OFFICERS OF THE 36TH ILLINOIS

The Meaning of Battle Losses ❖

This loss utterly destroyed the army. The Federals at Chickamauga withstood a loss practically the same—thirty per cent.—and still successfully defied the Confederates to attack them in Chattanooga.

The percentage of loss in battle by an entire army is, of course, obtained by including all present—those participating slightly, or even not at all, as well as those who bore the brunt of the fight.

Bearing this in mind, the reader will note to the credit of these troops that the dreadful losses sustained at Sharpsburg by the Fifteenth Massachusetts, Twenty-eighth Pennsylvania, Ninth New York, Twelfth Massachusetts, First Delaware, and other regiments; at Stone's River, December 31, 1862, by the Eighteenth United States Infantry, Twenty-second Illinois, and other regiments; at Gettysburg, by the Twenty-fourth Michigan, One hundred and eleventh New York, First Minnesota, One hundred and twenty-sixth New York, and One hundred and fifty-first Pennsylvania, were all suffered while the Federals were winning victories—suffered fighting, not in retreating.

So, also, the losses at the Wilderness of the Second Vermont, Fourth Vermont, and Ninety-third New York, occurred when the Federals, for the most part, held their ground. And nearly all the astonishing losses of the Confederate regiments were suffered when they were either winning victories or stubbornly holding on to the field of battle.

Altogether, the casualties in the greatest of the battles of the Civil War, whether considered in the aggregate or in the tragic light of regimental losses, make up a wonderful record.

In " *Étude sur les caractères généraux de la guerre d'Extrème Orient,*" par Le Capitaine Breveté F. Cullmann, Paris, 1909, the percentage of Federal losses at Gettysburg is given

[124]

COMMANDERS OF UNION BRIGADES CONSPICUOUS FOR LOSSES

These brigades from the Armies of the Potomac, the Cumberland, and the Tennessee, are mentioned specifically by Colonel William F. Fox, on account of their notable losses in action.

Iron Brigade	Michigan Cavalry Brigade	Harker's Brigade	Vermont Brigade
SOLOMON MEREDITH	PETER STAGG	LUTHER P. BRADLEY	LEWIS A. GRANT
Originally Colonel of the 19th Indiana.	Originally Colonel of the 1st Michigan Cavalry.	Originally Colonel of the 51st Illinois.	Originally Colonel of the 5th Vermont.

First New Jersey Brigade	Iowa Brigade	Willich's Brigade	Opdycke's Brigade
WILLIAM H. PENROSE	WILLIAM W. BELKNAP	AUGUST WILLICH	EMERSON OPDYCKE
Originally Colonel of the 15th New Jersey.	Originally Colonel of the 15th Iowa.	Originally Colonel of the 32d Indiana.	Originally Colonel of the 125th Ohio.

 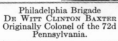

Excelsior Brigade	Philadelphia Brigade	Irish Brigade	Steedman's Brigade
JOSEPH B. CARR	DE WITT CLINTON BAXTER	THOMAS FRANCIS MEAGHER	JAMES B. STEEDMAN
Originally Colonel of the 2d New York.	Originally Colonel of the 72d Pennsylvania.	Commanded the Brigade in 1862.	Originally Colonel of the 14th Ohio.

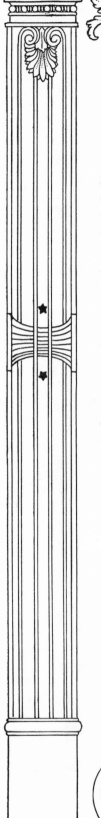

The Meaning of Battle Losses ❖ ❖ ❖

as twenty-three, the Confederate loss as thirty-two; the Japanese loss at Mukden as 14.1 and at Lio-Yang as 18.5. These were the bloodiest of the much lauded Japanese victories. This fighting does not compare with that in the American Civil War.

In the great Franco-Prussian war there is but one battle in which the percentage of the victor's loss is at all in the same class in the American Civil War, and that is Vionville, 1870, where the victor's loss was twenty-two, as compared with twenty-seven at Chickamauga. So it may be said fairly that, for a century, the world has seen no such stubborn fighter as the American soldier.

In studying the statistics of the various regiments whose losses are tabulated in this volume, the reader will discover that very many of these were suffered in great battles, the nature of which has been told briefly; and he must remember that neither of the armies suffered at any time any such signal defeat as would account for very heavy losses. The First Manassas (Bull Run) is no exception to this. The Confederates did not follow, and their losses in killed and wounded were heavier than those of the Federals.

What some of the foreign military experts think of us as fighters we may learn by extracts taken from their writings, italicizing at will. The late Lieutenant-Colonel Henderson was professor of military art and history at the Staff College of Great Britain. He says, in his " The Science of War ":

The War of Secession was waged on so vast a scale, employed so large a part of the manhood of both North and South America, aroused to such a degree the sympathies of the entire nation, and, in its brilliant achievements, both by land and sea, bears such splendid testimony to the energy and fortitude of their race, that in the minds of the American people it has roused *an interest which shows no sign of abating.*

Further on in the same essay he states:

Now, if there is one thing more than another apparent to the student of the Civil War, *it is that the soldiers on both sides were exceedingly well matched in courage and endurance.*

[126]

WILLIAM T. WOFFORD
Led his Brigade in the Maryland, Gettysburg, Wilderness and Shenandoah Campaigns.

DANIEL S. DONELSON
Led his Brigade in the Tennessee Campaign, notably at Murfreesboro.

ROBERT H. ANDERSON
Colonel of the 5th Georgia Cavalry; Promoted Brigadier-General July 26, 1864.

JAMES H. LANE
Led his Brigade at Fredericksburg, Gettysburg and in the Wilderness Campaign.

WILLIAM B. BATE
Led his Brigade in Bragg's Tennessee Campaigns, notably at Chickamauga.

ROGER ATKINSON PRYOR
Fought his Brigade on the Peninsula, where it bore a conspicuous part at Seven Pines.

CADMUS M. WILCOX
Led his Brigade at Manassas, Fredericksburg, Chancellorsville and Gettysburg.

WINFIELD SCOTT FEATHERSTON
Originally Colonel of the 17th Mississippi; Promoted for Gallantry at Ball's Bluff; Led his Brigade on the Peninsula.

HENRY L. BENNING
Led his Brigade in the Principal Battles of Longstreet's Corps, including Gettysburg, Chickamauga and the Wilderness.

EDWARD AYLESWORTH PERRY
Commanded a Regiment on the Peninsula; was wounded at Frayser's Farm; Led his Brigade at Gettysburg and the Wilderness.

COMMANDERS OF
CONFEDERATE BRIGADES WHICH SUFFERED HEAVILY IN BATTLE

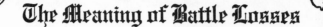

The Meaning of Battle Losses

The forces here credited with these "brilliant achievements" in 1861–65 are now thoroughly united, and would stand shoulder to shoulder against a foreign foe. Our population has increased threefold, while our military resources, our capacity to equip and to convey food to armies, to manufacture arms, and to build ships, even in the interior if need be, has increased tenfold. Our rivers still traverse the land, but the art of mining waters, practised with some success by the Confederates, has developed until no foe would think of exploiting these rivers with vessels in advance of troops.

Aye, but the spirit of our people, say the alarmists—we have lost patriotism, become commercialized, money-mad, and have now no militant instinct. To an old Confederate this prattle about our people being "commercialized" is especially amusing. It carries him back to 1860–61. In the hot sectional animosities that brought on the war he had imbibed that same idea about the North—the "Yankee" now worshiped "the Almighty Dollar," and in his all-absorbing struggle for it had lost the spirit that animated his forefathers at Lexington, Bunker Hill, and Saratoga. When the news of Manassas came, many an ambitious Confederate who was so unfortunate as not to have been there, felt like going into mourning. He was never to have a chance to "flesh his maiden sword." But the young Confederate was miscalculating. The exasperated North roused itself, after Manassas, like an angry lion pricked by the spear of the hunter, and soon we were to hear its roar.

In reference to inexperienced volunteers, it must be said, as every veteran of the Civil War knows, that it was not always the oldest regiments that were the bravest. In the gallant, though finally unsuccessful, assault that was made by the Federals at Salem Church, May 3, 1863, just where the Confederate line was broken for a time, the official reports show that the One hundred and twenty-first New York was in the fore-

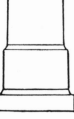

MAJ.-GEN. JAMES B. MCPHERSON
Atlanta, July 22, 1864.

MAJ.-GEN. JOS. K. MANSFIELD
Antietam, September 18, 1864.

MAJ.-GEN. JOHN SEDGWICK
Spotsylvania, May 9, 1864.

MAJ.-GEN. JOHN F. REYNOLDS
Gettysburg, July 1, 1863.

FEDERAL GENERALS KILLED IN BATTLE—GROUP No. 1—ARMY AND CORPS COMMANDERS

On this and the following six pages are portraits of the fifty-one Union generals killed in battle. Beneath each portrait is the date and place of death, or mortal wounding. Since no such pictorial necrology existed to aid the editors of this History, many questions arose—such as the determination of the actual rank of an officer at a given date, or the precise circumstances of death in certain instances. The list of Colonel W. F. Fox, presented in his work on "Regimental Losses in the Civil War," has been followed.

front, and its gallant Colonel Upton in his report says this was the regiment's first battle. Its loss, as officially reported, was two hundred and twenty-two killed and wounded.

At Fredericksburg, December 13, 1862, Franklin with the Federal left broke through Jackson's lines. The Confederates restored their line after heavy losses, and in this counterstroke a North Carolina regiment, fresh from home, drove headlong through the Northern lines and was with difficulty recalled. The apology of one of its privates, when it got back into line, caused a laugh all through the army. "If we had a-knowed how to fight like you fellows, we could have done better!"

In the work: "*Der Bürgerkrieg in den Nordamerikanischen Staaten,*" by Major Scheibert, of the German Engineer Corps, the author says:

After the European cavalry had been discredited in the wars of 1854 and 1859, the American mounted troops brought genuine joy to the heart of every true cavalryman, showing by their service and bravery that a better future might yet be in store for the European cavalry. We could not help sympathizing with the rise of the true spirit of knighthood without fear or blame, and with the many gallant deeds which promised better results.

We could multiply indefinitely these extracts, but space forbids. From the preface to the work of Cecil Battine, Captain, Fifteenth, The King's, Hussars, entitled: "The Crisis of the Confederacy, and History of Gettysburg and the Wilderness," the following is taken:

The history of the American Civil War still remains the most important theme for the student and the statesman because it was waged between adversaries of the highest intelligence and courage, who fought by land and sea over an enormous area with every device within the reach of human ingenuity, and who had to create every organization needed for the purpose after the struggle had begun. The admiration which the valor of the Confederate soldiers fighting against superior numbers and resources excited in Europe; the dazzling genius

PHILIP KEARNY
Chantilly
September 1, 1862.

FEDERAL
GENERALS KILLED
IN BATTLE

GROUP No. 2

ISAAC I. STEVENS
Chantilly
September 1, 1862.

ISRAEL B. RICHARDSON
Antietam
November 3, 1862.

MAJOR–GENERALS
COMMANDING
DIVISIONS
AND CORPS

AMIEL W. WHIPPLE
Chancellorsville
May, 7, 1863.

HIRAM G. BERRY
Chancellorsville
May 3, 1863.

JESSE L. RENO
South Mountain
September 14, 1862.

of some of the Confederate generals, and, in some measure, jealousy at the power of the United States have ranged the sympathies of the world during the war and ever since to a large degree on the side of the vanquished. Justice has hardly been done to the armies which arose time and again from sanguinary repulses, and *from disasters more demoralizing than any repulse in the field, because they were caused by political and military incapacity in high places, to redeem which the soldiers freely shed their blood, as it seemed, in vain.* If the heroic endurance of the Southern people and the fiery valor of the Southern armies thrill us to-day with wonder and admiration, the stubborn tenacity and courage which succeeded in preserving intact the heritage of the American nation, and which triumphed over foes so formidable, are not less worthy of praise and imitation. *The Americans still hold the world's record for hard fighting.*

This extract brings to mind that what impressed the Confederate in Lee's army with most admiration for the Army of the Potomac was, not its brave stand at Malvern Hill following a series of disasters, not its dogged perseverance when attacking an impregnable position at Marye's Heights, not its indomitable spirit at the "bloody angle," Spotsylvania, but the fact that no mistakes of its generals or of the authorities at Washington ever caused it to lose heart. Always and everywhere it fought bravely when given a chance. There never was but one Bull Run. Three successive changes were made in its commanders, from Yorktown to the Wilderness, and yet that gallant army never lost faith in itself, as the following incident illustrates. In the winter of 1863–64, the writer, then an officer in Lee's army, met between the picket lines near Orange Court House, Virginia, a lieutenant of a New York regiment. During our conversation the lieutenant said, " Well, we are on the road to Richmond again." " Yes," was the reply; " but you will never get there." " Oh, yes, we will after a while," said the lieutenant, " and if you will swap generals with us, we'll be there in three weeks." Just before we parted, the lieutenant proposed, " Here's my toast: May the best man win! " and we drank it heartily.

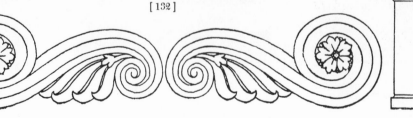

BRIG.-GEN.
THOMAS WILLIAMS
Baton Rouge, August 5, 1862.

BRIG.-GEN. ISAAC P. RODMAN
Antietam, September 30, 1862.

BRIG.-GEN.
WILLIAM H. L. WALLACE
Shiloh, April 10, 1862.

FEDERAL GENERALS KILLED IN BATTLE, GROUP No. 3

BRIG.-GEN.
JAMES E. JACKSON
Chaplin Hills, October 8, 1862.

BREVET MAJ.-GEN. JAMES S. WADSWORTH
Wilderness, May 8, 1864.

BREVET MAJ.-GEN.
DAVID A. RUSSELL
Opequon, September 19, 1864.

The Meaning of Battle Losses

Major G. W. Redway, referring to the volunteers of the Army of the Potomac, 1864, writes as follows:

The American volunteer who had survived such battles as Bull Run, Shiloh, Antietam, and the Seven Days' fighting around Richmond, was probably *such a soldier as the world had never seen before.* He needed no instruction as to his duty in the field, and, in fact, often exercised the functions of instructor both to officers and men less experienced than himself.

The impressions Federal and Confederate soldiers made on foreign critics were not lost on themselves. They were testing each other's courage, endurance, and patriotism, and coming to understand the situation as well. Four-fifths of the Confederates had never owned a slave. It was not slavery—both armies were fighting for the preservation of the same free institutions, for what each believed to be his Constitutional rights.

The first step toward reunion was being taken when picket shooting was stopped; and the armies of Northern Virginia and of the Potomac went far beyond that, when encamped on opposite banks of the Rappahannock, near Fredericksburg, during the winter and spring of 1862–63. They chatted, traded tobacco for sugar and coffee, and frequently visited each other across the narrow stream. A Confederate officer riding along the bank visiting his outposts was often saluted by a picket across the river, within easy gunshot. Similar compliments passed between pickets in gray and officers in blue. These soldiers were testifying their respect for each other, with little idea, on the part of the Confederates, that they would ever again be fellow countrymen.

Eventually both generals, Hooker and Lee, issued orders strictly forbidding all intercommunication. Just after these orders, an incident occurred which the writer long ago gave to the newspapers in the hope, which proved vain, that he might hear from the Union soldier. A Confederate officer

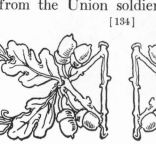

BREVET BRIG.-GEN.
JAMES A. MULLIGAN
Winchester, July 26, 1864.

BRIG.-GEN.
THOS. G. STEVENSON
Spotsylvania, May 10, 1864.

BREVET MAJ.-GEN.
THOMAS A. SMYTH
Farmville, April 9, 1865

BRIG.-GEN.
ROBT. L. McCOOK
Decherd, Tenn., August 6, 1862.

FEDERAL

GENERALS

KILLED

IN BATTLE

GROUP No. 4

BRIG.-GEN.
NATHANIEL LYON
Wilson's Creek, August 10, 1861.

BRIG.-GEN.
HENRY BOHLEN
Freeman's Ford, August 22, 1865.

MAJ.-GEN.
GEO. C. STRONG
Fort Wagner, July 30, 1863.

BREVET MAJ.-GEN.
S. K. ZOOK
Gettysburg, July 3, 1863.

BREVET MAJ.-GEN.
FREDERICK WINTHROP
Five Forks, April 1, 1865.

BREVET MAJ.-GEN.
ALEXANDER HAYS
Wilderness, May 5, 1864.

rode suddenly out of the woods on to his picket-post at Scott's dam, just above Banks' Ford. A Federal soldier was nearing the south bank of the river, newspaper in hand. The soldier reluctantly came ashore, insisting that he should be allowed to return; the Confederate pickets had promised it. "Yes," was the reply, "but they violated orders, and you violated orders on your side when you came over, and I happen to know it. Orders must be obeyed. You are my prisoner." The soldier, who was a big, manly fellow, stood straight as an arrow, looked the officer in the face, and with tears in his eyes, said: "Colonel, shoot me, if you want to, but for God's sake don't take me prisoner. I have been in the army only six weeks. I have never been in battle, and if I am taken prisoner under these circumstances, I will never get over it—it will always be believed that I deserted."

The officer hesitated for a moment, and then said, "Give me that paper and go, and tell your people you are the last man that will ever come over here and get back." Such an incident at the outset of the war would have been inconceivable.

It was in this spirit of kindly regard for each other that the war between the two armies went on, from Fredericksburg to Appomattox. It manifested itself with increasing tenderness after every bloody battle. It inspired Grant when he said to Lee, "Your men will need their horses to make a crop." It animated Grant's soldiers when they gave no cheer at the surrender, and when they divided their rations with the men who, in tears, laid down their arms. It did not die when the Confederates accepted the results of the war.

Time has only hallowed the memory of the glorious manhood displayed in those days by the men of both armies. The soldiers, had their sentiments prevailed, would soon have bound up the wounds of war, as they did those received in battle But politicians, for a time, interfered.

ELON J. FARNSWORTH
Gettysburg
July 3, 1863.

STEPHEN H. WEED
Gettysburg
July 2, 1863.

EDW. P. CHAPIN
Port Hudson
May 27, 1863.

VINCENT STRONG
Gettysburg
July 7, 1863.

CONRAD F. JACKSON
Fredericksburg
December 13, 1862.

FEDERAL

GENERALS

KILLED IN

BATTLE

GROUP No. 5

BRIGADIER–

GENERALS

PLEASANT A. HACKLEMAN
Corinth
October 3, 1862.

JOSHUA W. SILL
Stone's River
December 31, 1862.

GEO. D. BAYARD
Fredericksburg
December 14, 1862.

WM. R. TERRILL
Perryville
October 8, 1862.

GEO. W. TAYLOR
Manassas (Second Bull Run)
August 31, 1862.

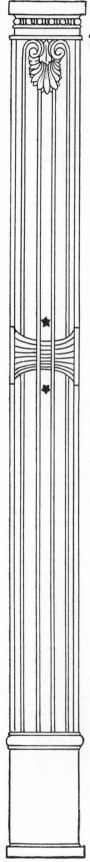

The Meaning of Battle Losses ❖ ❖ ❖

Of untold benefit have been the meeting of the Philadelphia Brigade and Pickett's men at Gettysburg, the visits of Massachusetts soldiers to Richmond, and of Virginia Confederates to Boston, and many similar occasions. These, coupled with the strewing of flowers, in 1867, by Southern women at Columbus, Mississippi, on the graves of Union soldiers, which brought from a Northern man that beautiful poem, "The Blue and the Gray," and a thousand similar incidents, have resulted in those acts that passed in Congress by unanimous votes, one providing for a Confederate section in Arlington Cemetery, the other looking to the care of the Confederate dead at Arlington and around the Federal prisons in the North.

Presidents Cleveland, McKinley, Roosevelt, and Taft have each and all, by deeds and words, had their full share in the work of perfect reunion. And all over the land there are monuments to the dead of the Civil War, bearing inscriptions that will outlast the marble and bronze upon which they are written. Such is the legend on the monument built by the State of Pennsylvania to its dead at Vicksburg, "Here brothers fought for their principles, here heroes died to save their country, and a united people will forever cherish the precious legacy of their noble manhood."

Another such is on a monument erected by the State of New Jersey, and the survivors of the Twenty-third New Jersey Volunteers at Salem Church, Virginia. On one side is an appropriate inscription to their own dead; on the other, a bronze tablet bearing this magnanimous tribute, "To the brave Alabama boys who were our opponents on this field and whose memory we honor, this tablet is dedicated." That is a tribute, not by a Government, but directly by the men who fought to the men who fought them. It is truly noble.

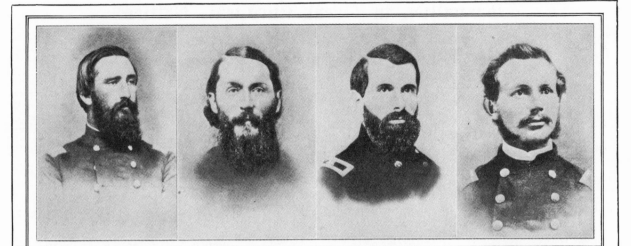

WILLIAM P. SANDERS
Knoxville
November 19, 1863.

WILLIAM H. LYTLE
Chickamauga
September 20, 1863.

JAMES C. RICE
Spotsylvania
May 10, 1864.

CHARLES G. HARKER
Kenesaw Mountain
June 27, 1864.

FEDERAL GENERALS

KILLED IN BATTLE

GROUP No. 6

BRIGADIER–GENERALS

HIRAM BURNHAM
Fort Harrison
September 30, 1864.

SAMUEL A. RICE
Jenkins' Ferry
July 6, 1864.

DANIEL McCOOK
Kenesaw Mountain
July 17, 1864.

J. H. KITCHING
Cedar Creek
Died January 10, 1865.

DANIEL D. BIDWELL
Cedar Creek
October 19, 1864.

Casualties in Great European Battles

COMPILED FROM HENDERSON'S "STONEWALL JACKSON AND THE AMERICAN CIVIL WAR"

LIST OF KILLED AND WOUNDED (EXCLUDING PRISONERS)

THE VICTORIOUS SIDE IS GIVEN FIRST IN EACH CASE

BATTLE	NUMBER OF TROOPS		KILLED AND WOUNDED	TOTAL	TOTAL PERCENTAGE	PERCENTAGE OF VICTOR
Blenheim, 1704............	Allies,	56,000	11,000	31,000	26	19
	French,	60,000	20,000			
Oudenarde, 1708...........	Allies,	85,000	10,000	20,000	11	11
	French,	85,000	10,000			
Malplaquet, 1709..........	Allies,	100,000	14,000	34,000	17	14
	French,	100,000	20,000			
Prague, 1757..............	Prussians,	64,000	12,000	22,000	17	18
	Austrians,	60,000	10,000			
Zorndorf, 1758............	Prussians,	32,760	12,000	32,000	38	37
	Russians,	52,000	20,000			
Kunnersdorf, 1759.........	Allies,	70,000	14,000	31,000	27	20
	Prussians,	43,000	17,000			
Torgau, 1760..............	Prussians,	46,000	12,000	24,000	22	26
	Austrians,	60,000	12,000			
Austerlitz, 1805...........	French,	65,000	9,000	25,000	16	13
	Allies,	83,000	16,000			
Eylau, 1807...............	French,	70,000	20,000	42,000	33	28
	Russians,	63,500	22,000			
Heilsberg, 1807............	Russians,	84,000	10,000	22,000	13	11
	French,	85,000	12,000			
Friedland, 1807............	French,	75,000	10,000	34,000	23	13
	Russians,	67,000	24,000			
Aspern, 1809..............	Austrians,	75,000	20,000	45,000	26	26
	French,	95,000	25,000			
Wagram, 1809..............	French,	220,000	22,000	44,000	11	10
	Austrians,	150,000	22,000			
Borodino, 1812............	French,	125,000	30,000	75,000	28	24
	Russians,	138,000	45,000			
Bautzen, 1813.............	French,	190,000	12,000	24,000	8	6
	Allies,	110,000	12,000			
Leipsic, 1813.............	Allies,	290,000	42,000	92,000	20	14
	French,	150,000	50,000			
Ligny, 1815..............	French,	73,000	12,000	24,000	15	16
	Prussians,	86,000	12,000			
Waterloo, 1815............	Allies,	100,000	20,000	42,000	24	20
	French,	70,000	22,000			
Solferino, 1859............	Allies,	135,000	16,500	31,500	10	11
	Austrians,	160,000	15,000			
Königgrätz, 1866..........	Prussians,	211,000	8,894	26,894	6	4
	Austrians,	206,000	18,000			
Vionville, 1870............	Germans,	70,000	15,800	32,800	19	22
	French,	98,000	17,000			
Gravelotte, 1870..........	Germans,	200,000	20,000	30,000	9	10
	French,	120,000	10,000			
Plevna, September 11, 1877..	Turks,	35,000	16,000	19,000	16	8
	Russians,	80,000	3,000			

GRIFFIN A. STEDMAN, JR.
Petersburg
Died August 6, 1864.

GEO. D. WELLS
Cedar Creek
October 13, 1864.

SYLVESTER G. HILL
Nashville
December 15, 1864.

FEDERAL GENERALS KILLED IN BATTLE—GROUP No. 7

ARTHUR H. DUTTON
Bermuda Hundred
Died June 4, 1864.

CHARLES R. LOWELL
Cedar Creek
October 20, 1864.

THEODORE READ
High Bridge
April 6, 1865.

TABULAR STATEMENT OF LOSSES IN BOTH THE UNION AND CONFEDERATE ARMIES IN THE PRINCIPAL BATTLES OF THE CIVIL WAR, 1861-1865, COMPILED FROM OFFICIAL REPORTS BY MARCUS J. WRIGHT, CHIEF OF THE DIVISION OF CONFEDERATE RECORDS, U. S. WAR DEPARTMENT

	Union Army				Confederate Army			
	Killed	Wounded	Missing	Total	Killed	Wounded	Missing	Total
Bull Run, Va., July 21, 1861	481	1,011	1,216	2,708	387	1,582	12	1,981
Wilson's Creek, Mo., Aug. 10, 1861	223	721	291	1,235	257	900	27	1,184
Fort Donelson, Tenn., Feb. 12-16, 1862	500	2,108	224	2,832	2,000	....	14,623	16,623
Pea Ridge, Ark., Mar. 7, 1862	203	980	201	1,384	600	....	200	800
Shiloh, Tenn., Apr. 6-7, 1862	1,754	8,408	2,885	13,047	1,723	8,012	959	10,694
Williamsburg, Va., May 4-5, 1862	456	1,410	373	2,249	1,570	....	133	1,703
Fair Oaks, Va., May 31-June 1, 1862	790	3,594	647	5,031	980	4,749	405	6,134
Mechanicsville, Va., June 26, 1862	49	207	105	361	1,484	....	....	....
Gaines' Mill, Va., June 27, 1862	894	3,107	2,836	6,837	8,751	....	....	....
Peach Orchard, Savage Station, Va., June 29, 1862								
White Oak Swamp, Glendale, Va., June 30, 1862	724	4,245	3,067	8,036	8,602	....	875	9,477
Malvern Hill, Va., July 1, 1862								
Seven Days, Va., June 25-July 1, 1862	1,734	8,062	6,075	15,849	3,478	16,261	875	20,614
Cedar Mountain, Va., Aug. 9, 1862	314	1,445	594	2,353	231	1,107	....	1,338
Manassas and Chantilly, Va., Aug. 27-Sept. 2, 1862	1,724	8,372	5,958	16,054	1,481	7,627	89	9,197
Richmond, Ky., Aug. 29-30, 1862	206	844	4,303	5,353	78	372	1	451
South Mountain, Md., Sept. 14, 1862	325	1,403	85	1,813	325	1,560	800	2,685
Antietam, or Sharpsburg, Md., Sept. 16-17, 1862	2,108	9,549	753	12,390	2,700	9,024	1,800	13,524
Corinth, Miss., Oct. 3-4, 1862	355	1,841	324	2,520	473	1,997	1,763	4,233
Perryville, Ky., Oct. 8, 1862	845	2,851	515	4,211	510	2,635	251	3,396
Prairie Grove, Ark., Dec. 7, 1862	175	813	263	1,251	164	817	336	1,317
Fredericksburg, Va., Dec. 13, 1862	1,284	9,600	1,769	12,653	595	4,061	653	5,309
Stone's River, or Murfreesboro, Tenn., Dec. 31, 1862, and Jan. 2, 1863	1,677	7,543	3,686	12,906	1,294	7,945	2,476	11,715
Arkansas Post, Ark., Jan. 11, 1863	134	898	29	1,061	28	81	4,791	4,900
Chancellorsville and Fredericksburg, Va., May 1-4, 1863	1,575	9,594	5,676	16,792	1,665	9,081	2,018	12,764

CONFEDERATE
GENERALS
KILLED
IN
BATTLE

GROUP NO. 1
ARMY
AND CORPS
COMMANDERS

On this page and fol-
lowing are portraits
of all the 73 general
officers of the Confed-
eracy killed in battle,
with the exception of
"Stonewall" Jack-
son, portraits of whom
appear in a preceding
chapter of this vol-
ume (See Index also).

GENERAL ALBERT SIDNEY JOHNSTON
Shiloh
April 6, 1862.

LIEUT.-GENERAL LEONIDAS POLK
Pine Mountain
June 14, 1864.

LIEUT.-GENERAL AMBROSE POWELL HILL
Petersburg
April 2, 1865.

Continued from page 142

Champion's Hill, Miss., May 16, 1863	410	1,844	187	2,441	381	1,769	1,670	3,851
Assault on Vicksburg, Miss., May 22, 1863	502	2,550	147	3,199	Full reports not available			
Port Hudson, La., May 27, 1863	293	1,545	157	1,995	....	235	....	
Port Hudson, La., June 14, 1863	203	1,401	188	1,792	22	25		47
Gettysburg, Pa., July 1–3, 1863	3,155	14,529	5,365	23,049	3,903	18,735	5,425	28,063
Fort Wagner, S. C., July 18, 1863	246	880	389	1,515	36	133	5	174
Chickamauga, Ga., Sept. 19–20, 1863	1,657	9,756	4,757	16,170	2,312	14,674	1,468	18,484
Chattanooga, Tenn., Nov. 23–25, 1863	753	4,722	349	5,824	361	2,160	4,146	6,667
Mine Run, Va., Nov. 27–Dec. 1, 1863	173	1,099	381	1,653	110	570	65	745
Pleasant Hill, La., Apr. 9, 1864	150	844	375	1,369	....	987	4,720	5,707
Wilderness, Va., May 5–7, 1864	2,246	12,137	3,383	17,666	Reports of losses not complete			
Spotsylvania, Va., May 10, 1864	753	3,347		4,100	Reports incomplete			
Spotsylvania, Va., May 12, 1864		6,020	800	6,820	Records of losses not shown			
Drewry's Bluff, Va., May 12–16, 1864	390	2,380	1,390	4,160	Reports incomplete			
Cold Harbor, Va., June 1–3, 1864	12,000				Reports incomplete			
Petersburg, Va., June 15–30, 1864	2,013	9,935	4,621	16,569	Estimated loss in Hill's Corps and Field and Kershaw's divisions, 2,970			
Atlanta Campaign, Ga., May, 1864 (including Buzzard's Roost, Snake Creek Gap and New Hope Church)	1,058		1,240	2,298	Killed and wounded, 9,187			
Assault on Kenesaw Mt., Ga., June 27, 1864	1,999		52	2,051	270		172	342
Tupelo, Miss., July 13–15, 1864	77	559	38	674	210	1,116	....	1,326
Atlanta, Ga., July 22, 1864 (Hood's attack)	430	1,599	1,733	3,722	2,890		851	3,741
Jonesboro, Ga., Aug. 31, 1864		179			1,640			
Jonesboro, Ga., Sept. 1, 1864	233	946	105	1,274	No full return of losses			
Winchester, Va., Sept. 19, 1864	697	3,983	338	5,018	276	1,827	1,818	3,921
Chaffin's Farm and Forts Harrison and Gilmer, Va., Sept. 29–30, 1864	383	2,299	645	3,327	No full report of losses			
Cedar Creek, Va., Oct. 19, 1864	644	3,430	1,591	5,665	320	1,540	1,050	2,910
Franklin, Tenn., Nov. 30, 1864	189	1,033	1,104	2,336	1,750	3,800	702	6,252
Nashville, Tenn., Dec. 15–16, 1864	387	2,562	112	3,061	No report of killed and wounded			
Bentonville, N. C., Mar. 19, 1865	139	794	170	1,103	195	1,313	610	2,118
Appomattox, Va., Mar. 29–Apr. 9, 1865	1,316	7,750	1,714	10,780	No report of losses			
Petersburg, Va., Apr. 2, 1865	625	3,189	326	4,140	No report of losses			

WILLIAM D. PENDER
Gettysburg
July 18, 1863.

J. E. B. STUART
Yellow Tavern
May 12, 1864.

STEPHEN D. RAMSEUR
Cedar Creek
October 19, 1864.

CONFEDERATE

GENERALS

KILLED

IN BATTLE

GROUP

No. 2

MAJOR–

GENERALS

W. H. T. WALKER
Atlanta
July 22, 1864.

PATRICK R. CLEBURNE
Franklin
November 30, 1864.

ROBERT E. RODES
Opequon
September 19, 1864.

Summary of Union Troops Furnished by the Several States and Territories

STATES AND TERRITORIES	White Troops	Sailors and Marines	Colored Troops	Indian Nations	Aggregate	Total Deaths, All Causes
Alabama	2,578	....	....	....	2,578	345
Arkansas	8,289	....	....	....	8,289	1,713
California	15,725	....	....	....	15,725	573
Colorado	4,903	....	....	....	4,903	323
Connecticut	51,937	2,163	1,784	....	55,864	5,354
Dakota	206	....	....	....	206	6
Delaware	11,236	94	954	....	12,284	882
District of Columbia	11,912	1,353	3,269	....	16,534	290
Florida	1,290	....	....	....	1,990	215
Georgia	....	....	....	....	....	15
Illinois	255,057	2,224	1,811	....	259,092	34,834
Indiana	193,748	1,078	1,537	....	196,363	26,672
Iowa	75,797	5	440	....	76,242	13,001
Kansas	18,069	....	2,080	....	20,149	2,630
Kentucky	51,743	314	23,703	....	75,760	10,774
Louisiana	5,224	....	....	....	5,224	945
Maine	64,973	5,030	104	....	70,107	9,398
Maryland	33,995	3,925	8,718	....	46,638	2,982
Massachusetts	122,781	19,983	2,966	....	146,730	13,942
Michigan	85,479	498	1,387	....	87,364	14,753
Minnesota	23,913	3	104	....	24,020	2,584
Mississippi	545	....	....	....	545	78
Missouri	100,616	151	8,344	....	109,111	13,885
Nebraska	3,157	....	....	....	3,157	239
Nevada	1,080	....	....	....	1,080	33
New Hampshire	32,930	882	125	....	33,937	4,882
New Jersey	67,500	8,129	1,185	....	76,814	5,754
New Mexico	6,561	....	....	....	6,561	277
New York	409,561	35,164	4,125	....	448,850	46,534
North Carolina	3,156	....	....	....	3,156	360
Ohio	304,814	3,274	5,092	....	313,180	35,475
Oregon	1,810	....	....	....	1,810	45
Pennsylvania	315,017	14,307	8,612	....	337,936	33,183
Rhode Island	19,521	1,878	1,837	....	23,236	1,321
Tennessee	31,092	....	....	....	31,092	8,777
Texas	1,965	....	....	....	1,965	151
Vermont	32,549	619	120	....	33,288	5,224
Virginia	....	....	....	....	....	42
Washington Territory	964	....	....	....	964	22
West Virginia	31,872	133	196	....	32,068	4,017
Wisconsin	91,029	....	165	....	91,327	12,301
Indian Nations	....	....	....	3,530	3,530	1,018
Regular Army	....	....	....	....	....	5,798
Colored Troops	....	....	*99,337	....	99,337	**36,847
Veteran Volunteers	....	....	....	....	....	106
U. S. Volunteers***	....	....	....	....	....	243
U. S. Sharpshooters and Engineers	....	....	....	....	....	552
Veteran Reserves	....	....	....	....	....	1,672
Generals and Staffs	....	....	....	....	....	239
Miscellaneous—Bands, etc	....	....	....	....	....	232
	2,494,592	101,207	178,975	3,530	2,778,304	359,528

* Colored troops recruited in the Southern States.
** Includes all the deaths in the 178,975 Colored Troops.
*** Ex-Confederate Soldiers.
Eighty-six thousand seven hundred and twenty-four drafted men paid commutation and were exempted from service.

BRIG.-GEN.
BENJAMIN McCULLOCH
Pea Ridge, March 7, 1862.

BRIG.-GEN.
BARNARD E. BEE
First Bull Run, July 21, 1861.

MAJ.-GEN.
JOHN PEGRAM
Hatcher's Run, February 6, 1865.

CONFEDERATE GENERALS
KILLED IN BATTLE

GROUP No. 3

BRIG.-GEN.
FELIX K. ZOLLICOFFER
Mill Springs, January 19, 1862.

BRIG.-GEN.
FRANCIS S. BARTOW
First Bull Run, July 21, 1861.

BRIG.-GEN.
ROBERT SELDEN GARNETT
Rich Mountain, July 13, 1861.

DEATHS FROM ALL CAUSES IN UNION ARMIES

Cause	Officers	Enlisted Men	Total
Killed and died of wounds........................	6,365	103,705	110,070
Died of disease...............................	2,712	197,008	199,720
In prison...................................	83	24,873	24,866
Accidents..................................	142	3,972	4,114
Drowning..................................	106	4,838	4,944
Sunstroke..................................	5	308	313
Murdered...................................	37	483	520
Killed after capture...........................	14	90	104
Suicide....................................	26	365	391
Military execution............................	....	267	267
Executed by enemy...........................	4	60	64
Causes unclassified...........................	62	1,972	2,034
Cause not stated.............................	28	12,093	12,121
Totals..................................	9,584	349,944	359,528

DEATHS IN CONFEDERATE ARMIES

A tabulation of Confederate losses as compiled from the muster-rolls on file in the Bureau of Confederate Archives. (In the report for 1865–66, made by General James B. Fry, United States Provost Marshal-General.) These returns are incomplete, and nearly all the Alabama rolls are missing. Still the figures show that at least 74,524 Confederate soldiers were killed or died of wounds, and that 59,297 died of disease.

STATE	KILLED			DIED OF WOUNDS			DIED OF DISEASE		
	Officers	Enlisted Men	Total	Officers	Enlisted Men	Total	Officers	Enlisted Men	Total
Virginia............	266	5,062	5,328	200	2,319	2,519	168	6,779	6,947
North Carolina.....	677	13,845	14,522	330	4,821	5,151	541	20,061	20,602
South Carolina.....	360	8,827	9,187	257	3,478	3,735	79	4,681	4,760
Georgia...........	172	5,381	5,553	140	1,579	1,719	107	3,595	3,702
Florida...........	47	746	793	16	490	506	17	1,030	1,047
Alabama.........	14	538	552	9	181	190	8	716	724
Mississippi........	122	5,685	5,807	75	2,576	2,651	103	6,704	6,807
Louisiana.........	70	2,548	2,618	42	826	868	32	3,027	3,059
Texas............	28	1,320	1,348	13	1,228	1,241	10	1,250	1,260
Arkansas.........	104	2,061	2,165	27	888	915	74	3,708	3,782
Tennessee........	99	2,016	2,115	49	825	874	72	3,353	3,425
Regular C. S. Army.	35	972	1,007	27	441	468	25	1,015	1,040
Border States......	92	1,867	1,959	61	672	733	58	2,084	2,142
Totals........	2,086	50,868	52,954	1,246	20,324	21,570	1,294	58,003	59,297

Colonel W. F. Fox, the authority on Civil War Statistics, states: "If the Confederate rolls could have been completed, and then revised—as has been done with the rolls of the Union regiments—the number of killed, as shown above (74,524), would be largely increased. As it is, the extent of such increase must remain a matter of conjecture. The Union rolls were examined at the same time, and a similar tabulation of the number killed appears, also, in General Fry's report. But this latter number was increased 15,000 by a subsequent revision based upon the papers known as "final statements" and upon newly-acquired information received through affidavits filed at the Pension Bureau."

WM. Y. SLACK
Pea Ridge
March 8, 1862.

ADLEY H. GLADDEN
Shiloh
April 11, 1862.

ROBERT HATTON
Fair Oaks
June 1, 1862.

RICHARD GRIFFITH
Savage Station
June 30, 1862.

GEORGE B. ANDERSON
Antietam
Sept. 17, 1862.

CONFEDERATE

GENERALS KILLED

IN BATTLE

GROUP No. 4

TWELVE BRIGADIER-

GENERALS

HENRY LITTLE
Iuka
September 19, 1862.

L. O'B. BRANCH
Antietam
September 17, 1862.

TURNER ASHBY
Harrisonburg
June 6, 1862.

WILLIAM E. STARKE
Antietam
September 17, 1862.

JAMES McINTOSH
Pea Ridge
March 7, 1862.

CHARLES S. WINDER
Cedar Mountain
August 9, 1862.

SAMUEL GARLAND, JR.
South Mountain
September 14, 1862.

TABULAR STATEMENT OF ORGANIZATIONS IN THE UNION SERVICE

	REGIMENTS	BATTALIONS	COMPANIES	BATTERIES
Cavalry	272	45	78	...
Heavy artillery	61	8	36	...
Light artillery	...	9	...	432
Engineers	13	1	7	...
Sharpshooters	4	3	35	...
Infantry	2,144	60	351	...
Totals	2,494	126	507	432

SUMMARY OF ORGANIZATIONS IN THE CONFEDERATE ARMY

Any attempt to present in statistical form the strength of the Confederate armies is manifestly impossible, as was explained by General Marcus J. Wright in his introductory chapter in Volume I of the PHOTOGRAPHIC HISTORY. The same conditions also render futile any accurate comparison of the troops furnished to the Confederate armies by the various states of the South. Nevertheless, by tabulating the various organizations and bearing in mind the limitations of the method as well as the original data, a slight basis is afforded to gain some idea of the relative numbers contributed by the different States. Furthermore, the numbers of the organizations when summarized are of interest in comparison with those given above.

No complete official roll of regiments and other organizations in the Confederate army is to be found either in the archives of the United States War Department or published in the War Records, and it is difficult, if not impossible, to give either an accurate list or the total number. Various lists have been compiled by private individuals, but none of these show absolute accuracy, and all differ among themselves. A list prepared by Colonel Henry Stone, a member of the Military Historical Society of Massachusetts, was made the basis of the following table by Colonel Thomas L. Livermore, which is published in his volume "Numbers and Losses in the Civil War." This list General Wright states is as accurate as can be found.

TABLE MADE BY COLONEL LIVERMORE FROM COLONEL STONE'S LIST

	INFANTRY				CAVALRY				ARTILLERY		
	Regiments	Legions	Battalions	Companies	Regiments	Legions	Battalions	Companies	Regiments	Battalions	Companies
Alabama	55	..	18	4	6	..	18	10	..	2	17
Arkansas	42	..	14	2	4	..	5	4	..	2	16
Florida	9	..	1	16	2	..	3	6	..	1	15
Georgia	67	3	14	9	7	..	21	...	..	..	...
Kentucky	9	..	...	..	11	..	1	...	..	..	...
Louisiana	33	..	22	..	3	..	13	8	5	3	19
Mississippi	53	..	21	..	25	1	4	...	..	1	9
Missouri	30	..	...	..	7	..	...	...	..	..	...
North Carolina	74	1	12	4	6	..	12	2	2	..	9
South Carolina	53	3	14	8	7	..	7	13	3	3	25
Tennessee	78	..	24	..	10	..	11	17	..	1	35
Texas	35	1	4	14	33	..	8	15	2	..	24
Virginia	99	1	19	5	16	..	40	26	4	12	58
Confederate or Prov. Army	5	..	...	..	...	..	...	...	..	..	...
Total	642	9	163	62	137	1	143	101	16	25	227

MAXCY GREGG
Fredericksburg,
December 13, 1862.

E. D. TRACY
Port Gibson
May 1, 1863.

THOMAS R. R. COBB
Fredericksburg
December 13, 1862.

LLOYD TILGHMAN
Champion's Hill
May 16, 1863.

GROUP No. 5

CONFEDERATE GENERALS

KILLED IN BATTLE

ROGER W. HANSON
Stone's River
December 30, 1862

E. F. PAXTON
Chancellorsville
May 3, 1863.

JAMES E. RAINS
Stone's River,
Dec. 31, 1862.

LEWIS A. ARMISTEAD
Gettysburg
July 3, 1863.

WILLIAM BARKSDALE
Gettysburg
July 2, 1863.

MARTIN E. GREEN
Vicksburg
June 27, 1863.

Regimental Casualties in the Union Army

IN any discussion of the total or relative casualties suffered by a military organization in a war, or in any particular engagement, it must be borne in mind that the entire subject is one around which many questions center. The general consideration has been discussed by Colonel Hilary A. Herbert in the preceding chapter. It now remains to give the readers of the PHOTOGRAPHIC HISTORY some few exact statistics of the losses suffered in both great armies.

In the official records there are summarized with considerable completeness the enlistments and casualties for the various regiments and other organizations of the Union army. The reports for the most part are complete and comprehensive, admitting of full discussion, yet often there is great difficulty in reducing the vast amount of material to a common denominator for purposes of comparison. The problem is to consider the various elements in their relations one to another. Thus, it is possible to take those regiments where the number killed or died of wounds during the entire period of service stood at a maximum in comparison with other organizations. Furthermore, it is possible to consider such casualties relatively, depending upon the strength of the organization, and this latter method gives a clear indication of the efficiency of the regiment during its entire period of service. Large total losses mean that the regiment was at the fore-front of the fighting in many battles and not necessarily unduly exposed at one particular action.

Such is the list to be found on page 154, compiled from the authoritative work of Lieutenant-Colonel William F. Fox, U. S. V.—" Regimental Losses in the Civil War." It is, indeed, a record of valor; the fifty regiments here listed are entitled to places of high honor on the scroll of history. It is, all things considered, the most useful basis of making a comparison of the services of the different regiments, and it is one which unfortunately cannot be made for the regiments comprising the Confederate army, on account of the absence of suitable rosters and reports.

Now, if we should consider the maximum percentage of casualties based on the total of killed, wounded, and missing, a similar roll could be constructed. It would be headed by the First Minnesota Infantry, which, at the battle of Gettysburg, with 262 men engaged on the second day, lost 168 wounded and 47 killed, or a percentage of 82. In fact, other regiments standing at the top of such a list are worthy of note, and a few such, as listed by Colonel Fox, are given in the table at the bottom of this page.

The tabular statement on page 154 must be considered, therefore, as suggestive rather than complete. The selection of fifty regiments is an arbitrary one; for, of over two thousand regiments in the Union army, 45 infantry regiments lost over 200 men killed or mortally wounded in action during the war. In fact, Colonel Fox has compiled a list of 300 fighting regiments, which lost over 130 who were killed and died of wounds during the war, or which, with a smaller enrollment, suffered an equivalent percentage of casualties.

REGIMENT	BATTLE	Killed	Wounded	Missing	Total	Engaged	Per Cent.
1st Minnesota.............	Gettysburg.............	47	168	—	215*	262	82.0
141st Pennsylvania.......	Gettysburg.............	25	103	21	149	198	75.7
101st New York..........	Bull Run..............	6	101	17	124	168	73.8
25th Massachusetts	Cold Harbor...........	53	139	28	220	310	70.0
36th Wisconsin (4 Cos.)....	Bethesda Church........	20	108	38	166	240	69.0
20th Massachusetts.......	Fredericksburg..........	25	138	—	163	238	68.4
8th Vermont.............	Cedar Creek...........	17	66	23	106	156	67.9
81st Pennsylvania........	Fredericksburg..........	15	141	20	176	261	67.4
12th Massachusetts.......	Antietam..............	49	165	10	224	334	67.0
1st Maine H. A..........	Petersburg.............	115	489	28	632	950	66.5
9th Louisiana Colored.....	Milliken's Bend........	62	130	—	192	300	64.0
5th New Hampshire.......	Fredericksburg..........	20	154	19	193	303	63.6

* Action of July 2d,—8 companies engaged; total casualties at Gettysburg were 224.

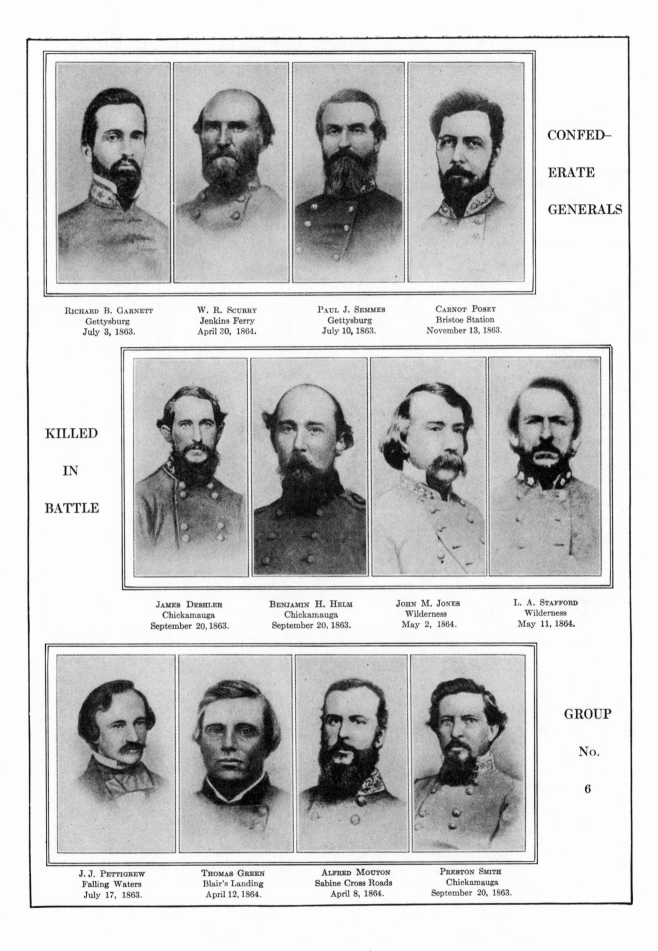

CONFED–

ERATE

GENERALS

RICHARD B. GARNETT
Gettysburg
July 3, 1863.

W. R. SCURRY
Jenkins Ferry
April 30, 1864.

PAUL J. SEMMES
Gettysburg
July 10, 1863.

CARNOT POSEY
Bristoe Station
November 13, 1863.

KILLED

IN

BATTLE

JAMES DESHLER
Chickamauga
September 20, 1863.

BENJAMIN H. HELM
Chickamauga
September 20, 1863.

JOHN M. JONES
Wilderness
May 2, 1864.

L. A. STAFFORD
Wilderness
May 11, 1864.

GROUP

No.

6

J. J. PETTIGREW
Falling Waters
July 17, 1863.

THOMAS GREEN
Blair's Landing
April 12, 1864.

ALFRED MOUTON
Sabine Cross Roads
April 8, 1864.

PRESTON SMITH
Chickamauga
September 20, 1863.

Casualties of Fifty Union Regiments During Entire Term of Service

KILLED AND DIED OF WOUNDS—MAXIMUM PERCENTAGES OF ENROLLMENT

COMPILED FROM FOX'S "REGIMENTAL LOSSES IN THE CIVIL WAR"

REGIMENT	DIVISION	CORPS	Enrolled	Killed	Per Cent.
2d Wisconsin	Wadsworth's	First	1,203	238	19.7
1st Maine H. A.	Birney's	Second	2,202	423	19.2
57th Massachusetts	Stevenson's	Ninth	1,052	201	19.1
140th Pennsylvania	Barlow's	Second	1,132	198	17.4
26th Wisconsin	Schurz's	Eleventh	1,089	188	17.2
7th Wisconsin	Wadsworth's	First	1,630	281	17.2
69th New York	Hancock's	Second	1,513	259	17.1
11th Penn. Reserves	Crawford's	Fifth	1,179	196	16.6
142d Pennsylvania	Doubleday's	First	935	155	16.5
141st Pennsylvania	Birney's	Third	1,037	167	16.1
19th Indiana	Wadsworth's	First	1,246	199	15.9
121st New York	Wright's	Sixth	1,426	226	15.8
7th Michigan	Gibbon's	Second	1,315	208	15.8
148th Pennsylvania	Barlow's	Second	1,339	210	15.6
83d Pennsylvania	Griffin's	Fifth	1,808	282	15.5
22d Massachusetts	Griffin's	Fifth	1,393	216	15.5
36th Wisconsin	Gibbon's	Second	1,014	157	15.4
27th Indiana	Williams'	Twelfth	1,101	169	15.3
5th Kentucky	T. J. Wood's	Fourth	1,020	157	15.3
27th Michigan	Willcox's	Ninth	1,485	225	15.1
79th U. S. Colored	Thayer's	Seventh	1,249	188	15.0
17th Maine	Birney's	Third	1,371	207	15.0
1st Minnesota	Gibbon's	Second	1,242	187	15.0
93d Illinois	Quinby's	Seventeenth	1,011	151	14.9
36th Illinois	Sheridan's	Fourth	1,376	204	14.8
8th Penn. Reserves	Crawford's	Fifth	1,062	158	14.8
126th New York	Barlow's	Second	1,036	153	14.7
49th Pennsylvania	Wright's	Sixth	1,313	193	14.6
9th Illinois	Dodge's	Sixteenth	1,493	216	14.4
20th Indiana	Birney's	Third	1,403	201	14.3
15th Kentucky	Johnson's	Fourteenth	956	137	14.3
2d Massachusetts	Williams'	Twelfth	1,305	187	14.3
55th Illinois	Blair's	Fifteenth	1,099	157	14.2
4th Michigan	Griffin's	Fifth	1,325	189	14.2
15th Massachusetts	Gibbon's	Second	1,701	241	14.1
15th New Jersey	Wright's	Sixth	1,702	240	14.1
145th Pennsylvania	Barlow's	Second	1,456	205	14.1
28th Massachusetts	Barlow's	Second	1,778	250	14.0
1st Michigan	Morell's	Fifth	1,329	187	14.0
8th New York H. A.	Gibbon's	Second	2,575	361	14.0
7th West Virginia	Gibbon's	Second	1,008	142	14.0
37th Wisconsin	Willcox's	Ninth	1,110	156	14.0
5th Michigan	Birney's	Third	1,883	263	13.9
10th Penn. Reserves	Crawford's	Fifth	1,150	160	13.9
13th Penn. Reserves	Crawford's	Fifth	1,165	162	13.9
63d Pennsylvania	Birney's	Third	1,341	186	13.8
5th Vermont	Getty's	Sixth	1,533	213	13.8
6th Iowa	Corse's	Sixteenth	1,102	152	13.7
155th New York	Gibbon's	Second	830	114	13.7
49th Ohio	T. J. Wood's	Fourth	1,468	202	13.7

ABNER PERRIN
Spotsylvania
May 12, 1864.

W. E. JONES
Piedmont
June 5, 1864.

GEORGE DOLES
Bethesda Church
May 30, 1864.

ROBERT H. ANDERSON
Antietam
October 6, 1862.

JOHN H. MORGAN
Greenville
September 4, 1864.

JOHN R. CHAMBLISS, JR.
Deep Bottom
August 16, 1864.

CONFEDERATE

GENERALS

KILLED

IN BATTLE

GROUP No. 7

BRIGADIER–

GENERALS

JUNIUS DANIEL
Spotsylvania
Died May 13, 1864.

JAMES B. GORDON
Yellow Tavern
May 11, 1864.

J. C. SAUNDERS
Weldon Railroad
August 21, 1864.

MICAH JENKINS
Wilderness
May 6, 1864.

C. H. STEVENS
Peach Tree Creek
July 20, 1864.

SAMUEL BENTON
Ezra Church
July 29, 1864.

Some Casualties of Confederate Regiments

By General Marcus J. Wright, Confederate States Army

AT the time when Lieutenant-Colonel William F. Fox, U. S. V., published his valuable and exceedingly accurate work, entitled "Regimental Losses of the American Civil War, 1861–1865," many regimental reports were missing or inaccessible, so that this work, in many respects a standard as far as Confederate material was concerned, necessarily is incomplete.

No compilation of statistics exists corresponding to that given for the Union armies on a preceding page, and but little exact statistical information of a broad character is available. Therefore, it seems desirable here to give on a following page a table from Colonel Fox's book, which shows remarkable percentages of losses in Confederate regiments at particular engagements. This list contains only a few of the many instances of regiments suffering a heavy percentage of loss. The list is compiled from the few cases in which the official Confederate reports on file in the United States War Department mention the number of effectives taken into action as well as the actual losses.

Because of these statistical deficiencies, no complete catalogue of distinguished Confederate regiments based on the records of battlefield casualties is possible. This is especially regrettable to those who recall the conspicuous services of many organizations from the very outset.

In addition to Colonel Fox's table we give a few other notable instances. At the first battle of Bull Run, the 33d Virginia lost 45 killed and 101 wounded, and the 27th Virginia lost 19 killed and 122 wounded. Hampton's Legion lost 19 killed and 100 wounded.

The 2d Georgia had the longest service of any infantry regiment from that State. In the Seven Days' around Richmond, with 271 men in the field, it lost 120. At Malvern Hill, it lost 81 men and about the same number at Gettysburg.

At Mills Springs, Ky., the 15th Mississippi Regiment lost 46 killed and 153 wounded. The 8th Kentucky regiment at Fort Donelson, Tenn., lost 27 killed and 72 wounded. The 4th Tennessee, at Shiloh, lost 36 killed and 183 wounded, while the 4th Kentucky lost 30 killed and 183 wounded. The 12th Mississippi, at Fair Oaks, Va., lost 41 killed and 152 wounded. Hampton's Legion, a South Carolina organization, at Fair Oaks lost 21 killed and 122 wounded. The 20th North Carolina lost, at Gaines' Mill, 70 killed and 202 wounded. At Gaines' Mill and Glendale the 14th Alabama lost 71 killed and 253 wounded, the 19th Mississippi 58 killed and 264 wounded, the 14th Louisiana 51 killed and 192 wounded, and the 12th Mississippi 34 killed and 186 wounded. At Malvern Hill, the 2d Louisiana lost 30 killed and 152 wounded. The 21st Virginia lost, at Cedar Mountain, Va., 37 killed and 85 wounded.

At Manassas (Second Bull Run), Va., the 5th Texas lost 15 killed and 224 wounded; the 2d Louisiana lost 25 killed and 86 wounded. At Richmond, Ky., the 2d Tennessee lost 17 killed and 95 wounded. At Antietam, or Sharpsburg, the 13th Georgia lost 48 killed and 169 wounded; the 48th North Carolina lost 31 killed and 186 wounded. At Iuka, Miss., the 3d Texas, dismounted cavalry, lost 22 killed and 74 wounded. At Corinth, Miss., the casualties of the 35th Mississippi were 32 killed and 110 wounded, and of the 6th Missouri, 31 were killed and 130 wounded. At Chaplin Hills, Ky., from the 1st Tennessee regiment, 49 were killed and 129 wounded.

At Fredericksburg, Va., the 57th North Carolina lost 32 killed, 192 wounded, and the 48th North Carolina 17 killed and 161 wounded. At Stone's River, the 29th Mississippi lost 34 killed and 202 wounded.

At Chancellorsville, Va., the losses of the 37th North Carolina were 34 killed and 193 wounded; the 2d North Carolina, 47 killed and 167 wounded. At Vicksburg, Miss., the 3d Louisiana lost 49 killed, 119 wounded, and the 6th Missouri lost 33 killed and 134 wounded. At Helena, Ark., the 7th Missouri lost 16 killed and 125 wounded. At Gettysburg, the 42d Mississippi lost 60 killed and 205 wounded, and the 1st Maryland, with 400 present for duty, had 52 killed and 140 wounded.

At Charleston Harbor, the 21st South Carolina lost 14 killed and 112 wounded, and the 25th South Carolina 16 killed and 124 wounded. At the bloody battle of Chickamauga, Alabama regiments suffered great losses.

ARCHIBALD GRACIE, JR.
Petersburg Trenches
December 2, 1864.

JOHN ADAMS
Franklin
November 30, 1864.

H. B. GRANBERRY
Franklin
November 30, 1864.

JAMES DEARING
High Bridge
April 6, 1865.

CONFEDERATE

GENERALS

KILLED

IN

BATTLE—

GROUP No. 8—

BRIGADIER-

GENERALS

JOHN DUNOVANT
Vaughn Road,
October 1, 1864.

JOHN GREGG
Darbytown Road,
October 7, 1864.

STEPHEN ELLIOTT, JR.
Petersburg
Died in 1864.

OSCAR F. STRAHL
Franklin
November 30, 1864.

ARCHIBALD C. GODWIN
Opequon
September 19, 1864.

S. R. GIST
Franklin
November 30, 1864.

VICTOR J. GIRARDEY
Petersburg
August 16, 1864.

Casualties of Fifty Confederate Regiments

From Fox's "Regimental Losses in the Civil War"

Showing Remarkable Percentages of Losses at Particular Engagements Based on Official Reports

Note—This list does not aim to include all the notable instances of remarkable casualties of regiments in the Confederate Army. It was based by Colonel Fox on available records where the numbers taken into action as well as the casualties were specified in official reports. The list is suggestive rather than complete, as many regiments omitted might with propriety claim to be included in any roll of "Fifty Fighting Regiments."

REGIMENT	BATTLE	DIVISION	Present	Killed	Wounded	Missing	Per Cent.
1st Texas	Antietam	Hood's	226	45	141	..	82.3
21st Georgia	Manassas	Ewell's	242	38	146	..	76.0
26th North Carolina	Gettysburg	Heth's	820	86	502	..	71.7
6th Mississippi	Shiloh	Hardee's	425	61	239	..	70.5
8th Tennessee	Stone's River	Cheatham's	444	41	265	..	68.2
10th Tennessee	Chickamauga	Johnson's	328	44	180	..	68.0
Palmetto Sharpshooters	Glendale	Longstreet's	375	39	215	..	67.7
17th South Carolina	Manassas	Evans'	284	25	164	1	66.9
23d South Carolina	Manassas	Evans'	225	27	122	..	66.2
44th Georgia	Mechanicsville	D. H. Hill's	514	71	264	..	65.1
2d N. C. Battalion	Gettysburg	Rodes'	240	29	124	..	63.7
16th Mississippi	Antietam	Anderson's	228	27	117	..	63.1
27th North Carolina	Antietam	Walker's	325	31	168	..	61.2
6th Alabama	Seven Pines	D. H. Hill's	632	91	277	5	59.0
15th Virginia	Antietam	McLaws'	128	11	64	..	58.5
8th Georgia	Antietam	Hood's	176	13	72	16	57.3
1st S. C. Rifles	Gaines' Mill	A. P. Hill's	537	81	225	..	56.9
10th Georgia	Antietam	McLaws'	148	15	69	..	56.7
18th North Carolina	Seven Days	A. P. Hill's	396	45	179	..	56.5
3d Alabama	Malvern Hill	D. H. Hill's	354	37	163	..	56.4
17th Virginia	Antietam	Pickett's	55	7	24	..	56.3
7th North Carolina	Seven Days	A. P. Hill's	450	35	218	..	56.2
12th Tennessee	Stone's River	Cheatham's	292	18	137	9	56.1
9th Georgia	Gettysburg	Hood's	340	27	162	..	55.0
5th Georgia	Chickamauga	Cheatham's	353	27	167	..	54.9
16th Tennessee	Stone's River	Cheatham's	377	36	155	16	54.9
4th North Carolina	Seven Pines	D. H. Hill's	678	77	286	6	54.4
27th Tennessee	Shiloh	Hardee's	350	27	115	48	54.2
12th South Carolina	Manassas	A. P. Hill's	270	23	121	2	54.0
4th Virginia	Manassas	Jackson's	180	18	79	..	53.8
4th Texas	Antietam	Hood's	200	10	97	..	53.5
27th Tennessee	Perryville	Cleburne's	210	16	84	12	53.3
1st South Carolina	Manassas	A. P. Hill's	283	25	126	..	53.3
49th Virginia	Fair Oaks	D. H. Hill's	424	32	170	22	52.8
12th Alabama	Fair Oaks	D. H. Hill's	408	59	156	..	52.6
7th South Carolina	Antietam	McLaws'	268	23	117	..	52.2
7th Texas	Raymond	John Gregg's	306	22	136	..	51.6
6th South Carolina	Fair Oaks	D. H. Hill's	521	88	181	..	51.6
15th Georgia	Gettysburg	Hood's	335	19	152	..	51.0
11th Alabama	Glendale	Longstreet's	357	49	121	11	50.7
17th Georgia	Manassas	Hood's	200	10	91	..	50.5
3d North Carolina	Gettysburg	Johnson's	312	29	127	..	50.0
4th Virginia	Chancellorsville	Trimble's	355	14	155	3	48.4
1st Maryland	Gettysburg	Johnson's	400	52	140	..	48.0
8th Mississippi	Stone's River	Jackson's	282	20	113	..	47.1
32d Virginia	Antietam	McLaws'	158	15	57	..	45.5
18th Mississippi	Antietam	McLaws'	186	10	73	..	44.6
14th South Carolina	Gaines' Mill	A. P. Hill's	500	18	197	..	43.0
33d North Carolina	Chancellorsville	A. P. Hill's	480	32	167	..	41.4
5th Alabama	Malvern Hill	D. H. Hill's	225	26	66	..	40.8

VI

FEDERAL ARMIES, CORPS AND LEADERS

THE SECOND CORPS, ARMY OF THE POTOMAC

MARCHING DOWN PENNSYLVANIA AVENUE IN 1865—THE SECOND CORPS HAD
A RECORD OF LONGER CONTINUOUS SERVICE, A LARGER ORGANIZATION,
HARDEST FIGHTING, AND GREATEST NUMBER OF CASUALTIES, THAN ANY OTHER
IN THE EASTERN ARMIES—IT CONTAINED THE REGIMENT WHICH SUSTAINED
THE LARGEST PERCENTAGE OF LOSS IN ANY ONE ACTION; THE REGIMENT
WHICH SUSTAINED THE GREATEST NUMERICAL LOSS IN ANY ONE ACTION; AND
THE REGIMENT WHICH SUSTAINED THE GREATEST NUMERICAL LOSS DURING
ITS TERM OF SERVICE—OF THE HUNDRED UNION REGIMENTS WHICH LOST
THE MOST MEN IN BATTLE, THIRTY-FIVE BELONGED TO THE SECOND CORPS

"FIGHTING JOE HOOKER" WITH HIS STAFF

"Fighting Joe Hooker" was a man of handsome physique and intense personal magnetism. He graduated at West Point in 1837 in the same class with Jubal A. Early and Braxton Bragg. Having fought through the Mexican War, he resigned from the army in 1853. On May 17, 1861, he was appointed brigadier-general of volunteers, and on May 5, 1862, major-general of volunteers. He was active throughout the Peninsular campaign, and at Bristoe Station, Second Bull Run, Chantilly, South Mountain and Antietam. He commanded the center grand division of the Army of the Potomac at Fredericksburg. At last, on January 26, 1863, he was assigned by President Lincoln to the command of the Army of the Potomac. On the 4th of May, 1863, his right flank was surprised by Jackson at Chancellorsville, and his 90,000 soldiers were forced to recross the Rappahannock. While fighting in the East he was wounded at

[160]

WALKER, THE ARTIST CAPTAIN R. H. HALL   GENERAL   GENERAL   COLONEL
    LIEUTENANT   MAJOR WILLIAM   JOSEPH   DANIEL   JAMES D.
SAMUEL W. TAYLOR   H. LAWRENCE   HOOKER   BUTTERFIELD   FESSENDEN

ON THE SPOT WHENCE HE DIRECTED HIS "BATTLE ABOVE THE CLOUDS"

Antietam, and stunned at Chancellorsville by a cannon-ball which struck a pillar against which he was leaning.   In September, 1863, he was sent with the Eleventh and Twelfth Corps to reënforce Rosecrans at Chattanooga.   On November 24th, in the "battle among the clouds" at the head of his new command, he led a charge against the Confederate artillery and infantry posted on Lookout Mountain.   For his conduct on this occasion he was brevetted major-general in the regular army.   He further distinguished himself under Sherman at Dalton and Resaca, and in the attack on Atlanta.   At his own request (July 30, 1864) he was placed on waiting orders September 28th, when he was put in command of the Northern Department.   He retired from active service October 15, 1868, with the full rank of major-general in the regular army.   General Hooker died at Garden City, Long Island, New York, October 31, 1879.

THE ARMY OF GEORGIA—ON PARADE, GENERAL SLOCUM AT THE HEAD

Very different from the march through Georgia and the Carolinas was this magnificent parade of the Army of Georgia down Pennsylvania Avenue. In front ride General Slocum and his staff. Behind come the long straight lines of men who proved the Confederacy a hollow shell with all of its fighting men at the front. Eagerly crowding close to the line of march are the citizens of Washington who had alternately clamored for action, and shaken in their boots when the daring Confederate leaders pressed close to the Northern capital. Many a heartfelt prayer of thanks and relief was offered when mothers saw their boys march past, unscathed by the war and about to reënter civil life. Many a tear fell for those who could not be there to share the glory.

At Gaines' Mill, Slocum's Division of the Sixth Corps was sent to the support of General Porter, and lost 2,021 out of less than 8,000 present in the hot engagement. It was in front of Fredericksburg May 3, 1863, under General Sedgwick, that the Corps made its most brilliant display of dash and daring. It carried at the point of the bayonet Marye's Heights, the strong position before which there had fallen, gloriously but in vain, nearly 13,000 men the previous December. Most of the Corps was held in reserve at Gettysburg, and its casualties there were slight, but it added again to its laurels at Rappahannock Sta-

THE SIXTH ARMY CORPS IN THE GRAND
REVIEW—THE CORPS THAT SAVED
WASHINGTON FROM CAPTURE

tion. In the battles of the Wilderness and Spotsylvania it encountered its hardest fighting, the percentage of killed of the Fifteenth New Jersey in the latter battle being equaled in only one instance during the whole war. At Cold Harbor it suffered heavily again, and the appearance of two of its divisions at Fort Stevens checked Early's advance on Washington. It pursued Early up the Shenandoah, and fought at Opequon and Cedar Creek. In the final assault on Petersburg it played an important part. It was no less prominent in its final appearance at the Grand Review in Washington.

THE NINETEENTH ARMY CORPS

THE TWENTIETH ARMY CORPS

The Armies of the United States in the Civil War

BY THE PROVISIONS of the Constitution, the President of the United States is commander-in-chief of the army and navy. During the Civil War, this function was exercised in no small degree by President Lincoln. As Secretaries of War, he had in his cabinet Simon Cameron, from March 4, 1861, to January 14, 1862; and Edward M. Stanton, who served from January 15, 1862, throughout Lincoln's administration, and also under Johnson until May 28, 1868, except for a short interval during which he was suspended. There were four generals-in-chief of the armies: Brevet Lieutenant-General Scott, Major-Generals McClellan and Halleck, and Lieutenant-General Grant. The last named has been considered in previous pages of this volume, but the lives and services of the other three are summarized below, in addition to the treatment received in other volumes. (CONSULT INDEX.) This is true of all the army leaders not separately described in the pages that follow. The Index will refer to treatment in other volumes.

LIEUTENANT-GENERAL WINFIELD SCOTT was born near Petersburg, Virginia, June 13, 1786. After being graduated from William and Mary College, he studied law, was admitted to the bar, and then entered the army at the age of twenty-two. His career was one of bravery and incident. He was captured by the British, but exchanged in 1813, fought in the battle of Lundy's Lane, and was severely wounded. After the close of the war he was raised to the rank of major-general, and in 1841 succeeded General Macomb as commander of the United States army. In the war with Mexico, he won great fame and was nominated by the Whigs for President in 1852; but he carried only four States. In 1855, Congress revived the rank of lieutenant-general and conferred it by brevet upon Scott, the appointment being dated March 29, 1847, the day of his brilliant capture of Vera Cruz. It was evident that his age and infirmities would prevent his taking any active part in the Civil War, and on November 1, 1861, he was retired from the chief command of the army of the United States. He wrote an autobiography, and made a European trip in 1864, dying May 29, 1866, at West Point, New York.

MAJOR-GENERAL HENRY WAGER HALLECK (U.S.M.A. 1839) was born in Westernville, New York, January 16, 1815. He served in California and on the Pacific coast during the Mexican War. He retired from the army with the rank of captain in 1854 to practise law, but after the outbreak of the Civil War reentered the regular service, with the grade of major-general. He was in command of the Department of Missouri (afterward Department of Mississippi) from November 19, 1861, to July 11, 1862, when he became general-in-chief of all the armies. Grant succeeded him, March 9, 1864, and Halleck was his chief-of-staff until the close of the war. He continued in the army as head, successively, of the Military Division of the James, the Department of the Pacific, and Department of the South until his death at Louisville, Kentucky, January 9, 1872.

MAJOR-GENERAL GEORGE BRINTON McCLELLAN (U.S.M.A. 1846) was born in Philadelphia, December 3, 1826. He served in the Engineer Corps during the Mexican War, distinguished himself by gallant service, and reached the rank of captain in 1855, having been so brevetted in 1847. He became assistant instructor in practical engineering at West Point, later accompanied the Red River exploring expedition, and was sent on a secret mission to Santo Domingo. During the Crimean War, he was one of a commission of three appointed by Congress to study and report upon the whole art of European warfare. He remained some time with the British forces. McClellan's report was a model of comprehensive accuracy and conciseness, and showed him to be a master of siege-tactics. In 1857, McClellan resigned his army commission to devote himself to the practice of engineering. He became vice-president of the Illinois Central Railroad Company, and later president of the Eastern Division of the Ohio and Missouri Railroad. He made his home in Cincinnati until the outbreak of the Civil War, when he tendered his services to his country and was made major-general of volunteers, April 21, 1861. The Department of the Ohio was constituted, and McClellan took command, May 13th, his appointment as major-general dating from the following day. He drove the Confederates from northwestern Virginia and saved that section to the Union, an accomplishment of the most vital importance, since, in the event of the establishment of the Confederacy, the Union territory would have been contracted at

The upper photograph, as beautifully "composed" as a classic painting, shows General and Mrs. Scott at their home, Elizabeth, New Jersey, in 1862. A closer portrait study of the general appears below. Winfield Scott became the first general-in-chief of the United States Army during the Civil War, being already in that position when the war broke out. He was then nearly seventy-five years old. The aged hero owed his exalted rank and his military fame to his dashing and vigorous achievements as commander in the Mexican War. He directed until retired by his own request in November, 1861. Scott possessed an imposing figure and courage equal to every danger. He was exacting in discipline—that power which the French call "the glory of the soldier and the strength of armies.

Major-General Henry Wager Halleck assumed command of the Army and Department of Missouri in 1861, and from his headquarters at St. Louis directed the operations of the forces which early in 1862 compelled the Confederates to evacuate Kentucky and Central and West Tennessee. After he assumed control of all the armies as successor to McClellan in July, 1862, he made his headquarters in Washington, performing duties similar to those of a chief-of-staff in a modern army. His military decisions in particular crises as Fredericksburg, Chancellorsville and Gettysburg were not always approved by critics; nevertheless, he bore a reputation for genius as a commander. He was succeeded in the duties of general-in-chief in February, 1864, by Lieutenant-General Ulysses S. Grant.

SCOTT AND HALLECK—TWO GENERALS-IN-CHIEF OF THE UNITED STATES ARMY

this point into a neck but little more than one hundred miles in width. After this success, McClellan was placed, July 25, 1861, at the head of the newly created District (afterward Department) of the Potomac, and began the organization and training of the army of that name. From November 5, 1861 to March 11th of the following year, he was general-in-chief of the armies of the United States, and after the latter date continued in command of the Army of the Potomac until November 9, 1862, when he was replaced by Major-General A. E. Burnside. He took no further part in the war. His removal was due to dissatisfaction with his methods that gradually developed among President Lincoln and his advisers. The failure of the army to capture Richmond in the Peninsula campaign, and the non-pursuit of Lee immediately after Antietam were the chief reasons. As the nominee of the Democratic party, he was defeated for the presidency in 1864, and his resignation from the army was accepted on November 8th. He now spent several years abroad, returning to live in New Jersey, of which State he became governor in 1877. Aside from his military abilities, McClellan was a man of fine tastes in literature and art, and also took an active interest in promoting the manufacturing industries of the State. He wrote his autobiography, and several works of a military nature. His death occurred October 29, 1885, at Orange.

Army of the Potomac

BY THE CONSOLIDATION of the Department of Washington and the Department of Northeastern Virginia, July 25, 1861, the Military District of the Potomac was constituted and placed under command of Major-General George B. McClellan. On August 15, 1861, the Department, or Army of the Potomac was created from it, and as such it was known thereafter. Major-General McClellan assumed command of this army August 20, 1861. As then constituted, it was organized in fourteen brigades composed largely of the troops (regular army and volunteer) of the Department of Northeastern Virginia, under Brigadier-General Irvin McDowell, and new organizations. Most of these brigades had artillery and some of them cavalry. McClellan immediately applied his military knowledge to remodeling the army, and in October a new organization was announced. The division was now the unit, and there were fourteen, including one stationed at Baltimore. There were also one provisional brigade, a provost-guard, a cavalry command, and a cavalry reserve. During the winter of 1861–62, the Army of the Potomac was thoroughly drilled. A new organization was announced in March, 1862, and this the army retained, except while Burnside created the grand division, until it was discontinued, June 28, 1865. The corps were the units, and their number varied from time to time. There were also the provost-guard, the guard for general headquarters, a full artillery, and cavalry reserve. A cavalry division was formed in July, 1862, and reorganized as a cavalry corps in February, 1863. The successive commanders of the Army of the Potomac were: Major-General George B. McClellan to November 9, 1862; Major-General A. E. Burnside to January 26, 1863; Major-General Joseph Hooker to June 28, 1863, being succeeded by Major-General George G. Meade, who remained at its head until it was discontinued, June 28, 1865, except for a short interval in January, 1865, when Major-General John G. Parke was in temporary command.

MAJOR-GENERAL AMBROSE EVERETT BURNSIDE (U.S.M.A. 1847) was born in Liberty, Indiana, May 23, 1824. He served in the artillery with the rank of first lieutenant, resigned his commission, in 1853, to take up the manufacture of a breech-loading rifle which he had invented. At the outbreak of the Civil War he was an officer of the Illinois Central Railroad Company. For gallant service at Bull Run he was made brigadier-general of volunteers, and in March, 1862, major-general of volunteers. He organized an expeditionary corps in December, 1861, and this was merged in the Department of North Carolina, of which Burnside was the head from January to July, 1862. He captured Roanoke Island and occupied New Berne. From these troops and others was organized, July 22, 1862, the Ninth Corps, with Burnside at its head. He served under McClellan at South Mountain, and at Antietam, where he commanded the left wing, and succeeded him in the command of the Army of the Potomac. Later, Major-General Burnside was assigned to command of the Department of the Ohio. Burnside and the Ninth Corps were with Grant in the

ANOTHER GENERAL–IN–CHIEF
McCLELLAN, WITH HIS WIFE

Major-General George Brinton McClellan began his war career as commander of the Department of Ohio. After he had defeated and scattered the Confederate forces commanded by General Robert E. Lee, securing West Virginia to the Union, he was appointed general-in-chief of the United States Armies as successor to General Scott, in November, 1861. He planned and directed the expeditions which, under General A. E. Burnside captured the coast of North Carolina, under Butler and Farragut opened up the lower Mississippi, and in Kentucky and Tennessee resulted in the capture of Fort Donelson. He led the Army of the Potomac in the Peninsula and Antietam campaigns. Meade, its last commander, said: "Had there been no McClellan there could have been no Grant."

Virginia campaign of 1864. Major-General Burnside resigned his commission at the close of the war and resumed his career as a railroad projector and manager. He was governor of Rhode Island from 1866 to 1869, and senator from 1875 until his death, which occurred September 3, 1881, at Bristol, Rhode Island.

MAJOR-GENERAL JOSEPH HOOKER (U.S.M.A. 1837) was born in Hadley, Massachusetts, November 13, 1814. He entered the artillery and was brevetted lieutenant-colonel for distinguished services in the Mexican War. He resigned his commission in 1853. At the outbreak of the Civil War he was living in California as a farmer and civil engineer. He tendered his services to the Government and was appointed brigadier-general of volunteers. In March, 1862, he was made a division commander in the Army of the Potomac, with a promotion to major-general of volunteers in May. An appointment as brigadier-general of the regular army followed the battle of Antietam, in which he was wounded. In September, 1862, he rose to corps commander, and was at the head of the Center Grand Division in Burnside's organization. He was commander of the Army of the Potomac from January 26, 1863, to June 28th. Later, he exhibited great gallantry as corps commander at Lookout Mountain, and

in the Atlanta campaign. On October 1, 1864, he was placed at the head of the Northern Department, and served at the head of other departments until he was retired, as the result of a paralytic stroke, with full rank of major-general, in October, 1868. His death occurred at Garden City, New York, October 31, 1879.

MAJOR-GENERAL GEORGE GORDON MEADE (U. S.M.A. 1835) was born in Cadiz, Spain, December 31, 1815, while his father was American naval agent at that city. He saw service in the Seminole War, and then resigned in 1836 to take up the practice of civil engineering. He reentered the army and served with the Topographical Engineer Corps during the Mexican War. He was afterward employed on river and harbor improvements, lighthouse construction, and the survey of the Great Lakes, until the Civil War broke out, when he was commissioned brigadier-general of volunteers and put in command of a brigade in the Pennsylvania Reserve in the Army of the Potomac. Later, he commanded the First and Fifth corps and was made general commanding of the army, June 28, 1863. He was in chief command at Gettysburg. On August 18, 1864, he received a commission as major-general in the regular army, and served therein until his death, in Philadelphia, November 6, 1872.

Army of the Tennessee

THE TROOPS in the Military District of Cairo were under the command of Brigadier-General U. S. Grant from August 1, 1861, until February, 1862. The District of West Tennessee was organized February 17, 1862, and Grant was at its head until October 16th. His forces were known as the Army of West Tennessee, and were included in those of the Department of Mississippi, under Major-General Halleck. With this force, consisting of six divisions and some unassigned troops, Grant fought the battle of Shiloh. On October 16, 1862, the Department of Tennessee was created to include Cairo, western Kentucky and Tennessee, and northern Mississippi. Grant was commander until October 24, 1863, when the Military Division of the Mississippi was organized to include the Departments of the Ohio, Tennessee, Cumberland, and of Arkansas. The troops in the Department of Tennessee were designated the Thirteenth Army Corps until December 18, 1862,

when they were reorganized into the Thirteenth, Fifteenth, Sixteenth, and Seventeenth corps. Succeeding Grant, this force, usually called the Army of the Tennessee, was successively commanded by Major-Generals W. T. Sherman, James B. McPherson, John A. Logan, and O. O. Howard. This army took part in the capture of Vicksburg, battle of Chattanooga, Atlanta campaign, and Sherman's campaigns in Georgia and the Carolinas. A detachment of it was with the Red River expedition, in 1864.

MAJOR-GENERAL JAMES BIRDSEYE MCPHERSON (U.S.M.A. 1853) was born in Sandusky, Ohio, November 14, 1828. He practised engineering in the Government employ and also taught it at West Point. When the war broke out, he raised a force of engineers, and later he was aide to Major-General Halleck. In December, 1862, he was given command of the Seventeenth Corps. His services

AMBROSE EVERETT BURNSIDE
Commander of the Army of the Potomac During
the Fredericksburg Campaign, November, 1862, to January, 1863.

GEORGE GORDON MEADE
Commander of the Army of the Potomac in the
Gettysburg Campaign, also in the Wilderness
Campaign and Siege of Petersburg.

MAJOR–GENERALS

BURNSIDE,

HOOKER,

MEADE

COMMANDERS

OF

THE ARMY OF

THE POTOMAC

JOSEPH HOOKER
Commander of the Army of the Potomac During the Chan-
cellorsville Campaign and the Opening of the
Gettysburg Campaign.

in reenforcing Rosecrans after Corinth, October, 1862, won him the rank of major-general of volunteers, and after the fall of Vicksburg he received the commission of brigadier-general of the regular army. He succeeded Major-General William T. Sherman in the command of the Army of the Tennessee, March 12, 1864, and was killed at the battle of Atlanta, July 22, 1864.

MAJOR-GENERAL JOHN A. LOGAN was born in Jackson County, Illinois, February 9, 1826. He served in the Mexican War, rising from a private to the rank of second lieutenant. He was afterward admitted to the bar and finally reached Congress. During his term here the Civil War broke out and he enlisted and fought at Bull Run. Returning to the West, he raised the Thirty-first Illinois Infantry, afterward becoming its colonel. He was wounded at Fort Donelson and shortly afterward was made major-general of volunteers. In the Vicksburg campaigns he commanded a division of the Seventeenth Corps. In 1863, he took command of the Fifteenth Corps and served in the Atlanta campaign and led his troops through the Carolinas. He was made head of the Department of the Tennessee May 19, 1865. He was elected to the United States Senate in 1871, and was defeated for the vice-presidency of the United States on the Republican ticket of 1884. He died in Washington, December 26, 1886.

MAJOR-GENERAL OLIVER OTIS HOWARD (U.S. M.A. 1854) was born in Leeds, Maine, November 8, 1830. He served as chief of ordnance, and as first lieutenant taught mathematics at West Point until the Civil War broke out, when he left the regular army to command the Third Maine Volunteers. He headed a brigade in the first battle of Bull Run and was promoted to brigadier-general of volunteers in September, 1861. At Fair Oaks, where he lost his right arm, he achieved distinction as an able fighter. After Antietam, he commanded a division of the Second Corps, and later, as major-general of volunteers, the corps itself for a short time. On April 2, 1863, the Eleventh Corps was given him, and it was these troops that were so badly routed by " Stonewall " Jackson at Chancellorsville. In September, 1863, Howard and his corps were transferred to the Army of the Cumberland, in which he became leader of the Fourth Corps, April, 1864. Howard's services at Gettysburg, Lookout Mountain, and Missionary Ridge were conspicuous. He accompanied Sherman to the relief of Knoxville, and fought in all the battles of the Atlanta campaign, succeeding Major-General McPherson to the command of the Army of the Tennessee, and marching with Sherman through Georgia and the Carolinas. After the close of the war he commanded the Nez Percé Indian expedition of 1877, the Bannock, and Piute campaigns, and from 1880 to 1882, was superintendent of the Military Academy, West Point. He was (1865–74) commissioner of the Bureau of Refugees, Freedmen, and Abandoned Lands, and in 1895 founded the Lincoln Memorial University and the industrial school at Cumberland Gap, Tennessee. Major-General Howard was a noted total-abstinence advocate and was much interested in Sunday-school work. He was retired with full rank in 1894, and he died at Burlington, Vermont, October, 26, 1909.

Army of the Ohio and Army of the Cumberland

THE DEPARTMENT OF KENTUCKY, which constituted the whole of that State within a hundred miles of the Ohio River, was merged in the Department of the Cumberland, comprising the States of Kentucky and Tennessee, August 15, 1861. On November 9th, it was renamed the Department of the Ohio, the States of Ohio, Michigan, and Indiana being added. The troops in this region (over whom McClellan, Rosecrans, O. M. Mitchel, Robert Anderson, and W. T. Sherman had, at different times and places, control) were now organized into the Army of the Ohio, with Major-General Don Carlos Buell in command. Although the department was merged into that of Mississippi in March, 1862, the Army of the Ohio retained its name. This was the body that brought such timely assistance to Grant at Shiloh and drove Bragg out of Kentucky. The army was organized into three corps in September, 1862, but the following month (October 24th) the Department of the Cumberland was recreated to consist of eastern Tennessee, Alabama, and Georgia, and the Army of the Ohio, which had operated chiefly in that region, now became officially the Fourteenth Army Corps, but better known as the Army of the Cumberland. On October 30th, Buell was

GEORGE HENRY THOMAS
Commander of the Army of the Cumberland in the Ten-
nessee and Georgia Campaigns, including Stone's
River, Chickamauga, Chattanooga and Atlanta.

JOHN ALEXANDER LOGAN
Commander of the Army of the Tennessee in Front of
Atlanta. He subsequently resumed Command of a
Corps and Led it Through the Carolinas.

MAJOR–GENERALS

THOMAS

LOGAN

HOWARD

ARMY OF THE

CUMBERLAND

AND ARMY OF

THE TENNESSEE

OLIVER OTIS HOWARD
Commander of the Army of the Tennessee in Part
of the Atlanta Campaign and in the March
Through Georgia and the Carolinas.

replaced by Major-General W. S. Rosecrans, and the Fourteenth Corps was reorganized into the Right Wing, Center, and Left Wing, later the Fourteenth, Twentieth, and Twenty-first Army corps. The last two were afterward consolidated as the Fourth Corps. With this army, Rosecrans fought the battle of Stone's River, drove Bragg across the Tennessee, and was defeated at Chickamauga. Major-General George H. Thomas succeeded to the command October 20, 1863. The army distinguished itself on Missionary Ridge and through the Atlanta campaign (as a part of the Military Division of the Mississippi), and in the campaign against Hood in Tennessee. The army had four divisions of cavalry. It had a reserve corps for a short time, and received two corps from the Army of the Potomac, which were finally consolidated into the reorganized Twentieth Corps.

MAJOR-GENERAL DON CARLOS BUELL (U.S. M.A. 1841) was born March 23, 1818, near Marietta, Ohio, and served in the Mexican War. When the Civil War broke out he assisted in the organization of volunteers, and in November, 1861, took charge of the Department and Army of the Ohio. He was soon raised to the rank of major-general of volunteers. His last service in this army was the driving of Bragg out of Kentucky, for this, with the preceding Tennessee campaign during the summer of 1862, aroused such criticism that he was replaced, October 30th, by Major-General Rosecrans and tried before a military commission. An adverse report was handed in, and Buell resigned from the army June 1, 1864. He then became president of the Green River Iron Company, and, 1885-89, was pension-agent at Louisville. He died near Rockport, Kentucky, November 19, 1898.

MAJOR-GENERAL WILLIAM STARKE ROSECRANS (U.S.M.A. 1842) was born at Kingston, Ohio, September 6, 1818. He served in the Engineer Corps and as assistant professor at West Point. In 1854, he resigned from the army to practise architecture and civil engineering, but at the outbreak of the Civil War he tendered his services to the Government and was made brigadier-general of the regular army, and major-general of volunteers in March, 1862. He succeeded McClellan at the head of the army of occupation in western Virginia after his victory at Rich Mountain, and held it until Major-General Fremont took charge of the Mountain Department, March 29, 1862. From June 26th until the end of October, Rose-

crans was Pope's successor in the Army of the Mississippi and, taking command of the District of Corinth, he defeated the Confederate forces at Iuka and Corinth. He now replaced Buell in the Army of the Cumberland. As general commanding he won the battle of Stone's River, but was defeated at Chickamauga, and was succeeded by Major-General George H. Thomas. He then spent a year in command of the Department of Missouri, during which he drove Price out of the State, and on December 9, 1864, was relieved of active command. After resigning his commission, in 1866, he was United States minister to Mexico, and was in Congress from 1881 to 1885. In 1889, Congress restored him to the rank and pay of brigadier-general. He died at Redondo, California, March 11, 1898.

MAJOR-GENERAL GEORGE HENRY THOMAS (U. S.M.A. 1840) was born in Southampton County, Virginia, July 31, 1816. He served in the Seminole and Mexican wars, and had risen to the grade of lieutenant-colonel when the Civil War broke out. In August, 1861, he was made brigadier-general of volunteers. His first services in the war were rendered in the Departments of Pennsylvania and of the Shenandoah. His division of the Army of the Ohio defeated the Confederate forces at Mill Springs, Kentucky, January 19, 1862. This victory first brought him into notice, and shortly afterward he was made major-general of volunteers. He was put at the head of the Center (Fourteenth Corps) of the reorganized Army of the Cumberland, and in October, 1863, he assumed the chief command, distinguishing himself at Missionary Ridge, in the Atlanta campaign, and in the crushing defeat of Bragg at Nashville. He was promoted to major-general in the regular army for his services at Nashville, December 15, 1864. He narrowly escaped this honor, for, impatient at his delay in attacking Hood—a delay occasioned by the very inclement weather—Grant had sent Major-General Logan to relieve him, and the latter was on the way. He had also shown himself a gallant fighter in the earlier battles of Stone's River, and Chickamauga, where he held the left wing of the army against tremendous odds. This feat is considered one of the most glorious of the whole war. With the right wing of the army routed and in utter confusion, Thomas kept his position against the whole of Bragg's army until ordered to withdraw. He declined the brevet of lieutenant-general, which President Johnson offered him in 1868. Two years later he died in San Francisco, March 28, 1870.

JOHN McALLISTER SCHOFIELD

Commander of the Army of the Frontier and of the
Department and Army of the Ohio.

DON CARLOS BUELL

Commander of the Army of the Ohio in the Shiloh
Campaign and Afterward of a Department.

JOHN POPE

Commander of the Army of Virginia, June to September, 1862, Including Second Bull Run.

WILLIAM STARKE ROSECRANS

Commander of the Army of the Ohio (Cumberland) in
the Campaign of Stone's River and Chickamauga.

COMMANDERS OF THE ARMIES OF THE OHIO AND VIRGINIA

Army of the Ohio

THE DEPARTMENT OF THE OHIO having been merged in that of Mississippi, March, 1862, it was recreated on August 19th, to consist of the States of Ohio, Michigan, Indiana, Illinois, Wisconsin, and Kentucky, east of the Tennessee River, and Major-General H. G. Wright was placed at the head. The troops of the department were scattered through many districts. Some of the brigades constituted the Army of Kentucky, of which Major-General Gordon Granger was in command. Wright was replaced March 25, 1863, by Major-General A. E. Burnside, and shortly afterward the troops in the department were reorganized into the Twenty-third Army Corps, and this force is the Army of the Ohio associated with the Knoxville, Atlanta, and Nashville campaigns. The Ninth Corps was attached to the department from March, 1863, to March, 1864. Burnside was succeeded in turn by Major-Generals J. G. Foster, J. M. Schofield, and George Stoneman. A cavalry division organized in April, 1864, was headed by Major-General Stoneman, and afterward by Colonels Capron and Garrard. On January 17, 1865, the troops still in the department (the Twenty-third Corps having gone to North Carolina) were annexed to the Department of the Cumberland.

MAJOR-GENERAL JOHN MCALLISTER SCHOFIELD (U.S.M.A. 1853) was born in Chautauqua County, New York, September 29, 1831. After garrison duty in Florida and South Carolina, he held the chair of natural philosophy at West Point and later at Washington University, St. Louis, where the outbreak of the Civil War found him. He had command of the District of St. Louis, Department of Missouri; Army of the Frontier; of a division in the Fourteenth Corps; the Department and Army of the Ohio, and of the Twenty-third Corps, which was transferred to North Carolina late in the war. He was made major-general of volunteers in November, 1862. His most noteworthy active services were rendered during the Atlanta campaign and at the battle of Franklin. After the Civil War he was Secretary of War *ad interim*, after the resignation of General Grant. He was commander of the United States army from 1888 to 1895, rising to the rank of lieutenant-general, at which he was retired in September, 1895. He died at St. Augustine, Florida, March 4, 1906.

Army of the Mississippi

THE ARMY OF THE MISSISSIPPI had a short existence, being organized February 23d, and discontinued October 26, 1862. Its first commander was Major-General John Pope, who was succeeded, June 26th, by Major-General W. S. Rosecrans. This army consisted of five divisions, a flotilla brigade, and several brigades of cavalry, and operated on the Mississippi in the spring of 1862, capturing Island No. 10; before Corinth in May, 1862, and at Iuka and Corinth in September and October, 1862. Most of the troops went into the Thirteenth Army Corps.

Army of Virginia

TO OBTAIN CLOSER ORGANIZATION in the various commands operating in Virginia, President Lincoln, on June 26, 1862, constituted the Army of Virginia out of Major-General Fremont's forces (Mountain Department), those of Major-General McDowell (Department of the Rappahannock), those of Major-General Banks (Department of the Shenandoah), and Brigadier-General Sturgis' brigade from the Military District of Washington. This last, an unorganized body of troops, did not join the army at once. Major-General John Pope was placed at the head of the new organization, which was divided into three corps. Exclusive of Sturgis' troops it numbered between forty and fifty thousand men, and was augmented later by troops from three corps of the Army of the Potomac. A corps of the Army of Virginia checked " Stonewall " Jackson's advance

Eugene A. Carr, Commander of the Army
of the Southwest; Led Troops at
Wilson's Creek and Pea Ridge.

FEDERAL

MAJOR–GENERALS

COMMANDING

ARMIES

Quincy Adams Gillmore, Commander of the
Department and Army of the South
at the Siege of Charleston.

Frederick Steele, Commander of the Army
of Arkansas; Engaged at Little
Rock.

Benjamin Franklin Butler, Commander of the Department and
Army of the Gulf in 1862, and
of the Army of the James
in 1864. With this Army
he Operated Against Rich-
mond in May and June.

Gordon Granger, Commander of the Army
of Kentucky in 1862; Noted at
Chickamauga.

James G. Blunt, Commander in Kansas
and of the Army of the Frontier; at
Prairie Grove.

OPERATING

ON THE GULF

AND ALONG THE

WESTERN FRONTIER

David Hunter, Head of a Division at Bull
Run and later of the Department
of the South.

at Cedar Mountain, on August 9th, but the entire organization was defeated at Manassas by Jackson and Longstreet, August 29th and 30th, and withdrew to the lines of Washington. On September 12th, the Army of Virginia was merged in the Army of the Potomac.

MAJOR-GENERAL JOHN POPE (U.S.M.A. 1842) was born in Louisville, Kentucky, March 16, 1822. He served in the Mexican War, rising to the rank of captain. After this he did much work on engineering service in connection with the development of the West. When the Civil War broke out, Pope was sent to Cairo, Illinois, and later to command the troops in northern Missouri. From February to June, 1862, he headed the newly created Army of the Mississippi, during which time he was made major-general of volunteers and brigadier-general of the regular army. His most notable achievement was the capture of Island No. 10, as a result of which he was put in command of the Army of Virginia, June 26, 1862. The reverse of Second Bull Run caused him to ask to be relieved of this command, and he was sent to the Department of the Northwest, to carry on the war against the Sioux Indians. He headed other departments in the West until he was retired, in 1886. His last command was the Department of the Pacific. He was brevetted major-general in March, 1865, for his services at Island No. 10, and received the full rank in 1882. Major-General Pope died at Sandusky, Ohio, September 23, 1892.

Army of the Southwest

CREATED December 25, 1861, from troops in portions of the Department of Missouri. It was merged in the District of Eastern Arkansas, Department of Tennessee, December 13, 1862, and was commanded during its existence by Brigadier-Generals S. R. Curtis, Frederick Steele, E. A. Carr, and W. A. Gorman. This army fought many minor but important engagements in Missouri and Arkansas, including Bentonville, Sugar Creek, and Pea Ridge.

MAJOR-GENERAL SAMUEL RYAN CURTIS (U.S. M.A. 1831) was born near Champlain, New York, February, 1807, and resigned from the army to become a civil engineer and, later, a lawyer. He served as colonel of volunteers in the Mexican War, and afterward went to Congress. He was made brigadier-general of volunteers in May, 1861, and was commander of the Army of the Southwest from December, 1861, to August, 1862. He conducted an active campaign against Van Dorn and Price, during which he won the battle of Pea Ridge, March 7-8, 1862, and was made major-general of volunteers that same month. Later, he was unable to hold Arkansas and was compelled to march to the Mississippi River. He was in command of the Department of Missouri, September, 1862, to May, 1863, and of Kansas, January, 1864, to January, 1865, after which he was at the head of that of the Northwest. He negotiated treaties with several Indian tribes, and was mustered out of the volunteer service April 30, 1866. He died at Council Bluffs, Iowa, December 26, 1866.

MAJOR-GENERAL FREDERICK STEELE (U.S.M. A. 1843) was born in Delhi, New York, January 14, 1819, and served in the Mexican War. He was a major when the Civil War broke out and rose to be major-general of volunteers in November, 1862. Steele served with distinction in Missouri, and was given a division in the Army of the Southwest in May, 1862. For a short time, he had command of the army itself. When it was broken up, he was finally transferred into the Department of the Tennessee, having a division on Sherman's Yazoo Expedition, McClernand's Army of the Mississippi, and the new Fifteenth Army Corps, with which he took part in the Vicksburg campaign. In August, 1863, he was given charge of the Arkansas Expedition, which developed into the Seventh Army Corps, at the head of which he remained until December, 1864. He was given a separate command in the district of West Florida, and assisted Major-General Gordon Granger at the final operations around Mobile. After muster-out from the volunteer service, he returned to the regular army as colonel, having already received the brevet of major-general for the capture of Little Rock. He died at San Mateo, California, January 12, 1868.

MAJOR-GENERAL EUGENE ASA CARR (U.S.M. A. 1850) was born in Erie County, New York, in

GEORGE CROOK

Commander of the Army of West Virginia in 1864. Later Crook led a Cavalry Division under Sheridan in the Appomattox Campaign at Five Forks and during the pursuit of Lee.

JOHN C. FREMONT

Commander of the Mountain Department and Army in West Virginia in 1862. Fremont was in Command in Missouri in 1861 and at one time gave orders to Brigadier-General Grant.

NATHANIEL PRENTISS BANKS

Commander of the Department and Army of the Shenandoah in 1862 and of the Army of the Gulf in 1863–4. With this Army Banks captured Port Hudson in 1863.

PHILIP HENRY SHERIDAN

Commander of the Army of Shenandoah in 1864. Sheridan Led a Division at Chickamauga and Chattanooga and Commanded the Cavalry Corps of the Army of the Potomac in the Wilderness Campaign.

HENRY WARNER SLOCUM

Commander of the Army of Georgia in the Carolinas. Slocum Commanded the Twelfth Corps, Army of the Potomac, at Chancellorsville and Gettysburg and the Twentieth Corps in Front of Atlanta.

JOHN A. McCLERNAND

Commander of the Army of the Mississippi in 1862–3. McClernand Led Troops at Shiloh and later Commanded the Army of the Mississippi operating against Vicksburg; Head of a Corps in Grant's Siege.

COMMANDERS OF THE ARMIES OF WEST VIRGINIA, SHENANDOAH, GEORGIA AND MISSISSIPPI

1830, and served in the mounted rifles in Indian warfare until the opening of the Civil War, when he became colonel in the Illinois cavalry. His appointment of brigadier-general of volunteers was dated March 7, 1862. His service was chiefly in the Southwest, in the Army of the Southwest, the Thirteenth, Sixteenth, and Seventeenth corps, the Districts of Arkansas, and of Little Rock. For short periods he was at the head of the Army of the Southwest and of the left wing of the Sixteenth Corps. His gallant and meritorious service in the field won him a medal of honor and successive brevets in the regular army, and he showed especial bravery and military ability at Wilson's Creek, Pea Ridge, Black River Bridge, and the capture of Little Rock. He was mustered out of the volunteer service in January, 1866, with the brevet of major-general in the regular army. He returned to the army, and continued in service on the frontier. In 1892, he was made brigadier-general and was retired February 15, 1893. He died in Washington, D. C., December 2, 1910.

Army of West Virginia

THE TROOPS in the Department of West Virginia were taken from the Eighth Army Corps when the department was reorganized, June 28, 1863. The department commanders were Brigadier-General B. F. Kelley, Major-Generals Franz Sigel, David Hunter, George Crook, Brigadier-General J. D. Stevenson, Brevet Major-General S. S. Carroll, and Major-Generals W. S. Hancock and W. H. Emory. In the campaign against Lieutenant-General Early (June-October, 1864), the two divisions (about seventy-five hundred men) under Crook were called the Army of West Virginia. This force was prominent at the Opequon, Fisher's Hill, Cedar Creek, and other engagements. After the campaign, the troops returned to the various districts in the department.

MAJOR-GENERAL DAVID HUNTER (U.S.M.A. 1822) was born in Washington, July 21, 1802, and rose to rank of major in the Mexican War. As brigadier-general of volunteers, he commanded the Second Division at Bull Run, where he was severely wounded. Shortly afterward, he was made major-general of volunteers. He succeeded Fremont in the Western Department, and was at the head of the Department of Kansas, November, 1861, to March, 1862, then of the South, until September, and of the Tenth Corps from January to June, 1863, and in May, 1864, he succeeded Major-General Sigel in the command of the Department of West Virginia. Hunter was the first general to enlist colored troops, and presided at the court which tried the Lincoln conspirators. He was retired in 1866, having been brevetted major-general, and died in Washington, February 2, 1886.

MAJOR-GENERAL GEORGE CROOK (U.S.M.A. 1852) was born near Dayton, Ohio, September 8, 1828. He spent the nine years before the opening of the Civil War in California. As brigadier-general of volunteers in the Army of the Cumberland, he commanded a division of cavalry. He succeeded Major-General David Hunter in the command of the Department of West Virginia in August, 1864, and shortly afterward was made major-general of volunteers. He was active in the Shenandoah campaign under Sheridan; also at Five Forks and Appomattox. In 1866, as lieutenant-colonel of the regular army, he was sent to the West, where he remained in constant warfare with the Indians for many years. He obtained charge of all the tribes and did much for their advancement. In 1888, he attained the rank of major-general, and died in Chicago, March 21, 1890.

Department of Virginia and North Carolina, Army of the James

THE DEPARTMENT OF VIRGINIA was created in May, 1861, and the troops therein were organized into the Seventh Army Corps on July 22, 1862. This corps was divided between Fort Monroe, Norfolk, Portsmouth, Yorktown, and other places. The Eighteenth Army Corps, created December 24, 1862, from troops in the Department of North Carolina was transferred to the Department of Virginia and North Carolina July 15, 1863, when the two departments were united, and the troops

Irvin McDowell Commanded the 1st
Corps in Front of Washington.

A. A. Humphreys Commanded the
2d Corps at Petersburg.

John Newton Commanded the 1st
Corps at Gettysburg and After.

Darius N. Couch Commanded the
2d Corps at Fredericksburg and
Chancellorsville.

Edwin Vose Sumner Commanded the
2d Corps on the Peninsula
and in Maryland.

Winfield Scott Hancock; Under Him
the Second Corps Earned the
Name "Old Guard."

FEDERAL MAJOR–GENERALS COMMANDING THE FIRST AND SECOND ARMY CORPS

therein were all merged in the Eighteenth Corps. This was reorganized in April, 1864, and the Tenth Corps being transferred from the Department of the South, the whole force was called the Army of the James. Its principal commander was Major-General Benjamin F. Butler, although Major-Generals E. O. C. Ord and D. B. Birney held command for short periods. On December 3, 1864, the two corps were discontinued, the white troops being formed into the Twenty-fourth Army Corps and the colored into the Twenty-fifth. On January 31, 1865, the two departments were again separated.

MAJOR-GENERAL BENJAMIN FRANKLIN BUTLER was born in Deerfield, New Hampshire, November 5, 1818, and was graduated from Waterville College in 1838. He practised law and entered political life. As a brigadier-general of the Massachusetts State Militia, he answered President Lincoln's call and was placed in command of the Department of Annapolis. In May, 1861, he was made major-general of volunteers and given the Department of Virginia, and in August led the troops that assisted in the capture of Forts Hatteras and Clark. On March 20, 1862, he was put in command of the Department of the Gulf and his troops occupied New Orleans on May 1st. His army gained possession of most of the lower Mississippi, and in December he was relieved by Major-General Banks. On November 1st, he assumed command of the Department of Virginia and North Carolina and personally led the Eighteenth Corps (Army of the James) until May 2, 1864. He was sent to New York city in October to cope with the anticipated disturbance during the presidential election. Following an unsuccessful expedition (December 1864) against Fort Fisher, he was removed by Lieutenant-General Grant. He was elected to Congress as a Republican, in 1866. In 1883, he was Democratic governor of Massachusetts, and in the following year was the unsuccessful presidential candidate of the Greenback-Labor and Anti-Monopolist parties. He died in Washington, January 11, 1893.

Army and Department of the Gulf

CONSTITUTED February 23, 1862, comprising, in a general way, the territory of the Gulf States occupied by the Federal troops. Major-General Benjamin F. Butler was the first commander. He was followed by Major-Generals N. P. Banks, S. A. Hurlbut, and E. R. S. Canby, who commanded after the close of the war. There were, at first, many separate bodies of troops scattered over the department. One of these, the Nineteenth Army Corps, was organized in January, 1863, and was discontinued as a corps in this department November 7, 1864. The Thirteenth Army Corps joined this army from that of the Tennessee in August, 1863, and remained until June, 1864. A detachment of the Sixteenth Corps, also from the Army of the Tennessee, joined for the Red River expedition, in March, 1864. On May 7, 1864, the Department of the Gulf was merged in the Military Division of West Mississippi, but retained a separate existence.

MAJOR-GENERAL NATHANIEL PRENTISS BANKS was born in Waltham, Massachusetts, January 30, 1816. He received a common-school education, practised law, and was a prominent member of Congress from 1853 to 1857. He was governor of Massachusetts from 1858 until 1861, and when the Civil War broke out he was president of the Illinois Central Railroad Company, but immediately offered his services to the Government. He was made major-general of volunteers, and was appointed to the command of the Department of Annapolis, and then to the Department of the Shenandoah. In the organization of the Army of the Potomac in March, 1862, he was assigned to the Fifth Corps, but his force was detached April 4, 1862, and remained in the Shenandoah Valley, where Banks had command until that corps was merged in the Army of Virginia, June 26, 1862. After the Army of Virginia was discontinued, Banks was at the head of the Military District of Washington until October 27, 1862. He succeeded Major-General B. F. Butler in command of the Department of the Gulf, and was actively engaged along the lower Mississippi and Red rivers. He resigned his commission after the disastrous Red River expedition of 1864, and was reelected to Congress. In 1890, owing to an increasing mental disorder, he was obliged to retire from public life. He died at his home in Waltham, September 1, 1894.

TWO COMMANDERS
OF THE
THIRD ARMY CORPS,
SICKLES
AND
HEINTZLEMAN

Daniel E. Sickles Commanded the Third Corps at Chancellorsville and Gettysburg.

S. P. Heintzelman Led the Third Corps at Fair Oaks and Second Bull Run.

FEDERAL

MAJOR–

GENERALS

W. H. French Commanded the Third Corps in the Mine Run Campaign.

COMMANDERS OF THE

THIRD AND FOURTH

ARMY CORPS

T. J. Wood Commanded the Fourth Corps (West) at Nashville, 1864.

Erasmus D. Keyes Commanded the Fourth Corps (East) on the Peninsula.

Army of Georgia

MAJOR-GENERAL EDWARD RICHARD SPRIGG CANBY (U.S.M.A. 1839) was born in Kentucky in 1819. Entering the army, he served in the Seminole and Mexican wars. When the Civil War broke out, he served first as colonel in New Mexico, held that territory for the Union, and prevented a Confederate invasion of California. Then, for some time, he was on special duty in the North and East. In May, 1864, with the rank of major-general of volunteers, he assumed command of the Military Division of West Mississippi. He captured Mobile, April 12, 1865, and the following month arranged for the surrender of the Confederate forces in the Trans-Mississippi Department. June 3, 1865, he succeeded to the command of the Army and Department of the Gulf. After the close of the war he was made brigadier-general in the regular army, and was put in command of the Department of the Columbia. While engaged in attempting to settle difficulties between the Government and the Modoc Indians, he was treacherously murdered by their chief, April 11, 1873.

MAJOR-GENERAL GORDON GRANGER (U.S.M.A. 1845) was born in New York city in 1821, and served in the Mexican War and on the Southwestern frontier. When the Civil War broke out,

he was made captain and rose through successive grades until his appointment of major-general of volunteers was dated September 17, 1862. He fought at Wilson's Creek, and later commanded the cavalry and had a brigade in the Army of the Mississippi. Then he had charge of the so-called Army of Kentucky, from August to October, 1862, and served in the Department of the Ohio until put in charge of the newly organized Reserve Corps of the Army of the Cumberland. At Chickamauga, he rendered most timely assistance to Thomas and won a brevet of lieutenant-colonel in the regular army. He was the first commander of the new Fourth Corps until April, 1864, when he was sent to command the district of South Alabama, the troops of which were merged in the Reserve Corps, Department of the Gulf (afterward called New Thirteenth Army Corps) of which Granger took command in January, 1865. He commanded the land forces at the fall of Forts Morgan and Gaines (August, 1864), and in the operations around Mobile that resulted in its capture, April, 1865. After the war, Major-General Granger was mustered out of the volunteer service and received the commission of colonel in the regular army. He was brevetted major-general in March, 1865. He died in Santa Fé, New Mexico, January 10, 1876.

Army of Georgia

THE FOURTEENTH AND TWENTIETH ARMY CORPS on the march to the sea and through the Carolinas (November 1864–April 1865) were so known. This force was commanded by Major-General Henry W. Slocum, and constituted the left wing of Sherman's army.

MAJOR-GENERAL HENRY WARNER SLOCUM (U.S.M.A. 1852) was born in Delphi, New York, September 24, 1827, and, beginning the practice of law at Syracuse, New York, he resigned his commission as first lieutenant in 1855. At the outbreak of the Civil War, he joined McDowell's troops as colonel of the Twenty-seventh New York Volunteers, and at Bull Run was severely wounded. In August, 1861, as brigadier-general of volunteers, he commanded a brigade of Franklin's Division of the Army of the Potomac, and later had a division in the Sixth Corps. At Gaines' Mill and Glendale, General Slocum took a prominent part, and after the battle of Malvern Hill he was pro-

moted. As major-general of volunteers, he was given the Twelfth Corps in October, 1862. He fought with the armies of the Potomac and of Virginia, and was sent by Major-General Meade to command the army on the first day of Gettysburg. He went West with his corps, and was commanding at Tullahoma during the battle of Chattanooga. For short periods, in 1864 and 1865, he had charge of the District of Vicksburg. In the Atlanta campaign, he was in command of the Twentieth Corps and during the march to the sea and the Georgia and Carolina campaigns, he was at the head of the Army of Georgia, which formed the left wing of General Sherman's army. At the battle of Bentonville, North Carolina, General Slocum repulsed Johnston's attack, and later was present at the surrender of the Confederate Army. He resigned his commission in 1865, and devoted himself to the law. He died in Brooklyn, New York, April 14, 1894.

Fitz John Porter Commanded the
Fifth Corps on the Peninsula.

George Sykes Commanded the Fifth
Corps at Gettysburg.

William Farrar Smith Led the
Sixth Corps at Fredericksburg.

FEDERAL MAJOR–GENERALS
COMMANDERS OF THE FIFTH AND SIXTH ARMY CORPS

Horatio G. Wright Commanded the
Sixth Corps in the Shenandoah
and Petersburg Campaigns.

William Buel Franklin Commanded
the Sixth Corps on the Peninsula
and at Antietam under McClellan.

Gouverneur Kemble Warren, Long
Associated with the Fifth Corps,
finally as Corps Commander.

Army of the Shenandoah

A FORCE belonging to the Middle Military Division, organized for Major-General P. H. Sheridan, in August, 1864, in order to drive Lieutenant-General Early from the Shenandoah valley. It consisted of the Sixth Corps from the Army of the Potomac, and a detachment of the Nineteenth Corps, Army of the Gulf. There was also a cavalry corps made up of two divisions of the cavalry of the Army of the Potomac. With it acted the troops of the Department of West Virginia, a force created from the Eighth Corps (Middle Department), and sometimes called the Army of West Virginia, under the command of Major-General George Crook. Major-General Wright of the Sixth Corps had charge of the Army of the Shenandoah for a few days in October, 1864, and Major-General A. T. A. Torbert assumed the command in February, 1865, when Sheridan rejoined the Army of the Potomac with the cavalry.

Army of the Frontier

THE FIELD FORCES in Missouri and Kansas were organized into the Army of the Frontier on October 12, 1862. It was commanded by Major-Generals J. M. Schofield and F. J. Herron, and by Major-General James G. Blunt temporarily. It was very active during its existence, and fought many minor engagements in the Southwest, including Clark's Mill, Missouri, and Prairie Grove, Arkansas, and the capture of Van Buren, Arkansas. The army went out of existence June 5, 1863, and its troops were scattered among the districts in Tennessee and Missouri.

MAJOR-GENERAL FRANCIS JAY HERRON was born in Pittsburgh, Pennsylvania, in 1837, and gave up his business career in Iowa to go to the front as lieutenant-colonel of an Iowa regiment. He served in the Army of the Southwest, and was captured at Pea Ridge after conduct that brought him great praise and a medal of honor. He was given a division of the Army of the Frontier, which he commanded at Prairie Grove. From March to June, 1863, he was, as major-general of volunteers, at the head of the army itself. Later, as division commander of the Thirteenth Corps, he was present at the fall of Vicksburg, and also held command in Texas and at Port Hudson. He received the surrender of the Confederate forces west of the Mississippi in May, 1865. He resigned from the service in June, 1865, and practised law in New Orleans and New York. He died January 8, 1902.

MAJOR-GENERAL JAMES G. BLUNT was born in Trenton, Maine, in 1826, and became a physician. He settled in Kansas, where he became prominent for his work in the anti-slavery movement. He went to the Civil War as lieutenant-colonel and was made brigadier-general of volunteers in April, 1862. He was placed at the head of the Department of Kansas on May 5, 1862, and when that department was merged in that of Missouri, on September 19th, he was given a division in the Army of the Frontier. On December 7th, his division and that of Brigadier-General F. J. Herron checked, at Prairie Grove, Arkansas, the advance of Major-General Hindman into Missouri. Blunt was senior officer in command of both divisions in the battle. From June, 1863 to January, 1864, he was at the head of the District of the Frontier, that army having been broken up. From October, 1864, to the end of the war he commanded the District of South Kansas. He died in Washington, D. C., July 25, 1881.

Army of the Mountain Department

CREATED March 11, 1862, from the Department of Western Virginia. On March 29th, Brigadier-General Rosecrans turned over the troops therein to Major-General John C. Fremont. This force co-operated with Banks and McDowell against "Stonewall" Jackson in the Shenandoah valley, and its principal engagements were those at McDowell and Cross Keys. On June 26, 1862, the Mountain Department became the First Corps, Army of Virginia.

John A. Dix Commanded the Seventh Corps (East) in 1862.

J. J. Reynolds Commanded the Seventh Corps (West) in 1864.

FEDERAL
MAJOR–
GENERALS
COMMANDERS
OF THE
SEVENTH,
EIGHTH
AND NINTH
ARMY
CORPS

Robert C. Schenck Commanded the Eighth Corps in 1863.

John E. Wool Commanded the Eighth Corps in 1862.

John G. Parke Commanded the Ninth Corps at Petersburg.

Orlando B. Willcox Commanded the Ninth Army Corps in 1863–4.

First Army Corps

MAJOR-GENERAL JOHN CHARLES FREMONT was born in Savannah, Georgia, January 21, 1813. He became professor of mathematics in the United States navy, and was commissioned second lieutenant in the Corps of Topographical Engineers, in 1838. He conducted several exploring expeditions to the Far West, during one of which he fomented a revolt against Mexican rule in California and raised the Bear Flag in that region. Later, he assisted in the Mexican War and was made civil governor of California by Commodore Stockton. Trouble arose between him and General Kearny, who had been charged with the establishment of the Government, which resulted in a court martial and Fremont's resignation from the army. He settled in California, represented that State in the Senate, and was the unsuccessful Republican candidate for President, in 1856. At the outbreak of the Civil War, he was appointed major-general, and on July 25, 1861, put at the head of the Western Department, with headquarters at St. Louis, where he made an attempt to free the slaves of Southern sympathizers. This act led to his removal in November, and the following March he was given command of the newly created Mountain Department. He refused to serve as corps commander under Major-General Pope when his troops were merged in the Army of Virginia. He resigned from the army in June, 1864. He became interested in railroad building and was governor of Arizona (1878–1882). In 1890, he was reappointed major-general and was retired with that rank on April 28th. He died July 13, 1890.

First Army Corps

THE FIRST ARMY CORPS was originally planned to consist of the troops of the Mountain Department, earlier known as the Department of Western Virginia, under command of Brigadier-General W. S. Rosecrans, but by order of the President, the First Corps, from troops of the Army of the Potomac, was placed under command of Major-General Irvin McDowell, March 13, 1862. On April 4th, the First Corps was discontinued and the troops sent to the Department of the Rappahannock, and then in turn merged in the Army of Virginia, as the Third Corps, on June 26, 1862. The First Corps, Army of the Potomac, was re-created September 12, 1862, from the troops of the Third Corps, Army of Virginia, coming successively under command of Major-General Joseph Hooker, Brigadier-General George G. Meade, Brigadier-General J. S. Wadsworth, Major-Generals J. F. Reynolds, Abner Doubleday, and John Newton. This corps rendered gallant service at South Mountain, Antietam, Fredericksburg, Chancellorsville, and Gettysburg, among the more important engagements. It was discontinued March 24, 1864, when it became merged in the Fifth Corps, Army of the Potomac.

MAJOR-GENERAL IRVIN MCDOWELL (U.S.M.A. 1838) was born in Columbus, Ohio, October 15, 1818. He rendered distinguished service in the Mexican War. As brigadier-general at the head of the Department of Northeastern Virginia, he had command of the Union army at First Bull Run. Afterward, with a commission of major-general of volunteers, he had a division in the Army of the Potomac. In further reorganizations and changes he headed his troops as commander of the First Corps, Army of the Potomac; Department of the Rappahannock, and Third Corps, Army of Virginia. His conspicuous services at Cedar Mountain won him the brevet of major-general, which full rank he attained in 1872. Immediately after Second Bull Run he was relieved from field service, and was president of several army boards. In July, 1864, he was placed at the head of the Department of the Pacific, and after the war held various commands. He was retired in 1882, and died in San Francisco, May 4, 1885.

MAJOR-GENERAL ABNER DOUBLEDAY (U.S. M.A. 1842) was born at Ballston Spa, New York, June 26, 1819, and served in the Mexican and Seminole wars. As captain of the artillery he was at Fort Sumter under Major Anderson, and fired upon the Confederates the first Federal gun of the Civil War. He served under Major-General Patterson in the Valley, and on February 3, 1862, was made brigadier-general of volunteers and placed in charge of the defenses of Washington. He had a brigade in the Third Corps, Army of Virginia, and afterward a division, which he retained when the corps again became the First

J. M. Brannan Commanded the
Tenth Corps in 1862–63.

W. T. H. Brooks Commanded
the Tenth Corps in 1864.

FEDERAL

MAJOR–

GENERALS

COMMANDERS

OF THE

TENTH ARMY CORPS

David B. Birney Commanded
the Tenth Corps in 1864.

Ormsby M. Mitchel Commanded the
Tenth Corps in 1862.

Alfred H. Terry Commanded the Tenth
Corps in 1864–65.

Corps, Army of the Potomac. In November, 1862, he became major-general of volunteers. He fought at Fredericksburg and Chancellorsville. When Reynolds was killed on the field of Gettysburg, the command of the First Corps fell upon him for the day, July 1, 1863, until he was succeeded by Major-General John Newton. After being mustered out of the volunteer service, he served as colonel in the regular army until he was retired in 1873. He had been brevetted brigadier and major-general in 1865. Major-General Doubleday was the author of several important military works. He died January 27, 1893, at Mendham, New Jersey.

MAJOR-GENERAL JOHN NEWTON (U.S.M.A. 1842) was born in Norfolk, Virginia, August 24, 1823. After graduation he taught engineering at West Point for three years, and then devoted himself to the construction of fortifications. The outbreak of the Civil War found him chief engineer of the Department of Pennsylvania, and he assisted in preparing the defenses of the national capital. The rank of brigadier-general of volunteers was given him in September, 1861, and he remained with the organization which was eventually the First Corps, Army of the Potomac, as brigade and division commander, being made major-general of volunteers in March, 1863. He succeeded to the command of the corps after Reynolds' death at Gettysburg, July 1, 1863, and led it until it was discontinued, March 24, 1864. His appointment as major-general of volunteers expired in April, 1864, and with his former title he succeeded Sheridan in a division of the Fourth Corps,

Army of the Cumberland. After the war, he continued in the regular army and reached the grade of brigadier-general in 1884, being retired in 1886. His most renowned achievement was the removal of the reefs at Hell Gate in the harbor of New York. General Newton was commissioner of public works, New York city, from 1887 to 1888, and then president of the Panama Railroad Company. He died, May 1, 1895.

MAJOR-GENERAL JOHN FULTON REYNOLDS (U.S.M.A. 1841) was born in Lancaster, Pennsylvania, September 20, 1820, and served in the Mexican War, and in the Rogue River Indian and Utah expeditions. At the outbreak of the Civil War, he was commandant at West Point, but with the rank of brigadier-general of volunteers took active part in the operations of the Army of the Potomac from August, 1861. He commanded a brigade of the Pennsylvania Reserves which was merged in the First Corps, Army of the Potomac. He went with McDowell to the Department of the Rappahannock but returned to the Army of the Potomac at the head of a brigade in the Fifth Corps, for the move to the James. He was taken prisoner at Glendale but was exchanged. The brigade joined the Third Corps, Army of Virginia, in which Reynolds commanded a division. Again with the Army of the Potomac, Reynolds was given the First Corps on September 29, 1862, and later was made major-general of volunteers. On the first day of Gettysburg, July 1, 1863, he was killed by a Confederate sharpshooter. Reynolds' loss was most keenly felt in the Federal army.

Second Army Corps

CREATED by the general order of March 3, 1862, chiefly from Sumner's and Blenker's divisions of the Army of the Potomac as constituted in October, 1861. Major-General Sumner was its first commander, and his successors were Major-Generals D. N. Couch, John Sedgwick, O. O. Howard, W. S. Hancock, G. K. Warren, D. B. Birney, A. A. Humphreys, Brevet Major-Generals Gershom Mott, N. A. Miles, and F. C. Barlow, and Brigadier-Generals John Gibbon, William Hays, and J. C. Caldwell. The Second Corps was with the Army of the Potomac all through the war and took part in all its great engagements. It suffered most severely at Antietam. It was discon-

tinued June 28, 1865. The Second Corps made a notable record for itself. One interesting fact is that until the battle of Spotsylvania, on May 10, 1864, it never lost a gun or a color.

MAJOR-GENERAL EDWIN VOSE SUMNER was born in Boston, January 30, 1797, enlisting in the army in 1819. He rendered distinguished service in the Black Hawk and Mexican wars, and was military governor of New Mexico from 1851 to 1853. As brigadier-general, he superseded Brevet Brigadier-General Albert Sidney Johnston in the command of the Department of the Pacific in April, 1861. He came East to participate in

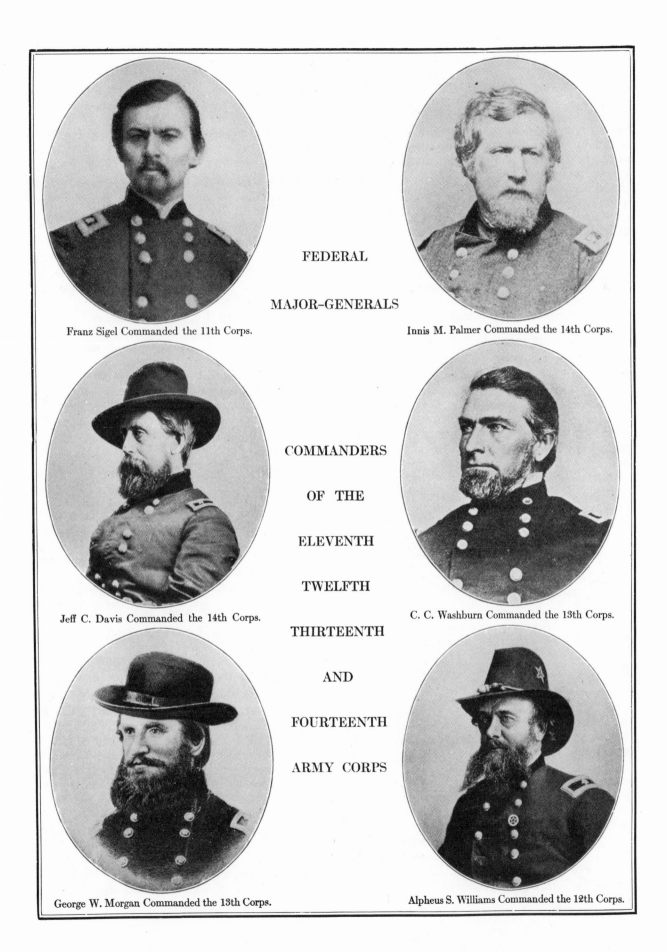

FEDERAL

MAJOR-GENERALS

Franz Sigel Commanded the 11th Corps.

Innis M. Palmer Commanded the 14th Corps.

COMMANDERS

OF THE

ELEVENTH

TWELFTH

THIRTEENTH

AND

FOURTEENTH

ARMY CORPS

Jeff C. Davis Commanded the 14th Corps.

C. C. Washburn Commanded the 13th Corps.

George W. Morgan Commanded the 13th Corps.

Alpheus S. Williams Commanded the 12th Corps.

the Civil War, and became the first commander of the Second Army Corps. He was made major-general of volunteers, July 4, 1862. He was wounded in the Peninsula campaign and also at Antietam. Upon Burnside's reorganization of the army, he commanded the Right Grand Division. When Hooker was put at the head, Major-General Sumner was relieved at his own request, and sent to the Department of Missouri. But he died on the way there, at Syracuse, New York, March 21, 1863.

MAJOR-GENERAL DARIUS NASH COUCH (U.S. M.A. 1846) was born in Putnam County, New York, July 23, 1822, and served in the Mexican and the Seminole wars, being brevetted first lieutenant in the former. In 1855, he resigned from the army and entered mercantile life in New York city, but returned to his profession at the opening of the Civil War as colonel of volunteers. He was identified with the Department and Army of the Potomac, first as brigade commander (August, 1861–March, 1862), then as division commander in the Fourth Army Corps to September, 1862, when he was made major-general of volunteers and his division was transferred to the Sixth Corps. In October, 1862, Couch was placed at the head of the Second Corps, which he led at Fredericksburg and at Chancellorsville. From June, 1863, to December, 1864, he was at the head of the Department of the Susquehanna, when he was given a division of the Twenty-third Army Corps, and fought at the battle of Nashville. He resigned from the army in 1865, and was defeated for governor of Massachusetts on the Democratic ticket in the same year. Subsequently, he was collector of the port of Boston, and quartermaster-general and adjutant-general of Connecticut. He died in Norwalk, Connecticut, February 12, 1897.

BRIGADIER-GENERAL WILLIAM HAYS (U.S.M.A. 1840) was born in Richmond, Virginia, in 1819, and served in the Mexican War. As lieutenant-colonel he had a brigade of horse artillery in the Army of the Potomac through the Peninsula campaign, the artillery reserve at Antietam, and the artillery of the Right Grand Division at Fredericksburg. In November, 1862, he was made brigadier-general of volunteers, and at Chancellorsville, in command of a brigade in the Second Army Corps he was wounded and captured. He was exchanged, and after the wounding of Hancock at Gettysburg, he had command

of the corps for a short time. Then he spent some time in the Department of the East and later had a brigade in the Second Corps. He died in Fort Independence, Boston Harbor, February 7, 1875.

MAJOR-GENERAL GERSHOM MOTT was born in Trenton, New Jersey, April 7, 1822, and served in the Mexican War. He went to the front in the Civil War as lieutenant-colonel of the Fifth New Jersey Infantry, and later became colonel of the Sixth New Jersey. In September, 1862, he was promoted to brigadier-general of volunteers, and had a brigade in the Third Corps from December, 1862, to March, 1864, and then had consecutively two divisions of the Second Corps. Several times he took command of the corps during the absence of Major-General Humphreys. Mott was brevetted major-general of volunteers in August, 1864, and received the title May 28, 1865, shortly before being mustered out. After the war, he was at one time treasurer of the State of New Jersey, and died in New York city, November 29, 1884.

MAJOR-GENERAL NELSON APPLETON MILES was born in Westminster, Massachusetts, August 8, 1839. He entered mercantile life, but went to the front in the Civil War as first lieutenant in the Twenty-second Massachusetts Infantry, and in May, 1862, he was made lieutenant-colonel of the Sixty-first New York Infantry. By September he had risen to a colonelcy of volunteers. He fought with the Army of the Potomac in all its battles and was wounded at Chancellorsville. From March to July, 1864, he had a brigade in the Second Corps and was made brigadier-general in May. The rank of major-general of volunteers was given him in October, 1865. After the war he entered the regular army as colonel, and his chief service was against the Indians in the West. In the Spanish-American War he commanded the United States army, and personally led the Porto Rico expedition, and upon the reorganization of the Army of the United States he was appointed lieutenant-general (1900), being retired with that rank three years later.

MAJOR-GENERAL WINFIELD SCOTT HANCOCK (U.S.M.A. 1844) was born in Montgomery Square, Pennsylvania, February 14, 1824. He served in the Mexican War and in the border troubles in Kansas, and had risen to the rank of captain when the Civil War broke out. He was

FEDERAL

MAJOR–

GENERALS

P. J. Osterhaus Commanded the Fifteenth
Corps in 1864.

S. A. Hurlbut Commanded the Sixteenth
Corps in 1863.

J. A. Mower Commanded the Seventeenth
Corps in the Carolinas.

J. G. Foster Commanded the Eighteenth
Army Corps in 1864.

COMMANDERS

OF THE

FIFTEENTH

SIXTEENTH

SEVENTEENTH

EIGHTEENTH

AND

NINETEENTH

ARMY CORPS

John H. Martindale Commanded the Eighteenth Corps in Front of Richmond.

William H. Emory Commanded the Nineteenth Corps in the Shenandoah Valley.

made brigadier-general of volunteers in September, 1861, and had a brigade in the Fourth Army Corps at Williamsburg, where McClellan called him " Hancock the Superb." At Antietam, he distinguished himself, and succeeded Richardson at the head of a division of the Second Corps. In November, 1862, he was made major-general of volunteers. His troops did noteworthy work at Fredericksburg and Chancellorsville, and Hancock received the Second Corps, in May, 1863. At Gettysburg, Meade sent him to take charge on the first day, after Reynolds' death, and on the third day he himself was severely wounded. In March, 1864, he resumed command of the Second Corps. He took charge of the Department of West Virginia and Middle Military Division in March, 1865. After the war, he became major-general in 1866, and commanded various departments. He was an unsuccessful candidate for the presidency against Garfield. Of Hancock, General Grant once said: " Hancock stands the most conspicuous figure of all the general officers who did not exercise a separate command. He commanded a corps longer than any other one, and his name was never mentioned as having committed in battle a blunder for which he was responsible." He died on Governor's Island, New York, February 9, 1886.

MAJOR-GENERAL ANDREW ATKINSON HUMPHREYS (U.S.M.A. 1831) was born in Philadelphia, November 2, 1810. He was closely associated with engineering and coast-survey work until the outbreak of the Civil War, when, as major, he became a member of Major-General McClellan's staff. In April, 1862, he was made brigadier-general of volunteers and was chief topographical engineer of the Army of the Potomac during the Peninsula campaign. He had a division of the Fifth Corps from September, 1862, to May, 1863, and fought at Fredericksburg and Chancellorsville. He was then given a division of the Third Corps, and after Gettysburg was promoted to major-general of volunteers and made General Meade's chief of staff. In the final campaign against Lee, he had the Second Corps (November, 1864, to June, 1865). After being mustered out of the volunteer service, September 1, 1866, he was made brigadier-general and placed at the head of the Engineer Corps of the United States army. He was retired in July, 1879, and died in Washington, December 27, 1883. He received brevets for gallant and meritorious services at the battles of Fredericksburg, Va., Gettysburg, Pa., and Sailors Creek, Va.

MAJOR-GENERAL JOHN GIBBON (U.S.M.A. 1847) was born in Holmesburg, Pennsylvania, April 27, 1827, and served in the Mexican War. Later, he was instructor in artillery practice and quartermaster at West Point. He had reached the grade of captain when the Civil War broke out, and became McDowell's chief of artillery. He was promoted to brigadier-general of volunteers in May, 1862. He had a brigade in the Third Corps, Army of Virginia, and a brigade and division in the First Corps, Army of the Potomac. He was given a division in the Second Army Corps, which he held for the most part until August, 1864. When Hancock was sent by Meade to take charge at Gettysburg on the first day, Gibbon was given temporary command of the corps and was seriously wounded. As major-general of volunteers, he had command of the Eighteenth and Twenty-fourth army corps for short periods. When mustered out of the volunteer service, he continued in the regular army as colonel, and rose to be brigadier-general in 1885. He did much Indian fighting, and in 1891 was retired from active service. He died in Baltimore, February 6, 1896.

MAJOR-GENERAL FRANCIS CHANNING BARLOW was born in Brooklyn, New York, October 19, 1834, and was a Harvard graduate of 1855. He enlisted as a private in the Twelfth New York Militia, and after the three months' service had expired, he returned to the field as lieutenant-colonel of the Sixty-first New York. His rise was rapid, due to ability displayed in the Army of the Potomac, and he was made brigadier-general of volunteers after the battle of Antietam (September, 1862), where he was badly wounded. He had a brigade in the Eleventh Corps at Chancellorsville, and a division at Gettysburg, when he was again badly wounded. On recovery, he was assigned to duty in the Department of the South and afterward given a division in the Second Army Corps, March 1864, and served until the Army of the Potomac was discontinued. He was made major-general of volunteers in May, 1865, for his conspicuous gallantry at the battle of Spotsylvania. In April and May, 1865, he had command of the Second Corps. General Barlow resigned from the army November 16, 1865, and returned to New York, where he entered political life and resumed the practice of law. He was secretary of state of New York 1865–1868, and attorney-general for New York from 1871 to 1873, in which capacity he conducted the prosecution of " Boss " Tweed and other municipal officials. He died in New York city, January 11, 1896.

TWENTIETH

TWENTY-FIRST

TWENTY-SECOND

TWENTY-THIRD

TWENTY-FOURTH

AND

TWENTY-FIFTH

CORPS

A. McD. McCook Commanded the
Twentieth Corps at Chickamauga.

Thos. L. Crittenden Commanded the
Twenty-first Corps in 1863.

C. C. Augur Commanded the Twenty-
second Corps at Port Hudson.

G. L. Hartsuff Commanded the Twenty-
third Corps in 1863.

E. O. C. Ord Commanded the Twenty-
fourth Corps in 1865.

Godfrey Weitzel Commanded the
Twenty-fifth Corps in 1864-5.

Third Army Corps

ON THE REORGANIZATION of the Army of the Potomac in March, 1862, a body of troops, chiefly from Heintzelman's, Porter's and Hooker's divisions of the earlier organization, was constituted the Third Army Corps. In May, Porter's men were transferred to the new provisional Fifth Army Corps. The future additions to the corps were chiefly from the Eighth and Twenty-second corps. The corps fought in the battles of the Army of the Potomac, and two divisions were sent to the assistance of the Army of Virginia at Second Bull Run and Chantilly. On March 24, 1864, it was merged in the Second Corps. Its commanders were Brigadier-Generals S. P. Heintzelman and George Stoneman, and Major-Generals D. E. Sickles, D. B. Birney, and W. H. French.

MAJOR-GENERAL SAMUEL PETER HEINTZELMAN (U.S.M.A. 1826) was born in Manheim, Pennsylvania, September 30, 1805, and served on the frontier, in Florida, in the Mexican War, and in California and Texas. At the opening of the Civil War he was promoted to a colonelcy, and became inspector-general of the defenses of Washington. In May, 1861, he was placed in command at Alexandria, Virginia. He headed the Third Division at Bull Run, and in subsequent organizations of the Army of the Potomac he had a brigade, a division, and afterward the Third Corps, which he commanded until November, 1862. His conduct at Fair Oaks won him a brevet of brigadier-general, for he was now major-general of volunteers. He fought through the Peninsula campaign, and was sent to assist Pope at Second Bull Run and Chantilly. He was in command of the defenses and later of the Department of Washington (Twenty-second Army Corps) from September, 1862, to October, 1863. After this, he took no active part in the war, but was commander of the Northern Department from January to October, 1864, and then served on court martials. He was mustered out of the volunteer service August, 1865, and was retired from the army with the rank of major-general, February 22, 1869. He died in Washington, May 3, 1880.

MAJOR-GENERAL GEORGE STONEMAN (U.S.M.A. 1846) was born in Busti, New York, August 8, 1822, and was captain in command at Fort Brown, Texas, when the Civil War broke out. He refused to obey the order of General Twiggs

to surrender the property of the United States Government to the State of Texas, and escaped by steamer to New York. His first active service in the Civil War was as major in the West Virginia campaign, and as brigadier-general of volunteers he had the cavalry command in the Army of the Potomac. It was his troops that brought on the action at Williamsburg in May, 1862. After the death of Major-General Kearny, at Chantilly, he succeeded eventually to the command of his division, and later succeeded Major-General Heintzelman in the command of the Third Army Corps, which he led at Fredericksburg. He was promoted to major-general of volunteers in command of the Cavalry Corps, Army of the Potomac, and led a famous raid toward Richmond during the Chancellorsville campaign. From January to April, 1864, he was in command of the Twenty-third Army Corps, and then received the cavalry division of the same organization. After a raid in the Atlanta campaign, in which he was captured and held prisoner for three months, he assumed command of the Department of the Ohio, and later the District of East Tennessee, where his operations were very successful, especially his raid into North Carolina, in April, 1865. He was retired from the regular army with the rank of colonel, in 1871, and went to California, of which State he was governor from 1883 to 1887. He died in Buffalo, New York, September 5, 1894.

MAJOR-GENERAL DANIEL EDGAR SICKLES was born in New York city, October 20, 1825. Admitted to the bar in 1846, he afterward served in the State legislature, the diplomatic service, and in Congress, where he was when the Civil War broke out. He raised the Excelsior Brigade of five New York regiments, which served in the Army of the Potomac with Sickles as brigadier-general of volunteers at its head. In March, 1862, it was incorporated in the Third Army Corps. He led his brigade through the Peninsula campaign, commanded a division at Fredericksburg and, as major-general of volunteers, the Third Corps at Chancellorsville and Gettysburg. In the latter battle he lost a leg on the second day. He continued in the army after the close of the war, and was retired with rank of major-general in 1869. He went on a secret diplomatic mission to South America in 1867, and was minister to Spain, 1869–1873. He was sheriff of New York County, in 1890, and Democratic member of Congress, 1892–94, as well as president of the New

John E. Phelps, of Arkansas— Colonel of the 2d Cavalry.   Marcus La Rue, of Arkansas— Promoted for Gallantry.   John B. Slough, of Colorado— Engaged in New Mexico.   Patrick E. Connor, of California—Colonel of the 3d Infantry.

FEDERAL GENERALS—No. 1—ARKANSAS (first two above). COLORADO (third above). CALIFORNIA (fourth above and six below).

James Shields, Brave Irish Soldier, A Friend of Lincoln.   George S. Evans, Originally Colonel of the 2d Cavalry.   George W. Bowie, Originally Colonel of the 5th Infantry.

Edward McGarry, Brevetted for Conspicuous Gallantry.   James W. Denver; Denver, Colo., Named After Him.   J. H. Carleton Commanded a Column in March Across Arizona.

This is the first of 29 groups embracing representative general officers of 34 states and territories. On preceding pages portraits appear of many leaders, including all the commanders of armies and army corps, and all generals killed in battle. Many others appear in preceding volumes, as identified with particular events or special branches, such as cavalry and artillery and the signal and medical corps. Information of every general officer can be found through the index and the roster concluding this volume.

Fourth Army Corps (Potomac)

York State Board of Civil Service Commissioners for several years.

MAJOR-GENERAL WILLIAM HENRY FRENCH (U.S.M.A. 1837) was born in Baltimore, January 13, 1815, and served in the Seminole and Mexican wars. In September, 1861, he was appointed brigadier-general of volunteers and major-general of volunteers the following year. He had a brigade in Sumner's Division, a division in the Second Corps, Army of the Potomac, and for a

short time a command in the Eighth Corps, that joined the Third Corps after the battle of Gettysburg. He was in command of the Third Corps, from July 7, 1863, to January 28, 1864, and again from February 17th to March 24, 1864. In May, 1864, he was mustered out of the volunteer service, and was brevetted major-general the following year. In the regular army he rose to the rank of colonel in 1877, and, in 1880, was retired from active service. He died in Baltimore, May 20, 1881.

Fourth Army Corps (Potomac)

CREATED March 3, 1862, chiefly from troops in Couch's, W. F. Smith's, and Casey's divisions of the earlier Army of the Potomac, together with some new organizations. It was commanded by Major-General E. D. Keyes. The corps fought through the Peninsula campaign and remained in that region when the rest of the Army of the Potomac withdrew. The troops were gradually sent to other corps of the army—to North Carolina, Washington, and other places, and the corps was discontinued on August 1, 1863.

MAJOR-GENERAL ERASMUS DARWIN KEYES (U.S.M.A. 1832) was born in Brimfield, Massachu-

setts, May 29, 1810. He did duty on the Western frontier until the Civil War began, when he was raised to a colonelcy and made brigadier-general of volunteers in May, 1861. He commanded a brigade at Bull Run, and eventually was put in command of the Fourth Army Corps when it was created. His appointment as major-general of volunteers was dated from the battle of Williamsburg, and he received a brevet of brigadier-general in the regular army for his gallant and meritorious service at Fair Oaks. He resigned from the army in May, 1864, and went to California. He died in Nice, France, October 11, 1895.

Fourth Army Corps (Cumberland)

THE TWENTIETH AND TWENTY-FIRST army corps were consolidated on September 28, 1863, and the new organization was designated the Fourth Army Corps—the first one of that name, in the Army of the Potomac, having passed out of existence. It was commanded by Major-Generals Gordon Granger, O. O. Howard, D. S. Stanley, and Brigadier-General T. J. Wood. The corps fought in the battle of Chattanooga, was sent to the relief of Knoxville, and took part in the Atlanta campaign. When Sherman turned back toward Atlanta from Gaylesville, Alabama, the Fourth Corps went into Tennessee for the campaign against Hood. It fought at Franklin and Nashville, and was discontinued April 1, 1865.

MAJOR-GENERAL DAVID SLOAN STANLEY (U.S.M.A. 1852) was born in Cedar Valley, Ohio, June

1, 1828. He distinguished himself by his services, at the beginning of the Civil War, in the Southwest, at Dug Springs and Wilson's Creek. As brigadier-general of volunteers he had a division in the Army of the Mississippi and fought at Island No. 10, Iuka, and Corinth. In November, 1862, he became chief of cavalry in the Army of the Cumberland, and soon afterward was made major-general of volunteers. In November, 1863, he received a division of the Fourth Corps and became its head in July, 1864, when Major-General Howard took command of the Army of the Tennessee. Major-General Stanley was wounded at Franklin, November 30, 1864, and this ended his active service in the war, although he again headed the corps from February to August, 1865. Later on, he was given a colonelcy in the regular army and fought against the Indians in the

Orris S. Ferry, of Connecticut, Colonel of the 5th Regiment, Later U. S. Senator.

Joseph R. Hawley, of Connecticut, Distinguished at the Battle of Olustee.

Henry W. Birge, of Connecticut, Commander of a Division in the 19th Corps.

Henry W. Wessells, of Connecticut, Led Troops on the Peninsula in 1862.

H. H. Lockwood, of Delaware, Commander of a Brigade at Gettysburg.

Robert O. Tyler, of Connecticut, Commanded Artillery at Fredericksburg.

Lorenzo Thomas, of Delaware, Adjutant-General of the United States Army.

FEDERAL

GENERALS

No. 2

John B. S. Todd, of Dakota Territory, Appointed Brigadier-General to Date from September 19, 1861.

Daniel Tyler, of Connecticut, Led the Advance at Bull Run, 1861.

CONNECTICUT

DAKOTA

DELAWARE

Northwest. He was made brigadier-general in 1884, and was retired in 1892. He died in Washington, D. C., March 13, 1902.

MAJOR-GENERAL THOMAS JOHN WOOD (U.S. M.A. 1845) was born in Mumfordville, Kentucky, September 25, 1823, and served in the Mexican War. As brigadier-general of volunteers he had a brigade and then a division in the Army of the Ohio, a division of the Left Wing (Fourteenth Corps), Army of the Cumberland, which was continued in the Twenty-first Corps

when the Left Wing was reorganized, and likewise in the Fourth Corps until it was discontinued. He had command of the Twenty-first and Fourth corps for short periods, succeeding Stanley in the latter at Franklin and leading it at Nashville. He was wounded at Stone's River and in the Atlanta campaign. He was made major-general of volunteers in January, 1865, and was mustered out of the volunteer service in 1866, having been brevetted major-general in 1865. He was retired in 1868, and died in Dayton, Ohio, February 25, 1906.

Fifth Army Corps

ON THE ORGANIZATION of the Army of the Potomac into corps, March 3, 1862, the Fifth Army Corps was created and given to Major-General N. P. Banks. But this corps was detached, April 4th, from the Army of the Potomac and assigned, with its commander, to the Department of the Shenandoah, and was made the Second Corps of the Army of Virginia, in June. On May 18th, a new Fifth Corps was created and existed provisionally until confirmed by the War Department. It was composed, at first, of Brigadier-General Porter's division of the Third Corps, and Brigadier-General Sykes' troops of the regular army. Other bodies of troops were added from time to time, and the First Corps was merged in it, when the Army of the Potomac was reorganized in March, 1864. It was commanded from time to time by Brigadier-General F. J. Porter, Major-General Joseph Hooker, Brigadier-General Daniel Butterfield, Major-Generals George G. Meade, Charles Griffin, George Sykes, and A. A. Humphreys, Brevet Major-General S. K. Crawford, and Major-General G. K. Warren. The corps fought in whole or in part through all the battles of the Army of the Potomac.

MAJOR-GENERAL FITZ JOHN PORTER (U.S.M.A. 1845) was born in Portsmouth, New Hampshire, June 13, 1822, served in the Mexican War, and afterward taught at West Point. He was assistant adjutant-general in Albert Sidney Johnston's Utah expedition, in 1857. When the Civil War broke out, he was appointed brigadier-general of volunteers and served as chief of staff to Patterson and Banks. He was given a division in the Army of the Potomac, and after it had been

assigned to the Third Corps it was made the basis of the Fifth Corps, of which Porter was given command on May 18, 1862, just before McClellan's advance to the Chickahominy. After fighting through the Peninsula campaign, Porter was made major-general of volunteers, and went with his corps to the assistance of Pope and the Army of Virginia. At Second Bull Run, his action on an order from Major-General Pope led to his dismissal from the army. After long years of struggle, in 1886 he succeeded in being restored to the army with the rank of colonel, and shortly afterward was retired. He was engaged in business in New York and held several municipal offices. He died in Morristown, New Jersey, May 21, 1901.

MAJOR-GENERAL DANIEL BUTTERFIELD was born in Utica, New York, October 31, 1831, and was graduated from Union College. Early in the Civil War he became colonel of the Twelfth New York Volunteers, and brigadier-general of volunteers, taking part in the campaigns of McClellan, Burnside, Hooker, and Pope. At Fredericksburg, he had command of the Fifth Army Corps, and afterward became chief-of-staff to the commanding general. He went with Hooker to Chattanooga in October, 1863, and was his chief-of-staff until given a division in the Twentieth Army Corps, which he commanded until July, 1864. At the close of the war he was mustered out of the volunteer service and was brevetted major-general in the United States Army. He resigned from the army in 1869, and was United States treasurer in New York city, 1869–1870. He died at Cold Spring, New York, July 17, 1901.

FEDERAL
GENERALS
No. 3

DISTRICT OF
COLUMBIA
(UPPER TWO)

ILLINOIS
(NINE BELOW)

George W. Getty Led a Division
in the Army of the Potomac.

Samuel Sprigg Carroll, Brevetted
for Gallantry at Spotsylvania.

Isham Nichols
Haynie, Orig-
inally Colonel
of the 48th Reg-
iment.

Joseph Adal-
mon Maltby,
Originally Col-
onel of the 45th
Regiment.

Thomas E. G. Ranson Commanded
the 16th Army Corps.

John F. Farnsworth, Originally
Colonel of the 8th Cavalry.

E. N. Kirk, Severely Wounded in Re-
sisting the Attack on Johnson's
Division at Stone's River.

Alexander C. McClurg, Chief of
Staff, 14th Army Corps.

Abner Clark Harding,
Promoted for Gallan-
try at Donelson.

Charles E. Hovey, a
Gallant Division
Commander.

John McArthur, Conspicuous
as a Division Commander.

MAJOR-GENERAL GOUVERNEUR KEMBLE WARREN (U.S.M.A. 1850) was born at Cold Spring, New York, January 8, 1830. He made a specialty of topographical engineering, and was assistant professor of mathematics at West Point until the beginning of the Civil War, when he came into active service as lieutenant-colonel of the Fifth New York Volunteers. His promotion was rapid, and he reached the rank of major-general of volunteers in May, 1863. He served as brigade and division commander in the Fifth Army Corps, and in January, 1863, became chief topographical engineer, and, later, chief engineer of the Army of the Potomac. His service to the Union cause in defending Little Round Top at Gettysburg won him a brevet of colonel in the regular army. For a short time after Gettysburg he was in command of the Second Corps, and from March, 1864, to April, 1865, of the Fifth Corps, Army of the Potomac; after which he served for a short time in the Department of Mississippi. He left the volunteer service in May, 1865, having received the brevet of major-general in the regular army, in which he remained until February 13, 1866, when he resigned. His last years were spent on surveys and harbor improvements, and he died at Newport, Rhode Island, August 8, 1882.

MAJOR-GENERAL GEORGE SYKES (U.S.M.A. 1842) was born in Dover, Delaware, October 9, 1822, and served in the Mexican and Seminole wars. As major, he entered the Civil War, and was commissioned brigadier-general of volunteers in September, 1861. He led a division of the Fifth Army Corps and was commander for several short periods, notably at the battle of Gettysburg. His commission of major-general of volunteers was dated November 29, 1862. In September–October, 1864, he was in command of the District of South Kansas. After leaving the volunteer service he was made colonel in the regular army, where he remained until he died in Brownsville, Texas, February 9, 1880.

MAJOR-GENERAL CHARLES GRIFFIN (U.S.M.A. 1847) was born in Licking County, Ohio, in 1826, and served in the Mexican War and on the frontier. He was captain when the Civil War broke out, at the head of the Fifth Artillery. His battery fought with great bravery at Bull Run. As brigadier-general of volunteers, he had a brigade and then a division in the Fifth Army Corps, and took part in most of its important battles. He was given command of the corps on April 1, 1865, from which dated his appointment as major-general of volunteers. He led his corps in the final operations against Petersburg, and at Lee's surrender he received the arms and colors of the Army of Northern Virginia. He was one of the commission to carry out the terms of the surrender. After the close of the war, as colonel in the regular army, he was in command of the Department of Texas, where, during an outbreak of yellow fever, he refused to leave his post. Contracting the disease, he died in Galveston, September 15, 1867.

Sixth Army Corps

THE CREATION of this corps was similar to that of the Fifth, on May 18, 1862. Its basis was Brigadier-General W. B. Franklin's division, which was transferred from the Department of the Rappahannock (McDowell's command) and Brigadier-General W. F. Smith's division of the Fourth Army Corps. Franklin was the first commander, and he was followed by Major-Generals W. F. Smith, John Sedgwick, Brigadier-General J. B. Ricketts, Major-General H. G. Wright, and Brevet Major-General G. W. Getty. One division of the corps was prominent at Gaines' Mill, where there were about twenty thousand men present for duty, and it was partially engaged at Second Bull Run, South Mountain, Antietam, and Fredericksburg.

In the last battle it was in the Left Grand Division. The corps carried Marye's Heights in the Chancellorsville campaign, but, excepting one brigade, it was held in reserve at Gettysburg. Several changes were made in the reorganization of March, 1864, and with about twenty-five thousand men at the opening of the Wilderness campaign, it fought with the Army of the Potomac as far as Petersburg, when it was sent to the defense of Washington. Afterward it joined the Army of the Shenandoah and was prominent at the Opequon, Fisher's Hill, and Cedar Creek. In December, 1864, the corps returned to Petersburg and continued with the Army of the Potomac until it was discontinued, June 28, 1865.

P. S. Post. Originally Colonel of the 59th Regiment, Led a Brigade at Stone's River and Nashville.

John W. Turner, Commander of a Division at Drewry's Bluff and in the Siege of Petersburg.

Julius White, Originally Colonel of the 37th Regiment.

James Grant Wilson, Originally Colonel of the 4th U. S. Cavalry.

August Mersy, Originally Colonel of the 9th Infantry.

Leonard F. Ross, Originally Colonel of the 17th Regiment.

Benjamin M. Prentiss, Noted for His Heroic Defense at Shiloh.

John Eugene Smith, Originally Colonel of the 45th Regiment.

Richard J. Oglesby, Conspicuous at Corinth, where He was Wounded.

John C. Black, Originally Colonel of the 37th Regiment.

Hasbrouck Davis Led his Command out of the Net at Harper's Ferry.

Elias S. Dennis, Originally Colonel of the 30th Regiment; Conspicuous at Mobile.

Michael K. Lawler Promoted for Gallant Service Throughout the War.

FEDERAL GENERALS—No. 4—ILLINOIS

Giles A. Smith Commander of a Division in Georgia and the Carolinas.

Seventh Army Corps

MAJOR-GENERAL WILLIAM BUEL FRANKLIN (U.S.M.A. 1843) was born in York, Pennsylvania, February 27, 1823, and served in the Mexican War. He was also an engineer, and taught at West Point. At the opening of the Civil War, as colonel, he had a brigade at Bull Run, and subsequently a division in the First Corps, Army of the Potomac, which formed the nucleus of the Sixth when it was ordered to McClellan on the Peninsula, after having gone with McDowell to the Department of the Rappahannock. Franklin rose to be major-general of volunteers, his commission being dated July 4, 1862. In Burnside's reorganization of the Army of the Potomac, he commanded the Left Grand Division at Fredericksburg. His conduct in this battle was unsatisfactory to Burnside, and Franklin was relieved from duty in the service. In August, 1863, he was put in command of the Nineteenth Army Corps, serving until May, 1864, and was wounded at Sabine Cross Roads on the Red River expedition. From December, 1864, to November, 1865, he was at the head of a board for retiring disabled officers. On the latter date he resigned from the volunteer service, and gave up the regular army, in which he had been brevetted major-general on March 15, 1866. He then became vice-president of the Colt Firearms Company, and was American commissioner-general to the Paris Exposition of 1889. He died in Hartford, Connecticut, March 8, 1903.

MAJOR-GENERAL JOHN SEDGWICK (U.S.M.A. 1837) was born in Cornwall, Connecticut, September 13, 1813. He served with great distinction in the Mexican and Seminole wars. At the outbreak of the Civil War, he was lieutenant-colonel in the cavalry, and he rose to major-general of volunteers by July, 1862. After having a brigade in the Army of the Potomac, he was given a division of the Second Corps, and it met with frightful loss at Antietam, where Sedgwick was twice wounded. After recovery he took command of the Second and Ninth corps for short periods, and in February, 1863, he became head of the Sixth Army Corps, with which his name is so nobly associated. His brave attack upon the heights of Fredericksburg in May, 1863, won him renown. At Gettysburg, which he reached by a forced march on the second day, the left wing of the army was under his command. He was killed by a Confederate sharpshooter near Spotsylvania Court House, May 9, 1864.

MAJOR-GENERAL HORATIO GOUVERNEUR WRIGHT (U.S.M.A. 1841) was born in Clinton, Connecticut, March 6, 1820. At the beginning of the Civil War he had the rank of captain, having been in the Engineers Corps since his graduation. He was chief engineer of the expedition that destroyed the Norfolk Navy-Yard and occupied the same position in the Port Royal expedition. He was division commander in the Department of the South, and was then placed at the head of the re-created Department of the Ohio in August, 1862. Later, he was division and corps commander of the Sixth Army Corps. Being sent by Grant to defend Washington, he took part in the Shenandoah campaign and rejoined the Army of the Potomac before Petersburg. He led the assault on April 2, 1865, which ended the siege. He was promoted to major-general of volunteers in May, 1864. He served on several important commissions after the war, being made brigadier-general in 1879, and was retired from the army in 1884. He died in Washington, July 2, 1899.

Seventh Army Corps

THE TROOPS in the Department of Virginia at Fort Monroe, Norfolk, Portsmouth, and elsewhere, were organized into the Seventh Army Corps, on July 22, 1862, which existed until discontinued on August 1, 1863, when the troops were merged in the Eighteenth Army Corps. It was commanded in turn by Major-General John A. Dix and Brigadier-Generals H. M. Naglee and G. W. Getty. Its principal engagements were the affair at Deserted House, Virginia, and the defense of Suffolk, when besieged by Longstreet in 1863. Its greatest strength, present for duty, was about thirty-three thousand.

MAJOR-GENERAL JOHN ADAMS DIX was born in Boscawen, New Hampshire, July 24, 1798. In 1812, he entered the United States army as a cadet, and continued in military service until 1828, when he settled in Cooperstown, New York, to practise law. He served one term in the United States Senate, and became Secretary of the Treasury under President Buchanan. On the outbreak of the Civil

Robert Francis Catterson, Originally Colonel of the 97th Regiment.

Silas Colgrove Forwarded Lee's "Lost Order" Before Antietam to McClellan.

Thomas T. Crittenden, Originally Colonel of the 6th Infantry.

Robert Sanford Foster, Brevetted for Gallantry.

Alvin P. Hovey, Gallant Division Commander.

Thomas John Lucas, Originally Colonel of the 16th Infantry.

George F. McGinnis, Originally Colonel of the 11th Infantry.

James W. McMillan, Originally Colonel 1st Artillery.

John F. Miller, Colonel of the 29th Regiment; wounded at Stone's River.

Charles Cruft, Conspicuous at Stone's River and Chattanooga.

Jeremiah C. Sullivan Fought in the Shenandoah and Vicksburg Campaigns.

Robert A. Cameron, Originally Colonel of the 34th Regiment.

W. P. Benton Commanded a Brigade at Pea Ridge.

F. Knefler, Originally Colonel of the 79th Regiment.

Walter Q. Gresham, Engaged in the Nashville Campaign.

William Grose Led a Brigade under Thomas.

FEDERAL GENERALS—No. 5—INDIANA

War, Dix was appointed major-general of volunteers, and was given command of the Department of Annapolis (afterward Maryland, and finally merged in the Department of Pennsylvania, July, 1861). Then he was given a division at Baltimore, which became part of the Army of the Potomac, when it was organized. On March 22, 1862, Dix's Division was organized with other troops into the Middle Department, which he headed until June, when he was transferred to the Department of Virginia, the troops of which were organized into the Seventh Army Corps, in July. In July, 1863, Dix was transferred to the Department of the East with headquarters at New York, and remained there until the end of the war. He was twice minister to France (1866-69) and was governor of New York, 1873-75. He died in New York city, April 21, 1879.

Seventh Army Corps (Department of Arkansas)

ANOTHER CORPS designated the Seventh was created on January 6, 1864, to consist of the troops in the Department of Arkansas. The command was given to Major-General Frederick Steele, who was succeeded by Major-General J. J. Reynolds in December, 1864. For a year from May, 1864, the corps was a unit of the Military Division of West Mississippi and was discontinued August 1, 1865. The principal fighting done by the Seventh Corps was in Steele's Arkansas Expedition, especially at Jenkins' Ferry.

MAJOR-GENERAL JOSEPH JONES REYNOLDS (U. S.M.A. 1843) was born in Flemingsburg, Kentucky, January 4, 1822. He taught at West Point and, after resigning, at Washington University, St. Louis, and finally engaged in business in Lafayette. Indiana. He entered the Civil War as colonel of the Tenth Indiana Volunteers, and reached the rank of major-general of volunteers in November, 1862. After active service in Western Virginia, he had a division in the Army of the Cumberland, and was chief-of-staff to Rosecrans in October, 1863. In December, he was put in command of the defenses of New Orleans, and on July 7, 1864, he took command of that portion of the Nineteenth Army Corps which remained in Louisiana, going from there to the head of the Gulf Reserve Corps. On December 22, 1864, he took command of the Seventh Army Corps (Arkansas) until it was discontinued, August 1, 1865. Mustered out of the volunteer service, he returned to the regular army as colonel in the cavalry and received the brevet of major-general. He was retired June 25, 1877, and died in Washington, February 25, 1899.

Eighth Army Corps

THE TROOPS in the Middle Department were organized into the Eighth Army Corps on July 22, 1862. The forces were stationed at various points in Maryland. Its first commander was Major-General John E. Wool, and he was succeeded by Major-Generals R. C. Schenck, Brevet Brigadier-General W. W. Morris, Brigadier-Generals E. B. Tyler, H. H. Lockwood, and Major-General Lewis Wallace. The Eighth Corps saw little active fighting except in West Virginia. Wallace was in command at the Monocacy (July 9, 1864), and the First Separate Brigade under Brigadier-General E. B. Tyler took part, but that battle was fought chiefly by a division of the Sixth Corps. The Eighth Corps was discontinued, August 1, 1865.

MAJOR-GENERAL JOHN ELLIS WOOL was born in Newburg, New York, February 20, 1787. He became a lawyer, but raised an infantry company at Troy and entered the War of 1812. He remained in the army, and in 1841 was raised to the rank of brigadier-general. He selected the American position at Buena Vista in the Mexican War, and for his skill and courage received a vote of thanks and a sword from Congress. He was in command of the Department of the East when the Civil War broke out, and was transferred, in August, 1861, to the Department of Virginia, where he succeeded in saving Fort Monroe to the Federal Government. In May, 1862, his troops occupied Norfolk and Portsmouth

JOHN EDWARDS
Colonel of the 18th Infantry.

ALEXANDER CHAMBERS
Promoted for Gallantry.

WILLIAM T. CLARK
Promoted at Atlanta.

FITZ-HENRY WARREN
Colonel of the 1st Cavalry.

CYRUS BUSSEY
Daring Leader of Cavalry.

JAMES B. WEAVER
Brevetted for Gallantry.

JAMES MADISON TUTTLE
Colonel of the 2d Infantry.

JAMES A. WILLIAMSON
Colonel of the 4th Infantry.

EDWARD HATCH
Brilliant Cavalry Commander.

JACOB G. LAUMAN
Conspicuous at Belmont.

MARCELLUS M. CROCKER
At Corinth and Vicksburg.

FEDERAL GENERALS

No. 6

IOWA

E. W. RICE
Colonel of the 19th Regiment.

JAMES G. GILBERT
Colonel of the 27th Infantry.

after the Confederate evacuation, and at this time he was made major-general. He was given command of the Middle Department in June, and headed the Eighth Army Corps when it was organized in July. In January, 1863, he went back to the Department of the East, which had been recreated, and remained there until July 18th. He was retired from the army on August 1, 1865, and died in Troy, New York, November 10, 1869.

MAJOR-GENERAL ROBERT CUMMING SCHENCK was born in Franklin, Ohio, October 4, 1809. He became a lawyer, and was minister to Brazil, 1851–53. When the Civil War broke out he was made brigadier-general of volunteers, and commanded a brigade at the battle of Bull Run. His force was transferred to the Department of Western Virginia, and he aided in saving that valuable region to the Union. In the new Mountain Department, Schenck had an independent brigade, and he commanded the Federal right at the battle of Cross Keys. He was given a division of the First Corps, Army of Virginia, when the Mountain troops were merged in that army. He was severely wounded at Second Bull Run, where his gallantry won him promotion to major-general of volunteers. After recovery, he was given the Eighth Army Corps (troops of the Middle Department), December 22, 1862. He resigned from

the army December 3, 1863, having been elected member of Congress, where he served until 1870. In 1871, he was a member of the commission which drew up the treaty of Washington, and from 1871 to 1876 was United States minister to Great Britain. He died in Washington, March 23, 1890.

MAJOR-GENERAL LEWIS WALLACE was born in Brookville, Indiana, April 10, 1827. He became a lawyer and served in the Mexican War. At the commencement of the Civil War he headed the Eleventh Indiana Infantry, and was made brigadier-general of volunteers in September, 1861. At Fort Donelson and Shiloh he was in command of a division, and after the former battle he was promoted to major-general of volunteers. In 1863, he superintended the construction of the defenses of Cincinnati. In March, 1864, he took command of the Eighth Army Corps and was defeated by Lieutenant-General Early at the Monocacy. He resigned from the army in November, 1865. After the war he was appointed Governor of New Mexico, and from 1881 to 1885 was United States minister to Turkey. Major-General Wallace was the author of "Ben-Hur," the "Prince of India," and other well-known books, in addition to enjoying great popularity as a lecturer. He died at Crawfordsville Indiana, February 15, 1905.

Ninth Army Corps

THE TROOPS that Major-General Burnside took with him to North Carolina in December, 1861, which were then known as Burnside's Expeditionary Corps and which made a record for themselves at Roanoke Island, New Berne, and elsewhere, were merged in the Department of North Carolina in April, 1862. They and some others from the Department of the South were transferred to the Army of the Potomac in July, and on the 22d, the Ninth Army Corps came into existence. At first, it contained less than five thousand men. Its commanders were Major-Generals Burnside, J. L. Reno, Brigadier-General J. D. Cox, Major-Generals John Sedgwick, W. F. Smith, J. G. Parke, Brigadier-General R. B. Potter, and Brevet Major-General O. B. Willcox. Two divisions went to the assistance of Pope, and fought at Second Bull Run and Chantilly. Afterward,

the corps distinguished itself at South Mountain, Antietam, and Fredericksburg. After the latter battle, Burnside was transferred to the Department of the Ohio (March, 1863) and two divisions of the corps (one having gone to the Seventh) went West with him. The corps took part in the siege of Vicksburg, and was itself besieged in Knoxville, where it suffered great hardships. Early in 1864, the corps was ordered East for reorganization, with Burnside at the head. At the end of May, it became part of the Army of the Potomac, having acted as a separate command through the earlier battles of Grant's campaign. It was very prominent in the siege of Petersburg, and the famous mine was constructed and exploded in front of its lines. The flags of the Ninth Corps were the first that were shown on the public buildings of Petersburg. In June, 1865, the corps was

FEDERAL
GENERALS
No. 7

KANSAS
(THREE TO LEFT AND
EXTREME RIGHT
SECOND ROW)

LOUISIANA
(EXTREME RIGHT
THIRD ROW)

KENTUCKY
(TEN REMAINING)

GEORGE W. DEITZLER
Originally Colonel of the 1st Infantry.

THOMAS EWING, JR.
Originally Colonel of the 11th Cavalry.

THOMAS MOONLIGHT
Originally Colonel of the 11th Cavalry.

SPEED S. FRY
Noted for his Encounter at
Mill Springs.

STEPHEN G. BURBRIDGE
Cavalry Leader in the Morgan
Campaigns.

JOHN T. CROXTON
Led a Brigade in Tennessee and
Georgia.

POWELL CLAYTON
Of Kansas—Later Governor of
Arkansas.

EDWARD H. HOBSON
Noted for the Pursuit of Morgan's
Raiders.

WALTER C. WHITTAKER
Commander of a Brigade at
Chickamauga.

THEOPHILUS T. GARRARD
Defender of Kentucky and East
Tennessee.

D. J. KEILY
Of Louisiana—Colonel of the
Second Cavalry.

JAMES M. SHACKELFORD
Prominent in the Pursuit of Morgan's Raiders.

WILLIAM NELSON
Commanded a Division in Buell's
Army at Shiloh.

JEREMIAH T. BOYLE
Defender of Kentucky and
Tennessee.

N. B. BUFORD
Leader of Cavalry in Kentucky
and Tennessee.

transferred to the Department of Washington and was discontinued on August 1st. This organization is often referred to as the "wandering corps," for it fought in seven States.

MAJOR-GENERAL JESSE LEE RENO (U.S.M.A. 1846) was born in Wheeling, West Virginia, June 20, 1823, and served in the Mexican War, where he was severely wounded at Chapultepec. He was a captain when the Civil War broke out, but was commissioned brigadier-general of volunteers and commanded a brigade in Burnside's Expeditionary Corps, a division in the Department of North Carolina, and the same in the Ninth Army Corps, when it was created. He fought at Roanoke Island, New Berne, Camden, Manassas, and Chantilly and was placed in command of the Ninth Corps, September 3, 1862. He was killed at South Mountain on the 14th. His commission of major-general of volunteers was dated July 18, 1862.

MAJOR-GENERAL JOHN GRUBB PARKE (U.S. M.A. 1849) was born in Chester County, Pennsylvania, September 22, 1827, and entered the Corps of Topographical Engineers. He was first lieutenant when the Civil War broke out, and his commission of brigadier-general of volunteers was dated November 23, 1861. He commanded a brigade in Burnside's expedition to North Carolina, and later had a division in the Ninth Corps. As major-general of volunteers he was Burnside's chief-of-staff at Antietam and Fredericksburg. He went with the corps to the West as its commander, fought through the Vicksburg campaign, and was at the siege of Knoxville. He also commanded the corps after August, 1864, in the operations around Petersburg. He was in command of the Twenty-second Army Corps and at Alexandria, in 1865. After the war he rose to the rank of colonel in the regular army, with the brevet of major-general. He was engaged in engineering, and as superintendent of West Point until he was retired in July, 1889. He died in Washington, December 16, 1900.

BREVET MAJOR-GENERAL ORLANDO BOLIVAR WILLCOX (U.S.M.A. 1847) was born in Detroit, Michigan, April 16, 1823. He served in Texas, in Florida, and in the Mexican War, resigning his commission of first lieutenant in 1857 and taking up the practice of law. He hastened to the front at the outbreak of the war, as colonel of the First

Michigan Infantry, and was present at the occupation of Alexandria (May 24, 1861). He commanded a brigade at the battle of Bull Run, where he was severely wounded and captured. For his services here he was made brigadier-general of volunteers. He was exchanged (February, 1862), and later had a division of the Ninth Army Corps; and headed the corps itself at the battle of Fredericksburg. For a short time he was stationed in Indiana and Michigan, and had charge of the district of East Tennessee. He served again with the Ninth Corps in the Knoxville campaign and was at its head for a short period. As division commander he fought through the Wilderness campaign and in the last operations of the Army of the Potomac until July, 1865, except for short periods when he was at the head of the corps. He received the surrender of Petersburg. In August, 1864, he was brevetted major-general of volunteers. After being mustered out of the volunteer service, he became a colonel in the regular army and brigadier-general in 1886. The following year he was retired, and he died at Coburg, Ontario, May 10, 1907.

MAJOR-GENERAL JACOB DOLSON COX was born in Montreal, Canada, October 27, 1828. He became a lawyer and a member of the Ohio State Senate. He entered the Civil War as brigadier-general in the Ohio militia, and was made brigadier-general of volunteers in May, 1861. After distinguished service in western Virginia and under Pope, he succeeded to the command of the Ninth Army Corps upon the death of Major-General Reno, at South Mountain. He was in command of forces in West Virginia and of the Military District of Ohio in 1862-63. On March 4, 1863, his appointment of major-general of volunteers, which dated from October 6, 1862, expired, and it was renewed December 7, 1864. He received a division of the Twenty-third Army Corps in April, 1864, and during the Atlanta and Tennessee campaigns was several times in command of the corps itself. After the battle of Nashville, the corps was moved to North Carolina, where Major-General Cox served in various capacities, and finally as head of the corps from April to June, 1865. In 1866, he resigned from the volunteer service. From 1866 to 1868, he was governor of Ohio, and President Grant's Secretary of the Interior in 1869. He was prominent in politics, finance, and the law until his death, which occurred at Magnolia, Massachusetts, August 4, 1900.

Jonathan P. Cilley, Gallant
Cavalry Leader.

Selden Connor, Colonel
of the 19th Regiment.

Joshua L. Chamberlain, Active at Round Top.

L. G. Estes, Promoted at
the Close of the War.

Cyrus Hamlin, Colonel of the
80th U. S. Colored Infantry.

James D. Fessenden, Brevetted for Meritorious Service.

Francis Fessenden, Active in
the Red River Campaign.

George L. Beal, Brevetted for
Conspicuous Gallantry.

Albion P. Howe, Leader of the Light
Division at the Storming of
Marye's Heights, May 3, 1863.

Joseph Dickinson, Brevetted for
Gallantry on Staff Duty
at Gettysburg.

FEDERAL GENERALS

Neal Dow, Captured and Exchanged for a
Son of Gen. R. E. Lee.

No. 8—MAINE

Tenth Army Corps

CREATED September 3, 1863, to consist of the troops in the Department of the South. Its commanders were Brigadier-General John M. Brannan, and Major-Generals O. M. Mitchel, David Hunter, and Q. A. Gillmore. It took part in the various operations around Charleston Harbor, and in February, 1864, one division went to Florida, where it suffered severely in the battle of Olustee. In April, 1864, the corps entered the Army of the James, in which its commanders were Brigadier-General A. H. Terry, Major-General Q. A. Gillmore, Brigadier-General W. H. T. Brooks, Major-General D. B. Birney, and Brigadier-General Adelbert Ames. It fought around Drewry's Bluff, and two divisions went to Cold Harbor, forming a third division of the Eighteenth Corps. After this, the corps fought at Deep Bottom, Darbytown Road, and Fair Oaks. It was discontinued December 3, 1864 and merged in the new Twenty-fourth Corps. One division and a brigade of the Twenty-fourth, under Major-General Terry, went to Fort Fisher, and, after its capture, the Tenth Corps was reorganized March 27, 1865, in the Department of North Carolina, from Terry's troops. Besides Major-General Terry, Brevet Major-General Adelbert Ames had command from May 13 to August 1, 1865, when the corps was discontinued.

MAJOR-GENERAL ORMSBY McKNIGHT MITCHEL (U.S.M.A. 1829) was born in Union County, Kentucky, August 28, 1810, and served as assistant professor of mathematics at West Point until 1831, later becoming professor of mathematics, philosophy, and astronomy at Cincinnati College. For a time he practised law. He was director of the Dudley Observatory at Albany, New York, when the Civil War broke out, and entered the army, receiving a commission of brigadier-general of volunteers. From September to November, 1861, he was at the head of the Department of the Ohio, and had a division in the Army of the Ohio, December, 1861, to July, 1862, during which he made a brilliant expedition into Alabama, and won promotion to major-general of volunteers. In September, he was placed at the head of the Tenth Army Corps and died at Hilton Head, South Carolina, of yellow fever, October 27, 1862. He made several important astronomical discoveries.

BREVET MAJOR-GENERAL JOHN MILTON BRANNAN (U.S.M.A. 1841) was born in the District of Columbia in 1819, and served in the Mexican

War. He had reached the rank of captain when the Civil War broke out, and was promoted to brigadier-general of volunteers in September, 1861. He was commander of the Department of Key West from February, 1862, until it was merged, the following month, in the Department of the South, of which he was twice in command, as well as temporarily at the head of the Tenth Army Corps between September, 1862, and January, 1863. During this period he led the St. John's River expedition and took part in the battle of Pocotaligo. After this, he commanded divisions in the Twenty-first and Fourteenth corps. He reorganized the artillery in the Army of the Cumberland, and placed the artillery for the defense of Atlanta. He was mustered out of the volunteer service, having been brevetted major-general of volunteers, in May, 1866, and continued in the regular army as lieutenant-colonel and colonel, but with the brevet of major-general, serving at various posts until he was retired in April, 1882. He died in New York city, December 16, 1892.

MAJOR-GENERAL QUINCY ADAMS GILLMORE (U.S.M.A. 1849) was born at Black River, Ohio, February 28, 1825. He entered the Engineer Corps, and served as assistant instructor in engineering at West Point. Before the Civil War broke out he had done much work on fortifications and other engineering projects connected with the army. As captain and chief engineer, he accompanied Burnside to North Carolina, and later planned the details of the successful attack on Fort Pulaski, which feat won him the rank of brigadier-general of volunteers. After this, he held a command in West Virginia and also served in the Department of the Ohio. In June, 1863, he took command of the Tenth Army Corps and held it for a year, participating in the operations around Charleston Harbor, Bermuda Hundred, and the battle of Drewry's Bluff. His commission of major-general of volunteers was dated July 10, 1863. He went to the defense of Washington against Early with the Nineteenth Corps in July, 1864. Resigning from the volunteer service after the war, he rose to rank of colonel in the regular army and was connected with many great engineering projects until his death, which occurred at Brooklyn, New York, April 7, 1888.

MAJOR-GENERAL ALFRED HOWE TERRY was born in Hartford, Connecticut, November 10, 1827. He was colonel of the Second Connecticut

Charles H. Smith, Conspicuous as a
Cavalry Leader.

George F. Shepley, Originally Colonel
of the 20th Regiment.

Elias Spear, Colonel of the 20th
Regiment.

FEDERAL GENERALS—No. 9—MAINE (ABOVE) MARYLAND (BELOW)

Frank Nickerson, Originally
Colonel of the 4th
Regiment.

Daniel White, Brevetted for
Gallantry at the
Wilderness.

Nathaniel J. Jackson, Originally Colonel of the 1st
and 5th Infantry.

Cuvier Grover, Division
Leader in the East and
in the West.

James M. Deems, Brevetted for
Gallantry.

John R. Kenly, Originally Colonel of
the 1st Regiment.

James Cooper, In Command of Maryland Volunteers in 1861.

Volunteers at Bull Run. He returned home to raise the Seventh Connecticut Volunteers, and with this regiment served under Brigadier-General T. W. Sherman at the capture of Port Royal and under Major-General Hunter at Fort Pulaski, which he then commanded. Being raised to brigadier-general of volunteers in April, 1862, he commanded several districts in the Department of the South (Tenth Army Corps), and took command of this corps when it was transferred to the Army of the James, in April, 1864. As brevet major-general of volunteers he headed the Twenty-fourth Army Corps which was organized out of the Tenth, December, 1864, to January, 1865. On the latter date, he was put in command of the provisional corps organized for the capture of Fort Fisher and Wilmington. After these events had taken place, his corps became the reorganized Tenth Corps, and Major-General Terry was in command until May 13, 1865, when he took charge of Richmond. After leaving the volunteer service, he rose to the rank of major-general in the regular army (1886) and was retired in April, 1888. He died in New Haven, Connecticut, December 16, 1890. For the capture of Fort Fisher he was tendered the thanks of Congress.

Major-General William Thomas Harbaugh Brooks (U.S.M.A. 1841) was born in New Lisbon, Ohio, January 28, 1821, and served in the Seminole and Mexican wars, and in Texas and New Mexico. He had reached the rank of captain when the Civil War broke out, and was made brigadier-general of volunteers in September, 1861. He commanded a brigade in the Sixth Army Corps until October, 1862, and a division until after the Chancellorsville campaign, when, as major-general of volunteers, he was at the head of the Department of the Monongahela until Grant's operations against Lee and Richmond began. His commission of major-general of volunteers having expired, Brigadier-General Brooks was then in command of a division of the Eighteenth Army Corps, and on June 21, 1864, was put at the head of the Tenth Corps. He resigned from the volunteer service the following month, and died in Huntsville, Alabama, July 19, 1870.

Major-General David Bell Birney was born in Huntsville, Alabama, May 29, 1825. He practised law in Philadelphia until 1861, when he entered the Federal army as lieutenant-colonel of a Pennsylvania regiment and reached the rank of brigadier-general of volunteers, in February, 1862. He had a brigade in the Third Army Corps through the Peninsula campaign and was with Pope at Second Bull Run and Chantilly, taking the division temporarily after Brigadier-General Kearny was killed. As major-general of volunteers, he had a division at Fredericksburg and Chancellorsville and commanded the Third Corps at Gettysburg after Major-General Sickles was wounded, holding it from time to time until February, 1864. In the new organization of the Army of the Potomac (March, 1864), he had a division in the Second Corps until July, when he was given command of the Tenth Corps, Army of the James. While in this position he contracted a fever, and died in Philadelphia, October 18, 1864.

Eleventh Army Corps

When the Army of Virginia was discontinued, September 12, 1862, its First Corps, which had been the troops of the Mountain Department under Rosecrans and Fremont, and had been led by Sigel in the Pope campaign, was merged in the Army of the Potomac as the Eleventh Corps. It remained on the line of Manassas during the Antietam campaign, did not reach Fredericksburg in time for the battle, and at Chancellorsville was badly routed by "Stonewall" Jackson, because its commander allowed himself to be surprised. In this battle about twelve thousand troops were present. It was one of the two corps heavily engaged on the first day at Gettysburg. After that battle, one division was sent to Charleston Harbor, and the other two went with Hooker to Tennessee to assist Grant in the Chattanooga campaign. These two divisions then went with Sherman to the relief of Knoxville, and shared all the great hardships of the march. In April, 1864, these troops were merged in the new Twentieth Army Corps, for the Atlanta campaign. The leaders of the Eleventh Corps were Major-General Franz Sigel, Brigadier-General J. H. Stahel, Major-General Carl Schurz, Brigadier-General A. von Steinwehr, and Major-General O. O. Howard.

Stephen M. Weld, Jr., Leader of Colored Troops at the Crater Battle.

William F. Bartlett Led His Brigade at the Crater and Was Captured.

Oliver Edwards Led a Brigade at the "Bloody Angle," Spotsylvania; Brevetted for Gallantry at Sailor's Creek.

Edward F. Jones, Commander of the 6th Massachusetts on Its Memorable March Through Baltimore, April, '61.

Frederick W. Lander, One of the Early Heroes of the War.

Charles J. Paine, Noted Leader of Colored Troops.

George H. Gordon Led a Charge at Cedar Mountain.

Charles P. Stone, Later Distinguished in the Service of Egypt.

Albert Ordway, Promoted at the Close of the War.

Henry L. Eustis, Originally Colonel of the 10th Regiment.

N. A. Miles Commanded a Brigade at Chancellorsville and Later Led a Division in the Army of the Potomac.

FEDERAL GENERALS—No. 10—MASSACHUSETTS

Twelfth Army Corps

MAJOR-GENERAL FRANZ SIGEL was born in Sinsheim, Baden, November 18, 1824, and was graduated from the Military School at Carlsruhe, becoming a champion of German unity and minister of war to the revolutionary Government of 1848, which was overthrown by Prussia. Later, having withdrawn to Switzerland, the Government expelled him, and he emigrated to America in 1852. He taught in a military institute in St. Louis and edited a military periodical. When the Civil War broke out, he organized the Third Missouri Infantry and an artillery battery, and after assisting Captain Lyon in the capture of Camp Jackson, he served in Missouri, at Carthage and at Springfield. As brigadier-general of volunteers, he was conspicuous for his bravery at Pea Ridge, and as major-general of volunteers was placed in command of Harper's Ferry in June, 1862. Then he served in the Army of Virginia, in command of its First Corps, out of which the Eleventh Corps, Army of the Potomac, was created. He relinquished the latter in January, 1863. On March 10, 1864, he succeeded Brigadier-General B. F. Kelley in the command of the Department of West Virginia, but after the defeat at New Market, May 15th, he was relieved by Major-General Hunter and given the division at Harper's Ferry, where he successfully held out against Lieutenant-General Early. In July, 1864, he was relieved from his command, and he resigned from the army in May, 1865. After the war, he edited a German paper in Baltimore, and later was register and United States pension-agent in New York city. He was well known as a lecturer and editor of the "New York Monthly," a German periodical. He died in New York city, August 21, 1902.

MAJOR-GENERAL CARL SCHURZ was born in Cologne, Prussia, March 2, 1829, studying there in the gymnasium and later at the University of Bonn. He was engaged in the revolutionary movement in 1848, and was compelled to seek refuge in Switzerland. In 1852, he came to the United States and settled in Philadelphia, later going to Milwaukee, Wisconsin, where he began the practice of law. Lincoln appointed him United States minister to Spain, but he resigned to take part in the Civil War. As brigadier-general of volunteers, he commanded a division of the First Corps, Army of Virginia, at Second Bull Run, and at Chancellorsville a division of the Eleventh Corps. At Gettysburg he had command, as major-general of volunteers, of the Eleventh Corps, temporarily, and again in January and February, 1864. At Chattanooga, he took an active part. In March, 1864, he was put in charge of a corps of instruction near Nashville, and at the close of the war was chief-of-staff to Major-General Slocum in the Army of Georgia. He resigned from the volunteer service in May, 1865, and became a newspaper correspondent in Washington, and, in 1866, founded the *Detroit Post*. He was senator from Missouri (1869-1875), and Secretary of the Interior from 1877 to 1881, and editor of the New York *Evening Post* from 1881 to 1884. He was an enthusiastic advocate of civil-service reform and other political movements. He was a writer and speaker of note, and died in New York city, May 14, 1906.

Twelfth Army Corps

CREATED September 12, 1862, from the Second Corps, Army of Virginia, the troops of which, under Major-General N. P. Banks, had been in the Department of the Shenandoah, and in earlier organizations of the Army of the Potomac. It was the smallest corps in the army, and in the early days contained about twelve thousand men. The command was given to Major-General J. F. K. Mansfield, who was killed at Antietam, the first battle of the new corps. Its next battle was that of Chancellorsville where, with the Third, it bore the real brunt of the fight. After Gettysburg, in which we remember the Twelfth by its gallant defense of Culps' Hill, it went with Hooker to Tennessee where one division opened the line of supplies to the starving Army of the Cumberland and fought "the battle in the clouds" on Lookout Mountain. In April, 1864, the Twelfth Corps was merged in the newly formed Twentieth, for the Atlanta campaign. After Mansfield's death, the command of the Twelfth Corps was held by Major-General H. W. Slocum except for very brief periods, when it was headed by Brigadier-General A. S. Williams, the senior division commander. In its short career, the corps is said to have never lost a gun or a color.

JOHN C. PALFREY
Chief Engineer of the 13th
Army Corps.

EDWARD W. HINKS
Originally Colonel of the 8th
Infantry.

MASSACHUSETTS

(ABOVE)

CHARLES DEVENS
Colonel of the 15th Regiment.
Later Commanded Division.

GEORGE L. ANDREWS
Engaged in the Siege and Capture
of Port Hudson.

MICHIGAN

(BELOW)

J. M. OLIVER
Originally Colonel of the
15th Regiment.

HENRY BAXTER
Promoted for Gallantry at
the Wilderness.

JOSEPH T. COPELAND
Originally Colonel of the
5th Cavalry.

FEDERAL

GENERALS

No. 11

WM. R. SHAFTER
Later Commander at Santiago, Cuba.

CHARLES C. DOOLITTLE
Originally Colonel of the 18th Infantry;
Promoted for Merit.

BYRON R. PIERCE
Originally Colonel of the
3d Infantry.

HENRY A. MORROW
"Here to fight, not to surrender"—Gettysburg, July 1.

RALPH ELY
Leader of the Brigade which
was first in Petersburg.

Thirteenth Army Corps

MAJOR-GENERAL JOSEPH KING FENNO MANSFIELD (U.S.M.A. 1822) was born in New Haven, Connecticut, December 22, 1803, and served in the Mexican War and in the Engineer Corps. From May, 1861, to March, 1862, he had charge of the Department of Washington, and as brigadier-general of volunteers commanded the District of Suffolk of the Seventh Army Corps, and captured the town of Norfolk in May. As major-general of volunteers, he was put at the head of the newly formed Twelfth Army Corps on September 12, 1862, and was mortally wounded at Antietam, on the 17th.

BREVET MAJOR-GENERAL ALPHEUS STARKEY WILLIAMS was born in Saybrook, Connecticut, September 10, 1810, was graduated from Yale College, and held various political positions in Detroit where he also practised law. As colonel of a Michigan regiment, when the Civil War broke out, he was made brigadier-general of volunteers and headed a brigade in the Department of Pennsylvania. Passing through the various organizations of the Army of the Potomac, he was given a division in the Fifth Corps, which became the Second Corps, Army of Virginia, and the Twelfth Corps, Army of the Potomac, and finally was merged in the Twentieth Corps, Army of the Cumberland. Williams was the only general to lead the same division through the whole of the war, although at various times he temporarily headed the corps in which he was placed. He was corps commander at Antietam, after Mansfield fell; at Gettysburg, and also on the march to the sea and in the campaign through the Carolinas. His brevet of major-general of volunteers for marked ability and energy, was dated January 12, 1865, and a year later he was mustered out of the service. After the war, he was United States minister to San Salvador (1866–69), and member of Congress from 1874 until his death, which occurred in Washington, December 21, 1878.

Thirteenth Army Corps

ON OCTOBER 24, 1862, the troops in the newly created Department of the Tennessee, under Major-General Grant, were designated the Thirteenth Army Corps, and Major-General W. T. Sherman was put in command. The troops were scattered in many districts. Sherman organized four of the divisions into the Yazoo Expedition, and started on the campaign that ended in failure at Chickasaw Bluffs, December 29, 1862. On December 18th, the corps was subdivided, and the Army of the Tennessee now consisted of the Thirteenth, Fifteenth, Sixteenth, and Seventeenth corps. Brigadier-General Morgan succeeded Sherman, who commanded the whole department, at the head of the new Thirteenth Army Corps. The corps went with Major-General McClernand (January 4-12, 1863) on the expedition to Arkansas Post, the expedition being known as McClernard's Army of the Mississippi, in which the Thirteenth Corps became the First Corps for that period. Following Morgan, the commanders of the Thirteenth Corps were Major-Generals J. A. McClernand, E. O. C. Ord (who succeeded when McClernand was relieved at Vicksburg), and C. C. Washburn. One division fought the battle of Helena (July 4, 1863), and the battle of Port Gibson (May 1, 1863) was fought almost entirely by it.

After Vicksburg, the corps invested Jackson, and on August 7th it was transferred to the Army of the Gulf, where its chief active service (two divisions) took place in the Red River campaign of 1864. New commanders of the corps while in the Army of the Gulf were Major-General N. J. T. Dana, and Brigadier-Generals T. E. G. Ransom, R. A. Cameron, M. K. Lawler, and W. P. Benton. On June 11, 1864, the troops of the corps were transferred to other commands, but they were largely brought together again for the Reserve Corps, Army of the Gulf, in December, 1864, out of which on February 18, 1865, a new Thirteenth Army Corps was created, which, under command of General Gordon Granger, took part in the capture of Mobile, in April, 1865. The corps was discontinued at Galveston, Texas, July 20, 1865.

BRIGADIER-GENERAL GEORGE WASHINGTON MORGAN was born in Washington County, Pennsylvania, September 20, 1820. He did not graduate from West Point, which he entered in 1841, but took up the practice of law in Mount Vernon, Ohio. But he went to the Mexican War and was brevetted brigadier-general. Entering the diplomatic service, he was consul at Marseilles and minister to Portugal. When the Civil War broke

EGBERT B. BROWN
Originally of the 7th
Regiment.

JOHN D. STEVENSON
Originally Colonel of the
7th Regiment.

ISAAC F. SHEPHARD
Originally Colonel of the
3d Regiment.

JOSEPH CONRAD
Noted Brigade Commander.

GABRIEL R. PAUL
Gallant Figure at Gettysburg.

JOHN ELISHA PHELPS
Originally Colonel of the
2d Kansas Cavalry.

CLINTON B. FISK
Originally Colonel of
the 33d Regiment.

LEWIS B. PARSONS
Promoted at the Close
of the War.

JOHN McNEIL
Originally Colonel of the 3d
Infantry.

FEDERAL GENERALS—No. 12

MISSOURI (ABOVE)

MICHIGAN (MIDDLE ONE BELOW)

MINNESOTA (FOUR REMAINING BELOW)

ALEXANDER ASBOTH
Promoted at the End of
the War.

NAPOLEON J. T. DANA
Commander of a Brigade
in the Peninsula.

C. C. ANDREWS
Organizer and Division
Commander.

WILLIAM SANBORN
Promoted for Conspicuous
Gallantry.

STEPHEN MILLER
Colonel of the 7th Regiment;
Governor in 1863.

WILLIS A. GORMAN
First Commander of
the 1st Minnesota.

out he returned, and was made brigadier-general of volunteers in November, 1861. He served first under Buell and then as division commander in the Department of the Tennessee (Thirteenth Army Corps). He commanded a division in the Yazoo Expedition, and was the first commander of the reorganized Thirteenth Corps which he led at the capture of Arkansas Post (January, 1863). Ill-health compelled him to resign from the service in June, 1863. In 1868 and 1870, he was a member of Congress. He died at Old Point Comfort, Virginia, July 26, 1893.

MAJOR-GENERAL JOHN ALEXANDER McCLERNAND was born in Breckinridge County, Kentucky, May 30, 1812. He became a lawyer and served in the Black Hawk War as private. He was a member of Congress when the Civil War broke out and resigned to enter it, being made brigadier-general of volunteers in May, 1861. He first distinguished himself at Belmont, November 7, 1861. After Fort Donelson, he was made major-general of volunteers in the Army of West Tennessee, and commanded a division at Shiloh. On January 4, 1863, he replaced Sherman in command of the Yazoo Expedition which, under the name of McClernand's Army of the Mississippi, together with the Mississippi Squadron, captured Arkansas Post, January 11th. Grant removed McClernand from the command, and he was placed at the head of the Thirteenth Army Corps, of which he was in turn relieved on June 19th, during the siege of Vicksburg. He commanded this corps again for a short time in 1864, while it was serving in the Army of the Gulf. He resigned his commission on November 30, 1864, and resumed the practice of law. He died at Springfield, Illinois, September 20, 1900.

MAJOR-GENERAL CADWALLADER COLDEN WASHBURN was born in Livermore, Maine, April 22, 1818. He settled in Wisconsin as a lawyer and financier. At the outbreak of the war he raised the Second Wisconsin Cavalry, and as its colonel was successful under Major-General Curtis in Arkansas. He rose to the rank of major-general of volunteers in November, 1862, and later headed divisions in the Army of the Tennessee. He was the first commander of the reorganized Thirteenth Army Corps, and went with it from the Army of the Tennessee to that of the Gulf. After that, he was at the head of the District of West Tennessee, and resigned from the volunteer service in May, 1865. Later on, he was member of Congress and governor of Wisconsin. He died at Eureka Springs, Arkansas, May 14, 1882.

BREVET MAJOR-GENERAL THOMAS EDWARD GREENFIELD RANSOM was born in Norwich, Vermont, November 29, 1834. He became a captain in an Illinois regiment in April, 1861, and was made brigadier-general of volunteers in November, 1862. He fought at Fort Donelson and Shiloh, and was for a time on Grant's staff. He commanded a brigade in the Seventeenth Army Corps during the Vicksburg campaign, and a detachment of the Thirteenth Army Corps on the Red River expedition, in 1864. He was wounded at Sabine Cross Roads. In the Atlanta campaign, he commanded a division of the Sixteenth Army Corps and headed that and the Seventeenth for short periods. On October 10th, he was obliged to give up the Seventeenth Corps on account of illness, and he died, October 29th, near Rome, Georgia. The brevet of major-general of volunteers had been conferred on him in September, a few weeks before his death.

Fourteenth Army Corps

THE ORGANIZATION of the Army of the Ohio into three corps, in September, 1862, was changed on October 24th, when this force became the Army of the Cumberland, and consisted of the Fourteenth Army Corps, with Major-General Rosecrans at its head. In November, the Fourteenth Corps was divided into the Right Wing, Center, and Left Wing, and on January 9, 1863, the Center was designated the Fourteenth Army Corps, with Major-General George H. Thomas in command.

The corps fought at Stone's River and won its greatest fame at Chickamauga. It also distinguished itself at Missionary Ridge. It was prominent in the Atlanta campaign, and was one of the two corps of the Army of Georgia in the march to the sea and the campaign through the Carolinas. It was discontinued August 1, 1865. Besides Thomas, it was commanded by Major-Generals John M. Palmer, Jeff. C. Davis, and Brigadier-General R. W. Johnson.

Gilman Marston, Colonel of the 10th Regiment.

Simon G. Griffin, Leader at the Crater Battle.

Joab N. Patterson, Colonel of the 2d Regiment.

Joseph H. Potter, Promoted for Gallantry.

John L. Thompson, Colonel of the 1st Cavalry.

FEDERAL GENERALS—No. 13—NEW .HAMPSHIRE (ABOVE) NEW JERSEY (BELOW)

Joseph W. Revere, Originally Colonel of the 7th Regiment. Promoted in 1862.

Gershom Mott, Active as a Division Commander in the Wilderness Campaign.

Ranald S. Mackenzie, Dashing Cavalry Leader in the Army of the Potomac.

Horatio P. VanCleve, Division Leader at Stone's River and Chickamauga.

Geo. W. Mindil, Originally Colonel of the 33d New Jersey.

Lewis C. Arnold, Active Commander in Florida.

William Birney, Brevetted for Gallantry in Action.

Edward Burd Grubb, Brevetted at the Close of the War.

Fifteenth Army Corps

MAJOR-GENERAL JOHN MCAULEY PALMER was born at Eagle Creek, Kentucky, September 13, 1817, and became a lawyer and politician. He entered the Civil War as colonel of volunteers and was major-general of volunteers before the end of 1862. His first service was with Fremont and Pope in Missouri, and later he was given a division of the Army of the Cumberland. For a short time during the Tullahoma campaign he headed the Twenty-first Corps. During the Atlanta campaign he was in command of the Fourteenth Corps until August, 1864. Later, he was in charge of the Department of Kentucky. After the war, he was governor of Illinois, United States senator, and candidate of the Gold Democrats for President, in 1896. He died in Springfield, Illinois, September 25, 1900.

BREVET MAJOR-GENERAL JEFFERSON COLUMBUS DAVIS was born in Clarke County, Indiana, March 2, 1828, and served as a volunteer in the Mexican War. After this he entered the regular army. He was a lieutenant at Fort Sumter when the Civil War broke out. Later on, he became captain and then colonel of an Indiana Regiment, and led a division in the Army of the Southwest at Pea Ridge. As brigadier-general of volunteers, he served as division commander in Pope's Army of the Mississippi and also in that of the Cumberland, and took command of the Fourteenth Army Corps, August 22, 1864, and led it through Georgia and the Carolinas until the close of the war. He remained in the regular army as colonel,

and was at one time commander of the United States troops in Alaska, and also was at the head of the troops that quelled the Modoc uprising of 1873, after the murder of Canby. He received the brevet of major-general in 1865. He died in Chicago, November 30, 1879.

BREVET MAJOR-GENERAL RICHARD W. JOHNSON (U.S.M.A. 1849) was born in Livingston County, Kentucky, February 7, 1827, and saw his first service on the frontier. He entered the Civil War as captain of cavalry, becoming colonel of a Kentucky regiment. He served in the Army of the Cumberland and its prior organizations. His commission as brigadier-general of volunteers was dated October 19, 1861. As cavalry commander, he was captured by Morgan in August, 1862. He commanded a division at Stone's River, Chickamauga, and Chattanooga, and was severely wounded at New Hope Church. For a short time in August, 1864, he headed the Fourteenth Army Corps. Then he took charge of the cavalry forces in the Army of the Cumberland, and headed a division at Nashville, for which service he received a brevet of major-general in the regular army. After the war he entered the regular army as major in the Fourth Cavalry, also serving as provost-marshal-general and judge advocate in several departments. He was professor of military science in the University of Minnesota, 1869-71. He retired as major-general in 1867, and after 1875 had the rank of brigadier-general. He died in St. Paul, Minnesota, April 21, 1897.

Fifteenth Army Corps

Two DIVISIONS and some district troops of the Thirteenth Corps, Army of the Tennessee, were constituted the Fifteenth, on December 18, 1862. In two divisions, it was on Sherman's Yazoo Expedition and was also known as the Second Corps, McClernand's Army of the Mississippi, from January 4 to January 12, 1863. The commanders of the Fifteenth Corps were Major-Generals W. T. Sherman, F. P. Blair, Jr., John A. Logan, Brigadier-General M. L. Smith, and Major-Generals P. J. Osterhaus and W. B. Hazen. The corps took part in the Vicksburg campaign, the battle of Chattanooga, the relief of Knoxville, the Atlanta campaign, and the last campaigns of Sherman. After the Grand Review of May 24, 1865, the corps

went to Louisville, Kentucky, and one division served with the army of occupation at Little Rock, Arkansas. The corps was discontinued August 1, 1865.

MAJOR-GENERAL PETER JOSEPH OSTERHAUS was born in Coblenz, Germany, in 1823, and served as an officer in the Prussian army. He came to St. Louis, and in 1861 entered the Union army as major of volunteers. Later, as colonel, he had a brigade in the Army of the Southwest, and at Pea Ridge he commanded a division. Passing into the Army of the Tennessee as brigadier-general of volunteers, he commanded divisions in the Thirteenth and Fifteenth corps, taking part in the

FEDERAL GENERALS
No. 14
NEW MEXICO
(LEFT)
NEBRASKA
(RIGHT)
NEW YORK
(BELOW)

Christopher Carson (Kit Carson), of New Mexico, Famous Rocky Mountain Scout.

John M. Thayer, of Nebraska, an Important Division Commander.

Henry M. Judah, Conspicuous During Morgan's Raid of 1863.

J. J. Bartlett Received the Arms of Lee's Troops at Appomattox.

Gustavus A. De Russy, who was Brevetted for Gallantry.

Charles K. Graham Led a Brigade at Chancellorsville.

N. Martin Curtis, Promoted for Gallantry at Fort Fisher.

Romeyn B. Ayres, Active as a Division Commander.

Abram Duryee, First Colonel of Duryee's Zouaves.

John P. Hatch, Dashing Leader of Cavalry.

Henry A. Barnum, Conspicuous Brigade Leader.

Vicksburg campaign and assisting Hooker in the capture of Lookout Mountain. During the Atlanta campaign, he was made major-general of volunteers (July, 1864), and he commanded the Fifteenth Army Corps on the march to the sea. He was Major-General Canby's chief-of-staff in 1865. After the war he resigned from the service, and was American consul at Lyons, France. Thereafter, remaining in Europe, he made his home in Mannheim, Germany.

Sixteenth Army Corps

CREATED from three divisions and troops of several districts of the Thirteenth Army Corps on December 18, 1862, with Major-General S. A. Hurlbut in command. The corps was much divided during its existence, and divisions were several times exchanged for others in the Seventeenth Corps. Some of it saw service at Vicksburg, but little active fighting at that place. A division went with Sherman to Chattanooga. Two divisions were in the Atlanta campaign, and two on the Red River expedition of 1864. Some troops were sent to the Seventh Corps in Arkansas. The corps was officially discontinued on November 1, 1864, but the right wing, under Major-General A. J. Smith, known as "Detachment, Army of the Tennessee," assisted Thomas at Nashville. Besides Hurlbut, the command was held by Brigadier-General C. S. Hamilton and Major-General N. J. T. Dana. The left wing was commanded from time to time by Major-Generals C. S. Hamilton, R. J. Oglesby, Brigadier-General G. M. Dodge, Colonel A. Mersey, and Brigadier-Generals E. A. Carr and T. E. G. Ransom. The "Detachment," which included a division of the Seventeenth Army Corps, was, on February 18, 1865, designated the Sixteenth Corps, with Smith in command. The corps was now in the Military Division of West Mississippi and assisted in the last operations around Mobile. It was discontinued July 20, 1865.

MAJOR-GENERAL STEPHEN AUGUSTUS HURLBUT was born in Charleston, South Carolina, November 29, 1815, and was admitted to the bar in 1837. In 1845, he removed to Illinois and attained considerable prominence in politics. At the opening of the Civil War he was appointed a brigadier-general of volunteers, and commanded a division at Shiloh. Later, he was at the head of several districts in the department and was given command of the reorganized Sixteenth Corps, Army of the Tennessee, in December, 1862. In September, 1862, he was promoted to major-general of volunteers. He succeeded Major-General N. P. Banks in command of the Army and Department of the Gulf. He left the volunteer service at the end of the war, and at the time of his death, March 27, 1882, was United States minister to Peru.

MAJOR-GENERAL GRENVILLE MELLEN DODGE was born in Danvers, Massachusetts, April 12, 1831. He was a member of the Government survey in the West until the Civil War broke out, when he went to the front as colonel of the Fourth Iowa Infantry, in July, 1861. He fought with the Army of the Southwest, and, being transferred to the Department of Tennessee, he commanded the troops in several districts thereof, as well as divisions of the Thirteenth and Sixteenth corps, having been made brigadier-general of volunteers in March, 1862. In the summer of 1863, he was put in command of the left wing of the Sixteenth Army Corps as major-general of volunteers, and was wounded on August 19, 1864, at Jonesboro, Georgia, in the Atlanta campaign. In December, 1864, he succeeded Major-General Rosecrans in the Department of Missouri, and remained there until the close of the war. He resigned from the service in May, 1866, and became chief engineer of the Union Pacific and Texas Pacific railways. In 1866-67, he was member of Congress from Iowa. In 1898, he was at the head of the commission appointed to investigate the conduct of the Spanish-American war.

MAJOR-GENERAL ANDREW JACKSON SMITH (U. S.M.A. 1838) was born in Berks County, Pennsylvania, April 28, 1815, and served in the Mexican War and in the West. He was made major in the cavalry when the Civil War broke out. His appointment of brigadier-general of volunteers was dated March 17, 1862. He had a division in the Army of the Ohio, but his name is chiefly associated with the Army of the Tennessee. He commanded a division in the Thirteenth Corps and was with the Yazoo Expedition and McClernand's Army of the Mississippi, and took part in

William Dwight, Originally
Colonel of the 70th
Regiment.

Morgan H. Chrysler, Bre-
vetted for Meritorious
Services.

Hiram Berdan, Celebrated
Commander of Sharp-
shooters.

Schuyler Hamilton, Con-
spicuous at Island
No. 10.

Wladimir Krzyzanowski,
Originally Colonel of
the 58th Regiment.

Henry E. Davies, Daring
Cavalry Leader
in the East.

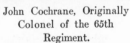

Joseph E. Hamblin, Origi-
nally Colonel of the
65th Volunteers.

John Cochrane, Originally
Colonel of the 65th
Regiment.

Philip Regis De Trobriand,
Prominent Brigade
Commander.

FEDERAL GENERALS

No. 15

NEW YORK

(Continued)

Thomas W. Egan, Prominent
Brigade Commander
in the East.

the siege of Vicksburg. He commanded the right wing of the Sixteenth Army Corps on the Red River expedition, and, as major-general of volunteers, in various operations in Tennessee and Mississippi during the Atlanta campaign. He took part in the battle of Nashville, and became commander of the reorganized Sixteenth Corps on February 18, 1865, participating in the closing operations around Mobile. He became Colonel of the Seventh U. S. Cavalry in 1866, and was retired in 1869. For a time he was postmaster of St. Louis. He died in St. Louis, January 30, 1897.

Seventeenth Army Corps

CREATED December 18, 1862, from troops in the Thirteenth Corps, Army of the Tennessee, and the command given to Major-General J. B. McPherson, with whose name it is closely linked. Divisions were exchanged with the Sixteenth Corps. It was prominent in the operations on the Mississippi before and after the fall of Vicksburg, and was a member of Sherman's Meridian expedition. After this the corps was divided: half remained in the Mississippi valley; the other two divisions went with Sherman to Atlanta. The Mississippi section was on the Red River expedition with Brigadier-General A. J. Smith and formed part of the detachment that fought at Nashville. It never rejoined the rest of the corps, which followed Sherman through Georgia and the Carolinas. On August 1, 1865, the corps was discontinued. Besides McPherson, it was commanded by Major-Generals F. P. Blair, Jr., J. A. Mower, Brigadier-Generals T. E. G. Ransom, M. D. Leggett, and W. W. Belknap.

MAJOR-GENERAL FRANCIS PRESTON BLAIR, JR., was born in Lexington, Kentucky, February 19, 1821, and became a lawyer and editor in St. Louis. He was a member of Congress for several years, and at the outbreak of the Civil War he was instrumental in saving Missouri to the Union. Entering the army as colonel, his commission of major-general of volunteers was dated November 29, 1862. He commanded a brigade on the Yazoo expedition, and afterward was division commander in the Fifteenth Army Corps, and headed it for a short time. In Sherman's campaigns to Atlanta and through Georgia and the Carolinas, he commanded the Seventeenth Army Corps. Resigning from the volunteer service in November, 1865, he was Democratic nominee for vice-president in 1868, and senator from Missouri, 1871-73. He died in St. Louis, July 8, 1875.

MAJOR-GENERAL JOSEPH ANTHONY MOWER was born in Woodstock, Vermont, August 22, 1827. He served as a private in the Mexican War and reentered the army as second lieutenant in 1855. After the Civil War broke out, he was promoted to a captaincy, became colonel of a Missouri regiment in May, 1862, and brigadier-general of volunteers in November of that year. He led his regiment in the attacks on Island No. 10, in other activities in Kentucky and Tennessee, and headed a brigade in the Army of the Mississippi at the time it was discontinued, passing thence to brigades in the Thirteenth, Sixteenth, and Fifteenth corps (Army of the Tennessee). With the latter, he served at the siege of Vicksburg. From December, 1863, to October, 1864, he commanded a brigade and then a division in the right wing of the Sixteenth Corps, and took part in the Red River expedition and in the operations in Mississippi and Tennessee while Sherman was fighting his way to Atlanta. In October, he joined Sherman's army at the head of a division of the Seventeenth Army Corps, and was its commander for a short time. In the closing days of the Carolina campaign he had command of the Twentieth Army Corps. Mower was appointed major-general of volunteers in August, 1864. After leaving the volunteer service he continued as colonel in the regular army, serving with the Thirty-ninth and Twenty-fifth infantry. He commanded the Department of Louisiana. He died in New Orleans, January 6, 1870.

Eighteenth Army Corps

ON DECEMBER 24, 1862, the troops in the Department of North Carolina were designated the Eighteenth Army Corps, and Major-General J. G. Foster was placed at its head. There were five divisions, at first. Two divisions were detached in February, 1863, and sent to the Tenth Corps,

John J. Peck, Commander on the Peninsula.

Charles H. Tompkins, Promoted in 1865.

Edward E. Potter, Brevetted for Gallantry.

William H. Morris, Colonel of the 6th Artillery.

Elisha G. Marshall Led a Brigade in the Crater Battle.

Robert Nugent, Originally Colonel of the 69th Regiment.

John C. Robinson Commanded a Division at Gettysburg.

James R. O'Beirne, Promoted from Major for Gallantry.

Rush C. Hawkins, Colonel of "Hawkins' Zouaves," 9th Infantry.

FEDERAL GENERALS

No. 16

NEW YORK (CONTINUED)

R. B. Potter, Commander of a Division at Crater Battle.

operating around Charleston Harbor. On July 15th, the Departments of Virginia and North Carolina were united, and on August 1st, the Seventh Corps, including Getty's division of the Ninth, was merged in the Eighteenth. The other commanders of the corps were Brigadier-General I. N. Palmer, Major-Generals B. F. Butler, W. F. Smith, Brigadier-General J. H. Martindale, Major-Generals E. O. C. Ord, John Gibbon, Brigadier-General C. A. Heckman, and Brevet Major-General Godfrey Weitzel. In April, 1864, this corps, with the Tenth, formed the Army of the James. It fought a series of battles after reaching Bermuda Hundred—especially that at Drewry's Bluff. Later in May, the corps joined the Army of the Potomac at Cold Harbor, in which battle it was very prominent. Then it returned to Bermuda Hundred and was very active in numerous engagements around Petersburg until December 3, 1864, when it was discontinued. The white troops were merged in the Twenty-fourth and the colored ones in the Twenty-fifth Corps.

MAJOR-GENERAL JOHN GRAY FOSTER (U.S. M.A. 1846) was born in Whitefield, New Hampshire, May 27, 1823. He rendered able service in the Mexican War, taught engineering at West Point, superintended Government works, and was one of the officers garrisoned at Fort Sumter during the siege. He distinguished himself at the capture of Roanoke Island and at New Berne; assumed chief command of the Department of North Carolina, the Department of Virginia and North Carolina, the Department and Army of the Ohio, and the Department of the South. He became major-general of volunteers in July, 1862. Being mustered out of the volunteer service in 1866, he, with the rank of lieutenant-colonel of engineers, continued his work on important engineering projects of the Government. He died in Nashua, New Hampshire, September 2, 1874.

BREVET MAJOR-GENERAL JOHN HENRY MARTINDALE (U.S.M.A. 1835) was born at Sandy Hill, New York, March 20, 1815. He resigned from the army the year after leaving West Point, but, offering his services at the outbreak of the Civil War, he was made brigadier-general of volunteers in August, 1861. He was brigade commander in several corps of the Army of the Potomac, and in February, 1863, took charge of the troops in the District of Washington—a portion of the Twenty-second Army Corps. In May, 1864, he was assigned to a division in the Eighteenth Army Corps, and for a short period in July, during the early

operations against Petersburg, he had command of the corps itself. On September 13th, he resigned from the service. The brevet of major-general of volunteers was conferred upon him on March 13, 1865, in recognition of his services at the battle of Malvern Hill (1862). He became attorney-general of the State of New York, and died at Nice, France, December 13, 1881.

MAJOR-GENERAL WILLIAM FARRAR SMITH (U. S.M.A. 1845) was born in St. Albans, Vermont, February 17, 1824, and taught mathematics at West Point. In the early days of the Civil War he served on the staffs of Major-Generals Butler and McDowell. His commission as major-general of volunteers was dated July 4, 1862, to which rank he was recommissioned March 9, 1864. After leading a brigade and division in the early organization of the Army of the Potomac, he had divisions in the Fourth and Sixth corps, and commanded the latter in the battle of Fredericksburg. After heading the Ninth Corps for a short time, he went to the Department of the Susquehanna and later—in 1863—became chief engineer of the Army of the Cumberland, where he rendered valuable assistance in the relief of Chattanooga. In May, 1864, he took command of the Eighteenth Corps in the Army of the James and led it at the battle of Cold Harbor, where it had joined the Army of the Potomac. He resigned from the volunteer service in 1865, and from the regular army in 1867, with the brevet of major-general. He became president of the International Telegraph Company, and was president of the board of Police Commissioners in New York City, 1877. After that, he practised civil engineering. He died in Philadelphia, February 28, 1903.

BRIGADIER-GENERAL CHARLES ADAMS HECKMAN was born in Easton, Pennsylvania, December 3, 1822. He served in the Mexican War, and went to the Civil War as lieutenant-colonel of the Ninth New Jersey Infantry. He became a colonel and had a brigade in the Department of North Carolina, where, after being made brigadier-general of volunteers, he had a division in the Eighteenth Army Corps. Later, he had charge of the District of Beaufort and the defenses of New Berne and at Newport News. On May 16, 1864, at the head of a brigade he was captured at Drewry's Bluff. He had temporary command of the Eighteenth Corps in September, 1864, and was temporary commander of the Twenty-fifth Army Corps, January-February, 1865. He resigned from the service in May, 1865, and died in Philadelphia, January 14, 1896.

Nelson Taylor, Originally Colonel
of the 72d Regiment.

John H. H. Ward, Originally Colonel
of the 38th Regiment.

Daniel Ullmann, Originally Colonel
of the 78th Regiment.

FEDERAL

GENERALS

No. 17

NEW YORK

(CONTINUED)

Adolph Von Steinwehr, Originally
Colonel of the 29th Infantry.

Emory Upton Led a Storming Column
at Spotsylvania.

Egbert L. Viele, Engaged at Fort
Pulaski and Norfolk.

Alexander Shaler Commanded a Brigade at Spotsylvania.

Nineteenth Army Corps

On January 5, 1863, the troops in the Department of the Gulf were constituted the Nineteenth Army Corps, with Major-General N. P. Banks in command. Its other leaders were Major-General W. B. Franklin, Brigadier-Generals W. H. Emory, B. S. Roberts, M. K. Lawler, and Major-General J. J. Reynolds. It operated in Louisiana, took part in the investment of Port Hudson, and did garrison duty until it went on the Red River expedition in March, 1864, where it was prominent at Sabine Cross Roads and in other engagements. In July, the First and Second divisions, under Emory, went to Virginia, and entered the Army of the Shenandoah and fought at the Opequon, Fisher's Hill, and Cedar Creek. This "detachment," as it was called until November 7th, was commanded by Brigadier-Generals W. H. Emory and Cuvier Grover, and after the campaign in the Shenandoah, it went, in different sections, to Savannah. Some of the troops were afterward attached to the Tenth Corps; others remained in Savannah until the corps was discontinued on March 20, 1865, and even longer. On November 7, 1864, the portion of the corps that had remained in Louisiana was discontinued, and the designation, Nineteenth Army Corps, passed to the divisions operating in the Shenandoah valley. Most of the troops in Louisiana were put in the Gulf Reserve Corps, which, in February, 1865, became the new Thirteenth Corps, and assisted at the capture of Mobile.

Major-General William Hemsley Emory (U.S.M.A. 1831) was born in Queen Anne's County, Maryland, September 9, 1811. He served in the Mexican War, and later was appointed astronomer to the commission which determined the boundary between Mexico and the United States. As colonel, he entered the Civil War in the cavalry of the Army of the Potomac, and, as brigadier-general of volunteers, had a brigade in the Fourth Army Corps after the Peninsula campaign. In 1863, he was sent to the Department of the Gulf, where, for a time, he was in charge of the defenses of New Orleans, and in May, 1864, he assumed command of the Nineteenth Army Corps. In July, with two divisions, he went to Washington and the Shenandoah valley to assist in the campaign against Early. He received the rank of major-general of volunteers in September, 1865, and commanded several departments after the war, being retired in 1876, as brigadier-general. He died in Washington, December 1, 1887.

Twentieth Army Corps

The right wing of the Army of the Cumberland was made the Twentieth Army Corps on January 9, 1863, under Brigadier-General A. McD. McCook, who held it until October 9, 1863, when it was merged in the Fourth Corps, which had been created on September 28th. It was prominent in the engagement at Liberty Gap, Tennessee, June 25th, during the advance of the army to Tullahoma, and eight of its brigades were in the battle of Chickamauga.

Major-General Alexander McDowell McCook (U.S.M.A. 1863) was born in Columbiana County, Ohio, April 22, 1831, and was the son of Major Daniel McCook, whose eight other sons also served in the Civil War. He did garrison duty in the West and was an instructor at West Point. He was colonel of the First Ohio at Bull Run, and then, as brigadier-general of volunteers, went to the Department of the Ohio, where he had a command, and, later, a division at Shiloh and elsewhere, until he headed the First Corps, Army of the Ohio, in the Kentucky campaign against Bragg. He had been made major-general of volunteers in July. He had command of the right wing (Army of the Cumberland), which bore the brunt of the attack at Stone's River. In the new organization of the army, he commanded the Twentieth Corps until after the battle of Chickamauga. Later, he had command of the northern defenses of Washington, and the District of Eastern Kansas. Retiring from the volunteer service, he resumed his rank of lieutenant-colonel in the regular army, serving with the Twenty-sixth and other infantry regiments. He was aide-de-camp to General Sherman from 1875 to 1880. In 1890 he was made brigadier-general, and became major-general, in 1894. He held several public positions of honor, and was retired in 1895. General McCook served on a commission to investigate the administration of the War Department during the Spanish war. He died in Dayton, Ohio, June 12, 1903.

John H. Ketcham, Promoted for Gallantry During the War.

George W. Von Schaack Led the Seventh New York in the Charge against the Stonewall at Fredericksburg.

Max Weber, in Command at Harper's Ferry in 1864.

Charles G. Halpinc (Miles O'Reilly), Poet and Author; Assistant Adjutant-General.

Charles H. Morgan, Promoted to Regular Rank for Gallantry in the Field.

Patrick H. Jones, Originally Colonel of the 154th Regiment.

Charles H. Van Wyck, Originally Colonel of the 56th Regiment.

Hiram C. Rogers, Chief of Staff to General H. W. Slocum.

FEDERAL GENERALS
No. 18

NEW YORK
(Continued)

Guy V. Henry, Originally Colonel of the 40th Regiment.

Twentieth Army Corps

A CORPS with the designation of Twentieth was created on April 4, 1864, from the troops of the Eleventh and Twelfth corps which, under Hooker, had joined the Army of the Cumberland in October, 1863. One division never joined the main body and finally engaged in Thomas' campaign against Hood in Tennessee, but the remainder followed the fortunes of the Atlanta campaign, and one of its brigades was the first to enter that city. On the march to the sea and the campaign through the Carolinas, the Twentieth Corps was part of Slocum's Army of Georgia. The corps commanders were Major-Generals Joseph Hooker, Henry W. Slocum, Joseph A. Mower, and Brigadier-General Alpheus S. Williams. The corps was discontinued on June 1, 1865.

Twenty-first Army Corps

THE LEFT WING of the Army of the Cumberland was made the Twenty-first Army Corps on January 9, 1863, and the command was given to Major-General T. L. Crittenden. Its other commanders were Brigadier-Generals T. J. Wood and Major-General J. M. Palmer. On October 9th, it was consolidated with the original Twentieth Corps and merged in the new Fourth Corps. The only battle the Twenty-first Corps participated in as an organization was Chickamauga, where one division fought with Thomas throughout the entire battle.

MAJOR-GENERAL THOMAS LEONIDAS CRITTENDEN was born in Russellville, Kentucky, May 15, 1815, and became a lawyer. He served in the Mexican War and later was United States consul at Liverpool, until 1853. In September, 1861, he was given a division in the Army of the Ohio under Buell, and was made major-general of volunteers for his conduct at Shiloh. In the campaign against Bragg, in Kentucky, he commanded the Second Corps, Army of the Ohio; the Left Wing, Army of the Cumberland, at Stone's River and the Twenty-first Army Corps at Chickamauga. For a short period, May–June, 1864, he led a division in the Ninth Corps. He resigned from the volunteer service in December, 1864, and after the war reentered the regular army as colonel. He received the brevet of brigadier-general in 1867, was retired in 1881, and died on Staten Island, New York, October 23, 1893.

Twenty-second Army Corps

CREATED February 2, 1863, and consisted of the troops occuping the defenses of Washington. It was first headed by Major-General S. P. Heintzelman, and he was succeeded by Major-Generals C. C. Augur and J. G. Parke. This corps saw active service only when it held the outer line of works during Lieutenant-General Early's attack on Washington, July 12, 1864. The roster of this corps was constantly changing as the troops were sent to reenforce other corps, so that it had no strong organization.

MAJOR-GENERAL CHRISTOPHER COLON AUGUR (U.S.M.A. 1843) was born in New York, July 10, 1821. He served in the Mexican War, and the campaign against the Oregon Indians. He entered the Civil War as major in the infantry, and was made brigadier of volunteers in November, 1861. He was severely wounded at Cedar Mountain, August 9, 1862, where he commanded a division in the Second Corps, Army of Virginia. He subsequently, as major-general of volunteers, had a division in the Nineteenth Corps, Army of the Gulf, from January to July, 1863, and in October was put in command of the Twenty-second Army Corps (Department of Washington) where he remained until the close of the war. He returned to the regular army in 1866, as colonel, and was made brigadier-general in 1869. He commanded several departments in the West and South and was retired in July, 1885. He died in Washington, D. C., January 16, 1898.

Samuel H. Hurst, Colonel of the 73d Regiment.

John W. Sprague, Originally Colonel of the 63d Regiment.

Charles F. Manderson, Originally Colonel of the 19th Infantry.

Eliakim P. Scammon, Colonel of the 23d Regiment.

Americus V. Rice, Originally Colonel of the 57th Regiment.

Thomas C. H. Smith, Promoted from the 1st Cavalry in 1862.

FEDERAL

GENERALS

No. 19—OHIO

Nathaniel C. McLean, Originally Colonel of the 7th Infantry.

E. B. Tyler, Originally Colonel of the 7th Infantry.

Twenty-third Army Corps

CREATED April 27, 1863, out of troops in the Department of the Ohio, then headed by Major-General A. E. Burnside. The regiments forming it had been stationed in Kentucky, and Major-General G. L. Hartsuff was placed in command. He was succeeded by Brigadier-Generals M. D. Manson, J. D. Cox, Major-Generals George Stoneman, and J. M. Schofield. The corps fought in Eastern Tennessee and was besieged in Knoxville. As the Army of the Ohio, it went on the Atlanta campaign and after the capture of that city, it returned to Tennessee and was prominent at Franklin and Nashville. The corps was then (except two divisions) moved to North Carolina and captured Wilmington in February, 1865. It joined Sherman's army at Goldsboro and marched with it to Washington. The corps was discontinued, August 1, 1865.

MAJOR-GENERAL GEORGE LUCAS HARTSUFF (U. S.M.A. 1852) was born in Tyre, New York, May 28, 1830, and served in Texas and Florida. He was at Fort Pickens from April to July, 1861, and then under Rosecrans. At Cedar Mountain, Manassas, and Antietam, he commanded a brigade, and in the last battle was severely wounded. In November, he was made major-general of volunteers, and after May, 1863, he was in command of the new Twenty-third Army Corps until September 24, 1863. Toward the end of the siege of Petersburg, he commanded the works at Bermuda Hundred. After leaving the volunteer service at the conclusion of the war he continued in the regular army, and was retired with the rank of major-general in June, 1871, on account of his wounds. He died in New York, May 16, 1874.

Twenty-fourth Army Corps

CREATED December 3, 1864, to consist of white troops of the Tenth and Eighteenth corps, Army of the James. Its first commander, Major-General E. O. C. Ord, headed it for only three days, and he was followed by Brevet Major-General A. H. Terry, Brigadier-General Charles Devens, Jr., Major-General John Gibbon, and Brevet Major-General John W. Turner. One division was sent to the operations against Fort Fisher, and its place was taken by one from the Eighth Army Corps. It was present at the final operations around Petersburg, and the pursuit of Lee. The corps was discontinued August 1, 1865.

MAJOR-GENERAL EDWARD OTHO CRESAP ORD (U.S.M.A. 1839) was born in Cumberland, Maryland, October 18, 1818. He served in the Seminole War and in various Indian expeditions in the far West. In 1859, he took part in the capture of

John Brown at Harper's Ferry. As brigadier-general of volunteers, he commanded a brigade in Buell's Division and the First Corps of the Army of the Potomac from October, 1861, to April, 1862, and had a division in the Department of the Rappahannock until June 10th. As major-general of volunteers, he commanded a division in the Army of West Tennessee. Then he assumed command of the Thirteenth Army Corps in the Armies of the Tennessee, and of the Gulf; of the Eighteenth Army Corps in the Department of Virginia and North Carolina, and of the Twenty-fourth Army Corps in the Army of the James, to the command of which army he succeeded Major-General B. F. Butler in January, 1865. He was wounded in the assault on Fort Harrison, but did not give up his command. Ord was retired with full rank of major-general in 1880, and died July 22, 1883, in Havana, Cuba.

Twenty-fifth Army Corps

CREATED December 3, 1864, to consist of the colored troops of the Tenth and Eighteenth corps, Army of the James. Its commanders were Major-General Godfrey Weitzel and Brigadier-General C.

A. Heckman. One division went with Terry to Fort Fisher; the others remained in Virginia, taking part in the final operations around Petersburg, and then formed the army of occupation in Texas.

James S. Robinson, Originally
Colonel of the 82d Regiment.

John G. Mitchell, Originally Colonel
of the 113th Regiment.

George W. Morgan, Commander of a
Division at Chickasaw Bluffs.

James W. Forsyth, Origi-
nally Colonel of the
18th U. S. Infantry.

FEDERAL GENERALS—

No. 20

OHIO

Ralph P. Buckland, Origi-
nally Colonel of the 72d
Regiment.

Benjamin Potts, Originally
Colonel of the 32d
Regiment.

Charles G. Gilbert, Corps
Commander at Perry-
ville under Gen. Buell.

Jacob Ammen, Originally
Colonel of the 24th Ohio;
Led a Brigade at Shiloh.

Thomas Smith, Originally
Colonel of the 54th
Regiment.

First Corps—Army of the Ohio

Its last regiments were mustered out on January 8, 1866. In February, 1865, it numbered about fourteen thousand troops.

MAJOR-GENERAL GODFREY WEITZEL (U.S.M. A. 1855) was born in Cincinnati, Ohio, November 1, 1835, and entered the Engineer Corps. At the opening of the Civil War, as first lieutenant, he served at the defense of Fort Pickens and was chief engineer of Butler's expedition to New Orleans, the capture of which city he planned and the acting mayor of which he became. As brigadier-general of volunteers, he had a brigade in the Department of the Gulf, and a brigade and division in the Nineteenth Army Corps at the siege of Port Hudson, where he commanded the right wing of Major-General Banks' forces. In May, 1864, he was given a division in the Eighteenth Army Corps, and later was chief engineer of the Army of the James, and constructed the fortifications at Bermuda Hundred and Deep Bottom. He was in command of the Eighteenth Army Corps from October to December, 1864, having been made major-general of volunteers. On the formation of the Twenty-fifth Army Corps (December, 1864) he was placed at its head and remained so, except for one short interval, until it was discontinued in January, 1866. He occupied Richmond, in April, 1865. After commanding a district in Texas, he was mustered out of the service, and returned to engineering work in the army. He became lieutenant-colonel of engineers in 1882. He had been brevetted major-general in the regular army in 1865. He died in Philadelphia, March 19, 1884.

First Corps—Army of the Ohio

THE ARMY OF THE OHIO was organized into three corps on September 29, 1862. The First was commanded by Major-General A. McDowell McCook. It bore the chief part in the battle of Perryville, Kentucky (October 8, 1862), and the campaign against Bragg in Kentucky. On October 24th, it was merged in the Fourteenth Corps, known as the Army of the Cumberland.

Second Corps—Army of the Ohio

THIS CORPS fought at Bardstown in the campaign against Bragg. It was headed by Major-General T. L. Crittenden. It constituted the right wing of the army, and was accompanied by Major-General George H. Thomas, who was second in command in the Army of the Ohio. Like the First Corps it had a brief existence, and it was merged in the Fourteenth Corps, October 24, 1862.

Third Corps—Army of the Ohio

THIS CORPS was commanded by Major-General C. C. Gilbert. It took part in the Kentucky campaign, but was only slightly engaged in Perryville. Its three divisions were commanded by Brigadier-Generals Schoepff, Mitchell, and Sheridan and Colonel Kennett. It was merged in the Fourteenth Corps, October 24, 1862.

Cavalry Corps—Military Division of the Mississippi

THE FIRST CAVALRY CORPS in the West was organized in October, 1864, with Brevet Major-General J. H. Wilson at its head. There were seven divisions, of which four took part in the battle of Nashville, December 15th and 16th. Wilson entered Alabama in March, 1865, and the corps fought its last engagement with Forrest at Columbus, Georgia, on April 16th. One division of this corps, under Brigadier-General Judson Kilpatrick, consisting of four brigades, accompanied Sherman's army through Georgia and the Carolinas, and was present at Bentonville and Johnston's surrender.

Emerson Opdycke, Brevetted for Gallantry at the Battle of Franklin.

Henry Van Ness Boynton, Decorated for Gallantry in Action.

Joseph Warren Keifer, Originally Colonel of the 110th Regiment.

FEDERAL GENERALS

No. 21

OHIO (CONTINUED)

John Beatty, Originally Colonel of the 3d Regiment of Infantry.

Joel A. Dewey, Originally Colonel of the 111th U. S. Colored Troops.

Hugh Ewing, Brevetted for Gallantry in 1865.

George P. Este, Originally Colonel of the 14th Infantry.

Catherinus P. Buckingham, Appointed in 1862.

Cavalry Forces—Department of the Cumberland

THE CAVALRY was a separate command in the Army of the Cumberland after the reorganization of January 9, 1863. It was headed in turn by Major-General D. S. Stanley and Brigadier-Generals R. B. Mitchell, W. L. Elliott, and R. W. Johnson. In October, 1864, this force was included in the newly formed Cavalry Corps of the Military Division of the Mississippi.

Reserve Corps—Army of the Cumberland

ORGANIZED June 8, 1863, and discontinued October 9th, when the troops were merged in the reorganized Fourth and Fourteenth corps. Major-General Gordon Granger was its commander. It served through the Tullahoma campaign, and went to the assistance of Thomas at Chickamauga.

Reserve Corps—Army of the Gulf

THE TROOPS of the Nineteenth Corps that were not sent to Washington and the Shenandoah valley were organized into the Reserve Corps of the Army of the Gulf, on December 5, 1864. It was commanded by Major-Generals J. J. Reynolds and Gordon Granger, and was merged in the reorganized Thirteenth Army Corps, February 18, 1865.

South Carolina Expeditional Corps

ORGANIZED under the command of Brigadier-General T. W. Sherman in September and October, 1861. It consisted of three brigades. This was the force that assisted the navy at the capture of Port Royal, occupying the abandoned works and garrisoning the base thus secured. It formed the nucleus of the Department of the South and the Tenth Army Corps.

BRIGADIER-GENERAL THOMAS WEST SHERMAN (U.S.M.A. 1836) was born at Newport, Rhode Island, March 26, 1813. He served in the Seminole War and as captain in the War with Mexico. At the opening of the Civil War, he was lieutenant in the artillery, and was promoted to brigadier-general of volunteers, May 17, 1861. He was placed at the head of the South Carolina Expeditional Corps and commanded the land forces in the operations around Port Royal. After that, he commanded a division in Grant's Army of West Tennessee. In September, 1862, he was put at the head of the Federal troops at Carrollton, Louisiana, in the Department of the Gulf, and in January, 1863, took charge of the defenses of New Orleans. He went with Banks to Port Hudson, in May, 1863, as division commander in the Nineteenth Army Corps. After that, he was again stationed at New Orleans with the reserve artillery and at the defenses of the city. After leaving the volunteer service at the close of the war, he was colonel of the Third Artillery, at Fort Adams, Rhode Island. On December 31, 1870, he was retired with full rank, of major-general. He died in Newport, March 16, 1879.

First Corps—Army of Virginia

CREATED June 26, 1862, from troops in the Mountain Department under Major-General Fremont, who, refusing to serve under Major-General Pope, was replaced by Major-General Franz Sigel. Brigadier-General R. C. Schenck headed the corps for short periods. After the close of Pope's Virginia campaign, it was merged in the Eleventh Corps, Army of the Potomac, September 12, 1862.

Franklin Sawyer, Originally Colonel of the 8th Regiment.

Anson G. McCook, Colonel of the 194th Regiment.

Henry M. Cist, Promoted for Gallantry at Stone's River.

Charles H. Grosvenor, Colonel of the 18th Veteran.

Timothy Stanley, Originally Colonel of the 18th Regiment.

Anson Stager, Conspicuous in the Telegraph Corps.

Henry C. Corbin, Colonel of Colored Infantry; Later Lieutenant-General of the United States Army.

William S. Smith, Originally Colonel of the 13th Regiment.

FEDERAL

GENERALS

—No. 22—

OHIO

William B. Woods, Originally Colonel of the 76th Regiment.

Robert K. Scott, Originally Colonel of the 68th Regiment.

Second Corps—Army of Virginia

CREATED June 26, 1862, from the troops in the Department of the Shenandoah. It was commanded by Major-General N. P. Banks, and later by Brigadier-General A. S. Williams. It defeated Jackson at Cedar Mountain and fought in the other battles of the campaign. When the Army of Virginia was discontinued it was merged in the Twelfth Corps, Army of the Potomac.

Third Corps—Army of Virginia

CREATED June 26, 1862, from the troops in the Department of the Rappahannock, previously the First Corps of the Army of the Potomac. It was commanded by Major-General Irvin McDowell and later by Brigadier-General J. B. Ricketts and Major-General Joseph Hooker. On the discontinuation of the Army of Virginia, it became again the First Corps of the Army of the Potomac.

Cavalry Corps—Army of the Potomac

A CAVALRY DIVISION under Brigadier-General A. Pleasonton was organized in July, 1862, and was with the Army of the Potomac, until February, 1863, when the Cavalry Corps was created with Major-General George Stoneman at its head. Its other commanders were Brigadier-Generals A. Pleasonton, D. McM. Gregg, Major-General P. H. Sheridan, Brigadier-General A. T. A. Torbert, Brevet Brigadier-General William Wells, Major-Generals Wesley Merritt and George Crook. Two divisions were transferred to the Army of the Shenandoah in August, 1864, and remained with it until til March, 1865. At first, the corps numbered over eleven thousand men. It saw constant active service; its most important battle being the one at Beverly Ford, Virginia, on June 9, 1863. Its hardest fighting took place in the Wilderness campaign of 1864. The corps was broken up in May, 1865.

MAJOR-GENERAL PHILIP HENRY SHERIDAN (U.S.M.A. 1853) was born in Albany, New York, March 6, 1831. After service in the West he became captain in May, 1861. He was on the staff of Halleck at Corinth, and in May, 1862, was made colonel of the Second Michigan Cavalry. Defeating Forrest's and repulsing Chalmer's superior force at Booneville, he was made brigadier-general of volunteers. In August, he defeated Falkner in Mississippi, and in September commanded a division in the Army of the Ohio, at Perryville and another in the Army of the Cumberland at Stone's River, for which service he was made major-general of volunteers and fought with great ability at Chickamauga and Missionary Ridge. In April, 1864, he was transferred to the command of the Cavalry Corps, Army of the Potomac, and in August he was put at the head of the Army of the Shenandoah and defeated Early at Cedar Creek. In December, 1864, he was made major-general in the regular army, lieutenant-general in March, 1869, and general June 1, 1888. He died in Nonquit, Massachusetts, August 5, 1888.

BREVET MAJOR-GENERAL ALFRED THOMAS ARCHIMEDES TORBERT (U.S.M.A. 1855) was born in Georgetown, Delaware, July 1, 1833. He entered the Civil War as colonel of the First New Jersey Volunteers, and commanded a brigade in the Sixth Army Corps. He had command of a division in the Sixth Corps, March–April, 1864, after which he had a division in the Cavalry Corps, and was given command of the Corps on August 6, 1864. He resigned in 1866, with the brevet of major-general of volunteers and served as United States consul-general at Havana in 1871. September 30, 1880, he was drowned in the wreck of the ill-fated steamer *Vera Cruz* off the Florida coast.

MAJOR-GENERAL WESLEY MERRITT (U.S.M.A. 1860) was born in New York, June 16, 1836. In 1861, he was at first, second and then first lieutenant of cavalry. He served throughout the Civil War, for the most part in the cavalry of the Army of the Potomac, where he rose to the command of the Cavalry Corps in the Shenandoah on January 26, 1865, and in the Army of the Potomac from March 25–May 22, 1865. After the war he served in various Indian campaigns, was superintendent of the United States Military Academy at West Point, and in May, 1898, was given command of the United States forces to be sent to the Philippines. He was first American military governor of those islands. He retired from the army in 1900 and died December 3, 1910.

VII

CONFEDERATE
ARMIES
AND
GENERALS

CONFEDERATES OF '61—AT THE BIRTH OF THE SOUTHERN ARMY, WHEN "GUARDS," "GRAYS," AND "RIFLES" ABOUNDED—THESE ARE THE "PELICAN RIFLES" OF BATON ROUGE, LOUISIANA, LATER MERGED INTO THE SEVENTH LOUISIANA VOLUNTEERS WHICH SUFFERED THE HEAVIEST LOSS OF ANY CONFEDERATE REGIMENT ENGAGED IN THE FIGHT AT PORT REPUBLIC, JUNE 9, 1862

The Armies of the Confederate States

THE permanent Constitution of the Confederate States of America provided that the President should be commander-in-chief of the army and navy, and of the militia of the several States when called into actual service. Accordingly, in any consideration of the Confederate army, the part played by President Davis must be borne in mind; also the fact that he previously had seen service in the United States army and that he had been Secretary of War of the United States. As Secretaries of War in the Confederate States Government there were associated with President Davis, the following: LeRoy Pope Walker, of Alabama, February 21, 1861, to September 17, 1861; Judah P. Benjamin, of Louisiana, September 17, 1861, to March 17, 1862; George W. Randolph, of Virginia, March 17, 1862, to November 17, 1862; Major-General Gustavus W. Smith, of Kentucky, November 17, 1862, to November 21, 1862; James A. Seddon, of Virginia, from November 21, 1862, to February 6, 1865; and Major-General John C. Breckinridge, of Kentucky, February 6, 1865, to the close of the war.

Unlike the Union army there were generals, both regular and of the provisional army, as well as lieutenant-generals; it being the intention that every commander of an army should rank as general, and every commander of a corps should rank as lieutenant-general. Such was the case with the generals mentioned in the biographical matter following in connection with the various armies and other organizations. An exception to this statement was General Samuel Cooper, who served at Richmond as adjutant and inspector-general.

GENERAL SAMUEL COOPER (U.S.M.A. 1815) was born in Hackensack, New Jersey, June 12, 1798, and served in the army, receiving the brevet of colonel for his services in the Mexican War. He resigned in March, 1861, to enter the service of the Confederacy. He was appointed general on May 16th, but, owing to his age, took no active part in the field. He was adjutant and inspector-general of the Confederate States army throughout the entire war, performing his duties with great thoroughness and ability. He died at Cameron, Virginia, December 3, 1876.

Army of the Shenandoah

MAJOR-GENERAL KENTON HARPER, of the Virginia State forces, had collected about two thousand Virginia volunteers at Harper's Ferry as early as April 21, 1861. He was relieved on the 28th by Colonel Thomas J. Jackson, and the mustering in of volunteers went rapidly on. On May 24th, Brigadier-General Joseph E. Johnston assumed command of the troops, and on June 30th, there were 10,654 present for duty, in four brigades and cavalry. This was the force that opposed Major-General Patterson in the Valley, and it was known as the Army of the Shenandoah. It took part in the engagement at Falling Waters, July 2d, and the skirmishes near Bunker Hill and Charlestown. Strengthened with eight Southern regiments, this army started for Manassas, on July 18th, and took part in the first battle of Bull Run. After this, it formed a part of the Confederate Army of the Potomac.

GENERAL JOSEPH EGGLESTON JOHNSTON (U.S.M.A. 1829) was born in Cherry Grove, near Farmville, Virginia, February 3, 1807. He served in the Black Hawk, Seminole, and Mexican wars, in the last of which he was twice severely wounded. He resigned his rank of brigadier-general to enter the Confederate service on April 20, 1861, and was given the rank of general in August. He was in command at Harper's Ferry after May 24th, and headed the Army of the Shenandoah. He brought his troops to Manassas and superseded Beauregard in the command, at Bull Run, joining his force to the Army of the Potomac. In command of the Army of Northern Virginia, he was severely wounded at Fair Oaks. In November, 1862, he was assigned to the head of the Department of Tennessee, but outside of an attempt to relieve Pemberton at Vicksburg in May, 1863, he saw no active service until he assumed command of the Army of Tennessee in December, 1863. He opposed Sherman during the Atlanta campaign of 1864, being superseded by General Hood on July 18th. His strategy was much criticised at the time, but it is now recognized that he displayed great ability during the campaign. In February, 1865, he was again given command of the Army of Tennessee,

**CONFEDERATE
GENERALS
FULL RANK
BEAUREGARD
AND
JOHNSTON**

All the officers who held the rank of General in the Confederate States Army are shown here, excepting Robert E. Lee, whose portrait has already appeared in this volume, and Albert Sidney Johnston, whose portrait appears among those killed in battle.

Pierre Gustave Toutant Beauregard received the Surrender of the First Federal Citadel — Fort Sumter; Fought in Defense of the Last Confederate Citadel—the City of Petersburg.

Joseph Eggleston Johnston commanded the First and the Last Great Aggressive Movements of Confederate Armies—Bull Run and Bentonville.

and attempted to prevent Sherman's advance through the Carolinas. Johnston's capitulation was agreed upon near Durham's Station, North Carolina, April 26, 1865. He was United States commissioner of railroads from 1885 to 1889. He died in Washington, March 21, 1891.

Army of the Peninsula

THE DEPARTMENT OF THE PENINSULA was established on May 26, 1861, and Colonel John B. Magruder was put in command. The troops therein were organized into divisions in November, and denominated the Army of the Peninsula. In December, the aggregate present was about sixteen thousand. On April 12, 1862, it was merged in the Army of Northern Virginia—constituting, under Major-General Magruder, the right wing of that army.

MAJOR-GENERAL JOHN BANKHEAD MAGRUDER (U.S.M.A. 1830) was born at Winchester, Virginia, August 15, 1810, and served in the Seminole and Mexican wars. He was stationed in Washington in 1861, and resigned in April to enter the Confederate service as colonel. He had charge of th' artillery in and around Richmond, and after May 21st, a division in the Department of the Peninsula, the troops of which were later designated the Army of the Peninsula. On June 10th, his division repelled the attack of Major-General B. F. Butler at Big Bethel, for which feat he was made brigadier-general. In October, he was promoted to major-general. Having fortified the Peninsula, he kept McClellan's army in check in April, 1862. On April 18th, his forces became the Right Wing of the Army of Northern Virginia, and he commanded it during the Peninsula campaign. Magruder was then appointed to the Trans-Mississippi Department, in order to prosecute the war more vigorously in the West, but the assignment was changed, and in October, 1862, he was given the District of Texas, which was afterward enlarged to include New Mexico and Arizona. Magruder recaptured Galveston, January 1, 1863, and kept the port open. After the war he served in the army of Maximilian, and after the fall of the Mexican empire settled in Houston, Texas, where he died, February 19, 1871.

Army of the Northwest

THE TROOPS assigned to operate in northwestern Virginia were placed under the command of Brigadier-General R. S. Garnett on June 8, 1861, and were subsequently known as the Army of the Northwest. This was the force that opposed McClellan and Rosecrans in West Virginia, and was defeated at Rich Mountain and other places. On July 13th, Garnett was killed while retreating, and Brigadier-General Henry R. Jackson was put in command, to be superseded, within a week, by Brigadier-General W. W. Loring. Early in 1862, dissension arose between Loring and T. J. Jackson, commanding the Valley District (Department of Northern Virginia), which led to the latter preferring charges against the commander of the Army of the Northwest. As a result, the Secretary of War, on February 9, 1862, divided the army, sending some of the regiments to Knoxville, some to the Aquia District, and the remainder to the Army of the Potomac (Department of Northern Virginia). After this, the forces under Brigadier-General Edward Johnson stationed at Camp Alleghany, and sometimes called the Army of the Alleghany, continued to be called the Army of the Northwest. Its aggregate strength in March, 1862, was about four thousand. It finally came under Jackson in the Valley District and passed into the Army of Northern Virginia.

BRIGADIER-GENERAL ROBERT SELDEN GARNETT (U.S.M.A. 1841) was born in Essex County, Virginia, December 16, 1819, and served in the Mexican War as aide to General Taylor. At the outbreak of the Civil War he entered the Confederate service, and in June, 1861, was appointed brigadier-general, with command of the Army of the Northwest. In the action at Carrick's Ford he was killed, June 13, 1861.

BRIGADIER-GENERAL HENRY ROOTES JACKSON was born in Athens, Georgia, June 24, 1820, and became a lawyer. He served in the Mexican War as colonel of the First Georgia Volunteers, and was *chargé d'affaires* at Vienna, in 1863. As United States district attorney for Georgia he aided in trying slave-trading cases. At the outbreak of the

JOHN BELL HOOD
To Paraphrase a Classic Eulogy, "None Led with More Glory than Hood, yet Many Led and There Was Much Glory."

EDMUND KIRBY SMITH
Skilful and Persistent Fighter Against Odds and Ever Indomitable in the Face of Reverses in the Field.

BRAXTON BRAGG
Leader in Three of the Fiercest Battles of the War and Carried the Southern Battle Line to Its Farthest North in the West; A Record of Four Years in the Field.

SAMUEL COOPER
Ranking Officer of the Army. All Commanding Generals Reported to Cooper and Received All Orders from Him. His Post and Duties were those of a Modern Cnief of Staff.

CONFEDERATE GENERALS—FULL RANK
HOOD, KIRBY SMITH, BRAGG AND COOPER

Army of the Potomac

Civil War he entered the Confederate Army as a brigadier-general, succeeding to temporary command of the Army of the Northwest after Brigadier-General Garnett was killed. He resigned his commission because he could not obtain leave of absence to take charge of the Georgia coast defenses, to which post he was called by the Governor of Georgia, who made him a major-general in command of the State troops. After these became part of the Confederate army, in 1862, Jackson received no commission until July, 1864, when he was assigned a brigade in the Army of Tennessee. During the battle of Nashville he was made prisoner and not released until the close of the war, when he returned to Savannah to practise law. He was United States minister to Mexico in 1885, and died in Savannah, May 23, 1898.

Major-General William Wing Loring was born in Wilmington, North Carolina, December 4, 1818, and served in the Seminole and Mexican wars. In the latter he lost an arm. Later, he was colonel of a regiment sent against the Indians in New Mexico. He resigned from the army to enter the Confederate service, and came into command of the Army of the Northwest, July 20, 1861. He was made major-general in February, 1862. His chief active service was in Kentucky, and in Mississippi, before and during the Vicksburg campaign; in that same State under Polk, and as division commander in the Army of Mississippi in the Atlanta campaign, and in the Army of Tennessee at Franklin and Nashville, and under Johnston in the Carolinas. After the war he went to Egypt, where he served as general in command of a division in the army of the Khedive. He died in New York city, December 30, 1886.

Major-General Edward Johnson (U.S.M. A. 1838) was born in Chesterfield County, Virginia, April 16, 1816, and served in the Mexican War. He entered the Confederate army and was made a brigadier-general, commanding the Northwest forces directly under Major-General T. J. Jackson, in May, 1862. The next year (February, 1863), he was made major-general. He had a division in the Second Corps, Army of Northern Virginia, and in September, 1864, was assigned to the division of the Second Corps, Army of Tennessee. He died in Richmond, Virginia, March 2, 1873.

Army of the Potomac

On May 24, 1861, Brigadier-General M. L. Bonham was placed in command of the troops on the line of Alexandria. On the 31st, he was relieved by Brigadier-General P. G. T. Beauregard. The forces here gathered were denominated the Army of the Potomac (afterward First Corps, Army of the Potomac) and consisted of six brigades, some unattached troops, and artillery, by the date of the battle of Bull Run. The Army of the Shenandoah joined this force on July 20th, when Johnston superseded Beauregard. The Department of Northern Virginia was created October 22, 1861, with Johnston at its head. It included the District of the Potomac (Beauregard); Valley District (T. J. Jackson), and Aquia District (T. H. Holmes.) In February, 1862, some of the troops in the Army of the Northwest came under Johnston's control, giving his entire command a strength of over eighty-two thousand. Beauregard had been sent to Kentucky on January 29th, and the troops in the Potomac district were now divided into four divisions with several separate detachments. On March 14th, the Army of the Potomac was denominated the Army of Northern Virginia. The total force then amounted to about fifty-five thousand.

General Pierre Gustave Toutant Beauregard (U.S.M.A. 1838) was born near New Orleans, May 28, 1818, and entered the Engineer Corps. He served with distinction in the Mexican War, and at the outbreak of the Civil War resigned his commission (February 20, 1861), to enter the Confederate army as a brigadier-general, being given command of the Confederate forces bombarding Fort Sumter. He took command of the Army of the Potomac on June 20th. After Bull Run he was made general. He was given the command of the Army of the Mississippi in March, 1862, and was second in command after A. S. Johnston joined his forces with it. After the latter's death at Shiloh, Beauregard remained at the head of the army until after the withdrawal from Corinth at the end of May. In 1863, he defended Charleston, and after May, 1864, cooperated with Lee in the defense of Petersburg and Richmond. He commanded the Confederate forces in the Carolinas in 1865, merging them with those under General J. E. Johnston, and surrendered his army to Sherman. After the war, he was a railroad president, adjutant-general of Louisiana, and manager of the State lottery. He died in New Orleans, February 20, 1893.

RICHARD STODDERT EWELL
A Battle Record from July 21, 1861, to April 6, 1865.
Fought Nearly Three Years on a Wooden Leg.

JAMES LONGSTREET
None Knew Better than Longstreet's Opponents How and
Where He Earned the Sobriquet "Lee's Warhorse."

JUBAL ANDERSON EARLY
Modest in Victory, Undaunted by Defeat, He Defended the
Shenandoah Against Enormous Odds.

DANIEL HARVEY HILL
Had No Superior as the Marshal of a Division in
Assault or Defense.

LIEUTENANT–GENERALS OF THE CONFEDERACY—GROUP No. 1

On this and the two pages following appear portraits of all officers who held the rank of Lieutenant-
General in the Confederate States Army, with the exception of "Stonewall" Jackson and
A. P. Hill, whose portraits have appeared among the general officers killed in battle.

Army of Northern Virginia

GENERAL J. E. JOHNSTON was wounded at Seven Pines, May 31, 1862, and Major-General G. W. Smith took command of the Army of Northern Virginia. On June 1st, General Robert E. Lee assumed command. In April, the forces on the Peninsula had been included in this army, and now the troops in eastern Virginia and North Carolina were made part of it. By the end of July, 1862, the division organization had been further concentrated into three commands, or corps, headed by Major-Generals T. J. Jackson, James Longstreet, and D. H. Hill, with cavalry under Brigadier-General J. E. B. Stuart, and artillery under Brigadier-General W. N. Pendleton. There was an aggregate present of about ninety-five thousand. Subsequently, the army took a more permanent form in two corps commanded by Jackson and Longstreet, with cavalry corps and artillery separate. Lieutenant-General A. P. Hill was given the Second Corps after Jackson's death, and on

May 30, 1863, this was divided, with additions from the First Corps, into the Second and Third corps, commanded by Lieutenant-Generals R. S. Ewell and A. P. Hill respectively. The army numbered about seventy thousand in the Gettysburg campaign. This organization of the main body of the army continued throughout the war, although other generals, for various reasons, commanded the corps from time to time. A new corps of North Carolina and Virginia troops under Lieutenant-General R. H. Anderson was added at the end of 1864. Longstreet's corps, with the exception of Pickett's division, was with the Army of Tennessee, and in eastern Tennessee, for a short period in 1863 and 1864, at and after the battle of Chickamauga. The last report of the army, February, 1865, showed an aggregate present of over seventy-three thousand. The Army of Northern Virginia laid down its arms at Appomattox Court House, April 9, 1865.

First Corps—Army of Northern Virginia

THE ORGANIZATION of the volunteer Confederate forces under Brigadier-General Beauregard into the First Corps, Army of the Potomac, was announced on June 20, 1861. There were then six brigades, which number was increased later to eight. The strength of the corps was about thirty thousand. A division organization was afterward adopted, and one of these divisions, commanded by Major-General Longstreet, was denominated the Center of Position, Army of Northern Virginia, at the opening of the Peninsula campaign. It contained about fourteen thousand men. As the Second Division (or Corps) of the army, the troops fought from Fair Oaks, where they were known as the Right Wing, through the Seven Days' battles. Toward the end of July, the army was further concentrated into commands of which one, consisting of six divisions, was headed by Longstreet, and this, during the campaign against Pope, was called the Right Wing or Longstreet's Corps. After the battle of Antietam, the corps was designated the First Corps, Army of Northern Virginia. In September, 1863, Lee sent the corps, with the exception of Pickett's division, to assist Bragg, and, as Longstreet's Corps, fought in the Army of Tennessee at Chickamauga and remained in East Tennessee until April, 1864, when it rejoined the Army of Virginia. Major-

General R. H. Anderson succeeded to the command of the corps after Longstreet was wounded at the battle of the Wilderness, May 6th. The latter returned to his corps, October 19th, and continued at the head until the surrender at Appomattox.

LIEUTENANT-GENERAL JAMES LONGSTREET (U. S. M. A. 1842) was born in Edgefield District, South Carolina, January 8, 1821, and served in the Mexican War, where he was severely wounded. In June, 1861, he resigned as major in the army and was appointed brigadier-general in the Confederate service. As major-general, he had a division, and, later, as lieutenant-general, the First Corps of the Army of Northern Virginia. In September, 1863, he was sent with part of his corps to Tennessee and took command of the left wing at the battle of Chickamauga. He was then placed at the head of the Department of East Tennessee and returned to Virginia in April, 1864. He was severely wounded at the battle of the Wilderness, May 6, 1864, but resumed command of the corps in October. After the war, he engaged in business in New Orleans and held several political offices. In 1880-81 he was American minister to Turkey, and in 1898 he was appointed United States railway commissioner. He died at Gainesville, Georgia, January 2, 1904.

Wade Hampton Fought from Bull Run to Bentonville. With J. E. B. Stuart's Cavalry he "Stood in the Way" of Sheridan at Trevilian Station in 1864.

Richard Henry Anderson Commanded a Brigade on the Peninsula; Later He Commanded a Division and, after the Wilderness, Longstreet's Corps.

John Brown Gordon. This Intrepid Leader of Forlorn Hope Assaults Rose from a Civilian Captain to the Second Highest Rank in the Army.

Leonidas Polk, Bishop and Soldier Both, to the End; He Fell on the Battlefield of Pine Mountain in the Defense of Atlanta.

William Joseph Hardee, On the Front Line for Four Years; Last Commander of the Defense of Charleston and Savannah.

Stephen Dill Lee Fought in Five States; with Beauregard at Charleston, April, 1861, and with Hood at Nashville, December, 1864.

LIEUTENANT-GENERALS OF THE CONFEDERACY—GROUP No. 2

Second Corps—Army of Northern Virginia

On September 25, 1861, Major-General G. W. Smith was assigned to the command of the Second Corps, Army of the Potomac, which was organized to consist of all the troops not hitherto assigned to the First Corps. After October 22d, the force was known as the Second Division and contained five brigades. It numbered almost twenty thousand men, and passed into the Reserve, Second Division, and D. H. Hill's Division of the Army of Northern Virginia. Most of these troops finally came under the command of Lieutenant-General T. J. Jackson and became known as the Second Corps of the Army of Northern Virginia, after the battle of Antietam. After Jackson's death, Lieutenant-General R. S. Ewell succeeded to the corps, after it had been temporarily headed by Stuart and A. P. Hill. On May 30, 1863, two divisions were detached to enter the Third Army Corps. The corps was commanded by Lieutenant-General J. A. Early in the Shenandoah campaign of 1864, and in the closing months of the war around Petersburg, by Lieutenant-General John B. Gordon.

Major-General Gustavus Woodson Smith (U.S.M.A. 1842) was born in Georgetown, Kentucky, January 1, 1822, and served in the Mexican War. He resigned from the army in 1854 to enter upon a Cuban expedition under Quitman, and afterward settled in New York City. At the outbreak of the Civil War he joined the Confederate forces at New Orleans, under Lovell. In September, 1861, he was appointed major-general and was given command of the Second Corps, Army of the Potomac, which was continued in the Army of Northern Virginia, until March 23, 1862, when he was put at the head of the Reserves. After Johnston was wounded at Fair Oaks, May 31st, Major-General Smith, who was leading the left wing, took command of the whole army, but was stricken by illness the following day and was succeeded by General Lee. In August, he took charge of the defenses of Richmond and was acting Secretary of War in November. In February, 1863, he resigned from the service, and on June 1, 1864, took command of the Georgia Militia. He was captured by Major-General J. H. Wilson at Marion in April, 1865. He died in New York, June 24, 1896.

Lieutenant-General Richard Stoddert Ewell (U.S.M.A. 1840) was born in Georgetown, District of Columbia, February 8, 1817, and served with distinction in the Mexican War. He joined the Confederate army in 1861, and was made major-general the following year. He fought as bri-gade and division commander with the Army of Northern Virginia, and was given command of the Second Corps after the death of Lieutenant-General T. J. Jackson, being made lieutenant-general in May, 1863. He was prominent in all its battles, and at Groveton he lost a leg. After June, 1864, when his corps was sent to the Shenandoah valley under Lieutenant-General J. A. Early, he was in command of the defenses of Richmond until the evacuation of that city. He died at Spring Hill, Tennessee, January 25, 1872.

Lieutenant-General Jubal Anderson Early (U.S.M.A. 1837) was born in Franklin County, Virginia, November 3, 1816, and served in the Seminole War of 1837, after which he resigned to take up the practice of law. In the Mexican War, he served as major of Virginia volunteers, and at the outbreak of the Civil War he entered the Confederate army as colonel, rising to the rank of lieutenant-general in May, 1864. He commanded a brigade at Bull Run, was wounded at Williamsburg, and had a division at Antietam and afterward. He had temporary command of both the Second and Third corps, Army of Northern Virginia, during the Wilderness campaign, and in June, 1864, was sent with the Second Army Corps to the Shenandoah valley, whence he made his way to Washington and attacked the city on July 12th. His forces were finally routed at Cedar Creek, October 19th, by Sheridan. He was relieved of the command of the Trans-Alleghany Department in March, 1865, after a defeat by Custer. After the war he practised law. He refused to take the oath of allegiance to the United States, and died in Lynchburg, Virginia, March 2, 1894. He is recognized as one of the ablest of the Confederate generals.

Lieutenant-General John Brown Gordon was born in Upson County, Georgia, February 6, 1832. He became a lawyer, but entered the Confederate service as lieutenant-colonel of an Alabama regiment, and rose to the rank of lieutenant-general before the close of the war. He was brigade and division commander in the Army of Northern Virginia, and was prominent in the Second Army Corps during Early's campaign in the Shenandoah valley. He was at the head of the Second Corps after January 31, 1865, and was in command of the left wing at the time of Lee's surrender. After the war, he became prominent in Georgia politics and was United States senator from that State, 1873–1880, and in 1891–1897.

ALEXANDER PETER STEWART

A Leader in Every Great Campaign
from Shiloh to Bentonville.

NATHAN BEDFORD FORREST

The American Murat and the King
of Mounted Raiders.

JOSEPH WHEELER

Masterful as Well as Indefatigable
and Indomitable Leader of Cavalry.

LIEUTENANT–GENERALS OF THE CONFEDERACY—GROUP No. 3

SIMON BOLIVAR
BUCKNER

Defender of His Native Kentucky in 1861 and in 1865;
Led a Corps to Victory
at Chickamauga.

RICHARD
TAYLOR

Skillful Defender of the
Trans-Mississippi
Territory.

THEOPHILUS HUNTER
HOLMES

Defender of the James River
in 1862 and Arkansas
in 1863.

JOHN CLIFFORD
PEMBERTON

Baffled the Assailants of
Vicksburg Through Three
Campaigns, Yielding to
only Heavy Odds.

From 1887 to 1890, he was governor of Georgia. He was commander-in-chief of the United Confed- erate Veterans after 1900. He died at Miami, Florida, January 9, 1904.

Third Corps—Army of Northern Virginia

CREATED from three divisions of the First and Second corps, Army of Northern Virginia, on May 30, 1863, and put under the command of Lieutenant-General A. P. Hill. Its first battle was Gettysburg. Hill was killed in front of Petersburg, April 2, 1865, and the corps was united with the First until the surrender at Appomattox.

LIEUTENANT-GENERAL AMBROSE POWELL HILL (U.S.M.A. 1847) was born in Culpeper County, Virginia, November 9, 1825, and served in the Mexican and Seminole wars. In 1861, he resigned from the army to enter the Confederate volunteers. He was appointed brigadier-general February 26, 1862, major-general in the following May and was one of the most efficient officers in the Confederate army, and rose to the command of the Third Corps, Army of Northern Virginia, when it was created in May, 1863, being made lieutenant-general at the same time. He was killed April 2, 1865.

Anderson's Corps—Army of Northern Virginia

ORGANIZED late in 1864 to consist of the divisions of Major-Generals R. F. Hoke and Bushrod R. Johnson, and a battalion of artillery under Colonel H. P. Jones. It contained an aggregate strength of about fourteen thousand. Hoke's division served with the First Army Corps and was sent to Wilmington, North Carolina, on December, 20, 1864. Johnson's division remained with the Army of Northern Virginia until the surrender at Appomattox.

LIEUTENANT-GENERAL RICHARD HERRON ANDERSON (U.S.M.A. 1842) was born in South Carolina, October 27, 1821, and served with distinction in the Mexican War. He resigned from the army in March, 1861, to enter the Confederate service. As colonel, he commanded the First South Carolina Infantry in the attack on Fort Sumter, and became brigadier-general in July, 1861. He destroyed a Union camp near Pensacola, in October, and in February, 1862, was as- signed to a brigade in Longstreet's Division in the Department of Northern Virginia. This he led with great distinction through the Peninsula campaign, being made major-general in July, 1862. He had a division in the First Corps, Army of Northern Virginia, at Second Bull Run and after. At Antietam, he was severely wounded, but he fought at Fredericksburg and Chancellorsville, and at Gettysburg he was in the Third Army Corps. After the wounding of Longstreet, in the battle of the Wilderness, Anderson was given command of the First Army Corps, receiving the appointment of lieutenant-general on June 1, 1864. In August, he was sent with an infantry division, one of cavalry, and a battalion of artillery to the assistance of Lieutenant-General Early in the Shenandoah, remaining there about a month. After the return of Longstreet to his corps, Anderson's Corps, consisting of two divisions, was organized, with Lieutenant-General Anderson at its head. He died at Beaufort, South Carolina, June 26, 1879.

Cavalry Corps—Army of Northern Virginia

THE VARIOUS TROOPS of cavalry in this army were finally gathered into a division of several brigades under the command of Brigadier-General J. E. B. Stuart. By the date of the battle of Gettysburg, July, 1863, the cavalry was organized in di- visions and the organization was known as the Cavalry Corps. After the death of Major-General J. E. B. Stuart, May, 1864, Major-General (later Lieutenant-General) Wade Hampton took command. Major-General Fitzhugh Lee also

Gustavus Woodson Smith, Defender
of Yorktown and Richmond.

John Bankhead Magruder, Defender
of the Virginia Peninsula in 1861.

William Wing Loring, with Robert
E. Lee in West Virginia in 1861.

Samuel Jones, Commander Florida,
Georgia and South Carolina.

Sterling Price Fought on Both Sides
of the Mississippi River.

Benjamin Franklin Cheatham, Brigade,
Division and Corps Commander.

Dabney Herndon Maury, Defender
of the Lower Mississippi in 1862-4.

John Cabel Breckinridge, Defender of
the Mississippi in 1861.

CONFEDERATE
MAJOR–GENERALS

CONSPICUOUS AS COMMANDERS
OF ARMIES OR ARMY CORPS

Earl Van Dorn, a Daring and Resourceful
Army Commander.

commanded several divisions at one time and was in command of the corps at Appomattox.

MAJOR-GENERAL JAMES EWELL BROWN STUART (U.S.M.A. 1854) was born in Patrick County, Virginia, February 6, 1833, and entered the Cavalry Corps of the United States army, serving in Kansas and against the Cheyenne Indians. He resigned his commission as captain in the army in May, 1861, to enter the Confederate service, as colonel of the First Virginia Cavalry, with which he fought under Johnston at Bull Run. He was made brigadier-general in September and major-general the following July. He had a brigade, and a division, and was placed at the head of the Cavalry Corps, Army of Northern Virginia, when it was organized, in the summer of 1863. Stuart proved himself to be a great cavalry leader, and his exploits won him much renown. Among his famous deeds were the ride around McClellan's army in June, 1862; the dash on Pope's headquarters at Catlett's Station, Virginia, and the raid on Manassas Junction in August; the expedition into Pennsylvania after Antietam, and the cooperation with Jackson at Chancellorsville. After the wounding of Jackson in that battle, he had temporary command of the Second Corps, Army of Northern Virginia. In the Wilderness campaign of 1864, he was very active, but was mortally wounded in an encounter with Sheridan's cavalry at Yellow Tavern. He died May 12, 1864.

LIEUTENANT-GENERAL WADE HAMPTON was born in Charleston, South Carolina, March 28, 1818. He was one of the largest slave-owners in the South. At the outbreak of the Civil War, he raised and equipped, in part, Hampton's South Carolina Legion, of which he was colonel. He was wounded at Fair Oaks, as brigadier-general at the head of a brigade, and thrice at Gettysburg, where he commanded a cavalry brigade. In August, 1863, he was made major-general with a di-

vision in the cavalry, and after the death of Stuart, he became head of the Cavalry Corps, Army of Northern Virginia. He made a famous raid on General Grant's commissariat, capturing some twenty-five hundred head of cattle. In February, 1865, he was made lieutenant-general, and commanded the cavalry in the Army of Tennessee, as well as a division of that of the Army of Northern Virginia. After the war, he strongly advocated the policy of conciliation. In 1876, he was governor of South Carolina; from 1878 to 1891, United States senator, and from 1893 to 1897, United States commissioner of railroads. He died in Columbia, South Carolina, April 11, 1902.

MAJOR-GENERAL FITZHUGH LEE (U.S.M.A. 1856) was born in Clermont, Virginia, November 19, 1835. He served against the Indians, and was cavalry instructor at West Point until he resigned his commission in May, 1861, to enter the Confederate service, becoming adjutant-general in Ewell's brigade. He was made major-general September 3, 1863. He had a brigade and division in the cavalry of the Army of Northern Virginia through all its campaigns, including that of Early in the Shenandoah in 1864, where he was wounded at the Opequon. He was in command of the Cavalry Corps, Army of Northern Virginia, from March, 1865, until the surrender, replacing Wade Hampton, who went to the Army of Tennessee. From 1886 to 1890 he was governor of Virginia, and, under appointment of President Cleveland, consul-general at Havana from 1896 to the outbreak of the Spanish-American War. President McKinley appointed him major-general of volunteers in 1898 and placed him at the head of the Seventh Army Corps. He was made military governor of Havana in 1899. Later, he commanded the Department of the Missouri. He received the rank of brigadier-general in February, 1901, and was retired the following month. He died in Washington, April 28, 1905.

Army of the Kanawha

THE CONFEDERATE FORCES assigned to operate in the Kanawha valley, West Virginia, were placed under the command of Brigadier-General John B. Floyd on August 11, 1861, and denominated the Army of the Kanawha. This force and one under Brigadier-General Henry A. Wise were its chief constituents. The troops took part in the en-

gagement at Carnifex Ferry. The strength of the command was about thirty-five hundred. Some of the troops were sent with Floyd to the Central Army of Kentucky, early in 1862, and formed one of its divisions. Several of the regiments were captured at Fort Donelson when this post capitulated to General Grant.

James T. Holtzclaw Led a Brigade of Alabamians.

John H. Kelly, a Gallant Boy General.

Cullen A. Battle Led a Brigade in Virginia.

Jonas M. Withers, Originally Colonel of the 3d Infantry.

CONFEDERATE GENERALS
No. 1—ALABAMA

This is the first of 25 groups embracing representative general officers of 14 States. On preceding pages of this volume appear portraits of all generals and lieutenant-generals, all generals killed in battle, also commanders of armies and army corps. Many appear in preceding volumes of this History as identified with particular events or special branches of the service, as cavalry and artillery. Information concerning every general officer may be found through the roster and index concluding this volume.

Edmund W. Pettus Became a Noted United States Senator.

James H. Clanton Led a Cavalry Brigade in Mississippi.

Charles M. Shelley Led a Brigade with Stewart.

Philip D. Roddey, Conspicuous Cavalry Leader.

Henry De Lamar Clayton, Originally Colonel of Infantry.

Army of Eastern Kentucky

BRIGADIER-GENERAL JOHN BUCHANAN FLOYD was born at Blacksburg, Virginia, June 1, 1807, and became a lawyer, practising in Arkansas and Virginia. He entered politics, and served in the Virginia legislature, and as governor of the State in 1850. He was Secretary of War in the Buchanan cabinet, where owing to his administrative methods he was requested to resign in 1860. At the opening of the Civil War he entered the Confederate army and was appointed brigadier-general in May, 1861.

He headed the force known as the Army of the Kanawha, and in February, 1862, was in command of Fort Donelson, Tennessee. He and Brigadier-General Gideon J. Pillow fled therefrom the night before the capitulation, leaving Brigadier-General Simon Bolivar Buckner to conduct the negotiations and surrender to General Grant. For this General Floyd was relieved of his command. In November, 1862, he was in command of the Virginia State Line, and died at Abingdon, Virginia, August 26, 1863.

Army of Eastern Kentucky

A TITLE applied to the troops under Brigadier-General Humphrey Marshall, consisting of the militia of Wise, Scott and Lee counties, in 1861. It was a small force of about fifteen hundred men, and was scattered by Federal troops under Brigadier-General James A. Garfield. Its chief action was at Pound Gap, March 16, 1862.

BRIGADIER - GENERAL HUMPHREY MARSHALL (U.S.M.A. 1832) was born in Frankfort, Kentucky, January 13, 1812. He resigned from the army the year after his graduation and became a lawyer. He went to the Mexican War as colonel of

cavalry, and led a charge at Buena Vista. In 1849, he became a member of Congress, and, after being commissioner to China in 1852, served again until 1859. He entered the Confederate service, being made brigadier-general in October, 1861. At the head of a small force, sometimes called the Army of Eastern Kentucky, he undertook the conquest of that region, but was driven from it by Brigadier-General James A. Garfield in March, 1862. After this, he had several commands in Virginia and resigned from the service in June, 1863. He resumed his practice of law and was elected member of the Confederate Congress from Kentucky. He died in Louisville, March 28, 1872.

Army of New Mexico

ORGANIZED December 14, 1861, to embrace all the forces on the Rio Grande above Fort Quitman, and those in the territories of New Mexico and Arizona. Its main object was the conquest of California. Brigadier-General H. H. Sibley was placed in command. He had about thirty-seven hundred men. His troops won the battle of Valverde, occupied Santa Fé and fought at Glorieta (or Apache Cañon). The army was forced to retreat into Texas, in April, 1862, by Federal troops under Colonel E. R. S. Canby. Sibley was relieved of the command in December, 1862.

BRIGADIER-GENERAL HENRY HOPKINS SIBLEY (U.S.M.A. 1838) was born at Natchitoches, Louis-

iana, May 23, 1816, and served in the Seminole and Mexican wars. He was the inventor of the famous Sibley tent. The outbreak of the Civil War found him on an Indian campaign in New Mexico, serving as a major of dragoons, but he accepted a commission as brigadier-general in the Confederate army and became commander of the Army of New Mexico. After his repulse at Glorieta, March 28, 1862, he was driven back into Texas. He continued his service at the head of various commands in Louisiana, south of the Red River. After the war he entered the service of the Khedive of Egypt, where he was, from 1869 to 1873, engaged in building coast and river defenses. He died at Fredericksburg, Virginia, August 23, 1886.

Army of Louisiana

AT THE BEGINNING of the war, the Louisiana State troops, commanded by Major-General Braxton Bragg and later by Colonel P. O. Hébert, were sometimes designated the Army of Louisiana.

BRIGADIER-GENERAL PAUL OCTAVE HÉBERT (U.S.M.A. 1840) was born in Bayou Goula, Herville Parish, Louisiana, November 12, 1818. He resigned from the army in 1845, reentering as

Young M. Moody, Command-
er of the District
of Florida.

Isham W. Garrott, Original
Colonel of 20th
Regiment.

William F. Perry Led a Noted
Brigade under
Longstreet.

William H. Forney Led an
Alabama Brigade in
Hill's Corps.

CONFEDERATE

GENERALS

No. 2

ALABAMA

William W. Allen Led a Cavalry
Division in Wheeler's Corps.

John H. Forney, One of the Defenders
of Vicksburg in 1863.

LeRoy P. Walker, First
Confederate Secretary
of War.

Sterling A. M. Wood Led
a Brigade at Chicka-
mauga.

James Cantey Commanded
the Garrison at
Mobile.

Zachary C. Deas Led a Brigade of Alabamians in
Tennessee.

lieutenant-colonel in the Mexican War, where he received the brevet of colonel for his gallant conduct at Molino del Rey. While governor of Louisiana, 1853 to 1856, he appointed his classmate, W. T. Sherman, to the head of the Louisiana Military Academy. When the Civil War broke out he succeeded Bragg in command of the Confederate

forces in Louisiana, and was appointed brigadier-general August 17, 1861. He was in special command of the defenses of New Orleans. Later, he commanded in turn the Department and District of Texas in the Trans-Mississippi. After the war he became state engineer of Louisiana. He died in New Orleans, August 29, 1880.

Army of Pensacola

THE FORCES at or near Pensacola, Florida, under Major-General Braxton Bragg, were designated the Army of Pensacola on October 22, 1861. Brigadier-General A. H. Gladden had temporary command in December, and Brigadier-General Samuel Jones took charge on January 27, 1862. The force then numbered eighty-one hundred men, divided among regiments from Alabama, Florida, Georgia, Louisiana, and Mississippi. On March 13th, the army was discontinued, the regiments entering the Army of the Mississippi or assigned for duty elsewhere. Pensacola was evacuated by the Confederate troops on the 9th of May.

BRIGADIER-GENERAL ADLEY H. GLADDEN was born in South Carolina. He entered the Confederate army and was appointed a brigadier-general from Louisiana in September, 1861. He had a brigade at Pensacola, and was in temporary command of the Army of Pensacola in December, 1861, and was given command of a brigade in the Second Corps, Army of the Mississippi. He was mortally wounded at Shiloh April 6, 1862.

MAJOR-GENERAL SAMUEL JONES (U.S.M.A. 1841) was born in Virginia, in 1820, and resigned his commission of captain in April, 1861, to enter the Confederate service. He was made major of artillery. He was acting adjutant-general of the Virginia forces in May and chief of artillery and ordnance in the Army of the Potomac from May to July, 1861. Appointed brigadier-general after the battle of Bull Run, he was assigned to the Army of Pensacola, in January, 1862, and the following month to the head of the Department of Alabama and West Florida. In April, he was given a division in the Army of the West, and in June, after having been appointed major-general in May, he was put at the head of a division in the Second Corps, Army of the Mississippi. After September, 1862, he commanded various departments in Tennessee and Virginia, being placed at the head of the Department of South Carolina, Georgia, and Florida, in April, 1864. At the close of the war he was in charge of the Department of Florida and South Georgia. He died in Washington, D. C., April 1, 1887.

Army of Mobile

ON JANUARY 27, 1862, the command of Brigadier-General Jones M. Withers, consisting of Alabama troops in and around the city of Mobile, was designated the Army of Mobile. Its strength was about ten thousand. It was subsequently commanded by Colonel J. B. Villepigue, temporarily, and Brigadier-General Samuel Jones, after March 15th. Many of the regiments entered the Army of the Mississippi and fought at Shiloh under Withers. More regiments were sent to that army, and on June 27, the Army of Mobile was discontinued.

MAJOR-GENERAL JONES MITCHELL WITHERS (U.S.M.A. 1835) was born in Madison County,

Alabama, January 12, 1814, and resigned from the army in 1848. He entered the Confederate service and received an appointment as brigadier-general in July, 1861. He was promoted to major-general after the battle of Shiloh. From January 27th to February 28, 1862, he was in command of the Army of Mobile. He then had a division in the Second Corps, Army of the Mississippi, and also the Reserve Corps for a time, and passed into the Right Wing and Polk's Corps, Army of Tennessee. He resigned his commission July 13, 1863, but his rank was restored within a few days, after which he assumed various commands in Alabama. He surrendered at Merid-

Thomas Churchill Commanded a Division in the Army of the West; Defender of Arkansas and Red River Region.

Thomas C. Hindman Commanded the Trans-Mississippi District in 1863; Led Troops at Shiloh and Chickamauga.

John F. Fagan, Originally Colonel of the 1st Arkansas Infantry; Conspicuous in the Attack on Helena, July 4, 1863.

CONFEDERATE

GENERALS

No. 3

ARKANSAS

Lucius E. Polk, Leader of a Charge at Murfreesboro.

Albert Pike, Commander of Indian Troops at Pea Ridge.

Albert Rust Led a Brigade in the Army of the West.

James C. Tappan Led a Brigade West of the Mississippi.

William L. Cabell Led a Brigade of Arkansas Cavalry.

John S. Roane, in Commission at Little Rock, Ark.

ian, Mississippi, May 11, 1865, and died March 13, 1890.

BRIGADIER-GENERAL JOHN BORDENAVE VILLE-PIGUE (U.S.M.A. 1854) was born in Camden, South Carolina, July 2, 1830, and resigned from the army in March, 1861, to enter the Confederate service. As colonel, he was temporarily in command of the Army of Mobile. He was appointed brigadier-general, March 18, 1862. He was in command at Fort Pillow at the time of Flag-Officer Davis's attack, May-June, 1862, and commanded a brigade at the battle of Corinth, October 4th. He died at Port Hudson, Louisiana, November 9, 1862, as the result of illness. Ville-pigue was considered one of the most promising young officers in the Confederate service, and his untimely death was greatly deplored.

Central Army of Kentucky

BRIGADIER-GENERAL S. B. BUCKNER assumed command of the forces in central Kentucky, September, 1861, and he was followed October 28th, by General Albert Sidney Johnston. The troops were organized in two divisions with a reserve, and a third division, under Brigadier-General John B. Floyd, was added later on. Major-General Hardee had temporary command, December, 1861-February, 1862. On March 29, 1862, the Central Army of Kentucky, whose strength was about twenty-three thousand, was consolidated with the Army of the Mississippi, under the latter designation, with General Johnston in command and General P. G. T. Beauregard second.

LIEUTENANT-GENERAL SIMON BOLIVAR BUCKNER (U.S.M.A. 1841) was born in Kentucky, April 1, 1823. He served in the Mexican War and taught at West Point. He resigned from the army in 1855, and returned to Kentucky to practise law. He entered the Confederate service in September, 1861, taking command in central Kentucky. He commanded a division of the Central Army of Kentucky at Bowling Green and at Fort Donelson. On February 16, 1862, he surrendered the fort and garrison of Fort Donelson and was sent to Fort Warren as a prisoner of war, being exchanged in August. He was then made major-general and had a division in Bragg's army and was given a temporary corps at Chickamauga. He was made lieutenant-general in September, 1864, and was commander in several districts of the Trans-Mississippi Department. He was elected governor of Kentucky in 1887, and in 1896 was the candidate of the Gold Democrats for Vice-President.

Army of East Tennessee—Army of Kentucky

IN FEBRUARY, 1862, Major-General E. Kirby Smith was sent to Knoxville to assume command of the troops in East Tennessee. With the army thus organized, it was intended to create a diversion in favor of General A. S. Johnston's operations with the Army of the Mississippi. The Army of East Tennessee was engaged in many minor engagements. On August 25th, the organization was designated the Army of Kentucky and was composed of three divisions. It led the advance in Bragg's invasion of Kentucky and was successful at the battle of Richmond, August 30th, raising great hopes for the Confederate conquest of Kentucky. On November 20, 1862, the Army of Kentucky was merged as Smith's Corps in the Army of Tennessee.

GENERAL EDMUND KIRBY SMITH (U.S.M.A. 1845) was born in St. Augustine, Florida, May 16, 1824, and served in the Mexican War, after which he was professor of mathematics at West Point. In April, 1861, he resigned his commission as captain to join the Confederates, becoming a brigadier-general in June. He was chief-of-staff to and had a brigade under General Joseph E. Johnston. He was seriously wounded at Bull Run. Early in 1862, as major-general, he was placed in command of the Army of East Tennessee (afterward Kentucky). In October of the same year he was made lieutenant-general and continued in the Department of East Tennessee. He was made general, and assumed command of the Trans-Mississippi Department in February, 1863. He surrendered his troops to Major-General Canby at Baton Rouge, May 26, 1865, having, the year before, defeated Major-General Banks in the Red

William N. R. Beall, District Commander in Mississippi and Louisiana.

Dandridge McRae Led a Brigade in Battles West of the Mississippi.

Alexander T. Hawthorne Led a Brigade in the Army of the Mississippi.

Daniel H. Reynolds Fought with Hood at Nashville.

Daniel C. Govan Commanded a Noted Brigade.

Evander McNair, Important Leader in the Army of Tennessee.

CONFEDERATE GENERALS

No. 4

ARKANSAS

Thomas P. Dockery Led a Cavalry Brigade.

Frank C. Armstrong, Brilliant Cavalry Commander.

River campaign. After the war, he devoted himself largely to education, becoming chancellor of the University of Nashville from 1870 to 1875, and later professor of mathematics at the University of the South. He died in Sewanee, Tennessee, March 28, 1893.

Army of the Mississippi

FROM TROOPS in the Western Department (Department No. 2) was created the Army of the Mississippi on March 5, 1862, and to General P. G. T. Beauregard was given the command. The army was divided into two corps headed by Major-Generals Leonidas Polk and Braxton Bragg. On March 29th, the army was joined to the Central Army of Kentucky with its three divisions, reserve corps, and cavalry. General A. S. Johnston, of the latter, took command of the Army of the Mississippi, that name having been preserved. Beauregard was second in command. The whole body was gathered at Corinth (except a force at Fort Pillow) in three corps, a reserve corps, and cavalry, and this was the organization that fought at Shiloh, when its strength was about forty thousand. The death of General Johnston placed the chief command upon General Beauregard, who was relieved June 27, 1862, by Major-General Hardee, and he, on August 15th, by Major-General Bragg. The army was transferred to Chattanooga in July. Major-General Polk had temporary command from September 28th to November 7, 1862, when, on the return of Bragg, the organization was called the Army of Tennessee.

GENERAL ALBERT SIDNEY JOHNSTON (U.S.M. A. 1826) was born in Washington, Mason County, Kentucky, February 3, 1803. He served in the Black Hawk War and resigned his commission in 1834. Two years later, he entered the army of the Texan Republic as a private, soon becoming a brigadier-general, and in 1838 was commander-in-chief of the army of Texas and Secretary of War. Later, he reentered the United States Army and served in the Mexican War with distinction. As colonel, he conducted an expedition against the Mormons in Utah in 1857, which won him a brevet of brigadier-general. He remained in command in Utah until February, 1860. At the outbreak of the Civil War, he was in command of the Department of the Pacific, but, by reason of his Southern sympathies, he resigned his commission to enter the Confederate service with the rank of general. He assumed command of Department No. 2, or Western Department, on September 15, 1861. In October he took immediate control of the Central Army of Kentucky, holding the line of Bowling Green, Kentucky, until February, 1862, against vastly superior numbers. On March 29, 1862, this army united with the Army of the Mississippi and Johnston took command of the new organization. He was killed on the battlefield of Shiloh, April 6, 1862, and his death was a stunning blow to the new Confederacy.

Third Corps—Army of the Mississippi

MAJOR-GENERAL W. J. HARDEE, who had been commander in northwestern Arkansas, was placed at the head of the Third Corps of the Army of the Mississippi on its reorganization, March 29, 1862. In August, the corps was merged in the Left Wing of the Army of the Mississippi.

Reserve Corps—Army of the Mississippi

COMMANDED by Major-General George B. Crittenden on March 29, 1862, and by Major-General J. C. Breckinridge after April 6th, and, later, by Brigadier-General Jones M. Withers. After Shiloh, and the siege of Corinth, the corps went to Louisiana and fought the battle of Baton Rouge, August 6, 1862, with the Federal troops under Brigadier-General Thomas Williams. Then it returned with Breckinridge to form the Army of Middle Tennessee and was merged in Hardee's (Second) Corps, Army of Tennessee, as the First Division, in November, 1862.

Jesse J. Finley Commanded a Brigade.

William G. M. Davis Led a Brigade of Cavalry.

Robert Bullock, Colonel of the 7th Regiment.

William Miller Commanded Reserve Forces in Florida.

J. Patton Anderson, Active Division Commander in the West.

CONFEDERATE
GENERALS

No. 5

FLORIDA

Martin L. Smith, One of the Defenders of Vicksburg.

Francis A. Shaup, Chief of Artillery, Army of Tennessee.

William S. Walker Commanded a South Carolina Brigade.

Theodore W. Brevard, Colonel of the 11th Regiment.

Army of Tennessee

THE JOINING of the Army of Kentucky with the Army of the Mississippi, on November 20, 1862, was the origin of the Army of Tennessee—the great Confederate army of the West. There were three corps and a division of cavalry, with an effective total of forty-seven thousand. General Braxton Bragg was in command. This army fought the battle of Stone's River, went through the Tullahoma campaign, and fought the battle of Chickamauga, assisted by Longstreet's Corps from the Army of Northern Virginia. It was driven from Chattanooga in November, 1863, by Grant's forces. After the battle of Chickamauga, the corps were reorganized several times. Bragg was removed from the command on December 2, 1863, and until General Johnston assumed it, on December 27th, both Hardee and Polk were in temporary command. Polk was sent to the Department of Alabama, Mississippi and East Louisiana before the end of December. The army spent the winter around Dalton, Georgia, and faced Sherman's advance in May, 1864, in two infantry and one cavalry corps. Polk brought back his divisions, which he called the Army of Mississippi, and these forces were consolidated with the Army of Tennessee on July 26th, after Polk had been killed. On July 18th, Johnston was replaced by General John B. Hood. After the capture of Atlanta, the army returned to Tennessee, and, failing to cut off Major-General Schofield's command at Franklin, was routed by Major-General Thomas at Nashville (December 15-16, 1864). In February, 1865, General Johnston was again placed in command of the Army of Tennessee, as well as the troops in South Carolina, Georgia, and Florida. The army had greatly dwindled. Lieutenant-General A. P. Stewart was at the actual head of the Army of Tennessee after March 16th, and Johnston's enlarged command included troops from the far South under Hardee, which, in February, had been organized in a corps, and those in North Carolina under Bragg. The aggregate present of the old Army of Tennessee was about twenty thousand. The army surrendered to Sherman in North Carolina, April 26, 1865.

GENERAL BRAXTON BRAGG (U.S.M.A. 1837) was born in Warren County, North Carolina, March 22, 1817, and served in the Seminole and Mexican wars. He resigned from the army in 1859, and became an extensive planter in Louisiana. On the secession of Louisiana, he was made a brigadier-general in the Confederate provisional army, and was the first commander of the military forces of Louisiana. After being appointed major-general in September, he took command of the forces in Alabama and West Florida from October, 1861, to February, 1862. He commanded the right wing of the Army of the Mississippi at Shiloh, and was made general after the death of Albert Sidney Johnston. He succeeded Beauregard as commander of the Army of the Mississippi (or Tennessee), and led it into Kentucky in September, 1862, and after his retreat therefrom, was defeated by Rosecrans at Stone's River (January, 1863). He in turn defeated Rosecrans at Chickamauga, but was driven from Chattanooga by Grant in November, 1863. Bragg was now relieved of the Army of Tennessee, and, later, was given control of the Confederate army's military operations at Richmond. As commander of the Department of North Carolina, he failed in attempts to check Sherman and prevent the fall of Wilmington. After February, 1865, he cooperated with Johnston and surrendered with the latter. Later on, he was state engineer of Alabama, and died in Galveston, Texas, September 27, 1876.

GENERAL JOHN BELL HOOD (U.S.M.A. 1853) was born in Owingsville, Kentucky, June 1, 1831, and fought against the Comanche Indians in Texas. He resigned from the army in April, 1861, to enter the Confederate service. After serving as captain in the cavalry and colonel of a Texas regiment, he received the appointment of brigadier-general in March, 1862. He was made major-general in October, 1862, after taking a conspicuous part in the Virginia campaigns. At Gettysburg, he commanded the largest division in Longstreet's Corps. In September, he went to Tennessee with Longstreet's Corps, which he commanded at Chickamauga, where he lost a leg. After the battle, he was given the rank of lieutenant-general, and at the head of the Second Corps in the Army of Tennessee, took part in the Atlanta campaign from May to July 18, 1864, when he succeeded Johnston in the command of the army with the temporary rank of general. He lost Atlanta, and, returning to Tennessee, was driven into Alabama by Major-General Thomas in the middle of December. In January, 1865, he was relieved of his command and was ordered to Richmond. After the war, he went to New Orleans, where he died, August 30, 1879.

Howell Cobb, Leader of Cobb's Georgia Legion.

G. T. Anderson Commanded a Brigade in Longstreet's Corps.

David E. Twiggs, in Command in East Louisiana in 1861.

Pierce M. B. Young, Brilliant Cavalry Leader.

Goode Bryan Led a Georgia Brigade in Longstreet's Corps.

Hugh W. Mercer Led a Georgia Brigade in the Army of Tennessee.

David R. Jones, Active Leader at Second Manassas and Sharpsburg.

William M. Brown, Defender of Savannah, December, 1864.

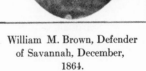

CONFEDERATE

GENERALS

No. 6

GEORGIA

Clement A. Evans, Leader in the Army of Northern Virginia.

Robert Toombs, Defender of Lee's Right Flank at Antietam.

First Corps—Army of the Mississippi and of Tennessee

MAJOR-GENERAL LEONIDAS POLK commanded from June, 1861, to March, 1862, the First Division in the Western Department (No. 2), the troops of which were scattered along the Mississippi from Columbus, Kentucky, to Memphis, and in the interior of Tennessee and Mississippi. It numbered about twenty-five thousand men. On the organization of the Army of the Mississippi in March, 1862, this division was called the First Grand Division, and after the consolidation with the Central Army of Kentucky, on March 29th, the First Corps, Army of the Mississippi. On August 15th, Polk's Corps was reorganized as the Right Wing in ten divisions, with over fifteen thousand present for duty. In the Army of Tennessee, the Right Wing became the First, or Polk's Corps. After the battle of Chickamauga, Polk was relieved of the command, and both corps of the army underwent reorganization. The leading corps was thereafter known as Hardee's, or Cheatham's Corps, from the names of its commanders.

LIEUTENANT-GENERAL LEONIDAS POLK (U.S. M.A. 1827) was born in Raleigh, North Carolina, April 10, 1806. He left the army for the church, and eventually became the first Protestant Episcopal Bishop of Louisiana, in 1841. In 1861, he entered the Confederate army and was made major-general in June. He was assigned to the command of the Western Department (No. 2); and in September he was replaced by General A. S. Johnston and given the First Division, Army of the Mississippi, with which he won the battle of Belmont in November. He led the First Corps at Shiloh, and later had temporary command of the army itself. In October, 1862, he was given the rank of lieutenant-general, and accompanied the Western Confederate army until after Chickamauga, where he commanded the Right Wing when he was temporarily suspended, but the charge of delay on his part was dismissed by President Davis. In the winter of 1863–64, he was in command of the Department of Alabama, Mississippi, and East Louisiana, and brought his forces, which he called the Army of Mississippi, to Georgia in May, 1864, to assist Johnston in opposing Sherman's advance to Atlanta. On Pine Mountain, near Marietta, Georgia, he was killed by a cannon-ball, June 14, 1864.

MAJOR-GENERAL BENJAMIN FRANKLIN CHEATHAM was born in Nashville, Tennessee, October 20, 1820. He entered the Mexican War, rising to the rank of colonel after distinguished service at Monterey and elsewhere. At the close of this war he became major-general of the Tennessee militia, and when the Civil War broke out he attached himself to the Confederate cause and organized the entire supply department for the Western troops. As brigadier-general, he served under Polk at Belmont, and had a division of the First Corps, Army of the Mississippi, at Shiloh, and was commander of the Right Wing of the same army during Bragg's invasion of Kentucky in 1862. He led his division at Stone's River, through the Tullahoma campaign, and at Chickamauga, and after that battle was head of Cheatham's Corps, an organization formed upon the departure of Polk from the army, and of which Hardee shortly afterward took command. In the Atlanta campaign he led a division in Hardee's Corps, and assumed command of the corps, which later was known as Cheatham's Corps, after the departure of Hardee for Savannah in October, 1864, with which he continued until the surrender at Durham Station. After the war he became a farmer in Tennessee, and was appointed postmaster of Nashville in 1885. He died there September 4, 1886.

MAJOR-GENERAL PATRICK ROMAYNE CLEBURNE was born in County Cork, Ireland, March 17, 1828. He ran away from Trinity College, Dublin, and enlisted in the Forty-first Foot. In 1855 he came to America, settling in Helena, Arkansas, where he practised law until the opening of the war. He entered the Confederate service as private, and rose to the rank of major-general, in 1862. He planned the capture of the United States arsenal in Arkansas, March, 1861. He was colonel of an Arkansas regiment, and at Shiloh, as brigadier-general, he commanded a brigade in the Third Corps, Army of the Mississippi. He was wounded at Perryville. At Murfreesboro and Chickamauga he commanded a division, and his troops formed the rear guard at Missionary Ridge. For his defense of Ringgold Gap, in the Atlanta campaign, he received the thanks of the Confederate Congress. Cleburne covered Hood's retreat at Jonesboro, and had temporary command of Hardee's Corps. He continued to hold his division in Cheatham's Corps, and at the battle of Franklin was killed, November 30, 1864. A brilliant charge at Chickamauga earned him the title of "Stonewall of the West," and it was he who initiated the Order of the Southern Cross and was among the first to urge the advantages to the Confederates of colored troops.

PHILIP COOK
Leader in Gordon's Attack
on Fort Stedman.

WILLIAM M. GARDNER
Commander of the Post of
Richmond, Va., in 1865.

JOHN K. JACKSON
Commanded a Reserve Corps
Army of the Mississippi.

CLAUDIUS C. WILSON
Led a Brigade in the
Army of Tennessee.

ISAAC M. ST. JOHN
Commissary General,
1865,

CONFEDERATE

GENERALS

No. 7—GEORGIA

(CONTINUED)

BRYAN M. THOMAS
Led a Brigade of Alabamians.

G. MOXLEY SORRELL
Staff Officer with Longstreet.

DUDLEY M. DUBOIS
Led a Brigade in Longstreet's Corps.

MARCELLUS A. STOVALL
Led a Brigade in
Hood's Corps.

LUCIUS J. GARTRELL
Led a Brigade in
Georgia Reserves.

HENRY C. WAYNE
Adjutant-General and
Inspector-General of
Georgia.

ALFRED CUMMING
Led a Brigade of
Georgians in the West.

JAMES P. SIMMS
Led a Georgia Brigade in
Longstreet's Corps.

WILLIAM R. BOGGS
Chief of Staff to Gen.
E. Kirby Smith.

Second Corps—Army of the Mississippi and of Tennessee

MAJOR-GENERAL BRAXTON BRAGG was given command of the Second Corps of the Army of the Mississippi on its organization, March 29, 1862. There were ten divisions, composed chiefly of Alabama, Mississippi, and Louisiana troops. In July, Major-General Samuel Jones had command, and on August 15th, when General Bragg resumed command of the whole army, his former corps passed to the control of Major-General Hardee. There was an aggregate present of about sixteen thousand men. On November 7th, the Left Wing, in an organization that had a short existence after August 15th, again became the Second (or Hardee's) Corps. In July, 1863, Lieutenant-General Hardee was relieved by Lieutenant-General D. H. Hill, who commanded at Chickamauga, and the later commanders were Major-Generals J. C. Breckinridge, T. C. Hindman, Lieutenant-General J. B. Hood, Major-General C. L. Stevenson and Lieutenant-General S. D. Lee. After 1864, the corps was known as Hood's, or Lee's Corps, Hardee having assumed command of the other corps.

LIEUTENANT-GENERAL WILLIAM JOSEPH HARDEE (U.S.M.A. 1838) was born in Savannah, Georgia, October 10, 1815, and served in the Seminole and Mexican wars. He resigned his commission of lieutenant-colonel in January, 1861, to join the Confederate forces, in which he was appointed a brigadier-general in June. He was given command of Fort Morgan, Mobile Bay, in March, and later, as major-general, was transferred to the Central Army of Kentucky, of which he had command from December, 1861, to February, 1862. He was given the Second Corps in the Army of the Mississippi and led the advance at Shiloh. He took part with this army as corps or wing commander in Bragg's invasion of Kentucky, at Stone's River, and at Chattanooga, having been made lieutenant-general in October, 1862. In the summer of 1863 he had charge of the defenses of Mississippi and Alabama. He had temporary command of the Army of Tennessee after Bragg was removed in December, 1863. He had a corps during the Atlanta campaign, and in October, 1864, he was placed in command of the Department of South Carolina, Georgia, and Florida. He was unable to prevent the capture of Savannah, and, in February, 1865, joined Johnston, serving in the Army of Tennessee, at the head of a corps formed from the troops in his department, until its surrender. After the war, he lived at Selma, Alabama, and died at Wytheville, Virginia, November 6, 1873.

LIEUTENANT-GENERAL DANIEL HARVEY HILL (U.S.M.A. 1842) was born at Hill's Iron Works, York District, South Carolina, July 12, 1821. He resigned from the army after the Mexican War, in which he had received the brevet of major, and was engaged in teaching until he entered the Confederate army, in 1861. As colonel of the First North Carolina Infantry, he showed marked talent at Big Bethel, June 10th, and was made brigadier-general the following month. As major-general, he had a division and later a command, or corps, in the Army of Northern Virginia, and fought through the Peninsula campaign. He was assigned to the Department of North Carolina in July, but fought with his division at South Mountain, where he held the Federal forces in check, and at Antietam. In July, 1863, he was made lieutenant-general, and replaced Lieutenant-General Hardee in command of the Second Corps, Army of Tennessee, which he led at Chickamauga, and of which he was relieved in November. With the rank of major-general, he took command of a division in Lee's Corps, Army of Tennessee, in March, 1865, and at the battle of Bentonville he led the corps itself. After the war, he became an editor, and from 1877 to 1884 was president of the Arkansas Industrial University. He died at Charlotte, North Carolina, September 25, 1889.

MAJOR-GENERAL CARTER LITTLEPAGE STEVENSON (U.S.M.A. 1838) was born near Fredericksburg, Virginia, September 21, 1817. He was dismissed from the army in June, 1861, having entered the Confederate service as lieutenant-colonel. He did duty at Cumberland Gap, from which he drove Brigadier-General G. W. Morgan away, and commanded a division in the Army of Tennessee. He rose to the rank of major-general in October, 1862. His division was with Pemberton's forces in the battle of Chickasaw Bayou, December 26, 1862. He fought at Chickamauga and in the Atlanta campaign onward with the Army of Tennessee, having on July, 1864, temporary command of Hood's Corps, before the appointment of Lieutenant-General S. D. Lee. He also assumed command of Lee's Corps, when the latter was wounded after the battle of Nashville, until the army had crossed the Tennessee. He died August 15, 1888.

MAJOR-GENERAL THOMAS CARMICHAEL HINDMAN was born in Tennessee, November, 1818. He became a lawyer and served in Congress. He fought in the Mexican War, and in 1860 was a

John S. Williams Commanded
a Cavalry Brigade.

INDIAN

TERRITORY

(ONE TO RIGHT)

KENTUCKY

(FIVE REMAINING)

Stand Watie, Indian Leader of Troops
at Pea Ridge.

Thomas H. Taylor Led a
Brigade in the Army of
Tennessee.

William Preston Led a Division
at the Battle of
Chickamauga.

CONFEDERATE

GENERALS

No. 8

James M. Hawes Com-
manded a Brigade West
of the Mississippi.

Humphrey Marshall, Confederate
Defender of Kentucky.

member of the Charleston Convention. He went to the Civil War as colonel of an Arkansas regiment, and served in the armies of the West and of the Mississippi. For his conduct at Shiloh he was made major-general. He was, at different times, division commander in the Army of Tennessee, and a temporary commander of the Second Corps, and was also at the head of the Trans-Mississippi District and that of Arkansas. He was defeated at Prairie Grove and at Newtonia. After the war, he went to Mexico, but returned to Arkansas and was murdered by one of his former soldiers at Helena, September 28, 1868.

Lieutenant-General Stephen Dill Lee (U. S.M.A. 1854) was born in Charleston, South Carolina, September 22, 1833. He resigned from the army in February, 1861, to enter the Confederate service as captain in the artillery, and rose to the rank of lieutenant-general June, 1864. He was one of the three men who called on Major Anderson, April 12, 1861, and demanded the surrender of Fort Sumter. He had a battalion in the Washington Artillery, and was prominent at Second Bull Run and at Antietam. He was then sent to the West and commanded a division at the battle of Chickasaw Bayou, December 27, 1862, driving back the Federal troops with great slaughter. He was among those who surrendered at Vicksburg, July 4, 1863, and in August was put at the head of the cavalry in the Department of Alabama, Mississippi, and East Louisiana, and fought at Tupelo and other places. In May, 1864, he succeeded Lieutenant-General Polk at the head of this department, remaining there until July, when he was assigned to the command of Hood's Corps, Army of Tennessee, General Hood having been placed at the head of the whole army. Henceforth it was known as Lee's Corps. He was wounded December 17, 1864, while protecting the rear of the army in the retreat from Nashville. After the war he became a planter in Mississippi; a member of the State legislature; and in 1880 he became president of the Mississippi Agricultural and Mechanical College. He was also at the head of the Vicksburg National Park, and was commander-in-chief of the United Confederate Veterans, after the death of Lieutenant-General John B. Gordon, in 1904. He died at Vicksburg, Mississippi, May 28, 1908.

Wheeler's Cavalry Corps—Army of Tennessee

On January 22, 1863, Major-General Joseph Wheeler was assigned to command all the cavalry in Middle Tennessee. On March 16th, the cavalry divisions in the Army of Tennessee were designated as corps, and were given the names of their respective commanders, Wheeler and Van Dorn. The corps were organized into divisions and brigades, and Wheeler's Corps, sometimes known as the Second Corps, had an aggregate present of nearly twelve thousand. It displayed great activity in Tennessee, making numerous raids and guarding the flanks of the army. After the battle of Chickamauga, it made a famous raid on Rosecrans' communications, October, 1863. It also operated on the flanks of the army during the Atlanta and other campaigns until the close of the war.

Lieutenant-General Joseph Wheeler (U. S.M.A. 1859) was born in Augusta, Georgia, September 10, 1836, and entered the mounted infantry, resigning, in 1861, to join the Confederate army, in which he reached the rank of major-general (January, 1863), and commander of the Second Cavalry Corps, Army of Tennessee. He was conspicuous as a raider, and was constantly employed in guarding the flanks of the army, cutting the Federal communications, covering retreats, and obtaining information for the army commanders. He was appointed lieutenant-general, February 28, 1865. After the war, he was a member of Congress from 1881 to 1899. He was commissioned major-general of volunteers in 1898, and went to the Spanish War, commanding the troops at Las Guasimas, and was senior field-officer at the battle of San Juan Hill. He was senior member of the commission which negotiated the surrender of Santiago. He served with the American troops during the insurrection in the Philippines from August, 1899, to January 24, 1900, and on June 13, 1900, was appointed brigadier-general of the United States army, being retired the following September. He died in Brooklyn, New York, January 25, 1906. General Wheeler made a unique reputation for himself as a cavalry leader, and in the Spanish war his services won universal acknowledgment as typical of the complete reunion of the North and South.

George B. Crosby Led a Brigade in
Mississippi and Louisiana.

Abraham Buford, Active Leader
of Cavalry.

Adam R. Johnson Led a Brigade of
Morgan's Cavalry.

CONFEDERATE GENERALS—No. 9—KENTUCKY (Continued)

Hyland B. Lyon Led a Brigade of
Cavalry in Forrest's Division.

Joseph H. Lewis Led a Brigade in
the Army of Tennessee.

George B. Hodge Commanded a
Brigade of Cavalry.

Van Dorn's Cavalry Corps—Army of Tennessee

On March 16, 1863, Major-General Van Dorn's Cavalry Division in the Army of Tennessee was called Van Dorn's, or the First Cavalry Corps. It had an average aggregate present of about eight thousand, and was a valuable adjunct to General Bragg's army.

Army of Middle Tennessee

When Major-General John C. Breckinridge assumed command of the forces around Murfreesboro on October 28, 1862, they were denominated the Army of Middle Tennessee. There were three brigades, with cavalry under Brigadier-General Forrest, who was shortly relieved by Brigadier-General Wheeler. When Bragg advanced from Chattanooga to oppose Rosecrans, the Army of Middle Tennessee became identified with a division of Hardee's Corps, Army of Tennessee.

Major-General John Cabell Breckinridge was born near Lexington, Kentucky, January 21, 1821, and became a lawyer. He served as major in the Mexican War. From 1857 to 1861, he was vice-president of the United States. In 1860, he was a candidate for the presidency, receiving the electoral votes of the Southern States, with the exception of Virginia, Kentucky, Tennessee, and Missouri. He was sent to the Senate, but left that body to join the Confederates. He was made brigadier-general in November, 1861, and major-general in April, 1862, after the battle of Shiloh. He had a command under General A. S. Johnston in the Central Army of Kentucky, and Army of the Mississippi, and led the reserve corps at Shiloh. After the siege of Corinth he took his force to Louisiana, and fought the battle of Baton Rouge, August 6, 1862. Later, he headed the Department and Army of Middle Tennessee. Rejoining the Army of Tennessee at the end of 1862, he fought at Stone's River, Chickamauga, and Chattanooga, at the head of a division in Hardee's Corps, and was its temporary commander for a period before the battle of Chattanooga. He was brought East after the opening of the Wilderness campaign, fought at Cold Harbor, and was second in command under Early in the Shenandoah. From February 6, 1865, to the downfall of the Confederacy, he was Secretary of War. He then went to Europe, but returned in 1868, and resumed the practice of law. He died in Lexington, Kentucky, May 17, 1875.

Missouri State Guard

On June 12, 1861, Governor C. F. Jackson of Missouri, in defiance of the United States military government, issued a call for fifty thousand of the State militia for active service. At the time of the flight of the governor and his followers to the extreme southwestern corner of the State, he was joined by Price. At that time, the whole Confederate State force amounted to about three thousand men. This Missouri State Guard was in command of Brigadier-Generals Sterling Price and M. M. Parsons from October 29, 1861, to March 17, 1862, when it merged in the Army of the West.

Army of the West

Major-General Earl Van Dorn assumed command of the troops in the Trans-Mississippi District of Western Department (No. 2), on January 29, 1862. Out of the force grew the Army of the West, so called after March 4th. It was largely composed of the Missouri State Guard. This army fought at Pea Ridge and elsewhere in Arkansas, and, being transferred across the Mississippi, was present at the siege of Corinth. The First Division was commanded by Major-General Sterling Price after March 22d, and the Second by Major-General Samuel Jones. It had three divisions after May, and a strength of over twenty thousand. On June 20th, Van Dorn was replaced by Major-General John P. McCown, who had commanded the Third Division, and he in turn by Major-General Price, on July 3d. The transfer of the Army of the Mississippi to Chattanooga at

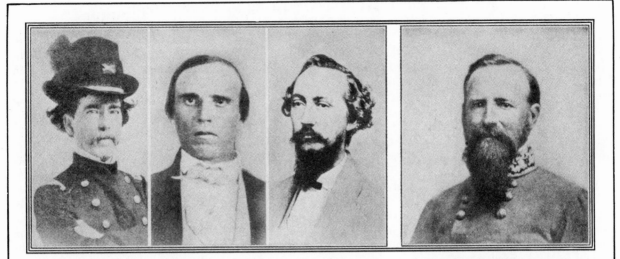

Paul O. Hébert Com-
manded the Army of
Lousiana Defend-
ing New Orleans.

Louis Hébert, Active
Commander in the
Southwest.

Thomas M. Scott, Orig-
inally Colonel of the
12th Regiment.

Franklin Gardner, Defender
of Port Hudson against
Banks in 1863.

CONFED–

ERATE

GENERALS

No. 10

LOUISI–

ANA

James P. Major Led a
Cavalry Brigade in
Louisiana.

Edward Higgins, Con-
spicuous at New Orleans
in 1862.

Henry H. Sibley, Con-
spicuous Leader in
New Mexico.

Albert G. Blanchard Led a Brigade
in the Army of Northern Virginia.

Zebulon York Commanded a
Brigade.

Allan Thomas Led a Brigade in the
Army of Northern Virginia.

the end of July, left the Army of the West in control of western Tennessee, and northern Mississippi. One division of the army fought the battle of Iuka, September 10th. On September 28th, a junction was made with Van Dorn's new command of troops in Mississippi, and the new organization was denominated the Army of West Tennessee. To Price was assigned a corps, which continued to be called, sometimes, the Army of the West.

MAJOR-GENERAL EARL VAN DORN (U.S.M.A. 1842) was born near Port Gibson, Mississippi, September 17, 1820, and served in the Mexican War and in several Indian campaigns. He resigned from the army, and was commissioned a colonel in the Confederate States army in March, 1861. His first commands were at New Orleans, and in the Department of Texas, where he forced the surrender of United States troops under Major Sibley and Colonel Reeve. He was made brigadier-general in June and major-general in September. In October and November, 1861, he commanded a division in the Army of the Potomac, and was assigned, in January, 1862, to the Trans-Mississippi District (Department No. 2), in which he had command of the Army of the West. He was defeated at Pea Ridge in March, and, with the Army of West Tennessee, at Corinth in October. After Pemberton assumed control of this force in the department in which Van Dorn was operating, he continued to command a cavalry division, at the

head of which he made a brilliant raid in Mississippi in December, 1862. In March, 1863, Van Dorn's cavalry division was designated a corps in the Army of Tennessee. On May 8, 1863, he was shot and killed by Doctor Peters, at Spring Hill, Tennessee, the result of a private quarrel.

MAJOR-GENERAL JOHN PORTER McCOWN (U. S.M.A. 1840) was born in Tennessee, in 1815, and served in the Mexican war, being brevetted captain for gallant conduct at Cerro Gordo. He resigned from the service in May, 1861, and entered the Confederate army, taking charge of the artillery in the provisional army of the State of Tennessee. As brigadier-general, he commanded a division of Polk's army at the battle of Belmont, November 7, 1861. After commanding at New Madrid, he had a division in the Army of the West, and was temporarily at the head of that force in June, 1862. He was placed in command of the Department of East Tennessee in September. Subsequently, he commanded a division of the Army of Kentucky, which fought with the Second Corps, Army of Tennessee, at the battle of Stone's River. In February, 1863, he was arrested on charges of conduct prejudicial to good order and military discipline and sent to Chattanooga, but was released. At the end of the war he fought with the Army of Tennessee in North Carolina. He died, January 22, 1879.

Army of West Tennessee—Army of Mississippi

MAJOR-GENERAL VAN DORN was transferred June 20, 1862, from the Army of the West to the Department of Southern Mississippi and East Louisiana. His troops occupied Vicksburg, and a force from the Reserve Corps of the Army of the Mississippi, under Major-General Breckinridge, fought the battle of Baton Rouge, August 6th. On September 28th, Van Dorn's troops joined the Army of the West to oppose Rosecrans' activities in northern Mississippi, and the combined force was denominated the Army of West Tennessee, with Van Dorn at the head. It fought the battle of Corinth (October 4th), and on December 7th its name was changed to the Army of Mississippi. It consisted of two corps, headed by Van Dorn and Price, the chief control having passed to Lieutenant-General John C. Pemberton, at the head of the Department of Mississippi and East Louisiana. Van Dorn, with his cavalry, made a famous raid in

northern Mississippi in December, capturing the Federal supply depot at Holly Springs. In January, 1863, the corps were changed into divisions. The title, Army of Mississippi, ceased to be used shortly after this date. The chief force under Pemberton surrendered at Vicksburg. Meanwhile, Van Dorn had been killed in Tennessee, May 8, 1863, and Price had been ordered to the Trans-Mississippi Department, February 27, 1863.

LIEUTENANT-GENERAL JOHN CLIFFORD PEMBERTON (U.S.M.A. 1837) was born in Philadelphia, August 10, 1814, and served in the Seminole and Mexican wars, making a noteworthy record in the artillery service. He entered the Confederate army in April, 1861, as major and chief of the Virginia artillery, being made brigadier-general in June. In November, 1861, he was transferred to South Carolina, and appointed major-general in

Johnson K. Duncan Commanded the
River Defenses below New Orleans.

Randall L. Gibson, Active Leader
in many Western Battles.

William R. Peck Commanded 9th Louisiana; Led a Charge at Appomattox.

CONFEDERATE

GENERALS—No. 11

LOUISIANA AND

MARYLAND

(Two Below.)

Daniel W. Adams, Noted Commander
in the Southwest.

St. John Lidell Led a Brigade in the
Army of the Mississippi.

Mansfield Lovell, Defender of the
Lower Mississippi in 1862.

William W. Mackall, Chief of Staff,
Army of Tennessee.

January, 1862, when his command was enlarged to include Georgia and East Florida. In October, he was advanced to the rank of lieutenant-general and sent to the Department of Mississippi and East Louisiana, where he took chief command of all the troops therein, including the Army of West Tennessee (or Mississippi) under Van Dorn and Price. He surrendered Vicksburg to Major-General Grant, July 4, 1863, and after exchange resigned his commission on account of criticism resulting from the surrender. In May, 1864, with the rank of lieutenant-colonel, he was given command of the artillery defenses at Richmond where he served until the close of the war. He became a farmer in Virginia, and died in Penllyn, Pennsylvania, July 13, 1881.

Southern Army—Trans-Mississippi Army

THE FORCES in the Department of West Louisiana and Texas were constituted the Southwestern Army, January 14, 1863, and the command was given to Lieutenant-General E. Kirby Smith. On February 9th, the command was enlarged so as to embrace the whole Trans-Mississippi Department, which, on May 26, 1862, had been separated from the Western Department (Department No. 2). Major-General T. H. Holmes had previously commanded in the Trans-Mississippi. Smith had about thirty thousand men, widely scattered from Fort Smith, Arkansas, to the Rio Grande. Major-General Holmes was defeated at Helena, July 4, 1863. The various portions of the army were constantly occupied in small engagements. These forces opposed the Federal Red River expedition in 1864. At the latest returns, in 1865, the aggregate present of the force was about forty-three thousand. They were the last Confederate troops to surrender, May 26, 1865.

LIEUTENANT-GENERAL THEOPHILUS HUNTER HOLMES (U.S.M.A. 1829) was born in Sampson County, North Carolina, in 1804, and fought in the Florida and Mexican wars. He resigned his commission of major in April, 1861, and entered the Confederate service, rising to the rank of lieutenant-general on October 10, 1862. On account of his age he saw little active service, but was placed at the head of various districts and departments throughout the Confederacy. On July 4, 1863, while in command of the District of Arkansas, Trans-Mississippi Department, he led an unsuccessful attack on Helena. He died in Fayetteville, North Carolina, June 20, 1880.

LIEUTENANT-GENERAL RICHARD TAYLOR, son of Zachary Taylor, was born in New Orleans, Louisiana, January 27, 1826. He was a Yale graduate and went to the Mexican War with General Taylor. He joined the Confederate army in 1861, serving first as colonel of the Ninth Louisiana Volunteers in the Army of the Potomac. He was promoted to brigadier-general in October, and served under " Stonewall " Jackson in the Shenandoah valley and in the Peninsula campaign. He was made major-general in July, 1862, and the following month was assigned to the command of the District of West Louisiana (Trans-Mississippi Department), where he remained until June, 1864. It was hoped that he would recover New Orleans. He occupied the Teche country during the winter of 1862–63. In the following spring and summer he fought against Weitzel and captured Brashear City. He reached the west bank of the Mississippi near New Orleans in July, but was driven back by Weitzel and Franklin. The following year he was instrumental in defeating the Red River expedition. In September, 1864, he was sent to command the Department of Alabama, Mississippi and East Louisiana, and surrendered to Major-General Canby, May 4, 1865. He died in New York City, April 12, 1879.

Army of Missouri

IN AUGUST, 1864, General E. Kirby Smith ordered Major-General Sterling Price to move into Missouri. It was expected that the various independent bands could be organized and bring at least twenty thousand recruits into the Confederate army. Price's force, consisting of the divisions of Fagan, Marmaduke, and Shelby, amounted to nearly twelve thousand men, and is variously called the Army of the Missouri, Price's Expeditionary Corps, and the Army in the Field. After a

John W. Frazer Commanded a Brigade.

Samuel J. Gholson Commanded a Brigade.

William F. Tucker Led a Brigade under Hood.

Benjamin G. Humphries Led a Brigade in Virginia.

William E. Baldwin, Commander of a Brigade at Mobile.

CONFEDERATE

GENERALS

No. 12

MISSISSIPPI

Jacob H. Sharp Led a Brigade in General Polk's Corps.

Claudius W. Sears, Originally Colonel of the 46th Regt.

Robert Lowry, Commander of a Brigade.

William F. Brantly Commanded a Brigade in Tennessee.

Douglas H. Cooper, Leader of Indian Troops.

very active campaign, Price was driven into Arkansas at the end of November by Major-Generals Rosecrans and Pleasanton, and the Army of the Missouri again became identified with the forces in the Trans-Mississippi Department.

MAJOR-GENERAL STERLING PRICE was born in Prince Edward County, Virginia, September 14, 1809. He settled in Missouri in 1830, and was a member of Congress in 1845, when he went to the Mexican War, in which he was made brigadier-general of volunteers. From 1853 to 1857, he was governor of the State, and president of the State Convention of 1853. He was made major-general of the Missouri militia in May, and assumed command of the Missouri State Guard, July 30, 1861. As major-general of the Confederate Army he commanded the Army of the West from July 2 to September 28, 1862, and later a corps of Van Dorn's Army of Mississippi. In February, 1863, he was ordered to the Trans-Mississippi Department, where he held various commands in Arkansas and elsewhere. His most noteworthy effort was the expedition into Missouri, August-December, 1864, in an attempt to gather a large number of recruits from the independent bands in that State. But Rosecrans drove him back to Arkansas. After the war he became interested in a colonization scheme in Mexico, but returned to the United States in 1866, and died in St. Louis, September 29, 1867.

Army of Mississippi

IN DECEMBER, 1863, Lieutenant-General Leonidas Polk, succeeding Pemberton, was put in command of the force of the Department of Alabama, Mississippi and East Louisiana. It had two divisions of cavalry and a strength of about twenty thousand. This is the force that contended with Major-General Sherman in Mississippi during the winter of 1864. In May, Polk joined the Army of Tennessee to oppose Sherman's advance to Atlanta, and he then denominated his troops the Army of Mississippi. Polk was killed on Pine Mountain, Georgia, June 14th, and was succeeded by Lieutenant-General A. P. Stewart. On July 26th, the Army of Mississippi was joined to the Army of Tennessee as Stewart's Corps.

LIEUTENANT - GENERAL ALEXANDER PETER STEWART (U.S.M.A. 1842) was born in Rogersville, Tennessee, October 12, 1821. He resigned from the army in 1845. He entered the Confederate service from Tennessee, rising to the rank of lieutenant-general in June, 1864, which rank was confirmed the following year. He had a brigade in Polk's command in the Western Department, and later a division in the Army of Tennessee. He was wounded at Ezra Church in the Atlanta campaign, and after Polk's death, he succeeded to the command of the Army of Mississippi, which later became a corps of the Army of Tennessee. On March 16, 1865, he was assigned to the command of the infantry and artillery in that army. He died at Biloxi, Mississippi, August 30, 1908.

MAJOR-GENERAL EDWARD CARY WALTHALL was born in Richmond, Virginia, April 4, 1831. He became a lawyer, practising in Coffeyville, Mississippi. He entered the Confederate service, in 1861, as lieutenant of the Fifteenth Mississippi Infantry, and in December, 1862, became brigadier-general, and major-general in June, 1864. He fought gallantly at Missionary Ridge and covered Hood's retreat at Nashville, where he prevented the capture of the Army of Tennessee by Thomas. In March, 1865, he had command of Stewart's Corps, Army of Tennessee, until the reorganization of April 9th, when he returned to the head of his division. After the war he became United States senator from Mississippi. He died in Washington, April 21, 1898.

Confederate Generals

MAJOR-GENERAL WILLIAM DORSEY PENDER (U.S.M.A. 1854) was born in Edgecombe County, North Carolina, February 6, 1834. He resigned from the army in March, 1861, to enter the Confederate service as colonel of the Sixth North Carolina Infantry. In June, 1862, he became brigadier-general and was made major-general in May, 1863. He was brigade and division commander in

Mark B. Lowrey Led a Brigade in Cleburne's Division in the Army of Tennessee.

Edward Cary Walthall, Conspicuous at Franklin; Later United States Senator.

Charles Clark Commanded a Division under General J. C. Breckinridge.

CONFEDERATE GENERALS—
No. 13—MISSISSIPPI

Samuel G. French, Leader of the Assault on Alatoona Pass in 1864.

William L. Brandon Commanded a Cavalry Brigade.

Nathaniel H. Harris, Colonel of the 19th Regiment.

Peter B. Stark Led a Cavalry Brigade in Forrest's Corps.

Samuel W. Ferguson Commanded a Cavalry Brigade.

George D. Johnston Led a Brigade under Bragg.

Joseph R. Davis Led a Brigade in R. E. Lee's Army.

Wirt Adams, a Conspicuous Cavalry Commander.

the Army of Northern Virginia, receiving his division on the organization of the Third Army Corps. He died in Staunton, Virginia, July 18, 1863, from wounds received upon the field of Gettysburg.

MAJOR-GENERAL STEPHEN DODSON RAMSEUR (U.S.M.A. 1860) was born in Lincolnton, North Carolina, May 31, 1837, and was assigned to the artillery at Fort Monroe. He resigned in April, 1861, to enter the Confederate service. He was made major in the North Carolina State artillery. He was present at the siege of Yorktown, and was placed at the head of a North Carolina regiment in April. He was severely wounded at Malvern Hill, but returned to the army during the winter of 1862-63, having been made brigadier-general in October. He led a brigade with great ability in the Second Army Corps at Chancellorsville and at Gettysburg. In the latter battle he was prominent in the capture of the town. The following year he was again wounded at Spotsylvania, and as major-general he succeeded to Early's division, when the latter was placed at the head of the Second Army Corps. He went to the Shenandoah valley with Early, and after taking a prominent part in all the principal engagements, he was captured, mortally wounded, at Cedar Creek on October 19, 1864.

MAJOR-GENERAL WILLIAM HENRY TALBOT WALKER (U.S.M.A. 1837) was born in Georgia in October, 1816. While serving in Florida he was thrice wounded in the battle of Okeechobee, December 25, 1837. He fought with great distinction in the Mexican War. Early in 1861, he joined the Confederate army, in which he rose to the rank of major-general in May, 1863. He had a brigade in the Second Corps, Army of the Mississippi, and later a command in the District of Georgia, under Beauregard. He was sent with a brigade to the assistance of Johnston in the latter's attempt to keep Grant from Vicksburg, in May, 1863. In August, he was given a division in Hill's Corps, Army of Tennessee, and commanded the reserves at Chickamauga, after which he was in Hardee's Corps in the Chattanooga and Atlanta campaigns until he was killed at Decatur, near Atlanta, July 22, 1864.

LIEUTENANT-GENERAL NATHAN BEDFORD FORREST was born near the site of Chapel Hill, Tennessee, July 13, 1821, and became a slave-trader at Memphis. In the summer of 1861, he joined the Tennessee mounted rifles as private, and a

month later raised and equipped a force of Confederate cavalry. He escaped with his battalion from Fort Donelson, and by the middle of 1862 he had become brigadier-general and was one of the most important officers in the Confederate army. At the head of his independent cavalry organization, he was active during Bragg's invasion of Kentucky and remained there some time. He was with the Army of Tennessee at Chickamauga, and in November, 1863, was made major-general and assigned to the command of all the cavalry in western Tennessee and northern Mississippi. In March and April, 1864, he advanced from Mississippi with a large force. He captured Union City with its garrison, and attacked Paducah, Kentucky. He fought with Sooy Smith, and retreating to Fort Pillow, captured the garrison there, amid great slaughter on April 12th. He then returned to Mississippi and began to operate against Sherman's lines of communication. He defeated Sturgis, at Guntown, on June 10th, but was put to rout by A. J. Smith, at Tupelo, on July 14th. In January, 1865, he was placed in command of the District of Mississippi and East Louisiana, and on February 28th was made lieutenant-general. He was defeated at Selma, Alabama, by the Federal cavalry-leader, J. H. Wilson, and surrendered his forces with those of Lieutenant-General Richard Taylor in May. After the war he conducted several large plantations. He died in Memphis, Tennessee, October 29, 1877.

MAJOR-GENERAL DABNEY HERNDON MAURY (U.S.M.A. 1846) was born in Fredericksburg, Virginia, May 20, 1822, and served in the Mexican War with distinction. He taught at West Point, and served in the West, being assistant adjutant-general in New Mexico when the Civil War broke out. He was dismissed from the service in June, 1861, having enlisted as captain in the Confederate cavalry. He served with the forces that later became the Army of the West, and after the battle of Pea Ridge was made brigadier-general. He had a division in the Army of the West, and commanded the whole force temporarily in June, 1862. As major-general, he had a division with Pemberton's forces in the battle with Sherman at Chickasaw Bayou, December 26, 1862. In 1863, he was placed at the head of the Department of East Tennessee, and in 1864-65, he was in command of the Department of the Gulf, surrendering at Meridian, Mississippi, May 11, 1865. He was the founder of the Southern Historical Society, and from 1886 to 1889 was American minister to Colombia. He died in Peoria, Illinois, January 11, 1900.

John B. Clark Commanded a Cavalry Brigade; Engaged at Pea Ridge.

John G. Walker, a Daring Leader in the Army of Northern Virginia.

Joseph O. Shelby, Cavalry Commander in Arkansas and Missouri Battles.

M. M. Parsons Led a Brigade in Price's Division; Defender of Red River.

Francis M. Cockrell, Distinguished in Missouri Campaigns; Later U. S. Senator.

CONFEDERATE

GENERALS—No. 14

MISSOURI

(ABOVE AND TO RIGHT)

NORTH CAROLINA

(BELOW)

John S. Marmaduke, Leader of Cavalry West of the Mississippi.

Daniel M. Frost Led a Brigade of State Guard under General Price.

John S. Bowen, Conspicuous at Port Gibson and Vicksburg in 1863.

James G. Martin Led a Brigade Defending Richmond in 1864–5.

Robert Ransom, Jr., One of the Defenders of Marye's Heights in 1862.

Richard C. Gatlin, Colonel of a Corps of Infantry, C. S. A., in 1861.

Bryan Grimes Led a Division in the Army of Northern Virginia.

Confederate Generals

BRIGADIER-GENERAL JOHN HUNT MORGAN was born in Huntsville, Alabama, June 1, 1826. He served in the Mexican War and joined the Confederate army in command of the Lexington Rifles, of Kentucky. He did scouting duty, and, as colonel, organized three cavalry companies known as Morgan's Squadron, which operated in Tennessee and Kentucky and fought at Shiloh. His invasion of Kentucky in July, 1862, prepared the way for Bragg. At Lexington, he routed a Union force and his frequent raids, especially the famous Christmas raid of 1862, were among the boldest Confederate exploits. His ability won him promotion to brigadier-general. In July, 1863, he made another raid into Kentucky. At Buffington Ford, about seven hundred of his men, hemmed in by Shackelton and Hobson, were forced to surrender, but Morgan escaped. At last he was captured by Shackelton at New Lisbon, July 26, 1863, but he and six fellow prisoners escaped from the Ohio State Penitentiary at Columbus, on November 27th, and joined the Confederate army in northern Georgia. In April, 1864, he was put at the head of the Department of Southwestern Virginia. Late in May, Morgan, with a few followers, went over into Kentucky, making a raid upon Lexington and dashing toward Frankfort, but Burbridge struck him a severe blow at Cynthiana, June 12th, and Morgan lost seven hundred men and one thousand horses. The early part of September found him in Greenville. While there the town was surprised and surrounded by Gillem's troops, and in attempting to escape Morgan was shot and killed September 4, 1864.

MAJOR-GENERAL LAFAYETTE McLAWS (U.S. M.A. 1842) was born in Augusta, Georgia, January 15, 1821. In March, 1861, he resigned from the army to enter the Confederate service, in which he reached the rank of major-general in May, 1862. He commanded a division in Magruder's command, Army of Northern Virginia, through the Seven Days' battle, and was then transferred to Longstreet's command, being identified as division commander with the First Army Corps through the Maryland campaign of 1862, and all the succeeding campaigns of the Army of Northern Virginia (including Chancellorsville) until September, 1863, when he went West with Longstreet and fought at Chickamauga and Knoxville. In May, 1864, he was sent to Georgia and South Carolina and being under Lieutenant-General Hardee eventually had a division in Hardee's Corps, when in February, 1865, the latter united his forces with the Army of Tennessee. After the war he

was collector of internal revenue and postmaster at Savannah, where he died, July 24, 1897.

BRIGADIER-GENERAL FELIX KIRK ZOLLICOFFER was born in Maury County, Tennessee, May 19, 1812. He became a printer and editor, interrupting the pursuit of this calling to serve in the Seminole War. In 1841, he was made associate editor of the Nashville *Banner*, was State comptroller from 1844 to 1849, and continued his political career in the State senate. He was a member of Congress from 1853 to 1859, and also a delegate to the Peace Conference held at Washington, 1861. In May of that year he was appointed major-general of the provisional army of Tennessee, and in July, after commanding an instruction camp, was made brigadier-general of the Confederate army and assigned to the District of East Tennessee. His forces were defeated by Brigadier-General Schoepf at Camp Wildcat, Kentucky, October 21st, and in an encounter with Brigadier-General Thomas at Logan's Cross Roads, or Mill Springs, Kentucky, January 19, 1862, he was killed.

MAJOR-GENERAL HENRY HETH (U.S.M.A. 1847) was born in Chesterfield County, Virginia, December 16, 1825. He rose to the rank of captain in the Tenth Infantry, from which he resigned, April 25, 1861, to enter the Confederate Army. He was made colonel of the Forty-fifth Virginia Infantry, June 17, 1861. He was commissioned brigadier-general, January 6, 1862, and major-general, May 24, 1863. After serving with his brigade in West Virginia under General Humphrey Marshall, and in the invasion of Kentucky under General Bragg, where he commanded a division of infantry and a brigade of cavalry, he came East, and commanded a division in the Gettysburg campaign. He was also in various campaigns with the Army of Northern Virginia, commanding a division in A. P. Hill's Third Army Corps. He surrendered at Appomattox, and died at Washington, D. C., September 26, 1899.

MAJOR-GENERAL JOSEPH B. KERSHAW was born at Camden, South Carolina, January 5, 1822. He was a member of the State Senate, 1852–57. He entered the Confederate service and was soon made colonel of the Second South Carolina regiment, and on February 15, 1862, he was appointed a brigadier-general. In that capacity he served on the Peninsula and in the Seven Days' battle. He also fought at Antietam, Fred-

Alfred M. Scales Led a North Carolina Brigade in Hill's Corps.

William P. Roberts Led a Brigade of Cavalry in Virginia.

John D. Barry, Colonel of the 18th North Carolina Regiment.

William McRae Led a North Carolina Brigade in Lee's Army.

William R. Cox Led a North Carolina Brigade in Ewell's Corps.

CONFED–
ERATE
GENERALS

No. 15
NORTH
CAROLINA

R. Leventhorpe, Defender of Fort Fisher.

Lawrence S. Baker, Colonel of the 1st Cavalry.

Thomas F. Toon Led a North Carolina Brigade in Lee's Army.

John R. Cooke, Engaged in Repelling Burnside at Fredericksburg.

Rufus Barringer Led a Brigade of Cavalry in Virginia.

Thomas L. Clingman Led a North Carolina Brigade in Lee's Army.

ericksburg, and Gettysburg, and with General Longstreet's Corps. He was engaged at the battle of Chickamauga, commanding a brigade in McLaws' Division of the Left Wing. Returning to the East he was prominent in the Wilderness campaign, and in the Shenandoah he was with Ewell's Corps at Sailors' Creek, when his command was captured on April 6, 1865, and he was released from Fort Warren, Mass., July 24, of the same year. He was elected President of the State Senate and later became a judge of the Circuit Court of South Carolina. General Kershaw died at Camden, South Carolina, April 13, 1894.

MAJOR-GENERAL CHARLES WILLIAM FIELD (U.S.M.A. 1849) was born in Woodford County, Kentucky, in 1818. He served in the Second Dragoons until May, 1861, when he resigned to enter the Confederate service, and was appointed brigadier-general on March 14, 1862. On February 12, 1864, he was appointed major-general. He served at Gaines' Mill, the Second Bull Run, the Wilderness, Spotsylvania, Drewry's Bluff, and in the campaign around Petersburg; being in command of Field's Division of the First Army Corps. General Field died in Washington, D. C., April 9, 1892.

MAJOR-GENERAL CADMUS MARCELLUS WILCOX (U.S.M.A. 1846) was born in Wayne County, North Carolina, May 29, 1826. He served with distinguished bravery in the Mexican War and was brevetted for gallantry and meritorious conduct at Chapultepec, acting as assistant instructor at West Point (1852–57) and becoming a Captain in 1860. On June 8, 1861, he resigned to enter the Confederate service. He was made a brigadier-general October 21, 1861, and served at Seven Pines, the Second Bull Run, and in the Antietam campaign; his name being associated with a brigade that achieved notable reputation during the war. It was composed of the Eighth, Ninth, Tenth, and Eleventh Alabama regiments and Thomas' Artillery, and was in Longstreet's division of the Army of Northern Virginia. It made a striking record in the Seven Days' battles, where it sustained a loss of 1055, or 57 per cent. of its entire number. Later this brigade was in General R. H. Anderson's division, to the command of which General Wilcox succeeded. He also participated at the battle of Gettysburg and served through a number of campaigns in the Army of Northern Virginia until the final surrender at Ap-

pomattox. He was appointed a major-general in 1863. From 1886 until his death, on December 2, 1890, he was chief of the Railroad Division of the General Land Office at Washington, D. C. He wrote a "History of the Mexican War," which is regarded as the standard military work on the subject.

MAJOR-GENERAL ROBERT E. RODES was born at Lynchburg, Virginia, March 29, 1829. He was graduated at the Virginia Military Institute at Lexington in 1848, and was a professor there until appointed captain of the Mobile Cadets early in 1861. He was made colonel of the Fifth Alabama and in October, 1861, was appointed brigadier-general. He served at the First Battle of Bull Run and at the battles of Seven Pines and Gaines' Mills, and distinguished himself in command of Rodes' Brigade, which was composed of Alabama troops in Hill's Division of Jackson's Corps, Army of Northern Virginia. On May 7, 1863, General Rodes was appointed major-general and he commanded a division at Chancellorsville and Gettysburg in Ewell's Second Corps of the Army of Northern Virginia. He also participated in the Wilderness campaign and in the operations in the Shenandoah valley, where he was killed in action at Winchester, September 19, 1864.

MAJOR-GENERAL GEORGE EDWARD PICKETT (U.S.M.A. 1846) was born at Richmond, Virginia, June 28, 1828. He served in the Mexican War, receiving the brevet of first lieutenant for gallant service at Contreras and Churubusco, and also the brevet of lieutenant for distinguished service at Chapultepec. He served with the regular army in the Territory of Washington, and at various posts in the West until June 25, 1861, when he resigned. He was appointed a colonel in the Confederate army, on July 23, and on January 14, 1862, he was appointed as brigadier-general. He served in command of a brigade in Longstreet's division of General Joseph E. Johnston's Army, and on October 11 he was made major-general, commanding a division in the Army of Northern Virginia. General Pickett made a memorable charge against the Federal front at Cemetery Hill on the third day of Gettysburg, his division having reached the field on that day. In September, 1863, General Pickett commanded the Department of North Carolina and operated against Drewry's Bluff in the following year, after his return to Virginia. He was defeated at Lynchburg in an attempt to

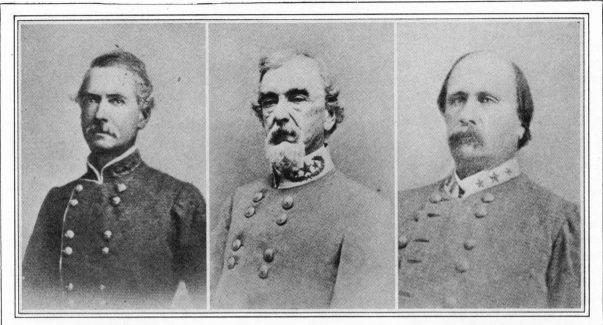

James H. Trapier, Commander at Fort
Moultrie and Sullivan's Island.

Benjamin Huger, Commander of a
Division at Seven Pines.

William H. Wallace, Originally Colonel
of the 18th Regiment.

CONFEDERATE

GENERALS

No. 16

SOUTH CAROLINA

Milledge L. Bonham Became Governor of
South Carolina.

Thomas F. Drayton Commanded a Military
District in South Carolina.

James Chestnut, Aide to Beauregard
at Fort Sumter.

Johnson Hagood, Defender of Richmond and Petersburg.

Arthur M. Manigault, Colonel 10th
Regiment.

oppose Sheridan's cavalry in March, 1865, and also at Dinwiddie Court House and Five Forks. He surrendered with the Army of Northern Virginia and at the conclusion of the war he settled in Richmond, where he died in 1875.

MAJOR-GENERAL WILLIAM HENRY FITZHUGH LEE was born at Arlington, Virginia, May 31, 1837, the second son of General Robert E. Lee. For two years he served as second lieutenant with the Sixth U. S. Infantry, resigning in May, 1859. At the outbreak of the Civil War he entered the Confederate Army in a Virginia cavalry regiment, was made a brigadier-general to rank from September 15, 1862, being promoted to major-general, April 23, 1864. During the Peninsula campaign General Lee, then colonel commanding the Ninth Virginia Cavalry, participated in Stuart's ride around McClellan's army. In the Chancellorsville campaign General Lee was in command of a body of cavalry which fought with the Union Cavalry of General Stoneman under the immediate command of General Averell. General Lee's brigade also participated in the Gettysburg campaign, forming one of the six brigades commanded by Major-General J. E. B. Stuart. General Lee with his cavalry opposed the advances of General Sheridan in his Trevilian raid when Wilson was sent out to cut the Weldon and South Side Road; and at the Petersburg campaign his cavalry participated actively, making many valiant assaults on the Federal lines. Before the surrender of Appomattox, General Lee with his cavalry aided General Gordon in keeping back the Union advances and protecting the wagon-trains of the Confederate army. He was paroled at Appomattox Court House, April 9, 1865, and died at Ravensworth, Fairfax County, Virginia, October 15, 1891.

MAJOR-GENERAL GEORGE WASHINGTON CUSTIS LEE (U.S.M.A. 1854) was born at Fortress Monroe, Virginia, September 16, 1832, and was the eldest son of General Robert E. Lee. Upon graduation from the United States Military Academy he joined the corps of engineers, in which he served until May 2, 1861, when he resigned to enter the Confederate Army. The greater part of his service was as aide to President Jefferson Davis. He was appointed major-general serving with the volunteer troops with temporary rank on February 7, 1865, the commission dating from October 20, 1864. On the same date he was also made full major-general. He was captured at Sailor's Creek, April 6, 1865, and was paroled six days later, which parole was extended until April 23, 1865.

In addition to serving as aide to President Davis, General Lee was in command of military forces in the city of Richmond. In the latter part of the war he commanded a division of Ewell's corps, and it was at this time that his division was captured along with that of General Kershaw. After the war he became professor of civil engineering at the Virginia Military Institute, and in 1871 he succeeded his father,—General Robert E. Lee,—as president of the Washington & Lee University. This position he held until 1897, when he became president emeritus.

MAJOR-GENERAL MATTHEW CALBRAITH BUTLER was born near Greenville, South Carolina, March 8, 1836. He was admitted to the South Carolina bar in 1856, and in addition to practising law was elected to the State legislature in 1859. At the outbreak of the Civil War he entered the Confederate Army as captain, and rose to the command of the Second South Carolina Cavalry, which fought a notable action at Brandy Station on June 10, 1863, in which Colonel Butler lost his right leg. He was appointed brigadier-general, September 2, 1863. In the following year General Butler had command of a brigade consisting of the Fourth, Fifth, and Sixth South Carolina Cavalry, which was included in General Wade Hampton's division and operated with the Army of Northern Virginia. General Butler participated in the battle of Trevilian Station on June 12, 1864, commanding General Hampton's division, where he was engaged with the cavalry of General Sheridan, and later broke through General J. H. Wilson's lines. General Butler was sent to resist the onward march of Sherman through North Carolina, and he participated in the battle of Bentonville. He had previously, December 7, 1864, been appointed major-general. After the surrender at Greensboro, General Butler was paroled, May 1, 1865. Entering politics again after the war, General Butler met with rapid advancement, and was United States Senator from South Carolina from 1877 to 1889. At the outbreak of the Spanish War he was made a major-general of volunteers, May 28, 1898, and served until honorably discharged, April 15, 1899. He was a member of the commission appointed by President McKinley to arrange for the evacuation of Cuba by the Spaniards. General Butler died at Columbus, S. C., April 14, 1909.

MAJOR-GENERAL WILLIAM MAHONE was born at Monroe, Southampton County, Virginia, December 1, 1826. Graduating from the Virginia Military Institute in 1847, he followed the profes-

John Bratton Led a Brigade in Longstreet's Corps.

Thomas M. Logan Led a Cavalry
Brigade in Lee's Army.

Nathan G. Evans, Commander of a
District on the Atlantic Coast.

CONFEDERATE

GENERALS

No. 17

SOUTH CAROLINA

Martin W. Gary, Originally Colonel
in Hampton's Legion.

James Connor Commanded a Brigade
in Lee's Army.

Ellison Capers Led a Brigade in the
Army of Tennessee.

John D. Kennedy Led a Brigade in
Longstreet's Corps.

John S. Preston, Chief of the Bureau
of Conscription.

sion of civil engineering until the outbreak of the Civil War, when he entered the Confederate Army. He participated in the capture of the Norfolk Navy Yard by the Virginia volunteers, raised and commanded the Sixth Virginia regiment and on November 16, 1861, he was appointed brigadier-general in the Confederate Army in March, 1864. In the battle of Seven Pines, General Mahone commanded a brigade in Huger's Division, while at Malvern Hill also his troops were engaged. General Mahone also fought in the Chancellorsville and Gettysburg campaigns, as well as in the Wilderness. At the North Anna on May 24th, General Mahone made a desperate attack on Warren's Corps, driving it back. On August 3, 1864, General Mahone was promoted to be major-general. He was active in the brilliant repulse of the Federal attack after the explosion of the mine at Petersburg and in the various operations about the Weldon Railroad. General Mahone was present at the last struggles of the war, and was paroled at Appomattox Court House, April 9, 1865. After the war he was made president of the Norfolk and Tennessee Railroad and became a leading figure in Virginia politics, being elected to the United States Senate in 1880, where he acted with the Republican party. He failed of re-election on the expiration of his term in 1887, and died at Washington, D. C., October 9, 1893.

VIII

THE ORGANIZATIONS
OF THE
VETERANS

THE GERM OF THE "G. A. R." IDEA

William W. Silkworth, of Long Branch, New Jersey, a veteran who had an opportunity to inspect some of the pictures reproduced in the PHOTOGRAPHIC HISTORY, recognized this group as Company B, 170th Regiment, New York Volunteers. "You cannot appreciate or understand fully my amazement and joy in the discovery," he wrote to the editors. "There right in the front of the picture sits my brother playing cards (You will note that he is left handed. We laid him away in front of Petersburg). With him is John Vandewater, Geo. Thomas and Wash. Keating. There is Charlie Thomas and all the rest as true as life. With the exception of two, I have not seen any of the boys for thirty years." It was at such moments as this, when the Federal soldiers played games and chatted and became

UNION RESERVES ON PICKET DUTY

acquainted, that the organization was being evolved which has grown into a leading national institution since its formation at Decatur, Illinois, on April 6, 1866. Between the men who had fought and marched and suffered together, who time out of mind had shared their last crust and saved each others' lives, who had nursed each other and cheered each other on when another step forward seemed to mean certain death, there arose a great love that extended to the widows and orphans of those whose dying words they had heard on the field of battle. Eve. since that time the organization has lent assistance to those reduced to need by the inexorable war. It admits to membership any soldier or sailor of the United States Army, Navy or Marine Corps, who served between April 12, 1861, and April 9, 1865.

The Grand Army of the Republic

By John E. Gilman, Commander-in-Chief, Grand Army of the Republic

AT the close of the Civil War, there were over a million men in the Union armies. Nearly two and a half million had served under the Stars and Stripes during the four long years of warfare, of whom three hundred and fifty-nine thousand had died. It was essential that those still in the service should disband and retire to civilian life. This was effected after a grand parade of the armies of the Potomac, the Tennessee, and of Georgia, on May 23 and 24, 1865, when one hundred and fifty thousand men marched through the wide avenues of Washington in review before the President and the commanding generals. From the glare and glory, the power and prestige of the soldier's career, they went into the obscurity of the peaceful pursuits of American citizenship, and in a few short months the vast armies of the United States had disappeared.

The great war was ended, but it would have been strange indeed if the memories of those years of storm and stress, the sacrifices of those who had fallen, the experiences of the march, the battlefield, and the camp, and the needs of their disabled comrades, and of the widows and the orphans had been forgotten.

Even before the war had ended, organizations of veterans of the Union armies had begun to be formed. The first veteran society formed, The Third Army Corps Union, was organized at the headquarters of General D. B. Birney, commander of the Third Army Corps, at a meeting of the officers of the corps, September 2, 1863. The main object, at that time, was to secure funds for embalming and sending home for burial the bodies of officers killed in battle or dying in hospitals at the front. General D. E. Sickles was its first president.

In April, 1865, the Society of the Army of the Tennessee was formed at Raleigh, North Carolina, membership being restricted to officers who had served with the old Army of the Tennessee. The object was declared to be " to keep alive that kindly and cordial feeling which has been one of the characteristics of this army during its career in the service." General Sherman was elected president in 1869, and continued to hold the office for many years.

After the war, many other veteran societies

were formed, composed not only of officers but of enlisted men of the various armies, corps, and regiments, as well as many naval organizations. Among them, the Military Order of the Loyal Legion of the United States was the first society formed by officers honorably discharged from the service. It was first thought of at a meeting of a group of officers who had met the day after the assassination of President Lincoln for the purpose of passing resolutions on his death. These resolutions were subsequently adopted, and it was determined to effect a permanent organization. This was done May 3, 1865, and a constitution and by-laws were, in part, adopted the same month. The titles of officers, the constitution, and general plan, were, in part, afterward adopted by the Grand Army of the Republic. The essential difference was that first-class membership of the Loyal Legion was restricted to officers.

Besides the foregoing organizations of veterans, there were others formed of a political nature, such as the Boys in Blue and other similar societies, and there were held in September, 1866, two political conventions of veterans of the army and navy. These political soldiers' clubs were the result of the times, for the controversy between Congress and President Johnson was at its height. In the East, after the fall elections of 1866, most of these political clubs of veterans were ready to disband. The desire for a permanent organization of veterans became strong. No post of the Grand Army had been organized east of Ohio prior to October, 1866. Posts were started, and inasmuch as eligibility to membership in the Grand Army was possessed by those who composed the membership of these political clubs, the Boys in Blue and similar clubs formed, in many places, the nucleus of the Grand Army posts.

This fact gave, in good part, a political tinge to the Grand Army during the first year or two of its existence, and to it was due, chiefly, the severe losses in membership that the order sustained for a short period. But, eventually, the political character was wholly eradicated, and the order recovered its standing and its losses.

During the winter of 1865–66, Major B. F. Stephenson, surgeon of the Fourteenth Illinois regiment, discussed with friends the matter of the

Galusha Pennypacker, Colonel of the 97th Regiment.

Joshua T. Owens, Colonel
of the 69th Regiment.

James A. Beaver, Colonel
of the 148th Regiment.

Isaac J. Wistar, Originally
Colonel of the 71st Reg't.

FEDERAL GENERALS

No. 23

PENNSYLVANIA

Joshua K. Sigfried, Originally Colonel of the 48th Regiment.

David H. Williams, Originally Colonel of the 82d Infantry.

John B. McIntosh, Origi-
nally Colonel of the 3d
Cavalry.

Frederick S. Stumbaugh,
Originally Colonel of
the 2d Infantry.

Thomas J. McKean Led
a Division at
Corinth.

Montgomery C. Meigs,
Quartermaster-General
of the Army.

formation of an organization of veteran soldiers. He had, previously, while the war was still continuing, talked over the formation of such an organization with his tent-mate, Chaplain William J. Rutledge of the same regiment, and both had agreed to undertake the work of starting such a project after the war was ended, if they survived.

At the national encampment in St. Louis, in 1887, it was stated by Fred. J. Dean, of Fort Scott, Arkansas, that in February, 1866, he, with Doctors Hamilton and George H. Allen, assisted Doctor Stephenson in compiling ritualistic work, constitution, and by-laws at Springfield, Illinois, and these four assumed the obligations of the Grand Army of the Republic at that time. It is conceded that the initiatory steps to constitute the order were taken in Illinois, and Doctor Stephenson's name is the first one connected with the systematic organization of the Grand Army. He and his coworkers were obligated in the work. Several other veterans joined with them, and a ritual was prepared.

The question of printing this ritual occasioned some anxiety on account of the desire to keep it secret, but this difficulty was solved by having it printed at the office of the Decatur (Illinois) *Tribune*, the proprietor of which, together with his compositors, were veterans. They were accordingly obligated, and the ritual was printed by them. Captain John S. Phelps, one of the active associates of Doctor Stephenson, who had gone to Decatur to supervise the work of printing the ritual, had met several of his comrades of the Forty-first Illinois and had sought their cooperation. One of them, Doctor J. W. Routh, who was acquainted with Doctor Stephenson, went to Springfield to consult the latter about organizing, and, with Captain M. F. Kanan, called upon Doctor Stephenson. They returned to Decatur to organize a post there, and at once set to work and secured a sufficient number of signatures to an application for a charter. They returned to Springfield to present the application in person. On April 6, 1866, Doctor Stephenson issued the charter, signing it as department commander of Illinois, thus creating the first post of the Grand Army of the Republic. The ritual was revised and a constitution written by a committee from this post, at the suggestion of Doctor Stephenson. The committee reported that the regulations and ritual had been presented to department headquarters and accepted. The plan of organization consisted of post, district, department, and national organizations, to be known as the Grand Army of the Republic.

The declaration of principles in the constitution, written by Adjutant-General Robert M. Woods, set forth that the soldiers of the volunteer army of the United States, during the war of 1861–65, actuated by patriotism and combined in fellowship, felt called upon to declare those principles and rules which should guide the patriotic freeman and Christian citizen, and to agree upon plans and laws which should govern them in a united and systematic working method to effect the preservation of the grand results of the war. These results included the preservation of fraternal feelings, the making of these ties advantageous to those in need of assistance, the providing for the support, care, and education of soldiers' orphans, and maintenance of their widows, the protection and assistance of disabled soldiers, and the " establishment and defense of the late soldiery of the United States, morally, socially, and politically, with a view to inculcate a proper appreciation of their services to the country, and to a recognition of such services and claims by the American people."

To this last section, the national encampment in Philadelphia, in 1868, added, " But this association does not design to make nominations for office or to use its influence as a secret organization for partisan purposes." The word " sailors " was added by the Indianapolis encampment. In May, 1869, the present form of rules and regulations was adopted.

Post No. 2 of the Department of Illinois was organized at Springfield, as stated by General Webber, in April, 1866.

In 1865, in Indiana, correspondence relating to the continuance of the Army Club, a society of veterans, had come to the hands of Governor Oliver P. Morton, of Indiana. He sent General R. S. Foster, of Indianapolis, to Springfield, to examine into Doctor Stephenson's plan of organization. General Foster met the latter, and was obligated by him. On his return, he obligated a number of his intimate comrades, and these he constituted as a department organization. The first post of this department was organized at Indianapolis, on the 22d of August, 1866.

Doctor Stephenson had issued, as department commander, General Orders No. 1, on April 1, 1866, at Springfield, in which he announced the following officers: General Jules C. Webber, aide-de-camp and chief of staff; Major Robert M. Woods, adjutant-general; Colonel John M. Snyder, quartermaster-general; Captain John S. Phelps, aide-de-camp, and Captain John A. Lightfoot, assistant adjutant-general, on duty at the de-

Thomas R. Rowley, Originally Colonel of the 102d Regiment.

Charles T. Campbell, Originally Colonel of the 1st Regiment of Artillery.

James Nagle, Originally Colonel of the 48th Regiment.

FEDERAL GENERALS— No. 24

Alexander Schimmelpfennig, Originally Colonel of the 14th Infantry.

PENNSYLVANIA

(CONTINUED)

George A. McCall, Commander of the Pennsylvania Reserves in the Seven Days.

Albert L. Lee Led a Cavalry Column in the Red River Campaign.

Joshua B. Howell, Originally Colonel of the 85th Regiment.

partment headquarters. On June 26, 1866, a call had been issued for a convention, to be held at Springfield, Illinois, July 12, 1866. The convention was held on this date and the Department of Illinois organized, General John M. Palmer being elected department commander. Doctor Stephenson was recognized, however, in the adoption of a resolution which proclaimed him as " the head and front of the organization." He continued to act as commander-in-chief.

In October, 1866, departments had been formed in Illinois, Wisconsin, Indiana, Iowa, and Minnesota, and posts had been organized in Ohio, Missouri, Kentucky, Arkansas, District of Columbia, Massachusetts, New York, and Pennsylvania. On October 31, 1866, Doctor Stephenson issued General Orders No. 13, directing a national convention to be held at Indianapolis, November 20, 1866, signing this order as commander-in-chief. In accordance with this order, the First National Encampment of the Grand Army of the Republic convened at Indianapolis on the date appointed, and was called to order by Commander-in-Chief Stephenson. A committee on permanent organization was appointed and its report nominating the officers of the convention was adopted, and General John M. Palmer became the presiding officer of the convention. The committee on constitution submitted a revised form of the constitution which, with a few amendments, was adopted. Resolutions were adopted calling the attention of Congress to the laws in regard to bounties, recommending the passage of a law making it obligatory for every citizen to give actual service when called upon in time of war, instead of providing a substitute, and suggesting, for the consideration of those in authority, the bestowal of positions of honor and profit upon worthy and competent soldiers and sailors. General S. A. Hurlbut, of Illinois, was elected commander-in-chief and Doctor Stephenson, adjutant-general.

The national organization of the Grand Army of the Republic was thus fairly started. The Second National Encampment was held at Philadelphia, January 15, 16, and 17, 1868, when General John A. Logan was elected commander-in-chief. At the Third National Encampment at Cincinnati, May 12 and 13, 1869, General Logan was reelected commander-in-chief. It appears from Adjutant-General Chipman's report at this encampment that, at the Philadelphia encampment in 1868, there were represented twenty-one departments, which claimed a total membership of over two hundred thousand. But there had been very few records kept, either in departments or at national headquarters, and there seems to have been very little communication between posts and headquarters. At the Cincinnati encampment, the adjutant-general reported that the aggregate number of departments was thirty-seven, and that the number of posts, reported and estimated, was 2050. At the encampment at Cincinnati, in 1869, the grade system of membership was adopted, establishing three grades of recruit, soldier, and veteran. This system met with serious opposition and was finally abandoned at the encampment at Boston, in 1871. It was claimed that to this system much of the great falling-off in membership was due. It is a fact that, at this period, there had been a large decrease in the numbers in the order, particularly in the West. But the cause of this may be laid to a variety of reasons. The order, at first, seems to have had a rapid growth. Because of the incompleteness of the records, it is impossible even to estimate what the strength of the membership in those early days was. But the real solidity of the order was not established until some years had passed.

On May 5, 1868, Commander-in-Chief Logan, by General Orders No. 11, had assigned May 30, 1868, as a memorial day which was to be devoted to the strewing of flowers on the graves of deceased comrades who had died in the defense of their country during the Civil War. The idea of Memorial Day had been suggested to Adjutant-General Chipman in a letter from some comrade then living in Cincinnati, whose name has been lost. At the encampment at Washington, in 1870, Memorial Day was established by an amendment to the rules and regulations. It has been made a holiday in many of the States, and is now observed throughout the country, not only by the Grand Army but by the people generally, for the decoration of the graves of the soldiers.

The first badge of the order was adopted in 1866. A change was made in October, 1868, in its design, and a further change in October, 1869. At the national encampment of 1873, the badge was adopted which is substantially the one that exists to-day, a few minor changes being made in 1886. It is now made from captured cannon purchased from the Government. The bronze button worn on the lapel of the coat was adopted in 1884.

The matter of pensions has, in the nature of things, occupied much of the time of the Grand Army encampments, both national and departmental. The order has kept careful watch over pension legislation; its recommendations have been conservative, and of late years have been adopted by Congress to a very great extent. Aid

William A. Quarles, Wounded in
Hood's Charge at Franklin.

George G. Dibrell, Leader of Cavalry
Opposing Sherman's March.

Alfred E. Jackson Commanded a
District of East Tennessee.

CONFEDERATE

GENERALS

No. 18

TENNESSEE

George Maney, Active Organizer and
Leader of Tennessee.

Bushrod R. Johnson, Conspicuous
in the West and in the East.

John P. McCown; At Belmont, in 1861.
Later Led a Division.

John C. Brown Led a Division in the
Army of Tennessee.

William H. Jackson Led a Brigade
of Forrest's Cavalry.

has been given to veterans and widows entitled to pensions, by cooperation with the Pension Office in obtaining and furnishing information for the adjudication of claims.

The Grand Army has been assisted in carrying out its purposes by its allied orders, the Woman's Relief Corps, the Sons of Veterans, the Daughters of Veterans, and the Ladies of the G. A. R. These organizations have adopted the principles and purposes that have actuated the Grand Army and have given much valued aid in the achievement of the results obtained.

The Grand Army of the Republic before the end of the nineteenth century had passed the zenith of its career. Its membership remained about the same in numbers after its first great leap and subsequent subsidence, varying between 25,000 and 50,000 from 1870 to 1880. During the decade between 1880 and 1890 it rose to its highest number of 409,-489. Since then it has decreased, through death, in very great part, until, at the national encampment of 1910, at Atlantic City, it had diminished to 213,901. Its posts exist throughout the length and breadth of the country, and even outside, and nearly every State has a department organization. Its influence is felt in every city, town, and village, and it has earned the good-will and support of the entire American people. Among its leaders have been some of the most prominent men of the country. Its commanders-in-chief have been:

B. F. Stephenson,	Illinois,	1866
S. A. Hurlbut,	Illinois,	1866–67
John A. Logan,	Illinois,	1868–70
Ambrose E. Burnside,	Rhode Island,	1871–72
Charles Devens,	Massachusetts,	1873–74
John F. Hartranft,	Pennsylvania,	1875–76
John C. Robinson,	New York,	1877–78
William Earnshaw,	Ohio,	1879
Louis Wagner,	Pennsylvania,	1880
George S. Merrill,	Massachusetts,	1881
Paul Van Dervoort,	Nebraska,	1882
Robert B. Beath,	Pennsylvania,	1883
John S. Kountz,	Ohio,	1884
S. S. Burdett,	Dist. of Columbia,	1885
Lucius Fairchild,	Wisconsin,	1886
John P. Rea,	Minnesota,	1887
William Warner,	Missouri,	1888
Russell A. Alger,	Michigan,	1889
Wheelock G. Veazey,	Vermont,	1890
John Palmer,	New York,	1891
A. G. Weissert,	Wisconsin,	1892
John G. B. Adams,	Massachusetts,	1893
Thomas G. Lawler,	Illinois,	1894
Ivan N. Walker,	Indiana,	1895
T. S. Clarkson,	Nebraska,	1896
John P. S. Gobin,	Pennsylvania,	1897
James A. Sexton,	Illinois,	1898
W. C. Johnson,	Ohio,	1899
Albert D. Shaw,	New York,	1899
Leo Rassieur,	Missouri,	1900
Ell Torrence,	Minnesota,	1901
Thomas J. Stewart,	Pennsylvania,	1902
John C. Black,	Illinois,	1903
Wilmon W. Blackmar,	Massachusetts,	1904
John R. King,	Maryland,	1904
James Tanner,	Dist. of Columbia,	1905
Robert B. Brown,	Ohio,	1906
Charles G. Burton,	Missouri,	1907
Henry M. Nevius,	New Jersey,	1908
Samuel R. Van Sant,	Minnesota,	1909
John E. Gilman,	Massachusetts,	1910
Hiram M. Trimble,	Illinois,	1911

The United Confederate Veterans

By S. A. Cunningham, Late Sergeant-Major, Confederate States Army, and Founder and Editor of "The Confederate Veteran"

THE organization known as the United Confederate Veterans was formed in New Orleans, June 10, 1889. The inception of the idea for a large and united association is credited to Colonel J. F. Shipp, a gallant Confederate, commander of N. B. Forrest Camp, of Chattanooga, Tennessee—the third organized—who was in successful business for years with a Union veteran. Colonel Shipp had gone to New Orleans in the interest of the Chattanooga and Chickamauga Mili-

tary Park, and there proposed a general organization of Confederates on the order of the Grand Army of the Republic, his idea being to bring into a general association the State organizations, one of which in Virginia, and another in Tennessee, had already been organized.

Following these suggestions, a circular was sent out from New Orleans in regard to the proposed organization, and the first meeting was held in that city on June 10, 1889, the organization being

ROBERT V. RICHARDSON
Commanded a Tennessee
Brigade.

SAMUEL R. ANDERSON
Commander of a Tennessee
Brigade.

BENJAMIN J. HILL
Provost-Marshal-General Army
of Tennessee.

JAMES A. SMITH
Led a Brigade in Cleburne's
Division.

ROBERT C. TYLER
Commander of the Garrison at West
Point, Georgia.

THOMAS B. SMITH
Led a Brigade in the Army of
Tennessee.

WILLIAM Y. C. HUMES
Commanded a Division of Wheeler's
Cavalry.

CONFEDERATE
GENERALS
No. 19
TENNESSEE

LUCIUS M. WALKER
Led a Calvary Brigade in the Army of the West.

ALEXANDER W. CAMPBELL
Led a Brigade of Forrest's Cavalry.

perfected under the name of United Confederate Veterans, with F. S. Washington, of New Orleans, as president, and J. A. Chalaron, secretary. A constitution was adopted, and Lieutenant-General John B. Gordon, of Georgia, was elected general and commander-in-chief. At this meeting there were representatives from the different Confederate organizations already in existence in the States of Louisiana, Mississippi and Tennessee.

While giving Colonel Shipp credit for suggesting the general organization of the United Confederate Veterans, the important part played by the Louisiana camps in furthering the association must be emphasized. The previously existing organizations became the first numbers in the larger association. The Army of Northern Virginia, of New Orleans, became Camp No. 1; Army of Tennessee, New Orleans, No. 2; and LeRoy Stafford Camp, Shreveport, No. 3. The N. B. Forrest Camp, of Chattanooga, Tennessee, became No. 4; while Fred. Ault Camp, of Knoxville, is No. 5. There are other camps, not among the first in the list, which are among the most prominent in the organization. For instance, Tennessee had an organization of bivouacs, the first and largest of which was Frank Cheatham, No. 1, of Nashville, but which is Camp No. 35, U. C. V. Then, Richmond, Virginia, had its R. E. Lee Camp, which has ever been of the most prominent, and was the leader in a great soldiers' home movement. In the U. C. V. camp-list, the R. E. Lee, of Richmond, is No. 181. The camps increased to a maximum of more than fifteen hundred, but with the passage of years many have ceased to be active.

While the organization was perfected in New Orleans, the first reunion of United Confederate Veterans was held in Chattanooga, Tennessee, July 3 to 5, 1890. To this reunion invitations were extended " to veterans of both armies and to citizens of the Republic," and the dates purposely included Independence Day.

The first comment both in the North and South was, " Why keep up the strife or the memory of it? " but it was realized that such utterances were from those who did not comprehend the scope of the organization of United Confederate Veterans, which, from the very outset, was clear in the minds of its founders. It was created on high lines, and its first commander was the gallant soldier, General John B. Gordon, at the time governor of Georgia, and later was United States senator. General Gordon was continued as commander-in-chief until his death.

The nature and object of the organization can-

not be explained better than by quoting from its constitution.

The first article declares:

" The object and purpose of this organization will be strictly social, literary, historical, and benevolent. It will endeavor to unite in a general federation all associations of the Confederate veterans, soldiers and sailors, now in existence or hereafter to be formed; to gather authentic data for an impartial history of the War between the States; to preserve the relics or memories of the same; to cherish the ties of friendship that exist among the men who have shared common dangers, common suffering and privations; to care for the disabled and extend a helping hand to the needy; to protect the widow and orphan, and to make and preserve the record of the services of every member and, as far as possible, of those of our comrades who have preceded us in eternity."

Likewise, the last article provides that neither discussion of political or religious subjects nor any political action shall be permitted in the organization, and that any association violating that provision shall forfeit its membership.

The notes thus struck in the constitution of the United Confederate Veterans were reechoed in the opening speech of the first commander-in-chief. General Gordon, addressing the Veterans and the public, said:

" Comrades, no argument is needed to secure for those objects your enthusiastic endorsement. They have burdened your thoughts for many years. You have cherished them in sorrow, poverty, and humiliation. In the face of misconstruction, you have held them in your hearts with the strength of religious convictions. No misjudgments can defeat your peaceful purposes for the future. Your aspirations have been lifted by the mere force and urgency of surrounding conditions to a plane far above the paltry consideration of partisan triumphs. The honor of the American Government, the just powers of the Federal Government, the equal rights of States, the integrity of the Constitutional Union, the sanctions of law, and the enforcement of order have no class of defenders more true and devoted than the ex-soldiers of the South and their worthy descendants. But you realize the great truth that a people without the memories of heroic suffering or sacrifice are a people without a history.

" To cherish such memories and recall such a past, whether crowned with success or consecrated in defeat, is to idealize principle and strengthen character, intensify love of country, and convert defeat and disaster into pillars of support for

Gideon J. Pillow, Opponent of Grant
in Grant's First Battle—Belmont.

William H. Carroll
Led a Brigade in
East Tennessee.

John C. Carter, Orig-
inally Colonel of the
38th Regiment.

John C. Vaughn, Com-
mander of a Cav-
alry Brigade.

George W. Gordon
Led a Brigade in
Army of Tennessee.

Alfred J. Vaughan Led
a Brigade in Gen-
eral Polk's Corps.

Henry B. Davidson
Led a Brigade of
Wheeler's Cavalry.

CONFEDERATE GENERALS

No. 20—TENNESSEE

Tyree H. Bell Led a Cavalry Command under Forrest.

William McComb Led a Brigade
in R. E. Lee's Army.

Joseph B. Palmer Led a Brigade in
General Polk's Corps.

future manhood and noble womanhood. Whether the Southern people, under their changed conditions, may ever hope to witness another civilization which shall equal that which began with their Washington and ended with their Lee, it is certainly true that devotion to their glorious past is not only the surest guarantee of future progress and the holiest bond of unity, but is also the strongest claim they can present to the confidence and respect of the other sections of the Union."

Referring to the new organization, General Gordon said:

" It is political in no sense, except so far as the word ' political ' is a synonym of the word ' patriotic.' It is a brotherhood over which the genius of philanthropy and patriotism, of truth and justice will preside; of philanthropy, because it will succor the disabled, help the needy, strengthen the weak, and cheer the disconsolate; of patriotism, because it will cherish the past glories of the dead Confederacy and transmute them into living inspirations for future service to the living Republic; of truth, because it will seek to gather and preserve, as witnesses for history, the unimpeachable facts which shall doom falsehood to die that truth may live; of justice, because it will cultivate national as well as Southern fraternity, and will condemn narrow-mindedness and prejudice and passion, and cultivate that broader and higher and nobler sentiment which would write on the grave of every soldier who fell on our side, ' Here lies an American hero, a martyr to the right as his conscience conceived it.' "

The reunions, thus happily inaugurated, became at once popular and have been held every year except the first appointment at Birmingham, Alabama, which was postponed from 1893 to 1894. Nc event in the South is comparable in widespread interest to these reunions. Only the large cities have been able to entertain the visitors, which range in number between fifty thousand and one hundred thousand.

The greatest of all gatherings was at Richmond, Virginia, June 30, 1907, when the superb monument to the only President of the Confederacy was unveiled. There were probably a hundred thousand people at the dedication. An idea of the magnitude of these reunion conventions and the interest in them may be had by reference to that held in Little Rock, Arkansas, in May, 1911, a city of a little more than thirty thousand inhabitants, wherein over a hundred thousand visitors were entertained during the three days.

No finer evidences of genuine patriotism can be found than in the proceedings of these conventions. In fact, there are no more faithful patriots. The Gray line of 1911 is not yet so thin as the press contributions make it. True, the veterans are growing feeble, but the joy of meeting comrades with whom they served in camp and battle for four years—many of whom had not seen one another in the interim—is insuppressible. It is not given to men in this life to become more attached to each other than are the Confederates. They had no pay-roll to look to, and often but scant rations, which they divided unstintedly. And their defeat increased their mutual sympathy.

Yet, on the other hand, there is a just appreciation of their adversaries. The great body of Confederate veterans esteem the men who fought them, far above the politician. They look confidently to the better class of Union veterans to cooperate with them in maintaining a truthful history. Maybe the time will come when the remnant of the soldiers, North and South, will confer together for the good of the country.

The Confederates have not pursued the excellent method of rotation in office in their organization, as have the Grand Army comrades. General John B. Gordon sought to retire repeatedly, but his comrades would not consent. At his death General Stephen D. Lee, next in rank, became commander-in-chief. It was a difficult place to fill, for there never was a more capable and charming man in any place than was General Gordon as commander-in-chief. However, General Lee was so loyal, so just, and so zealous a Christian that he grew rapidly in favor, and at his death there was widespread sorrow. He was succeeded by General Clement A. Evans, of Georgia, who possessed the same high qualities of Christian manhood, and he would have been continued through life, as were his predecessors, but a severe illness, which affected his throat, made a substitute necessary, so he and General W. L. Cabell, commander of the Trans-Mississippi Department from the beginning—their rank being about equal—were made honorary commanders-in-chief for life, and General George W. Gordon, a member of Congress from Tennessee, was chosen as active commander-in-chief in 1910. Generals Gordon, Cabell, and Evans died in 1911. Each had a military funeral in which U. S. Army officials took part.

Within a score of years there had developed a close and cordial cooperation between the veterans and such representative Southern organizations as the Confederated Southern Memorial Association, the United Sons of Confederate Veterans, and the United Daughters of the Confederacy. All are devoted to the highest patriotic ideals.

ROSTER

OF

GENERAL OFFICERS

BOTH UNION
AND CONFEDERATE

THE GENERAL-IN-CHIEF OF THE ARMIES OF THE UNITED STATES   A
PICTURE OF GRANT WITH HIS FAVORITE CHARGER "CINCINNATI"
TAKEN AT COLD HARBOR ON JUNE 4, 1864, IN THE MIDST OF THE
"HAMMERING POLICY" THAT IN TEN MONTHS TERMINATED THE WAR

General Officers of the Union Army

This roster includes in alphabetical order under the various grades the names of all general officers either of full rank or by brevet in the United States (Regular) Army and in the United States Volunteers during the Civil War. The highest rank attained, whether full or by brevet, only is given, in order to avoid duplications. It is, of course, understood that in most cases the actual rank next below that conferred by brevet was held either in the United States Army or the Volunteers. In some cases for distinguished gallantry or marked efficiency brevet rank higher than the next grade above was given. The date is that of the appointment.

LIEUTENANT-GENERAL
UNITED STATES ARMY
(*Full Rank*)

Grant, Ulysses S., Mar. 2, '64.

LIEUTENANT-GENERAL
UNITED STATES ARMY
(*By Brevet*)

Scott, Winfield, Mar. 29, '47.

MAJOR-GENERALS
UNITED STATES ARMY
(*Full Rank*)

Fremont, J. C., May 14, '61.
Halleck, H. W., Aug. 19, '61.
Hancock, W. S., July 26, '66.
McClellan, G. B., May 14, '61.
Meade, G. G., Aug. 18, '64.
Sheridan, P. H., Nov. 8, '64.
Sherman, Wm. T., Aug. 12, '64.
Thomas, Geo. H., Dec. 15, '64.
Wool, John E., May 16, '62.

MAJOR-GENERALS
UNITED STATES ARMY
(*By Brevet*)

Allen, Robert, Mar. 13, '65.
Ames, Adelbert, Mar. 13, '65.
Anderson, Robert, Feb. 3, '65.
Arnold, Richard, Mar. 13, '65.
Augur, Chris. C., Mar. 13, '65.
Averell, Wm. W., Mar. 13, '65.
Ayres, R. B., Mar. 13, '65.
Baird, Absalom, Mar. 13, '65.
Barnard, John G., Mar. 13, '65.
Barnes, Joseph K., Mar. 13, '65.
Barry, Wm. F., Mar. 13, '65.
Beckwith, Amos, Mar. 13, '65.
Benham, H. W., Mar. 13, '65.
Brannan, J. M., Mar. 13, '65.
Brice, Benj. W., Mar. 13, '65.
Brown, Harvey, Aug. 2, '66.
Buchanan, R. C., Mar. 13, '65.
Butterfield, D., Mar. 13, '65.
Canby, Ed. S. R., Mar. 13, '65.
Carleton, J. H., Mar. 13, '65.
Carlin, Wm. P., Mar. 13, '65.
Carr, Eugene A., Mar. 13, '65.
Carroll, Sam. S., Mar. 13, '65.
Casey, Silas, Mar. 13, '65.

Clarke, Henry F., Mar. 13, '65.
Cook, P. St. G., Mar. 13, '65.
Cram, Thomas J., Jan 13, '66.
Crawford, S. W., Mar. 13, '65.
Crook, George, Mar. 13, '65.
Crossman, G. H., Mar. 13, '65.
Cullum, Geo. W., Mar. 13, '65.
Custer, Geo. A., Mar. 13, '65.
Davidson, J. W., Mar. 13, '65.
Davis, Jef. C., Mar. 13, '65.
Delafield, Rich., Mar. 13, '65.
Donaldson, J. L., Mar. 13, '65.
Doubleday, A., Mar. 13, '65.
Dyer, Alex. B., Mar. 13, '65.
Easton, L. E., Mar. 13, '65.
Eaton, Amos B., Mar. 13, '65.
Elliott, W. L., Nov. 13, '65.
Emory, Wm. H., Mar. 13, '65.
Fessenden, F., Mar. 13, '65.
Foster, John G., Mar. 13, '65.
Franklin, Wm. B., Mar. 13, '65.
French, Wm. H., Mar. 13, '65.
Fry, James B., Mar. 13, '65.
Garrard, Kenner, Mar. 13, '65.
Getty, Geo. W., Mar. 13, '65.
Gibbon, John, Mar. 13, '65.
Gibbs, Alfred, Mar. 13, '65.
Gibson, Geo., May 30, '48.
Gillem, Alvan G., April 12, '65.
Gilmore, Q. A., Mar. 13, '65.
Granger, Gordon, Mar. 13, '65.
Granger, Robt. S., Mar. 13, '65.
Grierson, B. H., Mar. 2, '67.
Griffin, Charles, Mar. 13, '65.
Grover, Cuvier, Mar. 13, '65.
Hardie, James A., Mar. 13, '65.
Harney, Wm. S., Mar. 13, '65.
Hartsuff, G. L., Mar. 13, '65
Hatch, Edward, Mar. 2, '67.
Hawkins, J. P., Mar. 13, '65.
Hazen, Wm. B., Mar. 13, '65.
Heintzelman, S. P., Mar. 13, '65.
Hoffman, Wm. Mar. 13, '65.
Holt, Joseph, Mar. 13, '65.
Hooker, Joseph, Mar. 13, '65.
Howard, O. O., Mar. 13, '65.
Howe, A. P., Mar. 13, '65.
Humphreys, A. A., Mar. 13, '65.
Hunt, Henry J., Mar. 13, '65.
Hunter, David, Mar. 13, '65.
Ingalls, Rufus, Mar. 13, '65.
Johnson, R. W., Mar. 13, '65.
Kautz, August V., Mar. 13, '65.
Ketchum, Wm. S., Mar. 13, '65.

Kilpatrick, Judson, Mar. 13, '65.
King, John H., Mar. 13, '65.
Long, Eli, Mar. 13, '65.
McCook, A. McD., Mar. 13, '65.
McDowell, Irvin, Mar. 13,'65.
McIntosh, John B., Aug. 5, '62.
Marcy, R. B., Mar. 13, '65.
Meigs, Mont. C., July 5, '64.
Merritt, Wesley, Mar. 13, '65.
Miles, Nelson A., Mar. 2, '67.
Morris, Wm. W., Mar. 13, '65.
Mower, J. A., Mar. 13, '65.
Newton, John, Mar. 13, '65.
Nichols, Wm. A., Mar. 13, '65.
Ord, Ed. O. C., Mar. 13, '65.
Parke, John G., Mar. 13, '65.
Pennypacker, G., Mar. 2, '67.
Pleasonton, A., Mar. 13, '65.
Pope, John, Mar. 13, '65.
Ramsey, Geo. D., Mar. 13, '65.
Rawlins, John A., April 9, '65.
Reynolds, J. J., Mar. 2, '67.
Ricketts, J. B., Mar. 13, '65.
Ripley, Jas. W., Mar. 13, '65.
Robinson, J. C., Mar. 13, '65.
Rosecrans, W. S., Mar. 13, '65.
Rousseau, L. H., Mar. 28, '67.
Rucker, D. H., Mar. 13, '65.
Russell, David A., Sept. 19, '64.
Sackett, Delos B., Mar. 13, '65.
Schofield, J. M., Mar. 13, '65.
Schriver, E., Mar. 13, '65.
Seymour, T., Mar. 13, '65.
Sherman, T. W., Mar. 13, '65.
Shiras, Alex., Mar. 13, '65.
Sickles, Daniel E., Mar. 2, '67.
Simpson, M. D. L., Mar. 13, '65.
Smith, Andrew J., Mar. 13, '65.
Smith, Chas. H., Mar. 21, '67.
Smith, John E., Mar. 2, '67.
Smith, W. F., Mar. 13, '65.
Stanley, David S., Mar. 13, '65.
Steele, Frederick, Mar. 13, '65.
Stoneman, G., Mar. 13, '65.
Sturgis, S. D., Mar. 13, '65.
Sumner, Edwin V., May 6, '64.
Swayne, Wager, Mar. 2, '67.
Swords, Thomas, Mar. 13, '65.
Sykes, George, Mar. 13, '65.
Terry, Alfred H., Mar. 13, '65.
Thomas, Charles, Mar. 13, '65.
Thomas, Lorenzo, Mar. 13, '65.

Torbert, A. T. A., Mar. 13, '65.
Totten, J. G., April 21, '64.
Tower, Z. B., Mar. 13, '65.
Townsend, E. D., Mar. 13, '65.
Turner, J. W., Mar. 13, '65.
Tyler, Robt. O., Mar. 13, '65.
Upton, Emory, Mar. 13, '65.
Van Vliet, S., Mar. 13, '65.
Vinton, D. H., Mar. 13, '65.
Warren, G. K., Mar. 13, '65.
Webb, Alex. S., Mar. 13, '65.
Weitzel, G., Mar. 13, '65.
Wheaton, Frank, Mar. 13, '65.
Whipple, A. W., May 7, '63.
Whipple, Wm. D., Mar. 13, '65.
Willcox, O. B., Mar. 2, '67.
Williams, Seth, Mar. 13, '65.
Wilson, James H., Mar. 13, '65.
Wood, Thos. J., Mar. 13, '65.
Woodbury, D. P., Aug. 15, '64.
Woods, Chas. R., Mar. 13, '65.
Wright, H. G., Mar. 13, '65.

MAJOR-GENERALS
U. S. VOLUNTEERS
(*Full Rank*)

Banks, N. P., May 16, '61.
Barlow, F. C., May 25, '65.
Berry, H. G., Nov. 29, '62.
Birney, David D., May 3, '63.
Blair, Frank P., Nov. 29, '62.
Blunt, James G., Nov. 29, '62.
Brooks, W. T. H., June 10, '63.
Buell, Don Carlos, Mar. 21, '62.
Buford, John, July 1, '63.
Buford, N. B., Mar. 13, '65.
Burnside, A. E., Mar. 18, '62.
Butler, Benj. F., May 16, '61.
Cadwalader, G. B., Apr. 25, '62.
Clay, Cassius M., April 11, '62.
Couch, Darius N., July 4, '62.
Cox, Jacob Dolson, Oct. 6, '62.
Crittenden, T. L., July 17, '62.
Curtis, S. R., Nov. 21, '62.
Dana, N. J. T., Nov. 29, '62.
Davies, Henry E., May 4, '65.
Dix, John A., May 16, '61.
Dodge, G. M., June 7, '64.
Doubleday, A., Nov. 29, '62.
Garfield, J. A., Sept. 19, '63.
Hamilton, C. S., Sept. 18, '62.
Hamilton, S., Sept. 17, '62.
Herron, F. J., Nov. 29, '62.
Hitchcock, E. A., Feb. 10, '62.

Samuel P. Spear, Originally Colonel of the 11th Cavalry.

Roy Stone, Commander of the "Bucktail Brigade."

William A. Nichols, Promoted for Faithful Services in the War.

Israel Vogdes, Promoted for Gallantry in the Field.

S. B. M. Young, Originally Colonel 4th Cavalry; Later Commander of the U. S. Army.

John R. Brooke, Originally Colonel of the 54th Reg't, Army of the Potomac.

Pennock Huey, Originally Colonel of the 8th Cavalry, Army of the Potomac.

Henry J. Madill, Originally Colonel of the 141st Reg't, Noted at Gettysburg.

FEDERAL GENERALS—No. 25—PENNSYLVANIA

Andrew Porter, Commanded a Brigade at First Bull Run.

Thomas Welsh, Originally Colonel of the 45th Regiment.

Charles F. Smith, Originally Colonel of the 3d Infantry.

Thomas L. Kane, Organizer and Leader of "Kane's Bucktails."

Hurlbut, Stephen, Sept. 17, '62.
Kearny, Philip, July 4, '62.
Keyes, Erasmus D., May 5, '62.
Leggett, M. D., Aug. 21, '65.
Logan, John A., Nov. 29, '62.
McClernand, J. A., Mar. 21, '62.
McPherson, J. B., Oct. 8, '62.
Mansfield, J. K. F., July 18, '62.
Milroy, Robt. H., Nov. 29, '62.
Mitchell, Ormsby, April 11, '62.
Morell, Geo. W., July 4, '62.
Morgan, E. D., Sept. 28, '61.
Morris, Thos. A., Oct. 25, '62.
Mott, Gersham, May 26, '65.
Mower, Joseph A., Aug. 12, '64.
Negley, James S., Nov. 29, '62.
Nelson, William, July 17, '62.
Oglesby, R. J., Nov. 29, '62.
Osterhaus, P. J., July 23, '64.
Palmer, John M., Nov. 29, '62.
Peck, John J., July 4, '62.
Porter, Fitz John, July 4, '62.
Potter, Rbt. B., Sept. 29, '65.
Prentiss, B. M., Nov. 29, '62.
Reno, Jesse L., July 18, '62.
Reynolds, J. F., Nov. 29, '62.
Reynolds, Jos. J., Nov. 29, '62.
Richardson, I. B., July 4, '62.
Schenck, Robt. C. Aug. 30, '62.
Schurz, Carl, March 14, '63.
Sedgwick, John, July 4, '62.
Sigel, Franz, March 21, '62.
Slocum, Henry W., July 4, '62.
Smith, Chas. F., Mar. 21, '62.
Smith, Giles A., Nov. 24, '65.
Stahel, Julius H., Mar. 14, '63.
Steedman, Jas. B., April 30, '64.
Stevens, Isaac I., July 18, '62.
Strong, Geo. C., July 18, '63.
Wallace, Lewis, March 21, '62.
Washburn, C. C., Nov. 29, '62.

MAJOR–GENERALS
U. S. VOLUNTEERS
(By Brevet)

Abbott, Henry L., Mar. 13, '65.
Allen, Robert, Mar. 13, '65.
Alger, Russell A., June 11, '65.
Anderson, N. L., Mar. 13, '65.
Andrews, C. C., Mar. 9, '65.
Andrews, G. L., Mar. 26, '65.
Asboth, Alex., Mar. 13, '65.
Atkins, Smith D., Mar. 13, 'C5.
Avery, Robert, Mar. 13, '65.
Ayres, R. B., Aug. 1, '64.
Bailey, Joseph, Mar. 13, '65.
Baker, Benj. F., Mar. 13, '65.
Banning, H. B., Mar. 13, '65.
Barnes, James, Mar. 13, '65.
Barney, Lewis T., Mar. 13, '65.
Barnum, H. A., Mar. 13, '65.
Barry, H. W., Mar. 13, '65.
Bartlett, Jos. J., Aug. 1, '64.
Bartlett, Wm. F., Mar. 13, '65.
Baxter, Henry, April 1, '65.
Beal, Geo. L., Mar. 13, '65.
Beatty, Samuel, Mar. 13, '65.
Belknap, Wm. W., Mar. 13, '65.
Benton, Wm. P., Mar. 26, '65.
Birge, H. W., Feb. 25, '65.

Birney, Wm., Mar. 13, '65.
Bowen, James, Mar. 13, '65.
Brayman, Mason, Mar. 13, '65.
Brisbin, James, Mar. 13, '65.
Brooke, John R., Aug. 1, '64.
Buckland, R. P., Mar. 13, '64.
Bussey, Cyrus, Mar. 13, '65.
Byrne, James J., Mar. 13, '65.
Caldwell, John C., Aug. 19, '65.
Cameron, R. A., Mar. 13, '65.
Capehart, Henry, June 17, '65.
Carr, Joseph B., Mar. 13, '65.
Carter, Samuel P., Mar. 13, '65.
Catlin, Isaac S., Mar. 13, '65.
Chamberlain, J. L., Mar. 29, '65.
Chapin, Daniel, Aug. 17, '64.
Chapman, G. H., Mar. 13, '65.
Chetlain, A. L., June 18, '65.
Chrysler, M. H., Mar. 13, '65.
Clark, Wm. T., Nov. 24, '65.
Comstock, C. B., Nov. 26, '65.
Connor, P. E., Mar. 13, '65.
Cooke, John, Aug. 24, '65.
Cooper, Jos. A., Mar. 13, '65.
Cole, Geo. W., Mar. 13, '65.
Collis, C. H. T., Mar. 13, '65.
Corse, John M., Oct. 5, '64.
Coulter, Richard, April 6, '65.
Crawford, S. W., Aug. 1, '64.
Cross, Nelson, Mar. 13, '65.
Croxton, John T., April 27, '65.
Cruft, Charles, March 5, '65.
Curtis, N. M., Mar. 13, '65.
Cutler, Lys., Aug. 19, '64.
Davies, Thos. A., July 11, '65.
Dennis, Elias S., April 13, '65.
Dennison, A. W., Mar. 31, '65.
De Trobriand, P. R., Apr. 9, '65.
Devens, Chas., April 3, '65.
Devin, Thos. C., Mar. 13, '65.
Doolittle, C. C., June 13, '65.
Dornblazer, B., Mar. 13, '65.
Duncan, Sam'l A., Mar. 13, '65.
Duryee, Abram, Mar. 13, '65.
Duval, Isaac H., Mar. 13, '65.
Edwards, Oliver, April 5, '65.
Egan, Thos. W., Oct. 27, '64.
Ely, John, April 15, '65.
Ewing, Hugh, Mar. 13, 1865.
Ewing, Thos. Jr., Mar. 13, '65.
Ferrero, Edward, Dec. 2, '64.
Ferry, Orris S., May 23, '65.
Fessenden, J. D., Mar. 13, '65.
Fisk, Clinton B., Mar. 13, '65.
Force, M. F., Mar. 13, '65.
Foster, R. S., Mar. 31, '65.
Fuller, John W., Mar. 13, '65.
Geary, John W., Jan. 12, '65.
Gilbert, Jas. J., Mar. 26, '65.
Gleason, John H., Mar. 13, '65.
Gooding, O. P., Mar. 13, '65.
Gordon, Geo. H., April 9, '65.
Graham, C. K., Mar. 13, '65.
Grant, Lewis A., Oct. 19, '64.
Greene, George S., Mar. 13, '65.
Gregg, D. McM., Aug. 1, '64.
Gregg, John I., Mar. 13, '65.
Gregory, E. M., April 9, '66.
Gresham, W. Q., Mar. 13, '65.
Griffin, S. G., April 2, '65.
Grose, Wm., Aug. 15, '65.

Guss, Henry R., Mar. 13, '65.
Gwyn, James, April 1, '65.
Hamblin, J. E., April 5, '65.
Hamlin, Cyrus, Mar. 13, '65.
Harris, T. M., April 2, '65.
Hartranft, John F., Mar. 25, '65.
Hatch, John P., Mar. 13, '65.
Hawley, Jos. R., Sept. 28, '65.
Hayes, Joseph, Mar. 13, '65.
Hayes, Ruth. B., Mar. 13, '65.
Hays, Alex., May 5, '65.
Heath, H. H., Mar. 13, '65.
Hill, Chas. W., Mar. 13, '65.
Hinks, Edw. W., Mar. 13, '65.
Hovey, Chas. E., Mar. 13, '65.
Howe, Al. P., July 13, '65.
Jackson, N. J., Mar. 13, '65.
Jackson, R. H., Nov. 24, '65.
Jourdan, Jas., Mar. 13, '65.
Kane, Thos. L., Mar. 13, '65.
Keifer, J. W., April 9, '65.
Kelly, Benj. F., Mar. 13, '65.
Kenly, John R., Mar. 13, '65.
Ketcham, J. H., Mar. 13, '65.
Kiddoo, Jos. B., Sept. 4, '65.
Kimball, Nathan, Feb. 1, '65.
Kingsman, J. B., Mar. 13, '65.
Lanman, J. G., Mar. 13, '65.
Lawler, M. K., Mar. 13, '65.
Long, Eli, Mar. 13, '65.
Loring, Chas. G., July 17, '65.
Lucas, Thos. J., Mar. 26, '65.
Ludlow, Wm. H., Mar. 13, '65.
McAllister, Rbt., Mar. 13, '65.
McArthur, John, Dec. 15, '64.
McCallum, D. C., Mar. 13, '65.
McCook, E. M., Mar. 13, '65.
McCook, E. S., Mar. 13, '65.
McIvor, Jas. P., Mar. 13, '65.
McIntosh, J. B., Mar. 13, '65.
McKean, T. J., Mar. 13, '65.
McMahon, M. T., Mar. 13, '65.
McMillan, J. W., Mar. 5, '65.
McMillan, W. L., Mar. 13, '65.
McNeil, John, April 12, '65.
McQuade, Jas., Mar. 13, '65.
Mackenzie, R. S., Mar. 31, '65.
Macy, Geo. A., April 9, '65.
Madill, Henry J., Mar. 13, '65.
Marshall, E. G., Mar. 13, '65.
Martindale, J. H., Mar. 13, '65.
Maynadier, H. E., Mar. 13, '65.
Meredith, Sol., Aug. 14, '65.
Miller, John F., Mar. 13, '65.
Mindil, Geo. W., Mar. 13, '65.
Minty, R. H. G., Mar. 13, '65.
Mitchell, J. G., Mar. 13, '65.
Molineux, E. L., Mar. 13, '65.
Moore, M. F., Mar. 13, '63.
Morgan, Jas. D., Mar. 19, '65.
Morris, Wm. H., Mar. 13, '65.
Morrow, H. A., Mar. 13, '65.
Mulholland, St. C., Mar. 13, '65.
Neil, Thos. H., Mar. 13, '65.
Nye, Geo. H., Mar. 13, '65.
Oliver, John M., Mar. 13, '65.
Opdyke, Emer., Nov. 30, '64.
Osborn, Thos. O., Apr. 2, '65.
Paine, Chas. J., Jan. 15, '65.
Paine, Hal. E., Mar. 13, '65.
Palmer, I. M., Mar. 13, '65.
Parsons, L. B., Apr. 30, '65.

Patrick, M. R., Mar. 13, '65.
Pearson, A. L., May 1, '65.
Peck, Lewis M., Mar. 13, '65.
Pierce, B. R., Mar. 13, '65.
Pile, Wm. A., April 9, '65.
Plaisted, H. M., Mar. 13, '65.
Potter, Edw. E., Mar. 13, '65.
Potts, B. F., March 13, '65.
Powell, Wm. H., Mar. 13, '65.
Powers, Chas. J., Mar. 13, '65.
Ramsey, John, Mar. 13, '65.
Ransom, T. E. S., Sept. 1, '64.
Rice, Eliot W., Mar. 13, '65.
Runkle, Benj. P., Nov. 9, '65.
Roberts, Benj. S., Mar. 13, '65.
Robinson, J. C., June 27, '64.
Robinson, J. S., Mar. 13, '65.
Root, Adrian R., Mar. 13, '65.
Ruger, Thos. H., Nov. 30, '64.
Salomon, Fred'k, Mar. 13, '65.
Sanborn, John B., Feb. 10, '65.
Saxton, Rufus, Jan. 12, '65.
Scott, R. K., Dec. 5, '65.
Sewell, Wm. J., Mar. 13, '65.
Shaler, Alex., July 27, '65.
Shanks, J. P. C., Mar. 13, '65.
Sharpe, Geo. H., Mar. 13, '65.
Sibley, Henry H., Nov. 29, '65.
Sickle, H. G., Mar. 31, '65.
Slack, Jas. R., Mar. 13, '65.
Smith, G. C., Mar. 13, '65.
Smith, T. K., Mar. 13, '65.
Smyth, T. A., April 7, '65.
Spooner, B. U., Mar. 13, '65.
Sprague, J. W., Mar. 13, '65.
Stannard, Geo. J., Oct. 28, '64.
Stevenson, J. D., Mar. 13, '65.
Stoughton, W. L., Mar. 13, '65.
Sully, Alfred, Mar. 8, '65.
Thayer, John M., Mar. 13, '65.
Thomas, H. G., Mar. 13, '65.
Tibbetts, Wm. B., Mar. 13, '65.
Tidball, John C., April 2, '65.
Tillison, Davis, Mar. 13, '65.
Trowbridge, L. S., Mar. 13, '65.
Tyler, E. B., Mar. 13, '65.
Tyler, Robt. O., Aug. 1, '64.
Tyndale, Hector, Mar. 13, '65.
Ullman, Daniel, Mar. 13, '65.
Underwood, A. B., Aug. 13, '65.
Van Cleve, H. P., Mar. 13, '65.
Vandever, Wm., June 7, '65.
Veatch, Jas. C., Mar. 26, '65.
Voris, Alvin C., Nov. 15, '65.
Wadsworth, Jas. S., May 6, '64.
Walcutt, C. C., Mar. 13, '65.
Ward, Wm. T., Feb. 24, '65.
Warner Willard, Mar. 13, '65.
Warren, FitzH., Aug. 24, '65.
Washburn, H. D., July 26, '65.
Webster, Jos. D., Mar. 13, '65.
Wells, Wm., Mar. 13, '65.
West, Jas. R., Jan. 4, '66.
Wheaton, Frank, Oct. 19, '64.
Whitaker, W. C., Mar. 13, '65.
White, Julius, Mar. 13, '65.
Williams, A. S., Jan. 12, '65.
Williamson, J. A., Mar. 13, '65.
Willich, Aug., Oct. 21, '65.
Winthrop, Fred., April 1, '65.
Wood, Jas., Jr., Mar. 13, '65.
Woods, Wm. B., Mar. 13, '65.
Zook, S. K., July 2, '64.

Frank Wheaten, Brigade and
Division Commander in the
Army of the Potomac.

Richard Arnold, Originally
Colonel of the 5th Regi-
ment, U. S. Artillery.

George S. Greene Commanded
a Brigade at Antietam
and Gettysburg.

John G. Hazard, Originally
Major of the 1st Regi-
ment of Light Artillery.

FEDERAL GENERALS

No. 26

RHODE ISLAND

(ABOVE AND TO LEFT)

TENNESSEE

(BELOW AND TO RIGHT)

William Hays, Brevetted for
Gallantry on the Field.

Samuel P. Carter, Originally
Colonel 2d Regiment.

James A. Cooper, Originally
Colonel of the 6th
Regiment.

James G. Spears, Brevetted
Brigadier-General in
1862.

Robert Johnson, Originally
Colonel of the 1st
Cavalry.

William B. Campbell, Com-
missioned in 1862; Re-
signed in 1863.

The Union Generals

BRIGADIER-GENERALS
U. S. ARMY
(Full Rank)
Hammond, W. A., April 25, '62.
Taylor, Jos. P., Feb. 9, '63.

BRIGADIER-GENERALS
U. S. ARMY
(By Brevet)
Abercrombie, J. J., Mar. 13, '65.
Alexander, A. J., April 16, '65.
Alexander, B. S., Mar. 13, '65.
Alexander, E. B., Oct. '65.
Alvord, Ben., April 9, '65.
Arnold, Lewis G., Mar. 13, '65.
Babbitt, E. B., Mar. 13, '65.
Babcock, O. E., Mar. 13, '65.
Bache, H., Mar. 13, '65.
Badeau, Adam, Mar. 2, '67.
Barriger, J. W., Mar. 13, '65.
Beckwith, E. G., Mar. 13, '65.
Bell, George, April 9, '65.
Bingham, J. D., April 9, '65.
Blake, Geo. A. H., Mar. 13, '65.
Bomford, Jas. V., Mar. 13, '65.
Bonneville, B. L. E., Mar. 13, '65.
Bowers, Theo. S., April 9, '65.
Bradley, L. P., Mar. 2. '67.
Breck, Samuel, Mar. 13, '65.
Brewerton, H., Mar. 13, '65.
Brooks, Horace, Mar. 13, '65.
Brown, N. W., Oct. 15, '67.
Buell, Geo. P., Mar. 2, '67.
Burbank, Sid., Mar. 13, '65.
Burke, Martin, Mar. 13, '65.
Burns, Wm. W., Mar. 13, '65.
Burton, H. S., Mar. 13, '65.
Cady, Al., Mar. 13, '65.
Callender, F. D., April 9, '65.
Card, Benj. C., Mar. 13, '65.
Carrington, H. B., April 9, '65.
Churchill, Syl., Feb. 23, '47.
Clary, Rbt. E., Mar. 13, '65.
Clitz, Henry B., Mar. 13, '65.
Craig, Henry K., Mar. 13, '65.
Crane, Chas. H., Mar. 13, '65.
Crawford, S. W., Mar. 13, 65.
Cross, Osborn, Mar. 13, '65.
Cuyler, John M., April 9, '65.
Dana, James J., Mar. 13, '65.
Dandy, Geo. B., Mar. 13, '65.
Davis, N. H., Mar. 13, '65.
Dawson, Sam. K., Mar. 13, '65.
Day, Hannibal, Mar. 13, '65.
Dent, Fred. T., Mar. 13, '65.
DeRussey, R. E., Mar. 13, '65.
De Russy, G. A., Mar. 13, '65.
Dimick, Justin, Mar. 13, '65.
Drum, Rich. C., Mar. 13, ' 65.
Duane, Jas. C., Mar. 13, '65.
Duncan, Thos., Mar. 13, '65.
Dunn, W. McK., Mar. 13, '65.
Eastman, Seth, Aug. 9, '66.
Eaton, Joseph H., Mar. 13, '65.
Ekin, James A., Mar. 13, '65.
Finley, Clement, Mar. 13, '65.
Fitzhugh, C. L., Mar. 13, '65.
Forsyth, Jas. W., April 9, '65.
Fry, Cary H., Oct. 15, '67.

Gardner, John L., Mar. 13, '65.
Garland, John, Aug. 20, '47.
Gates, Wm., Mar. 13, '65.
Graham, L. P., Mar. 13, '65.
Graham, W. M., Mar. 13, '65.
Greene, James D., Mar. 13, '65.
Greene, Oliver D., Mar. 13, '65.
Grier, Wm. N., Mar. 13, '65.
Hagner, Peter V., Mar. 13, '65.
Haines, Thos. J., Mar. 13, '65.
Hardin, M. D., Mar. 13, '65.
Haskin, Jos. A., Mar. 13, '65.
Hayden, Julius, Mar. 13, '65.
Hays, William, Mar. 13, '65.
Hill, Bennett H., Jan. 31, '65.
Holabird, S. B., Mar. 13, '65.
Hunt, Lewis C., Mar. 13, '65.
Ibrie, George P., Mar. 2, '65.
Kelton, John C., Mar. 13, '65.
Kilburn, C. L., Mar. 13, '65.
Kingsbury, C. P., Mar. 13, '65.
Kirkham, R. W., Mar. 13, '65.
Leonard, H., Mar. 13, '65.
Leslie, Thos. J., Mar. 13, '65.
Loomis, Gus., Mar. 13, '65.
Lovell, Chas. S., Mar. 13, '65.
Lowe, Wm. W., Mar. 13, '65.
McAlester, M. D., April 9, '65.
McDougall, C., Mar. 13, '65.
McFerran, J. C., Mar. 13, '65.
McKeever, C., Mar. 13, '65.
McKibbin, D. B., Mar. 13, '65.
McLaughlin, N. B., Mar. 13, '65.
Mason, John S., Mar. 13, '65.
Maynadier, W., Mar. 13, '65.
Merchant, C. S., Mar. 13, '65.
Meyer, Albert J., Mar. 13, '65.
Michler, Nat., April 2, '65.
Miller, M. S., Mar. 13, '65.
Mills, Madison, Mar. 13, '65.
Moore, Tred., Mar. 13, '65.
Morgan, Chas. H., Mar. 13, '65.
Morgan, M. R., April 3, '65.
Morrison, P., Mar. 13, '65.
Morton, J. St. C., June, 17, '64.
Myers, Fred., Mar. 13, '65.
Myers, William, Mar. 13, '65.
Oakes, James, Mar. 30, '65.
Palfrey, John C., Mar. 26, '65.
Parker, Ely S., Mar. 2, '67.
Paul, G. R., Feb. 23, '65.
Pelouze, L. H., Mar. 13, '65.
Penrose, Wm. H., April 9, '65.
Perry, Alex. J., Mar. 13, '65.
Pitcher, Thos. G., Mar. 13, '65.
Poe, Orlando M., Mar. 13, '65.
Porter, Horace, Mar. 13, '65..
Potter, Jos. A., Mar. 13, '65.
Potter, Jos. H., Mar. 13, '65.
Prime, Fred'k E., Mar. 13, '65.
Prince, Henry, Mar. 13, '65.
Raynolds, Wm. F., Mar. 13, '65.
Reese, C. B., Mar. 13, '65.
Reeve, I. V. D., Mar. 13, '65.
Roberts, Jos., Mar. 13, '65.
Robertson, J. M., Mar. 13, '65.
Rodenbough, T. F., Mar. 13, '65.
Rodman, Thos. J., Mar. 13, '65.
Ruff, Chas. F., Mar. 13, '65.
Ruggles, Geo. D., Mar. 13, '65.

Satterlee, R. S., Sept. 2, '64.
Sawtelle, C. G., Mar. 13, '65.
Seawell, Wash., Mar. 13, '65.
Shepherd, O. L., Mar. 13, '65.
Sibley, Caleb C., Mar. 13, '65.
Sidell, Wm. H., Mar. 13, '65.
Simonson, J. S., Mar. 13, '65.
Simpson, J. H., Mar. 13, '65.
Slemmer, A. J., Mar. 13, '65.
Small, M. P., April 9, '65.
Smith, Joseph R., April 9, '65.
Sweitzer, N. B., Mar. 13, '65.
Thayer, Syl., May 31, '63.
Thom, George, Mar. 13, '65.
Thornton, W. A., Mar. 13, '65.
Tompkins, C. H., Mar. 13, '65.
Totten, James, Mar. 13, '65.
Townsend, Fred., Mar. 13, '65.
Trippler, Chas. S., Mar. 13, '65.
Vincent, T. M., Mar. 13, '65.
Vogdes, Israel B., April 9, '65.
Waite, C. A., Mar. 13, '65.
Wallen, Henry D., Mar. 13, '62.
Warner, Jas. M., April 9, '65.
Watkins, L. D., Mar. 13, '65.
Wessells, H. W., Mar. 13, '65.
Whiteley, R. H. K., Mar. 13, '65.
Williams, Rbt., Mar. 13, '65.
Wilson, Thos., Mar. 13, '65.
Wood, Rbt. C., Mar. 13, '65.
Woodruff, I. C., Mar. 13, '65.
Wright, George, Dec. 10, '64.
Wright, Jas. J. B., Mar. 13, '65.

BRIGADIER-GENERALS
U. S. VOLUNTEERS
(Full Rank)
Ammen, Jacob, July 16, '62.
Baker, Edw. D., May 17. '61.
Baker, L. C., April 26, '65.
Bayard, Geo. D., April 28, '62.
Beatty, John, Nov. 29, '62.
Biddle, Chas. J., Aug. 31, '61.
Bidwell, D. D., Aug. 11, '64.
Blenker, Louis, Aug. 9, '61.
Bohlen, Henry, April 28, '62.
Boyle, J. T., Nov. 4, '61.
Bragg, Edw. S., June 25, '64.
Bramlette, T. E., April 24, '63.
Briggs, Henry S., July 17, '62.
Brown, Egbert B., Nov. 29, '62.
Buckingham, C. P., July 16, '62.
Burbridge, S. G., June 9, '62.
Burnham, H., April 27, '64.
Busteed, Rich., Aug. 7, '62.
Campbell, C. T., Nov. 29, '62.
Campbell, W. B., June 30, '62.
Catterson, R. F., May 31, '65.
Chambers, Alex., Aug. 11, '63.
Champlin, S. G., Nov. 29, '62.
Chapin, Edw. P., June 27, '63.
Clayton, Powell, Aug. 1, '64.
Cluseret, G. P., Oct. 14, '62.
Cochrane, John, July 17, '62.
Conner, Seldon, June 11, '64.
Cooper, James, May 17, '61.
Cooper, Jos. A., July 21, '64.
Copeland, Jos. T., Nov. 29, '62.
Corcoran, M., July 21, '61.

Cowdin, Robt., Sept. 26, '62.
Craig, James, Mar. 21, '62.
Crittenden, T. T., April 28, '62.
Crocker, M. M., Nov. 29, '62.
Davis, E. J., Nov. 10, '64.
Deitzler, Geo. W., Nov. 29, '62.
Denver, Jas. W., Aug. 14, '61.
Dewey, J. A., Nov. 20, '65.
Dodge, Chas. C., Nov. 29, '62.
Dow, Neal, April 28, '62.
Duffie, Alfred N., June 23, '63.
Dumont, E., Sept. 3, '61.
Dwight, Wm., Nov. 29, '62.
Edwards, John, Sept. 26, '64.
Ellett, Alfred W., Nov. 1, '62.
Este, Geo. P., May 31, '65.
Eustis, H. L., Sept. 12, '63.
Ewing, Charles, Mar. 8, '65.
Fairchild, Lucius, Oct. 19, '65.
Farnsworth, E. J., June 29, '63.
Farnsworth, J. F., Nov. 29, '62.
Fry, Speed S., Mar. 21, '62.
Gamble, Wm., Sept. 25, '65.
Garrard, Th. T., Nov. 29, '62.
Gilbert, Chas. C., Sept. 9, '62.
Gorman, W. A., Sept. 7, '61.
Hackleman, P. A., April 28, '62.
Hamilton, A. J., Nov. 14, '62.
Harding, A. C., Mar. 13, '63.
Harker, Chas. G., Sept. 20, '63.
Harland, Edw., Nov. 29, '62.
Harrow, William, Nov. 29, '62.
Hascall, Milo S., April 25, '62.
Haupt, Herman, Sept. 5, '62.
Haynie, I. N., Nov. 29, '62.
Heckman, C. A., Nov. 29, '62.
Hicks, Thos. H., July 22, '62.
Hobson, Edw. H., Nov. 29, '62.
Hovey, A. P., April 28, '62.
Howell, J. B., Sept. 12, '64.
Jackson, C. F., July 17, '62.
Jackson, Jas. S., July 16, '62.
Jamison, C. D., Sept. 3, '61.
Johnson, Andrew, Mar. 4, '62.
Jones, Patrick H., Dec. 6, '64.
Judah, H. M., Mar. 21, '62.
Kaemerling, Guitar, Jan. 5, '64.
Keim, Wm. H., Dec. 20, '61.
Kiernan, James L., Aug. 1, '63.
King, Rufus, May 17, '61.
Kirby, Edmund, May 23, '63.
Kirk, E. N., Nov. 29, '62.
Knipe, Joseph F., Nov. 29, '62.
Krzyanowski, W., Nov. 29, '62.
Lander, F. W., May 17, '61.
Ledlie, James H., Dec. 24, '62.
Lee, Albert L., Nov. 29, '62.
Lightburn, J. A. J., Mar. 14, '63.
Lockwood, H. H., Aug. 8, '61.
Lowell, Chas. R., Oct. 19, '64.
Lyon, Nath'l., May 17, '61.
Lytle, William H., Nov. 29, '62.
McCall, G. A., May 17, '61.
McCandless, W., July 21, '64.
McCook, Daniel, July 16, '64.
McCook, R. L., Mar. 21, '62.
McGinnis, G. P., Nov. 29, '62.
McKinstry, J., Sept. 12, '61.
McLean, N. C., Nov. 29, '62.
Maltby, J. A., Aug. 4, '63.
Manson, M. D., Mar. 24, '62.
Marston, G., Nov. 29, '62.
Matthies, C. L., Nov. 29, '62.

TRUMAN SEYMOUR
Captain at Fort Sumter in 1861;
Later a Brigade Commander
in Army of the Potomac.

EDWIN H. STOUGHTON
Originally Colonel of the 4th
Vermont; Later commanded
the Second Vermont Brigade.

EDWARD H. RIPLEY
Commanded a Brigade in the
24th Corps.

ANDREW J. HAMILTON
Brigadier-General, 1862; Resigned, 1865.

GEORGE J. STANNARD
Led his Brigade against the
Flank of Pickett's Column
at Gettysburg.

JAMES M. WARNER
Colonel of the 1st Regiment
of Artillery.

JOHN W. PHELPS
Commander of a New England
Brigade in Operations on
the Gulf in 1861-2.

EDMUND J. DAVIS
Colonel 1st Texas Cavalry,
1862; Brigadier-General,
1864.

FEDERAL

GENERALS

No. 27—TEXAS

(TWO ABOVE)

VERMONT

(NINE TO LEFT)

B. S. ROBERTS
Colonel 4th Regiment.

GEORGE WRIGHT
Colonel 9th U. S. Infantry.

STEPHEN THOMAS
Colonel of the 8th Regiment.

Meagher, T. F., Feb. 3, '62.
Meredith, S. A., Nov. 29, '62.
Miller, Stephen, Oct. 26, '63.
Mitchell, R. B., April 8, '62.
Montgomery, W. R., May 17, '61.
Morgan, Geo. W., Nov. 12, '61.
Nagle, James, Sept. 10, '62.
Naglee, H. M., Feb. 4, '62.
Nickerson, F. S., Nov. 29, '62.
Orme, Wm. W., Nov. 29, '62.
Owens, Joshua T., Nov. 29, '62.
Paine, Eleazer, Sept. 3, '61.
Patterson, F. E., April 11, '62.
Phelps, John S., July 19, '62.
Phelps, John W., May 17, '61.
Piatt, Abraham, April 28, '62.
Plummer, J. B., Oct. 22, '61.
Porter, Andrew, May 17, '61.
Pratt, Calvin E., Sept. 10, '62.
Quinby, Isaac F., Mar. 17, '62.
Raum, Green B., Feb. 15, '65.
Reid, Hugh T., Mar. 13, '63.
Reilly, James W., July 30, '64.
Revere, J. W., Oct. 25, '62.
Rodman, Isaac P., April 28, '62.
Ross, Leonard F., April 25, '62.
Rowley, T. A., Nov. 29, '62.
Rice, Americus V., May 31, '65.
Rice, James C., Aug. 17, '63.
Rice, Samuel A., Aug. 4, '63.
Richardson, W. A., Sept. 3, '61.
Rutherford, F. S., June 27, '64.
Sanders, Wm. P., Oct. 18, '63.
Scammon, E. P., Oct. 15, '62.
Schimmelpfennig, Alex., Nov. 29, '62.
Schoepf, Albin, Sept. 30, '61.
Seward, W. H., Jr., Sept. 13, '64.
Shackelford, J. M., Jan. 2, '63.
Shepard, Isaac F., Oct. 27, '63.
Shepley, Geo. F., July 18, '62.
Sherman, F. T., July 21, '65.
Shields, James, Aug. 19, '61.
Sill, Joshua W., July 16, '62.
Slough, John B., Aug. 25, '62.
Smith, G. A., Sept. 19, '62.
Smith, Morgan L., July 16, 62.
Smith, T. C. H., Nov. 29, '62.
Smith, Wm. S., April 15, '62.
Spears, James G., Mar. 5, '62.
Spinola, F. B., June 8, '65.
Sprague, John W., July 21, '64.
Sprague, Wm., May 17, '61.
Starkweather, J. C., July 17, '63.
Stevenson, T. G., Mar. 14, '63.
Stokes, James H., July 20, '65.
Stolbrand, C. J., Feb. 18, '65.
Stone, C. P., May 17, '61.
Stoughton, E. H., Nov. 5, '62.
Strong, Wm. K., Sept. 28, '61.
Stuart, D., Nov. 29, '62.
Stumbaugh, F. S., Nov. 29, '62.
Sullivan, J. C., April 28, '62.
Sweeney, T. W., Nov. 29, '62.
Taylor, Geo. W., May 9, '62.
Taylor, Nelson, Sept. 7, '62.
Terrill, Wm. R., Sept. 9, '62.
Terry, Henry D., July 17, '62.
Thomas, Stephen, Feb. 1, '65.
Thurston, C. M., Sept. 7, '61.

Todd, John B. S., Sept. 19, '65.
Turchin, John B., July 17, '62.
Tuttle, James M., June 9, '62.
Tyler, Daniel, Mar. 13, '62.
Van Allen, J. H., April 15, '62.
Van Derveer, F., Oct. 4, '64.
Van Wyck, C. H., Sept. 27, '65.
Viele, Egbert L., Aug. 17, '61.
Vincent, Strong, July 3, '63.
Vinton, F. L., Sept. 19, '62.
Vogdes, Israel, Nov. 29, '62.
Von Steinwehr, Adolph, Oct. 12, '61.
Wade, M. S., Oct. 1, '61.
Wagner, Geo. D., Nov. 29, '62.
Wallace, W. H. L., Mar. 21, '62.
Ward, John H. H., Oct. 4, '62.
Weber, Max, April 28, '62.
Weed, Stephen H., June 6, '63.
Welsh, Thomas, Mar. 13, '63.
Wild, Edw. A., April 24, '63.
Williams, D. H., Nov. 29, '62.
Williams Thos., Sept. 28, '61.
Wistar, Isaac, Nov. 29, '62.

BRIGADIER–GENERALS
U. S. VOLUNTEERS
(By Brevet)

Abbott, Ira C., Mar. 13, '65.
Abbott, J. C., Jan. 5, '65.
Abert, Wm. S., Mar. 13, '65.
Acker, Geo. S., Mar. 13, '65.
Adams, A. W., Mar. 13, '65.
Adams, Chas. F., Mar. 13, '65.
Adams, Chas. P., Mar. 13, '65.
Adams, Chas. W., Feb. 13, '65.
Adams, Robt. N., Mar. 13, '65.
Adams, Will. A., Mar. 13, '65.
Agnus, Felix, Mar. 13, '65.
Albright, Chas., Mar. 7, '65.
Alden, Alonzo, Jan. 15, '65.
Allaire, A. J., June 28, '65.
Allcock, Thos. R., Mar. 13, '65.
Allen, Harrison, Mar. 13, '65.
Allen, Thos. S., Mar. 13, '65.
Ames, John W., Jan. 15, '65.
Ames, William, Mar. 13, '65.
Amory, Thos. J. C., Oct. 7, '64.
Anderson, A. L., Mar. 13, '65.
Anderson, J. F., April 2, '65.
Anderson, W. B., Mar. 13, '65.
Anthony, DeW. C., Mar. 13, '65.
Appleton, J. F., Mar. 13, '65.
Armstrong, S. C., Mar. 13, '65.
Askew, Franklin, July 14, '65.
Astor, John J., Jr., Mar. 13, '65.
Aukeny, Rollin V., Mar. 13, '65.
Averill, John T., Oct. 18, '65.
Avery, Mat. H., Mar. 13, '65.
Babcock, W., Sept. 19, '65.
Bailey, Silas M., Mar. 13, '65.
Baker, James H., Mar. 13, '65.
Balch, Joseph P., Mar. 13, '65.
Baldey, George, Mar. 13, '65.
Baldwin, Chas. P., April 1, '65.
Baldwin, Wm. H., Aug. 22, '65.
Ball, Wm. H., Oct. 19, '64.
Ballier, John F., July 13, '64.
Ballock, G. W., Mar. 13, '65.
Bangs, Isaac S., Mar. 13, '65.
Bankhead, H. C., April 1, '65.

Barber, G. M., Mar. 13, '65.
Barnes, Charles, Sept. 28, '65.
Barney, A. M., Mar. 11, '65.
Barney, B. G., Mar. 13, '65.
Barnett, James, Mar. 13, '65.
Barrett, Theo. H., Mar. 13, '65.
Barrett, W. W., Mar. 13, '65.
Barstow, Wilson, April 2, '65.
Barstow, S. F., Mar. 13, '65.
Bartholomew, O. A., Mar. 13, '65.
Bartlett, C. G., Mar. 13, '65.
Bartlett, Wm. C., Mar. 13, '65.
Barton, Wm. B., Mar. 13, '65.
Bassett, Isaac C., Dec. 12, '64.
Batchelder, R. N., Mar. 13, '65.
Bates, Delavan, July 30, '64.
Bates, Erastus N., Mar. 13, '65.
Baxter, D. W. C., Mar. 13, '65.
Beadis, John E., Mar. 13, '65.
Beadle, W. H. H., Mar. 16, '66.
Beaver, James A., Aug. 1, '64.
Bedel, John, Jan. 5, '65.
Beecher, James C., Mar. 13, '65.
Bell, John H., Nov. 30, '65.
Bell, J. W., Feb. 13, '65.
Bendix, John E., Mar. 13, '65.
Benedict, Lewis, April 9, '64.
Benjamin, W. H., Mar. 13, '65.
Bennett, John E., April 6, '65.
Bennett, T. W., Mar. 5, '65.
Bennett, Wm. T., May 25, '65.
Bentley, A. W., Mar. 13, '65.
Bentley, R. C., Mar. 13, '65.
Benton, Jr., T. H., Dec. 15, '64.
Berdan, Hiram, Mar. 13, '65.
Bertram, Henry, Mar. 13, '65.
Beveridge, J. L., Feb. 7, '65.
Biddle, James, Mar. 13, '65.
Biggs, Herman, Mar. 8, '65.
Biggs, Jonathan, Mar. 13, '65.
Biles, E. R., Mar. 13, '65.
Bingham, H. H., April 9, '65.
Bintliff, James, April 2, '65.
Bishop, J. W., June 7, '65.
Black, J. C., Mar. 13, '65.
Blackman, A. M., Oct. 27, '64.
Blair, C. W., Feb. 13, '65.
Blair, Louis J., Mar. 13, '65.
Blair, W. H., Mar. 13, '65.
Blaisdell, W., Jan. 23, '64.
Blakeslee, E., Mar. 13, '65.
Blanchard, J. W., Mar. 13, '65.
Blanden, L., Mar. 26, '65.
Bloomfield, Ira A., Mar. 13, '65.
Blunt, Asa P., Mar. 13, '65.
Bodine, R. L., Mar. 13, '65.
Bolinger, H. C., Mar. 13, '65.
Bolles, John A., July 17, '65.
Bolton, Wm. J., Mar. 13, '65.
Bond, John R., Mar. 13, '65.
Bonham, Edw., Mar. 13, '65.
Boughton, H., Mar. 11, '65.
Bouton, Edw., Feb. 28, '65.
Bowen, T. M., Feb. 13, '65.
Bowerman, R. N., April 1, '65.
Bowie, Geo. W., Mar. 13, '65.
Bowman, S. M., Mar. 13, '65.
Bowyer, Eli, Mar. 13, '65.
Boyd, Joseph F., Mar. 13, '65.
Boynton, H. V. N., Mar. 13, '65.

Boynton, H., Mar. 13, '65.
Bradshaw, R. C., Mar. 13, '65.
Brady, T. J., Mar. 13, '65.
Brailey, M. R., Mar. 13, '65.
Brayton, C. R., Mar. 13, '65.
Brewster, W. R., Dec. 2, '64.
Brinkerhoff, R., Sept. 20, '65.
Briscoe, Jas. C., Mar. 13, '65.
Broadhead, T. F., Aug. 30, '62.
Bronson, S., Sept. 28, '65.
Browne, T. M., Mar. 13, '65.
Browne, W. H., Mar. 13, '65.
Brown, C. E., Mar. 13, '65.
Brown, H. L., Sept. 3, '64.
Brown, J. M., Mar. 13, '65.
Brown, L. G., Mar. 13, '65.
Brown, O., Jan. 6, '66.
Brown, P. P., Mar. 13, '65.
Brown, S. B., Jr., Mar. 13, '65.
Brown, S. I., Mar. 13, '65.
Brown, T. F., Mar. 13, '65.
Brown, Wm. R., Mar. 13, '65.
Brownlow, J. P., Mar. 13, '65.
Bruce, John, Mar. 13, '65.
Brumback, J., Mar. 13, '65.
Brush, D. H., Mar. 13, '65.
Bukey, Van H., Mar. 13, '65.
Burke, J. W., Mar. 13, '65.
Burling, G. C., Mar. 13, '65.
Burnett, H. L., Mar. 13, '65.
Busey, S. T., April 9, '65.
Butler, T. H., Mar. 13, '65.
Callis, J. B., Mar. 13, '65.
Cameron, D., Mar. 13, '65.
Cameron, Hugh, Mar. 13, '65.
Campbell, C. J., Mar. 13, '65.
Campbell, E. L., June 2, '65.
Campbell, J. M., Mar. 13, '65.
Campbell, J. A., Mar. 13 '65.
Candy, Charles, Mar. 13, '65.
Capron, Horace, Feb. 13, '65.
Carle, James, Mar. 13, '65.
Carleton, C. A., Mar. 13, '65.
Carman, Ezra A., Mar. 13, '65.
Carnahan, R. H., Oct. 28, '65.
Carruth, Sumner, April 2, '65.
Carson, Chris., Mar. 13, '65.
Case, Henry, Mar. 16, '65.
Casement, J. S., Jan. 25, '65.
Cassidy, A. L., Mar. 13, '65.
Cavender, J. S., Mar. 13, '65.
Chamberlain, S. E., Feb. 24, '65.
Champion, T. E., Feb. 20, '65.
Chickering, T. E., Mar. 13, '65.
Chipman, H. L., Mar. 13, '65.
Chipman, N. P., Mar. 13, '65.
Christ, B. C., Aug. 1, '64.
Christensen, C. T., Mar. 13, '65.
Christian, W. H., Mar. 13, 'C5.
Churchill, M., Mar. 13, '65.
Cilly, J. P., June 2, '65.
Cist, H. M., Mar. 13, '65.
Clapp, D. E., Mar. 13, '65.
Clark, G. W., Mar. 13, '65.
Clark, J. S., Mar. 13, '65.
Clarke, Gideon, Mar. 13, '65.
Clarke, Wm. H., Mar. 13, '65.
Clay, Cecil, Mar. 13, '65.
Clendenin, D. R., Feb. 20, '65
Clough, J. M., Mar. 13, '65.
Coates, B. F., Mar. 13, '65.

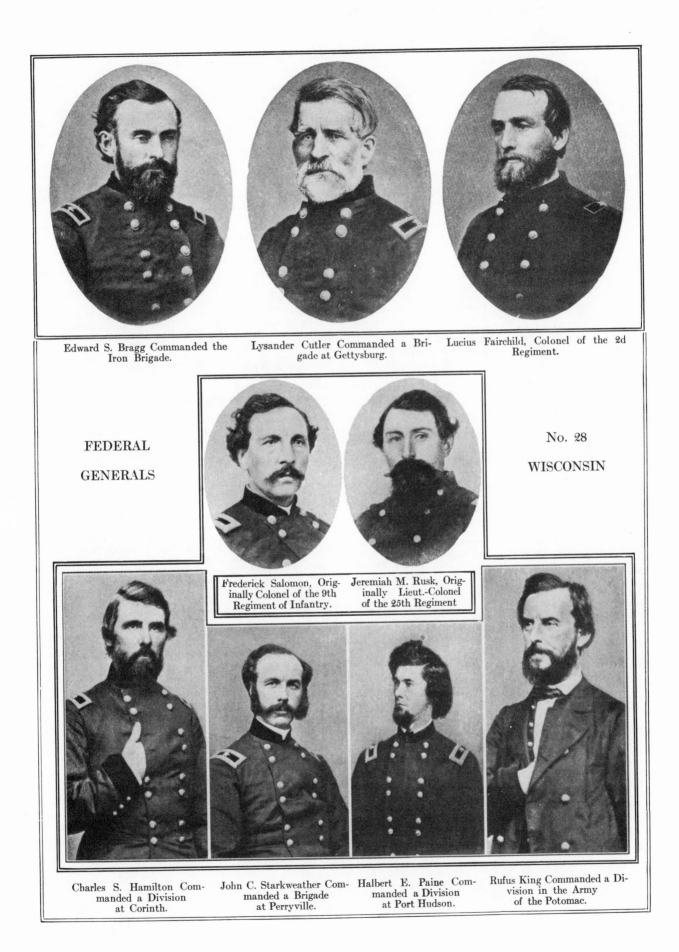

Edward S. Bragg Commanded the Iron Brigade.

Lysander Cutler Commanded a Brigade at Gettysburg.

Lucius Fairchild, Colonel of the 2d Regiment.

FEDERAL

GENERALS

No. 28

WISCONSIN

Frederick Salomon, Originally Colonel of the 9th Regiment of Infantry.

Jeremiah M. Rusk, Originally Lieut.-Colonel of the 25th Regiment

Charles S. Hamilton Commanded a Division at Corinth.

John C. Starkweather Commanded a Brigade at Perryville.

Halbert E. Paine Commanded a Division at Port Hudson.

Rufus King Commanded a Division in the Army of the Potomac.

Coates, J. H., Mar. 13, '65.
Cobb, Amasa, Mar. 13, '65.
Cobham, G. A., Jr., July 19, '64.
Coburn, J., Mar. 13, '65.
Cockerill, J. R., Mar. 13, '65.
Coggswell, W., Dec. 15, '64.
Coit, J. B., Mar. 13, '65.
Colgrove, Silas, Aug. 4, '64.
Collier, F. H., Mar. 13, '65.
Colville, Jr., W., Mar. 3, '65.
Comly, J. M., Mar. 13, '65.
Commager, H. S., Mar. 13, '65.
Congdon, J. A., Mar. 13, '65.
Conklin, J. T., Mar. 13, '65.
Conrad, J., Mar. 13, '65.
Cook, Edw. F., Mar. 13, '65.
Coon, D. E., Mar. 8, '65.
Corbin, H. C., Mar. 13, '65.
Coughlin, John, April 9, '65.
Cowan, B. R., Mar. 13, '65.
Cox, John C., July 4, '63.
Cox, Rob't C., April 2, '65.
Cram, Geo. H., Mar. 13, '62.
Cramer, F. L., Mar. 13, '65.
Crandal, F. M., Oct. 24, '65.
Crane, M. M., Mar. 13, '65.
Cranor, Jonathan, Mar. 3, '65.
Crawford, S. J., Mar. 13, '65.
Crocker, J. S., Mar. 13, '65.
Crowinshield, C., Mar. 13, '65.
Cummings, Alex., Apr. 19, '65.
Cummings, G. W., Mar. 13, '65.
Cummins, J. E., Mar. 13, '65.
Cunningham, J. A., Apr. 1, '65.
Curly, Thos., Mar. 13, '65.
Curtin, John J., Oct. 12, '64.
Curtis, A. R., Mar. 13, '65.
Curtis, G. S., Mar. 13, '65.
Curtis, J. F., Mar. 13, '65.
Curtis, Wm. B., Mar. 13, '65.
Curtiss, J. E., Mar. 13, '65.
Cutcheon, B. M., Mar. 13, '65.
Cutting, Wm., April 2, '65.
Cutts, R. D., Mar. 13, '65.
Daggett, A. S., Mar. 13, '65.
Daggett, Rufus, Jan. 15, '65.
Dana, E. L., July 26, '65.
Darr, Francis, Mar. 13, '65.
Dawson, A. R. Z., Nov. 21, '65.
Davis, E. P., Oct. 19, '64.
Davis, Hasbrook, Feb. 13, '65.
Davis, H. G., Mar. 13, '65.
Davis, W. W. H., Mar. 13, '65.
Day, Henry M., Mar. 26, '65.
Day, Nich. W., Mar. 13, '65.
Dayton, Oscar V., Mar. 13, '65.
Dawes, R. R., Mar. 18, '65.
Deems, J. M., Mar. 13, '65.
De Groat, C. H., Mar. 13, '65.
De Hart, R. P., Mar. 13, '65.
De Lacey, Wm., Mar. 13, '65.
De Land, C. V., Mar. 13, '65.
Dennis, John B., Mar. 13, '65.
Devereux, A. F., Mar. 13, '65.
De Witt, D. P., Mar. 13, '65.
Dick, Geo. F., Mar. 13, '65.
Dickerson, C. J., Mar. 13, '65.
Dickey, Wm. H., Mar. 13, '65.
Dickinson, Jos., Mar. 13, '65.
Dilworth, C. J., Mar. 13, '65.
Dimon, C. A. R., Mar. 13, '65.
Diven, Alex. S., Aug. 30, '64.
Diven, C. W., Mar. 25, '65.

Dixon, Wm. D., Mar. 13, '65.
Doan, A. W., Mar. 13, '65.
Dodd, Levi A., April 2, '65.
Dodge, Geo. S., Jan. 15, '65.
Donohue, M. T., Mar. 13, '65.
Doster, Wm. E., Mar. 13, '65.
Doubleday, U., Mar. 11, '65.
Dox, Ham. B., Feb. 13, '65.
Drake, Francis M., Feb. 22, '65.
Drake, Geo. B., Mar. 13, '65.
Draper, Alonzo G., Oct. 28, '64.
Draper, W. F., Mar. 13, '65.
Drew, C. W., Mar. 13, '65.
Ducat, A. C., Mar. 13, '65.
Dudley, N. A. M., Jan. 19, '65.
Dudley, Wm. W., Mar. 13, '65.
Duer, John O., July 12, '65.
Duff, Wm. L., Mar. 13, '65.
Dunham, T. H., Jr., Mar. 13, '65.
Dunlap, H. C., Mar. 13, '62.
Dunlap, James, Mar. 13, '65.
Duryea, Hiram, Mar. 13, '65.
Duryee, J. E., Mar. 13, '65.
Dustin, Daniel, Mar. 13, '65.
Dutton, A. H., May 16, '64.
Dutton, E. F., Mar. 16, '65.
Duval, Hiram F., Mar. 13, '65.
Dye, Wm. McE., Mar. 13, '65.
Dyer, Isaac, Mar. 13, '65.
Eaton, Chas. G., Mar. 13, '65.
Eaton, John, Jr., Mar. 13, '65.
Eckert, Thos. T., Mar. 13, '65.
Edgerton, A. J., Mar. 13, '65.
Edmonds, J. C., Mar. 13, '65.
Edwards, C. S., Mar. 13, '65.
Eggleston, B. B., Mar. 13, '62.
Eldridge, H. N., Mar. 13, '65.
Elliott, I. H., Mar. 13, '65.
Elliott, S. M., Mar. 13, '65.
Ellis, A. VanHorn, July 2, '63.
Ellis, Theo. G., Mar. 13, '65.
Elstner, G. R., Aug. 8, '64.
Elwell, J. J., Mar. 13, '65.
Ely, Ralph, April 2, '65.
Ely, Wm. C., April 13, '65.
Engleman, A., Mar. 13, '65.
Enochs, Wm. H., Mar. 13, '65.
Ent, W. H., Mar. 13, '65.
Enyart, D. A., Mar. 13, '62.
Erskine, Albert, Feb. 13, '65.
Estes, L. G., Mar. 13, '65.
Evans, George S., Mar. 13, '65.
Everett, Charles, Mar. 13, '65.
Fairchild, C., Mar. 13, '65.
Fairchild, H. S., Mar. 13, '65.
Fallows, Samuel, Oct. 24, '65.
Fardella, Enrico, Mar. 13, '65.
Farnum, J. E., Jan. 3, '66.
Farnsworth, A., Sept. 27, '65.
Farrar, B. G., Mar. 9, '65.
Fearing, Benj. D., Dec. 2, '64.
Fisher, Benj. F., Mar. 13, '65.
Fisher, Joseph W., Nov. 4, '65.
Fisk, Henry C., April 6, '65.
Fiske, Frank S., Mar. 13, '65.
Fiske, Wm. O., Mar. 13, '65.
Fitzsimmons, C., Mar. 13, '65.
Flanigan, Mark, Mar. 13, '65.
Fleming, R. E., Mar. 13, '64.
Fletcher, T. C., Mar. 13, '65.
Flood, Martin, Mar. 13, '65.
Flynn, John, Mar. 13, '65.

Fonda, John G., June 28, '65.
Ford, James H., Dec. 10, '65.
Forsyth, Geo. A., Feb. 13, '65.
Foster, Geo. P., Aug. 1, '64.
Foster, John A., Sept. 28, '65.
Foust, B. F., Mar. 13, '65.
Fowler, Edw. B., Mar. 13, '65.
Franchot, R., Mar. 13, '65.
Francine, Louis R., July 2, '63.
Frank, Paul, Mar. 13, '65.
Frankle, Jones, Sept. 3, '65.
Frazer, D., Mar. 13, '65.
Frazer, John, Mar. 13, '65.
Frederick, C. H., Mar. 13, '65.
French, W. B., Mar. 13, '65.
Frink, Henry A., Oct. 4, '65.
Frisbie, H. N., Mar. 13, '65.
Fritz, Peter, Jr., Mar. 13, '65.
Frizell, J. W., Mar. 13, '65.
Frohock, Wm. T., Mar. 13, '65.
Fuller, H. W., Mar. 13, '65.
Fullerton, J. S., Mar. 13, '65.
Funke, Otto, Feb. 13, '65.
Fyffe, Edw. P., Mar. 13, '65.
Gage, Joseph S., June 15, '65.
Gallagher, T. F., Mar. 13, '65.
Gallup, Geo. W., Mar. 13, '62.
Gansevoort, H. S., June 24, '64.
Gardiner, Alex., Sept. 19, '64.
Garrard, Israel, June 20, '65.
Garrard, Jephtha, Mar. 13, '65.
Gates, Theo. B., Mar. 13, '65.
Geddes, James L., June 5, '65.
Gerhardt, Joseph, Mar. 13, '65.
Gibson, H. G., Mar. 13, '65.
Gibson, Wm. H., Mar. 13, '65.
Giesy, Henry H., May 28, '64.
Gilbert, S. A., Mar. 13, '65.
Gilchrist, C. A., Mar. 26, '65.
Gile, Geo. W., May 6, '65.
Ginty, Geo. C., Sept. 28, '65.
Given, Josiah, Mar. 13, '65.
Given, William, Mar. 13, '65.
Glasgow, S. L., Dec. 19, '64.
Gleason, Newell, Mar. 13, '65.
Glenny, Wm., Mar. 13, '65.
Gobin, J. P. S., Mar. 13, '65.
Goddard, Wm., Mar. 13, '65.
Godman, J. H., Mar. 13, '65.
Goff, Nathan, Jr., Mar. 13, '65.
Goodell, A. A., Mar. 13, '65.
Goodyear, E. D. S., April 2, '65.
Gowan, Geo. W., April 2, '65.
Graham, Harvey, July 25, '65.
Graham, Samuel, Mar. 13, '65.
Granger, Geo. F., June 12, '65.
Greeley, Edwin S., Mar. 13, '65.
Green, Wm. M., May 14, '64.
Gregg, Wm. M., April 2, '65.
Grier, D. P., Mar. 26, '65.
Griffin, Dan'l F., Mar. 13, '65.
Grindlay, James, Mar. 13, '65.
Grosvenor, C. H., Mar. 13, '65.
Grosvenor, T. W., Feb. 13, '65.
Grover, Ira G., Mar. 13, '65.
Grubb, E. Burd, Mar. 13, '65.
Guiney, P. R., Mar. 13, '65.
Guppy, Joshua J., Mar. 13, '65.
Gurney, William, May 19, '65.
Hall, Caldwell K., Mar. 13, '65.
Hall, Cyrus, Mar. 13, '65.
Hall, H. Seymour, Mar. 13, '65.
Hall, Jas. A., Mar. 3, '65.

Hall, James F., Feb. 24, '65.
Hall, Jarius W., Mar. 13, '65.
Hall, Rob't M., Mar. 13, '65.
Hallowell, E. N., June 27, '65.
Halpine, C. G., Mar. 13, '65.
Hamilton, W. D., April 9, '65.
Hamlin, Chas., Mar. 13, '65.
Hammell, John S., Mar. 13, '65.
Hammond, J. H., Oct. 31, '64.
Hammond, John, Mar. 13, '65.
Hanbreght, H. A., June 7, '65.
Hanna, Wm., Mar. 13, '65.
Hardenbergh, J. B., Mar. 13, '65.
Harding, C., Jr., May 27, '65.
Harlin, E. B., Mar. 13, '65.
Harnden, Henry, Mar. 13, '65.
Harriman, Sam'l, April 2, '65.
Harriman, W., Mar. 13, '65.
Harris, A. L., Mar. 13, '65.
Harris, Benj. F., Mar. 13, '65.
Harris, Chas. L., Mar. 13, '65.
Harrison, Benj., Jan. 23, '65.
Harrison, M. LaRue, Mar. 13, '65.
Harrison, T. J., Jan. 31, '65.
Hart, James H., Mar. 13, '65.
Hart, O. H., Mar. 13, '65.
Hartshorne, W. R., Mar. 13, '65.
Hartsuff, Wm., Jan. 24, '64.
Hartwell, A. S., Dec. 30, '64.
Hartwell, C. A., Dec. 2, '65.
Haskill, L. F., Mar. 13, '65.
Hastings, R., Mar. 13, '65.
Haughton, Nath'l, Mar. 13, '65.
Hawkes, Geo. P., Mar. 13, '65.
Hawkins, I. R., Mar. 13, '65.
Hawkins, R. C., Mar. 13, '65.
Hawley, William, Mar. 16, '65.
Hayes, P. C., Mar. 13, '65.
Hayman, S. B., Mar. 13, '65.
Hays, E. L., Jan. 12, '65.
Hazard, J. G., Mar. 13, '65.
Healy, R. W., Mar. 13, '65.
Heath, Francis, Mar. 13, '65.
Heath, Thomas T., Dec. 15, '64.
Hedrick, J. M., Mar. 13, '65.
Heine, Wm., Mar. 13, '65.
Heinrichs, Gus., Mar. 13, '65.
Henderson, R. M., Mar. 13, '65.
Henderson, T. J., Nov. 30, '64.
Hendrickson, J., Mar. 13, '65.
Hennessey, J. A., Mar. 13, '65.
Henry, Guy V., Oct. 28, '64.
Henry, Wm. W., Mar. 7, '65.
Herrick, W. F., May 13, '65.
Herring, Chas., Mar. 13, '65.
Hickenlooper, A., Mar. 13, '65.
Hill, Jonathan A., April 9, '65.
Hill, Sylvester G., Dec. 15, '64.
Hillis, David B., Mar. 13, '65.
Hillyer, W. S., Mar. 13, '65.
Hitchcock, G. H., Mar. 13, '65.
Hobart, H. C., Jan. 12, '65.
Hobson, Wm., April 6, '65.
Hoffman, H. C., Mar. 13, '65.
Hoffman, Wm. J., Aug. 1, '64.
Hoge, Geo. B., Mar. 13, '65.
Hoge, George W., Mar. 13, '65.
Holbrook, M. T., Mar. 13, '65.
Holloway, E. S., Mar. 13, '65.

David H. Strother, of Virginia, Originally Colonel 3d West Virginia Cavalry.

Thomas M. Harris, of West Virginia, Originally Colonel of the 10th Infantry.

Lawrence P. Graham, of Virginia, Organized and Led a Cavalry Brigade in the Army of the Potomac.

FEDERAL GENERALS
No. 29
VIRGINIA AND
WEST VIRGINIA

Henry Capehart, of West Virginia, Colonel 1st Cavalry.

John W. Davidson, of Virginia, Promoted for the Capture of Little Rock.

James A. Hardie, of West Virginia, Brevetted for Distinguished Services.

Robert C. Buchanan, of District of Columbia, Brevetted for Gallantry.

WEST VIRGINIA
AND DISTRICT
OF COLUMBIA

Henry B. Carrington, Originally Colonel of the 18th West Virginia Infantry.

Richard H. Jackson, of District of Columbia, Brevetted for Gallantry During the War.

Holman, J. H., Mar. 13, '65.
Holt, Thomas, Mar. 13, '65.
Holter, M. J. W., Mar. 13, '65.
Hooker, A. E., Mar. 13, '65.
Horn, John W., Oct. 19, '64.
Hotchkiss, C. T., Mar. 13, '65.
Hough, John, March 13, '65.
Houghtaling, Chas., Feb. 13, '65.
Houghton, M. B., Mar. 13, '65.
Howard, Chas. H., Aug. 15, '65.
Howe, John H., Mar. 13, '65.
Howland, H. N., Mar. 13, '62.
Howland, Joseph, Mar. 13, '65.
Hoyt, Chas. H., Mar. 13, '65.
Hoyt, Geo. H., Mar. 13, '65.
Hoyt, Henry M., Mar. 13, '65.
Hubbard, James, April 6, '65.
Hubbard, L. F., Dec. 16, '64.
Hubbard, T. H., June 30, '65.
Hudnutt, Jos. O., Mar. 13, '65.
Hudson, John G., Mar. 13, '65.
Huey, Pennock, Mar. 13, '65.
Hugunin, J. R., Mar. 13, '65.
Humphrey, T. W., June 10, '65.
Humphrey, Wm., Aug. 1, '64.
Hunt, Lewis C., Mar. 13, '65.
Hunter, M. C., Mar. 13, '65.
Hurd, John R., Mar. 13, '65.
Hurst, Samuel H., Mar. 13, '65.
Hutchins, Rue P., Mar. 13, '65.
Hutchinson, F. S., May 24, '65.
Hyde, Thomas W., April 2, '65.
Ingraham, T., Oct. 2, '65.
Innes, Wm. P., Mar. 13, '65.
Irvine, Wm., March 13, '65.
Irvin, William H., Mar. 13, '65.
Ives, Brayton, March 13, '65.
Jacobs, Ferris, Jr., Mar. 13, '65.
Jackson, S. M., March 13, '64.
Jackson, Jos. C., Mar. 13, '65.
James, W. L., March 1, '66.
Jardine, Edw., Nov. 2, '65.
Jarvis, Dwight, Jr., Mar. 13, '65.
Jeffries, Noah L., Mar. 30, '65.
Jenkins, H., Jr., March 13, '65.
Jennison, S. P., March 13, '65.
Johnson, Chas. A., Mar. 13, '65.
Johnson, G. M. L., Mar. 13, '65.
Johnson, J. M., March 13, '65.
Johnson, Lewis, March 13, '65.
Johnson, Robert, Mar. 13, '65.
Johns, Thos. D., March 13, '65.
Jones, J. B., March 13, '65.
Jones, Edward F., Mar. 13, '65.
Jones, Fielder A., Mar. 13, '65.
Jones, John S., March 13, '65.
Jones, Samuel B., Mar. 31, '65.
Jones, Theodore, Mar. 13, '65.
Jones, Wells S., Mar. 13, '65.
Jones, Wm. P., March 13, '65.
Jordan, Thos. J., Feb. 25, '65.
Judson, R. W., July 28, '66.
Judson, Wm. R., Mar. 13, '65.
Karge, Jonah, March 13, '65.
Keily, D. J., March 13, '65.
Kellogg, John A., April 9, '65.
Kelly, John H., Feb. 13, '65.
Kennedy, R. P., March 13, '65.
Kent, Loren, March 22, '65.
Kennett, H. G., March 13, '65.
Ketner, James, March 13, '65.

Kidd, James H., Mar. 13, '65.
Kilgour, Wm. M., June 20, '65.
Kimball, John W., Mar. 13, '65.
Kimball, Wm. R., Mar. 13, '65.
Kimberly, R. L., Mar. 13, '65.
King, Adam E., Mar. 13, '65.
King, John F., March 13, '65.
King, Wm. S., March 13, '65.
Kingsbury, H. D., Mar. 10, '65.
Kinney, T. J., March 26, '65.
Kinsey, Wm. B., Mar. 13, '65.
Kirby, Byron, Sept. 6, '65.
Kirby, Dennis T., Mar. 13, '65.
Kirby, Isaac M., Jan. 12, '65.
Kise, Reuben C., Mar. 13, '65.
Kitchell, Edward, Mar. 13, '65.
Kitching, J. H., Aug. 1, '64.
Kneffner, Wm. C., Mar. 13, '65.
Knefler, Fred'k, Mar. 13, '65.
Knowles, Oliv. B., Mar. 13, '65.
Kozlay, E. A., March 13, '65.
Krez, Conrad, March 26, '65.
Lafflin, Byron, March 13, '65.
Lagow, C. B., March 13, '65.
La Grange, O. H., Mar. 13, '65.
La Motte, C. E., Mar. 13, '65.
Landram, Wm. J., Mar. 13, '62.
Lane, John Q., March 13, '65.
Langdon, E. Bassett, Mar. 13, '65.
Lansing, H. S., Mar. 13, '65.
Laselle, Wm. P., Mar. 13, '65.
Laughlin, R. G., Mar. 13, '65.
Latham, Geo. R., Mar. 13, '65.
Lawrence, A. G., Mar. 25, '65.
Lawrence, Wm. Henry, Mar. 13, '65.
Lawrence, Wm. Hudson, Mar. 13, '65.
Leake, Jos. B., March 13, '65.
Le Duc, Wm. G., Mar. 13, '65.
Lee, Horace C., Mar. 13, '65.
Lee, Edward M., Mar. 13, '65.
Lee, John C., March 13, '65.
Lee, Wm. R., March 13, '65.
Le Favour, H., March 13, '65.
Le Gendre, C. W., Mar. 13, '65.
Leech, Wm. A., Mar. 13, '65.
Leib, Herman, March 13, '65.
Leiper, Chas. L., Mar. 13, '65.
Lewis, Chas. W., Mar. 13, '65.
Lewis, John R., March 13, '65.
Lewis, W. D., Jr., Mar. 13, '65.
Lincoln, Wm. S., June 23, '65.
Locke, Fred'k. T., April 1, '65.
Lockman, J. T., March 13, '65.
Loomis, Cyrus O., June 20, '65.
Lord, T. Ellery, Mar. 13, '65.
Love, George M., Mar. 7, '65.
Lovell, Fred'k S., Oct. 11, '65.
Lindley, J. M., March 13, '65.
Lippincott, C. E., Feb. 17, '65.
Lippitt, Francis J., Mar. 3, '65.
Lister, Fred. W., Mar. 13, '65.
Litchfield, A. C., Mar. 13, '65.
Littell, John S., Jan. 15, '65.
Littlejohn, De Witt C., Mar. 13, '65.
Littlefield, M. S., Nov. 26, '65.
Livingston, R. R., June 21, '65.
Ludington, M. J., Mar. 13, '65.
Ludlow, Benj. C., Oct. 28, '64.
Lyle, Peter, Mar. 13, '65.

Lyman, Luke, Mar. 13, '65.
Lynch, Jas. C., Mar. 13, '65.
Lynch, Wm. F., Jan. 31, '65.
Lyon, Wm. P., Oct. 26, '65.
McArthur, W. M., Mar. 13, '65.
McBride, J. D., Mar. 13, '65.
McCall, W. H. H., April 2, '65.
McCalmont, A. B., Mar. 13, '65.
McCleery, Jas., Mar. 13, '65.
McCleunen, M. R., April 2, '65.
McClurg, A. C., Sept. 18, '65.
McConihe, John, June 1, '64.
McConihe, Sam., Mar. 13, '65.
McConnell, H. K., Mar. 13, '65.
McConnell, John, Mar. 13, '65.
McCook, A. G., Mar. 13, '65.
McCormick, Chas. C., Mar. 13, '65.
McCoy, Daniel, Mar. 13, '65.
McCoy, Rob't A., Mar. 13, '65.
McCoy, Thos. F., April 1, '65.
McCreary, D. B., Mar. 13, '65.
McCrillis, L., Sept. 4, '64.
McDougall, C. D., Feb. 25, '65.
McEwen, Matt., Mar. 13, '65.
McGarry, Ed., Mar. 13, '65.
McGowan, J. E., Mar. 13, '65.
McGregor, J. D., Mar. 13, '65.
McGroarty, S. J., May 1, '65.
McKenny, T. J., Mar. 13, '65.
McKibbin, G. H., Dec. 2, '64.
McLaren, R. N., Dec. 14, '65.
McMahon, J., June 30, '65.
McNary, Wm. H., Mar. 13, '65.
McNaught, T. A., Aug. 4, '65.
McNett, A. J., July 28, '65.
McNulta, John, Mar. 13, '65.
McQueen, A. G., Mar. 13, '65.
McQueston, J. C., Mar. 13, '65.
Mackey, A. J., Mar. 13, '65.
Macauley, Dan., Mar. 13, '65.
Magee, David W., Mar. 13, '65.
Malloy, Adam G., Mar. 13, '65.
Manderson, C. F., Mar. 13, '65.
Mank, Wm. G., Mar. 13, '65.
Mann, Orrin L., Mar. 13, '65.
Manning, S. H., Mar. 13, '65.
Mansfield, John, Mar. 13, '65.
Markoe, John, Mar. 13, '65.
Marple, Wm. W., Mar. 13, '65.
Marshall, W. R., Mar. 13, '65.
Martin, Jas. S., Feb. 28, '65.
Martin, John A., Mar. 13, '65.
Martin, Wm. H., June 8, '65.
Mason, Ed. C., June 3, '65.
Mather, T. S., Sept. 28, '65.
Matthews, J. A., April 2, '65.
Matthews, Sol. S., Mar. 13, '65.
Mattocks, C. P., Mar. 13, '65.
Maxwell, N. J., April 18, '65.
Maxwell, O. C., Mar. 13, '65.
May, Dwight, Mar. 13, '65.
Mehringer, John, Mar. 13, '65.
Merrill, Lewis, Mar. 13, '65.
Mersey, August, Mar. 13, '65.
Messer, John, Mar. 13, '65.
Meyers, Edw. S., Mar. 13, '65.
Michie, Peter S., Jan. 1, '65.
Miller, A. O., Mar. 13, '65.
Miller, Madison, Mar. 13, '65.
Mills, Jas. K., Mar. 13, '65.
Mintzer, Wm. M., Mar. 13, '65.
Mitchell, G. M., Aug. 22, '65.

Mitchell, W. G., Mar. 13, '65.
Mix, Elisha, Mar. 13, '65.
Mizner, H. R., Mar. 13, '65.
Mizner, John K., Mar. 13, '65.
Moffitt, Stephen, Mar. 13, '65.
Monroe, Geo. W., Mar. 13, '62.
Montgomery, M., Mar. 13, '65.
Moody, G., Jan. 12, '65.
Moon, John C., Nov. 21, '65.
Moonlight, Thos., Feb. 13, '65.
Moor, Augustus, Mar. 13, '65.
Moore, David, Feb. 21, '65.
Moore, Fred'k W., Mar. 26, '65.
Moore, Jesse H., May 15, '65.
Moore, Jon. B., Mar. 26, '65.
Moore, Tim. C., Mar. 13, '65.
Morehead, T. G., Mar. 13, '65.
Morgan, G. N., Mar. 13, '65.
Morgan, Thos. J., Mar. 13, '65.
Morgan, Wm. H., April 20, '65.
Morgan, Wm. H., Mar. 13, '65.
Morrill, John, Mar. 13, '65.
Morrison, D., Mar. 13, '65.
Morrison, Jos. J., Mar. 13, '65.
Morse, Henry B., Mar. 13, '65.
Mott, Sam'l R., Mar. 13, '65.
Mudgett, Wm. S., Mar. 13, '65.
Mulcahey, Thos., Mar. 13, '65.
Mulford, J. E., July 4, '64.
Mulligan, J. A., July 23, '65.
Mundee, Chas., April 2, '65.
Murphy, John K., Mar. 13, '65.
Murray, Benj. B., Mar. 13, '65.
Murray, Edw., Mar. 13, '65.
Murray, Ely H., Mar. 25, '65.
Murray, John B., Mar. 13, '65.
Mussey, R. D., Mar. 13, '65.
Myers, Geo. R., Mar. 13, '65.
Nase, Adam, Mar. 13, '65.
Neafie, Alfred, Mar. 13, '65.
Neff, Andrew J., Mar. 13, '65.
Neff, Geo. W., Mar. 13, '65.
Neide, Horace, Mar. 13, '65.
Nettleton, A. B., Mar. 13, '62.
Newbury, W. C., Mar. 13, '65.
Newport, R. M., Mar. 13, '65.
Nichols, Geo. F., Mar. 13, '65.
Nichols, Geo. S., Mar. 13, '65.
Niles, Nat., Mar. 13, '65.
Noble, John W., Mar. 13, '65.
Noble, Wm. H., Mar. 13, '65.
Northcott, R. S., Mar. 13, '65.
Norton, Chas. B., Mar. 13, '65.
Noyes, Edw. F., Mar. 13, '65.
Nugent, Robert, Mar. 13, '65.
O'Beirne, J. R., Sept. 26, '65.
O'Brien, Geo. M., Mar. 13, '65.
O'Dowd, John, Mar. 13, '65.
Oley, John H., Mar. 13, '65.
Oliphant, S. D., June 27, '65.
Oliver, Paul A., Mar. 8, '65.
Olmstead, W. A., April 9, '65.
Ordway, Albert, Mar. 13, '65.
Osband, E. D., Oct. 5, '64.
Osborn, F. A., Mar. 13, '65.
Otis, Calvin N., Mar. 13, '65.
Otis, Elwell S., Mar. 13, '65.
Otis, John L., Mar. 13, '65.
Ozburn, Lyndorf, Mar. 13, '65.
Packard, Jasper, Mar. 13, '65.
Painter, Wm., Mar. 13, '65.
Palfrey, F. W., Mar. 13, '65.
Palmer, Oliver H., Mar. 13, '65.

Walter P. Lane Led a Brigade of Cavalry West of the Mississippi.

William P. Hardeman Led a Brigade in Magruder's Army.

Lawrence S. Ross Commanded a Brigade in Wheeler's Cavalry.

Walter H. Stevens, Chief Engineer, Army of Northern Virginia.

Elkanah Greer Commanded the Reserve Corps, Trans-Mississippi Department.

A. P. Bagby, Originally Colonel of the 7th Cavalry; Later Led a Division.

John A. Wharton Commanded a Division of Wheeler's Cavalry in Tennessee.

James E. Harrison Commanded a Brigade of Polignac's Division in Louisiana.

William H. Young Led a Brigade in the Army of Tennessee.

John W. Whitfield Commanded a Brigade of Texas Cavalry.

Joseph L. Hogg Led a Brigade in the Army of the West.

Samuel Bell Maxcy, Originally Colonel of the 9th Infantry.

William Steele Led a Brigade at Shreveport in 1864.

CONFEDERATE GENERALS—No. 21—TEXAS

Palmer, Wm. J., Nov. 6, '64.
Partridge, F. W., Mar. 13, '65.
Partridge, B. F., Mar. 31, '65.
Parish, Chas. S., Mar. 13, '65.
Parrott, Jas. C., Mar. 13, '65.
Park, Sidney W., Mar. 13, '65.
Parkhurst, J. G., May 22, '65.
Pardee, D. A., Mar. 13, '65.
Pardee, Ario, Jr., Jan. 12, '65.
Parry, Aug. C., Mar. 13, '65.
Pattee, John, Mar. 13, '65.
Pattee, Jos. B., April 9, '65.
Patterson, R. F., Mar. 13, '65.
Patterson, R. E., Mar. 13, '65.
Patterson, J. N., Mar. 13, '65.
Patten, H. L., Sept. 10, '64.
Paul, Frank, Mar. 13, '65.
Payne, Eugene B., Mar. 13, '65.
Payne, Oliver H., Mar. 13, '65.
Pearsall, Uri B., Mar. 13, '65.
Pearson, Rbt. N., Mar. 13, '65.
Pearce, John S., Mar. 13, '65.
Pease, Phineas, Mar. 13, '65.
Pease, Wm. R., Mar. 13, '65.
Peck, Frank H., Sept. 19, '65.
Pennington, A. C. M., July 16, '65.
Perkins, H. W., Mar. 13, '65.
PerLee, Sam'l R., Mar. 13, '65.
Phelps, Chas. E., Mar. 13, '65.
Phelps, John E., Mar. 13, '65.
Phelps, W., Jr., Mar. 13, '65.
Phillips, Jesse L., Mar. 13, '65.
Pickett, Josiah, Mar. 13, '65.
Pierson, Chas. L., Mar. 13, '65.
Pierson, J. Fred., Mar. 13, '65.
Pierson, Wm. S., Mar. 13, '65.
Pierce, F. E., Mar. 13, '65.
Pinckney, Jos. C., Mar. 13, '65.
Pinto, F. E., Mar. 13, '64.
Platner, John S., Mar. 13, '65.
Pleasants, H., Mar. 13, '65.
Pollock, S. M., Mar. 13, '65.
Pomutz, Geo., Mar. 13, '65.
Pope, Ed. M., Mar. 13, '65.
Porter, Sam'l A., Mar. 13, '65.
Post, P. Sidney, Dec. 16, '64.
Potter, Carroll H., Mar. 13, '65.
Powell, Eugene, Mar. 13, '65.
Price, Francis, Mar. 13, '65.
Price, W. R., Mar. 13, '65.
Price, S. W., Mar. 13, '62.
Price, Rich'd B., Mar. 13, '65.
Pritchard, B. D., May 10, '65.
Proudfit, J. L., Mar. 13, '65.
Pratt, Benj. F., Mar. 13, '65.
Preston, S. M., Dec. 30, '65.
Prescott, Geo. L., June 18, '64.
Prevost, C. M., Mar. 13, '65.
Pugh, Isaac C., Mar. 10, '65.
Pulford, John, Mar. 13, '65.
Quincy, S. M., Mar. 13, '65.
Randall, Geo. W., Mar. 13, '65.
Randol, A. M., June 24, '65.
Ratliff, Rbt. W., Mar. 13, '65.
Raynor, Wm. H., Mar. 13, '65.
Read, S. Tyler, Mar. 13, '65.
Read, Theo., Sept. 29, '64.
Remick, D., Mar. 13, '65.
Reno, M. A., Mar. 13, '65.
Revere, W. R., Jr., Mar. 13, '65.
Revere, P. J., July 2, '65.

Reynolds, Jos. S., July 11, '65.
Richardson, H., Mar. 13, '65.
Richardson, W. P., Dec. 7, '64.
Richmond, Lewis, Mar. 13, '65.
Riggin, John, Mar. 13, '65.
Rinaker, J. I., Mar. 13, '65.
Ripley, Edw. H., Aug. 1, '64.
Ripley, Theo. A., Mar. 13, '65.
Risdon, O. C., Mar. 13, '65.
Ritchie, John, Feb. 21, '65.
Robbins, W. R., Mar. 13, '65.
Roberts, Chas. W., Mar. 13, '65.
Roberts, S. H., Oct. 28, '64.
Robeson, W. P., Jr., April 1, '65.
Robinson, G. D., Mar. 13, '65.
Robinson, H. L., Mar. 13, '65.
Robinson, M. S., Mar. 13, '65.
Robinson, W. A., Mar. 13, '65.
Robison, J. K., Mar. 13, '65.
Rockwell, A. P., Mar. 13, '65.
Rodgers, H., Jr., Mar. 13, '65.
Rodgers, H. C., Mar. 13, '65.
Rogers, Jas. C., Mar. 13, '65.
Rogers, George, Mar. 13, '65.
Rogers, Geo. C., Mar. 13, '65.
Rogers, Wm. F., Mar. 13, '65.
Roome, Chas., Mar. 13, '65.
Rose, Thos. E., July 22, '65.
Ross, Samuel, April 13, '65.
Ross, W. E. W., Mar. 11, '65.
Rowett, Rich'd, Mar. 13, '65.
Rowley, Wm. R., Mar. 13, '65.
Ruggles, Jas. M., Mar. 13, '65.
Rusk, Jer. M., Mar. 13, '65.
Rusling, Jas. F., Feb. 16, '66.
Russell, Chas. S., July 30, '64.
Russell, Hy. S., Mar. 13, '65.
Rust, John D., Mar. 13, '65.
Rust, H., Jr., Mar. 13, '65.
Rutherford, Allen, Mar. 13, '65.
Rutherford, G. V., Mar. 13, '65.
Rutherford, R. C., Mar. 13, '65.
Sackett, Wm. H., June 10, '64.
Salm Salm, F. P., April 13, '65.
Salomon, C. E., Mar. 13, '65.
Salomon, E. S., Mar. 13, '65.
Sanborn, Wm., Mar. 13, '65.
Sanders, A. H., Mar. 13, '65.
Sanders, H. T., April 19, '65.
Sanderson, T. W., Mar. 13, '65.
Sanford, E. S., Mar. 13, '65.
Sargent, H. B., Mar. 21, '64.
Sawyer, Frank, Mar. 13, '65.
Scates, W. B., Mar. 13, '65.
Schmitt, Wm. A., Mar. 13, '65.
Schneider, E. F., Mar. 13, '65.
Schofield, H., Mar. 13, '65.
Schofield, Geo. W., Jan. 26, '65.
Schwenk, S. K., July 24, '65.
Scribner, B. F., Aug. 8, '64.
Scott, Geo. W., Mar. 13, '65.
Scott, Rufus, Mar. 13, '65.
Seaver, Joel J., Mar. 13, '65.
Seawall, Thos. D., Mar. 13, '65.
Selfridge, J. L., Mar. 16, '65.
Serrell, Edw. W., Mar. 13, '65.
Sewall, F. D., July 21, '65.
Shaffer, G. T., Mar. 13, '65.
Shaffer, J. W., Mar. 13, '65.
Shafter, Wm. R., Mar. 13, '65.
Sharpe, Jacob, Mar. 13, '65.
Shaurman, N., Mar. 13, '65.

Shaw, Jas., Jr., Mar. 13, '65.
Shedd, Warren, Mar. 13, '65.
Sheets, Benj. F., Mar. 13, '65.
Sheets, Josiah A., Mar. 13, '65.
Sheldon, Chas. S., Mar. 13, '65.
Sheldon, L. A., Mar. 13, '65.
Shepherd, R. B., Mar. 13, '65.
Sherwood, I. R., Feb. 27, '65.
Sherwin, T., Jr., Mar. 13, '65.
Shoup, Sam'l, Mar. 13, '65.
Shunk, David, Feb. 9, '65.
Shurtleff, G. W., Mar. 13, '65.
Sickles, H. F., Mar. 13, '65.
Sigfried, J. K., Aug. 1, '64.
Simpson, S. P., Mar. 13, '65.
Sleven, P. S., Mar. 13, '65.
Slocum, Willard, Mar. 13, '65.
Smith, Arthur A., Mar. 13, '65.
Smith, Al. B., Mar. 13, '65.
Smith, Benj. F., Mar. 26, '65.
Smith, Chas. E., Mar. 13, '65.
Smith, E. W., Mar. 13, '65.
Smith, F. C., Mar. 13, '65.
Smith, Geo. W., Mar. 13, '65.
Smith, Gus. A., Mar. 13, '65.
Smith, Israel C., Mar. 13, '65.
Smith, James, Mar. 13, '65.
Smith, John C., June 20, '65.
Smith, Jos. S., July 11, '65.
Smith, Orlando, Mar. 13, '65.
Smith, Orlow, Mar. 13, '65.
Smith, Robert F., Mar. 13, '65.
Smith, Rbt. W., Feb. 13, '65.
Smith, Wm. J., July 16, '65.
Sniper, Gustavus, Mar. 13, '65.
Sowers, Edgar, Mar. 13, '65.
Sprague, A. B. R., Mar. 13, '65.
Sprague, Ezra T., June 20, '65.
Spalding, George, Mar. 21, '65.
Spaulding, Ira, April 9, '65.
Spaulding, O. L., June 25, '65.
Spencer, Geo. E., Mar. 13, '65.
Spear, Ellis, Mar. 13, '65.
Spear, Sam'l P., Mar. 13, '65.
Spicely, Wm. T., Aug. 26, '65.
Spurling, A. B., Mar. 26, '65.
Spofford, John P., Mar. 13, '65.
Stafford, Jacob A., Mar. 13, '65.
Stager, Anson, Mar. 13, '65.
Stagg, Peter, Mar. 30, '65.
Stanley, Tim. L., Mar. 13, '65.
Stanton, David L., April 1, '65.
Starbird, I. W., Mar. 13, '65.
Starring, F. A., Mar. 13, '65.
Stedman, G. A., Jr., Aug. 5, '64.
Stedman, Wm., Mar. 13, '65.
Steers, Wm. H. P., Mar. 13, '65.
Steiner, John A., Mar. 13, '65.
Stephenson, L., Jr., Mar. 13, '64.
Stevens, Aaron F., Dec. 8, '64.
Stevens, A. A., Mar. 7, '65.
Stevens, Hazard, April 2, '65.
Stevenson, R. H., Mar. 13, '65.
Stewart, Jas., Jr., Mar. 13, '65.
Stewart, W. S., Mar. 13, '65.
Stewart, Wm. W., Mar. 13, '65.
Stibbs, John H., Mar. 13, '65.
Stiles, Israel N., Jan. 31, '64.
Stockton, Jos., Mar. 13, '65.
Stokes, Wm. B., Mar. 13, '65.
Stone, Geo. A., Mar. 13, '65.

Stone, Roy, Sept. 7, '64.
Stone, Wm. M., Mar. 13, '65.
Stough, Wm., Mar. 13, '65.
Stoughton, C. B., Mar. 13, '65.
Stout, Alex. W., Mar. 13, '62.
Stratton, F. A., Mar. 13, '65.
Streight, Abel D., Mar. 13, '65.
Strickland, S. A., Mar. 13, '65.
Strong, Jas. C., Mar. 13, '65.
Strong, Thos. J., Mar. 13, '65.
Strong, Wm. E., Mar. 21, '65.
Strother, D. H., Aug. 23, '65.
Sumner, E. V., Jr., Mar. 13, '65.
Sullivan, P. J., Mar. 13, '65.
Sweet, Benj., Dec. 20, '64.
Sweitzer, J. B., Mar. 13, '65.
Swift, Fred. W., Mar. 13, '65.
Switzler, T. A., Mar. 13, '65.
Sypher, J. Hale, Mar. 13, '65.
Talbot, Thos. H., Mar. 13, '65.
Talley, Wm. C., Mar. 13, '65.
Tarbell, Jon., Mar. 13, '65.
Taylor, Ezra, Feb. 13, '65.
Taylor, J. E., Mar. 13, '65.
Taylor, John P., Aug. 4, '65.
Taylor, Thos. T., Mar. 13, '65.
Tevis, W. Carroll, Mar. 13, '65.
Tew, Geo. W., Mar. 13, '65.
Thomas, De Witt C., Mar. 13, '65.
Thomas, M. T., Feb. 10, '65.
Thomas, Samuel, Mar. 13, '65.
Thompson, C. R., April 13, '65.
Thompson, D., Mar. 13, '65.
Thompson, H. E., Mar. 13, '65.
Thompson, J. L., Mar. 13, '65.
Thompson, J. M., Mar. 13, '65.
Thompson, R., Mar. 13, '65.
Thompson, Wm., Mar. 13, '65.
Thorp, Thos. J., Mar. 13, '65.
Throop, Wm. A., Mar. 13, '65.
Thruston, G. P., Mar. 13, '65.
Thurston, W. H., Mar. 13, '65.
Tilden, Chas. W., Mar. 13, '65.
Tilghman, B. C., April 13, '65.
Tillson, John, Mar. 10, '65.
Tilton, Wm. S., Sept. 9, '64.
Titus, Herbert B., Mar. 13, '65.
Tompkins, C. H., Aug. 1, '64.
Tourtelotte, J. E., Mar. 13, '65.
Tracy, B. F., Mar. 13, '65.
Trauernicht, T., Mar. 13, '65.
Tremaine, H. E., Nov. 30, '65.
Trotter, F. E., Mar. 13, '65.
True, Jas. M., Mar. 6, '65.
Truex, William S., April 2, '65.
Trumbull, M. M., Mar. 13, '65.
Turley, John A., Mar. 13, '65.
Turner, Charles, Mar. 26, '65.
Van Antwerp, V., Feb. 13, '65.
VanBuren, D. T., Mar. 13, '65.
VanBuren, J. L., April 2, '65.
VanBuren, T. B., Mar. 13, '65.
Van Schrader, A., Mar. 13, '65.
Varney, Geo., Mar. 13, '65.
Van Petten, J. V., Mar. 13, '65.
Van Shaak, G. W., Mar. 13, '65.
Vail, Jacob G., Mar. 13, '65.
Vail, Nicholas J., Mar. 13, '65.
Vaughn, Sam'l K., Aug. 9, '65.
Vickers, David, Mar. 13, '65.
Vifquain, V., Mar. 13, '65.
Von Blessingh, L., Mar. 13, '65.

Richard M. Gano Led a Brigade of Morgan's Cavalry.

Matthew D. Ector Led a Brigade in the Army of Tennessee.

Richard Waterhouse Led a Brigade of Infantry and Cavalry.

Thomas Harrison Led a Brigade in the Army of Tennessee.

Felix H. Robertson Led a Brigade of Cavalry in the Army of Tennessee.

John C. Moore Led a Brigade in the Army of the West.

John R. Baylor, Conspicuous in Operations in Texas and New Mexico in 1861–62.

Henry E. McCulloch, Texas Brigade and District Commander.

Louis T. Wigfall, Bearer of a Flag of Truce at Fort Sumter.

Thomas N. Waul, Colonel of Waul's Texas Legion.

Jerome B. Robertson Led a Brigade in Hood's Division.

CONFEDERATE GENERALS

—No. 22—

TEXAS (Continued)

The Union Generals

Von Egloffstein, F. W., Mar. 13, '65.
Von Vegesack, E., Mar. 13, '65.
Vreeland, M. J., Mar. 13, '65.
Wade, Jas. F., Feb. 13, '64.
Wagner, Louis, Mar. 13, '65.
Waite, Charles, April 2, '65.
Waite, John M., Feb. 13, '65.
Wainwright, C. S., Aug. 1, '64.
Wainwright, W. P., Mar. 13, '65.
Walcutt, C. F., April 9, '65.
Walker, D. S., Mar. 13, '65.
Walker, F. A., Mar. 31, '65.
Walker, M. B., Mar. 27, '65.
Walker, Samuel, Mar. 13, '65.
Walker, Thos. M., July 5, '65.
Wallace, M. R. M., Mar. 13, '65.
Wangelin, Hugo, Mar. 13, '65.
Warner, D. B., Feb. 13, '65.
Ward, Durbin, Oct. 18, '65.
Ward, Geo. H., July 2, '63.
Ward, Henry C., Nov. 29, '65.
Ward, Lyman M., Mar. 13, '65.
Warner, A. J., Mar. 13, '65.
Warner, Edw. R., April 9, '65.
Warren, L. H., Mar. 13, '65.
Washburn, F., April 6, '65.
Washburn, G. A., Mar. 13, '65.

Wass, Ansell D., Mar. 13, '65.
Waters, L. H., June 18, '65.
Weaver, Jas. B., Mar. 13, '65.
Webber, Jules C., Mar. 13, '65.
Webber, A. W., Mar. 26, '65.
Weld, S. M., Jr., Mar. 13, '65.
Welles, Geo. E., Mar. 13, '65.
Wells, Geo. D., Oct. 12, '64.
Wells, Henry H., June 3, '65.
Wells, Milton, Mar. 13, '65.
Wentworth, M. F., Mar. 13, '65.
Welsh, William, Mar. 13, '65.
West, Edward W., Mar. 13, '65.
West, Francis H., Mar. 13, '65.
West, Geo. W., Dec. 2, '64.
West, Henry R., July 13, '65.
West, Robert M., April 1, '65.
Wever, Clark R., Feb. 9, '65.
Wheelock, Charles, Aug. 9, '64.
Wherry, Wm. M., April 2, '65.
White, Daniel, Mar. 13, '65.
Whitaker, E. W., Mar. 13, '65.
Whistler, J. N. G., Mar. 13, '65.
Whitbeck, H. N., Mar. 13, '65.
White, Carr B., Mar. 13, '65.
White, David B., Mar. 13, '65.
White, Frank, Mar. 13, '65.
White, Frank J., Mar. 13, '65.
White, Harry, Mar. 2, '65.

Whittier, Chas. A., April 9, '65.
Whittier, F. H., Mar. 13, '65.
Whittlesey, C. H., Mar. 13, '65.
Whittlesey, E., Mar. 13, '65.
Whittlesey, H. M., Mar. 13, '65.
Wilcox, Jas. A., Feb. 13, '65.
Wilcox, John S., Mar. 13, '65.
Wilder, John T., Aug. 7, '64.
Wildes, Thos. F., Mar. 11, '65.
Wildrick, A. C., April 2, '65.
Wiles, G. F., Mar. 13, '65.
Wiley, Aquila, Mar. 13, '65.
Wiley, Dan'l D., Mar. 13, '65.
Williams, A. W., Mar. 13, '65.
Williams, Jas. M., July 13, '65.
Williams, John, Mar. 13, '65.
Williams, R., Mar. 13, '65.
Williams, T. J., Sept. 22, '62.
Willian, John, April 9, '65.
Wilson, J. G., Mar. 13, '65.
Wilson, James, Mar. 13, '65.
Wilson, Lester S., Mar. 13, '65.
Wilson, Thomas, Mar. 13, '65.
Wilson, Wm. T., Mar. 13, '65.
Wilson, Wm., Nov. 13, '65.
Winkler, Fred. C., June 15, '65.
Winslow, Bradley, April 2, '65.
Winslow, E. F., Dec. 12, '64.
Winslow, R. E., Mar. 13, '65.

Wise, Geo. D., Mar. 13, '65.
Wisewell, M. N., Mar. 13, '65.
Wister, L., Mar. 13, '65.
Witcher, John S., Mar. 13, '65.
Withington, W. H., Mar. 13, '65.
Wolfe, Edw. H., Mar. 13, '65.
Wood, Oliver, Mar. 13, '65.
Wood, Wm. D., Mar. 13, '65.
Woodall, Daniel, June 15, '65.
Woodford, S. L., May 12, '65.
Woodhull, M. V. L., Mar. 13, '65.
Woodward, O. S., Mar. 13, '65.
Woolley, John, Mar. 13, '65.
Wormer, G. S., Mar. 13, '65.
Wright, Ed., Mar. 13, '65.
Wright, Elias, Jan. 15, '65.
Wright, John G., Mar. 13, '65.
Wright, Thos. F., Mar. 13, '65.
Yates, Henry, Jr., Mar. 13, '65.
Yeoman, S. B., Mar. 13, '65.
Yorke, Louis E., Mar. 13, '65.
Young, S. B. M., April 9, '65.
Young, Thos. L., Mar. 13, '65.
Zahm, Louis, Mar. 13, '62.
Ziegler, Geo. M., Mar. 13, '65.
Zinn, Geo., April 6, '65.
Zulick, Sam'l M., Mar. 13, '65.

D. B. Harris, Colonel in the
Engineer Corps; Chief En-
gineer at Charleston.

Armstead L. Long, Staff Officer to Lee and His
Authorized Biographer.

John B. Floyd, in Command in
West Virginia in 1861, later at Fort Donelson.

William L. Jackson, Originally Colonel of the
31st Regiment.

CONFEDERATE

GENERALS

No. 23

VIRGINIA

Albert G. Jenkins Led a Command in Southwest Vir-
ginia; Wounded at
Cloyd's Mountain.

Daniel Ruggles Commanded
a Division in General
Breckinridge's Army.

Camille J. Polignac, Defender
of the Red River Country,
Leading in many
Battles.

Montgomery D. Corse
Battled Heroically at
Five Forks and
Petersburg.

Richard L. T. Beale
Led a Brigade in
Lee's Army.

Henry H. Walker Led
a Virginia Brigade
in Lee's Army.

Joseph R. Anderson
Led a Brigade in
Lee's Army.

Thomas Jordan, Beaure-
gard's Chief of Staff;
Later Fought for
"Cuba Libre."

General Officers of the Confederate Army

A FULL ROSTER COMPILED FROM THE OFFICIAL RECORDS

The Confederate titles below derive authority through verification by General Marcus J. Wright, for many years in charge of Confederate records at the United States War Department, Washington. Some ranks appropriate to high commands, and fully justified, were never legally confirmed. In such cases, as those of Joseph Wheeler and John B. Gordon, General Wright has followed the strictest interpretation of the Confederate records below. As for the body of this History it has been thought best to employ the titles most commonly used, and found in the popular reference works. The highest rank attained is given in every case together with the date of the commission conferring such rank.

GENERALS

REGULAR

Beauregard, P. G. T., July 21, '61.
Bragg, Braxton, April 6, '62.
Cooper, Samuel, May 16, '61.
Johnston, A. S., May 30, '61.
Johnston, J. E., July 4, '61.
Lee, Robert E., June 14, '61.

GENERAL

PROVISIONAL ARMY

Smith, E. Kirby, Feb. 19, '64.

GENERALS

PROVISIONAL ARMY

(With Temporary Rank)

Hood, John B., July 18, '64.

LIEUTENANT-GENERALS

PROVISIONAL ARMY

Buckner, S. B., Sept. 20, '64.
Ewell, Richard S., May 23, '63.
Forrest, N. B., Feb. 28, '65.
Hampton, Wade, Feb. 14, '65.
Hardee, Wm. J., Oct. 10, '62.
Hill, Ambrose P., May 24, '63.
Hill, Daniel H., July 11, '63.
Holmes, T. H., Oct. 13, '62.
Jackson, T. J., Oct. 10, '62.
Lee, Stephen D., June 23, '64.
Longstreet, James, Oct. 9, '62.
Pemberton, J. C., Oct. 10, '62.
Polk, Leonidas, Oct. 10, '62.
Taylor, Richard, April 8, '64.

LIEUTENANT-GENERALS

PROVISIONAL ARMY

(With Temporary Rank)

Anderson, R. H., May 31, '64.
Early, Jubal A., May 31, '64.
Stewart, A. P., June 23, '64.

MAJOR-GENERALS

PROVISIONAL ARMY

Anderson, J. P., Feb. 17, '64.
Bate, William B., Feb. 23, '64.
Bowen, John S., May 25, '63.

Breckinridge, J. C., Apr. 14, '62.
Butler, M. C., Sept. 19, '64.
Cheatham, B. F., Mar. 10, '62.
Churchill, T. J., Mar. 17, '65.
Crittenden, G. B., Nov. 9, '61.
Cleburne, P. R., Dec. 13, '62.
Cobb, Howell, Sept. 9, '63.
Donelson, D. S., Jan. 17, '63.
Elzey, Arnold, Dec. 4, '62.
Fagan, James F., April 25, '64.
Field, Chas. W., Feb. 12, '64.
Forney, John H., Oct. 27, '62.
French, S. G., Aug. 31, '62.
Gardner, F., Dec. 13, '62.
Grimes, Bryan, Feb. 15, '65.
Gordon, John B., May 14, '64.
Heth, Henry, Oct. 10, '62.
Hindman, T. C., April 14, '62.
Hoke, Robert F., April 20, '64.
Huger, Benj., Oct. 7, '61.
Johnson, B. R., May 21, '64.
Johnson, Edward, Feb. 28, '63.
Jones, David R., Oct. 11, '62.
Jones, Samuel, Mar. 10, '62.
Kemper, J. L., Sept. 19, '64.
Kershaw, J. B., May 18, '64.
Lee, Fitzhugh, Aug. 3, '63.
Lee, G. W. Custis, Oct. 20, '64.
Lee, W. H. F., Apr. 23, '64.
Loring, W. W., Feb. 17, '62.
Lovell, Mansfield, Oct. 7, '61.
McCown, John P., Mar. 10, '62.
McLaws, L., May 23, '62.
Magruder, J. B., Oct. 7, '61.
Mahone, William, July 30, '64.
Marmaduke, J. S., Mar. 17, '65.
Martin, Will T., Nov. 10, '63.
Maury, D. H., Nov. 4, '62.
Polignac, C. J., April 8, '64.
Pender, W. D., May 27, '63.
Pickett, George E., Oct. 10, '62.
Price, Sterling, Mar. 6, '62.
Ransom, R., Jr., May 26, '63.
Rodes, Robert E., May 2, '63.
Smith, G. W., Sept. 19, '61.
Smith, Martin L., Nov. 4, '62.
Smith, William, Aug. 12, '63.
Stevenson, C. L., Oct. 10, '62.
Stuart, J. E. B., July 25, '62.
Taylor, Richard, July 28, '62.
Trimble, Isaac R., Jan. 17, '63.
Twiggs, D. E., May 22, '61.
Van Dorn, Earl, Sept. 19, '61.
Walker, John G., Nov. 8, '62.
Walker, W. H. T., May 23, '63.
Wharton, John A., Nov. 10, '63.
Wheeler, Joseph, Jan. 20, '64.
Whiting, W. H. C., Apr. 22, '63.
Withers, Jones M., April 6, '62.
Wilcox, C. M., Aug. 3, '63.

MAJOR-GENERALS

PROVISIONAL ARMY

(With Temporary Rank)

Allen, William W., Mar. 4, '65.
Brown, John C., Aug. 4, '64.
Clayton, Henry D., July 7, '64.
Lomax, L. L., Aug. 10, '64.
Ramseur, S. D., June 1, '64.
Rosser, T. L., Nov. 1, '64.
Walthall, E. C., July 6, '64.
Wright, A. R., Nov. 26, '64.
Young, P. M. B., Dec. 20, '64.

MAJOR-GENERAL

FOR SERVICE WITH VOLUNTEER TROOPS

(With Temporary Rank)

Gilmer, J. F., Aug. 25, '63.

BRIGADIER-GENERALS

PROVISIONAL ARMY

Adams, Daniel W., May 23, '62.
Adams, John, Dec. 29, '62.
Adams, Wirt, Sept. 25, '63.
Allen, Henry W., Aug. 19, '63.
Anderson, G. B., June 9, '62.
Anderson, J. R., Sept. 3, '61.
Anderson, S. R., July 9, '61.
Armistead, L. A., April 1, '62.
Armstrong, F. C., April 20, '63.
Anderson, G. T., Nov. 1, '62.
Archer, James J., June 3, '62.
Ashby, Turner, May 23, '62.
Baker, Alpheus, Mar. 5, '64.
Baker, L. S., July 23, '63.
Baldwin, W. E., Sept. 19, '62.
Barksdale, Wm., Aug. 12, '62.
Barringer, Rufus, June 1, '64.
Barton, Seth M., Mar. 11, '62.
Battle, Cullen A., Aug. 20, '63.
Beall, W. N. R., April 11, '62.
Beale, R. L. T., Jan. 6, '65.
Bee, Barnard E., June 17, '61.
Bee, Hamilton P., Mar. 4, '62.
Bell, Tyree H., Feb. 28, '65.
Benning, H. L., Jan. 17, '63.
Boggs, William R., Nov. 4, '62.
Bonham, M. L., April 23, '61.
Blanchard, A. G., Sept. 21, '61.
Buford, Abraham, Sept. 2, '62.
Branch, L. O. B., Nov. 16, '61.
Brandon, Wm. L., June 18, '64.
Bratton, John, May 6, '64.
Brevard, T. W., Mar. 22, '65.
Bryan, Goode, Aug. 29, '63.
Cabell, Wm. A., Jan. 20, '63.
Campbell, A. W., Mar. 1, '65.
Cantey, James, Jan. 8, '63.

Capers, Ellison, Mar. 1, '65.
Carroll, Wm. H., Oct. 26, '61.
Chalmers, J. R., Feb. 13, '62.
Chestnut, J., Jr., April 23, '64.
Clark, Charles, May 22, '61.
Clark, John B., Mar. 8, '64.
Clanton, J. H., Nov. 16, '63.
Clingman, T. L., May 17, '62.
Cobb, T. R. R., Nov. 1, '62.
Cockrell, F. M., July 18, '63.
Cocke, P. St. G., Oct. 21, '61.
Colston, R. E., Dec. 24, '61.
Cook, Philip, Aug. 5, '64.
Cooke, John R., Nov. 1, '62.
Cooper, D. H., May 2, '63.
Colquitt, A. H., Sept. 1, '62.
Corse, M. D., Nov. 1, '62.
Cosby, Geo. B., Jan. 20, '63.
Cumming, Alfred, Oct. 29, '62.
Daniel, Junius, Sept. 1, '62.
Davidson, H. B., Aug. 18, '63.
Davis, Wm. G. M., Nov. 4, '62.
Davis, J. R., Sept. 15, '62.
Deas, Z. C., Dec. 13, '62.
De Lagnel, J. A., April 15, '62.
Deshler, James, July 28, '63.
Dibrell, Geo. G., July 26, '64.
Dockery, T. P., Aug. 10, '63.
Doles, George, Nov. 1, '62.
Drayton, T. F., Sept. 25, '61.
Duke, Basil W., Sept. 15, '64.
Duncan, J. K., Jan. 7, 62.
Echols, John, April 16, '62.
Ector, M. D., Aug. 23, '62.
Evans, C. A., May 19, '64.
Evans, Nathan G., Oct. 21, '61.
Farney, Wm. H., Feb. 15, '65.
Featherson, W. S., Mar. 4, '62.
Ferguson, S. W., July 23, '63.
Finegan, Joseph, April 5, '62.
Finley, Jesse J., Nov. 16, '63.
Floyd, John B., May 23, '61.
Forney, John H., Mar. 10, '62.
Frazer, John W., May 19, '63.
Frost, Daniel M., Mar. 3, '62.
Gano, Rich. M., Mar. 17, '65.
Gardner, Wm. M., Nov. 14, '61.
Garland, Sam., Jr., May 23, '62.
Garnett, Rich. B., Nov. 14, '61.
Garnett, Robt. S., June 6, '61.
Garrott, I. W., May 28, '63.
Gartrell, Lucius J., Aug. 22, '64.
Gary, Martin W., May 19, '64.
Gatlin, Richard C., July 8, '61.
Gholson, S. J., May 6, '64.
Gist, States R., Mar. 20, '62.
Gladden, A. H., Sept. 30, '61.
Godwin, Arch. C., Aug. 5, '64.
Gordon, James B., Sept. 28, '63.
Govan, Dan'l C., Dec. 29, '63.

David A. Weisinger, Defender of the Petersburg Crater.

Gabriel C. Wharton, in the Shenandoah Valley in 1864.

Philip St. G. Cocke, First Defender of Virginia, in 1861.

Patrick T. Moore, in Command of Reserves Defending Richmond.

CONFEDERATE

GENERALS

No. 24

VIRGINIA

Edwin G. Lee, On Special Service.

James B. Terrell Led Pegram's Old Brigade at the Wilderness.

Robert H. Chilton, Lee's Adjutant-General.

Seth M. Barton Led a Brigade in Lee's Army.

George W. Randolph, Secretary of War in 1862.

William C. Wickham Fought Sheridan Before Richmond.

Eppa Hunton Led a Brigade in Pickett's Division.

The Confederate Generals

Gracie, Arch., Jr., Nov. 4, '63.
Gray, Henry, Mar. 17, '65.
Grayson, John B., Aug. 15, '61.
Green, Martin E., July 21, '62.
Green, Thomas, May 20, '63.
Greer, Elkanah, Oct. 8, '62.
Gregg, John, Aug. 29, '62
Gregg, Maxcy, Dec. 14, '61.
Griffith, Rich., Nov. 2, '61.
Hagood, Johnson, July 21,'62.
Hanson, Roger W., Dec. 13, '62.
Hardeman, W. P., Mar. 17, '65.
Harris, Nat. H., Jan. 20, '64.
Harrison, J. E., Dec. 22, '64.
Hays, Harry T., July 25, '62.
Hatton, Robert, May 23, '62.
Hawes, James M., Mar. 5, '62.
Hawthorne, A. T., Feb. 18, '64.
Helm, Ben. H., Mar. 14, '62.
Hebert, Louis, May 26, '62.
Hebert, Paul O., Aug. 17, '61.
Higgins, Edward, Oct. 29, '63.
Hodge, Geo. B., Nov. 20, '63.
Hogg, Joseph L., Feb. 14, '62.
Hoke, Robert F., Jan. 17, '63.
Hood, John B., Mar. 3, '62.
Huger, Benjamin, June 17,'61.
Humes, W. Y. C., Nov. 16, '63.
Humphreys, B. G., Aug. 12, '63.
Hunton, Eppa, Aug. 9, '63.
Iverson, Alfred, Nov. 1, '62.
Jackson, Alfred E., Feb. 9, '63.
Jackson, H. R., June 4, '61.
Jackson, John K., Feb. 13, '62.
Jackson, Wm. A., Dec. 19, '64.
Jackson, Wm. H., Dec. 29, '62.
Jenkins, Albert G., Aug. 5, '62.
Jenkins, Micah, July 22, '62.
Johnston, R. D., Sept. 1, '63.
Jones, John M., May 15, '63.
Jones, John R., June 23, '62.
Jones, William E., Sept. 19, '62.
Jordan, Thomas, April 14, '62.
Kelly, John H., Nov. 16, '63.
Kirkland, W. W., Aug. 29, '63.
Lane, James H., Nov. 1, '62.
Lane, Walter P., Mar. 17, '65.
Law, Evander M., Oct. 3, '62.
Lawton, Alex. R., April 13, '61.
Leadbetter, D., Feb. 27, '62.
Lee, Edwin G., Sept. 20, '64.
Lewis, Joseph H., Sept. 30, '63.
Liddell, St. J. R., July 12, '62.
Little, Henry, April 16, '62.
Logan, T. M., Feb. 15, '65.
Lowrey, Mark. P., Oct. 4, '63.
Lowry, Robert, Feb. 4, '65.
Lyon, Hylan B., June 14, '64.
McCausland, J., May 18, '64.
McComb, Wm., June 30, '65.
McCulloch, H. E., Mar. 14, '62.
McCullough, Ben., May 11, '61.
McGowan, S., Jan. 17, '63.
McIntosh, James, Jan. 24, '62.
McNair, Evander, Nov. 4, '62.
McRae, Dandridge, Nov. 5, '62.
Mackall, Wm. W., Feb. 27, '62.
Major, James P., July 21, '63.
Maney, George, April 16, '62.
Manigault, A. M., April 26, '63.
Marshall, H., Oct. 30, '61.
Martin, James G., May 15, '62.
Maxey, S. B., Mar. 4, '62.

Mercer, Hugh W., Oct. 29, '61.
Moody, Young M., Mar. 4, '65.
Moore, John C., May 26, '62.
Moore, P. T., Sept. 20, '64.
Morgan, John H., Dec. 11, '62.
Morgan, John T., June 6, '63.
Mouton, Alfred, April 16, '62.
Nelson, Allison, Sept. 12, '62.
Nicholls, F. T., Oct. 14, '62.
O'Neal, Ed. A., June 6, '63.
Parsons, M. M., Nov. 5, '62.
Paxton, E. F., Nov. 1, '61.
Peck, Wm. R., Feb. 18, '65.
Pegram, John, Nov. 7, '62.
Pendleton, W. N., Mar. 26, '62.
Perrin, Abner, Sept. 10, '63.
Perry, Ed. A., Aug. 28, '62.
Perry, Wm. F., Feb. 21, '65.
Pettigrew, J. J., Feb. 26, '62.
Pettus, E. W., Sept. 18, '63.
Pike, Albert, Aug. 15, '61.
Pillow, Gideon J., July 9, '61.
Polk, Lucius E., Dec. 13, '62.
Preston, William, April 14, '62.
Pryor, Roger A., April 16, '62.
Quarles, Wm. A., Aug. 25, '63.
Rains, G. J., Sept. 23, '61.
Rains, James E., Nov. 4, '62.
Randolph, G. W., Feb. 12, '62.
Ransom, M. W., June 13, '63.
Reynolds, A. W., Sept. 14, '63.
Richardson, R. V., Dec. 1, '63.
Ripley, Roswell S., Aug. 15, '61.
Roberts, Wm. P., Feb. 21, '65.
Robertson, B. H., June 9, '62.
Robertson, J. B., Nov. 1, '62.
Roddy, Philip D., Aug. 3, '63.
Roane, John S., Nov. 20, '62.
Ross, Lawrence S., Dec. 21, '63.
Ruggles, Daniel, Aug. 9, '61.
Rust, Albert, Mar. 4, '62.
Scales, Alfred M., June 3, '63.
Scott, T. M., May 10, '64.
Scurry, Wm. R., Sept. 12, '62.
Sears, Claudius W., Mar. 1, '64.
Semmes, Paul J., Mar. 11, '62.
Shelby, Joseph O., Dec. 15, '63.
Shoup, Francis A., Sept. 12, '62.
Sibley, H. H., June 17, '61.
Simms, James P., Dec. 4, '64.
Slack, William Y., April 12,'62.
Slaughter, J. E., Mar. 8, '62.
Smith, James A., Sept. 30, '63.
Smith, Preston, Oct. 27, '62.
Smith, Wm. D., Mar. 7, '62.
Stafford, Leroy A., Oct. 8, '63.
Starke, Peter B., Nov. 4, '64.
Starke, Wm. E., Aug. 6, '62.
Steele, William, Sept. 12, '62.
Sterling, A. M. W., Jan. 7, '62.
Steuart, Geo. H., Mar. 6, '62.
Stevens, C. H., Jan. 20, '64.
Stovall, M. A., April 23, '63.
Strahl, Otho F., July 28, '63.
Taliaferro, Wm. B., Mar. 4, '62.
Tappan, James C., Nov. 5, '62.
Taylor, T. H., Nov. 4, '62.
Thomas, Allen, Feb. 4, '64.
Thomas, Ed. L., Nov. 1, '62.
Toombs, Robert, July 19, '61.
Tilghman, Lloyd, Oct. 18, '61.
Tracy, Edward D., Aug. 16, '62.
Trapier, James H., Oct. 21, '61.

Tucker, Wm. F., Mar. 1, '64.
Tyler, Robert C., Feb. 23, '64.
Vance, Robert B., Mar. 4, '63.
Vaughn, A. J., Jr., Nov. 18, '63.
Vaughn, J. C., Sept. 22, '62.
Villepigue, J. B., Mar. 13, '62.
Walker, H. H., July 1, '63.
Walker, James A., May 15, '63.
Walker, Leroy P., Sept. 17, '61.
Walker, L. M., April 11, '62.
Walker, Wm. S., Oct. 30, '62.
Waterhouse, R., Mar. 17, '65.
Watie, Stand, May 6, '64.
Waul, Thomas N., Sept. 18, '63.
Wayne, Henry C., Dec. 16, '61.
Weisiger, D. A., July 30, '64.
Wharton, G. C., July 8, '63.
Whitfield, John W., May 9, '63.
Wickham, W. C., Sept. 1, '63.
Wigfall, Louis T., Oct. 2, '61.
Williams, John S., April 16,'62.
Wilson, C. C., Nov. 16, '63.
Winder, Chas. S., Mar. 1, '62.
Winder, John H., June 21, '61.
Wise, Henry A., June 5, '61.
Woffard, Wm. T., Jan. 17, '63.
Wood, S. A. M., Jan. 7, '62.
Wright, Marcus J., Dec. 13, '62.
Zollicoffer, Felix K., July 9,'61.

BRIGADIER-GENERALS OF ARTILLERY
PROVISIONAL ARMY

Alexander, Ed. P., Feb. 26, '64.
Long, A. L., Sept. 21, '63.
Walker, R. L., Feb. 18, '65.

BRIGADIER-GENERAL
(COMMISSARY GENERAL)
PROVISIONAL ARMY

St. John, Isaac M., Feb. 16, '65.

BRIGADIER-GENERALS
(Special Appointments)
PROVISIONAL ARMY

Imboden, John D., Jan. 28, '63.
Johnson, Adam R., June 1, '64.

BRIGADIER-GENERALS
(Special)
PROVISIONAL ARMY

Benton, Samuel, July 26, '64.
Chambliss, J. R., Jr., Dec. 19, '63.
Chilton, R. H., Oct. 20, '62.
Connor, James, June 1, '64.
Elliott, S., Jr., May 24, '64.
Fry, Birkett D., May 24, '64.
Gibson, R. L., Jan. 11, '64.
Goggin, James M., Dec. 4, '64.
Gorgas, Josiah, Nov. 10, '64.
Granberry, H. B., Feb. 29, '64.
Hodge, Geo. B., Aug. 2, '64.
Leventhorpe, C., Feb. 3, '65.
McRae, William, Nov. 4, '64.
Northrop, L. B., Nov. 26, '64.
Page, Richard L., Mar. 1, '64.
Payne, Wm. H., Nov. 1, '64.

Posey, Carnot, Nov. 1, '62.
Preston, John S., June 10, '64.
Reynolds, D. H., Mar. 5, '64.
Stevens, W. H., Aug. 28, '64.
Terry, William, May 19, '64.

BRIGADIER-GENERALS
PROVISIONAL ARMY
(With Temporary Rank)

Anderson, R. H., July 26, '64.
Barry, John D., Aug. 3, '64.
Brantly, Wm. F., July 26, '64.
Browne, Wm. M., Nov. 11, '64.
Bullock, Robert, Nov. 29, '64.
Carter, John C., July 7, '64.
Cox, William R., May 31, '64.
Dubose, D. M., Nov. 16, '64.
Dunnovant, John, Aug. 22, '64.
Girardey, V. J. B., July 30, '64.
Gordon, Geo. W., Aug. 15, '64.
Harrison, T., Jan. 14, '65.
Hill, Benjamin J., Nov. 30, '64.
Holtzclaw, J. T., July 7, '64.
Johnson, B. T., June 28, '64.
Johnson, G. D., July 26, '64.
Kennedy, J. D., Dec. 22, '64.
Lewis, Wm. G., May 31, '64.
Lilley, Robt. D., May 31, '64.
Miller, William, Aug. 2, '64.
Palmer, Joseph B., Nov. 15, '64.
Robertson, F. H., July 26, '64.
Sanders, J. C. C., May 31, '64.
Sharp, Jacob H., July 26, '64.
Shelley, Chas. M., Sept. 17, '64.
Smith, T. B., July 29, '64.
Sorrell, G. Moxley, Oct. 27, '64.
Terrill, James B., May 31, '64.
Terry, Wm. R., May 31, '64.
Toon, Thomas F., May 31, '64.
Wallace, Wm. H., Sept. 20, '64.
York, Zebulon, May 31, '64.
Young, Wm. H., Aug. 15, '64.

BRIGADIER-GENERALS
FOR SERVICE WITH VOLUNTEER TROOPS
(With Temporary Rank)

Armstrong, F. C., Jan. 20, '63.
Dearing, James, April 29, '64.
Thomas, Bryan M., Aug. 4, '64.

The following were assigned to duty as general officers by Gen. E. Kirby Smith commanding the Trans-Mississippi Department, and served as such.

Green, Cullen.
Gordon, B. Frank.
Harrison, G. P. J.
Jackman, S. D.
Lewis, Leven M.
Maclay, Robt. P.
Munford, Thomas T.
Pearce, N. B.
Randall, Horace.

Assigned to duty as brigadier-general by Major-General Fitzhugh Lee and served as such though not appointed by the President or confirmed.

Terrell, Alex. W., May 16, '65.

Richard L. Page Commanded the Defenses of Mobile Bay.

Carter L. Stevenson, Active Division Leader in the West.

Henry A. Wise, Defender of Petersburg in 1864.

CONFEDERATE GENERALS

No. 25

VIRGINIA (CONTINUED)

William Terry Led a Brigade in Lee's Army.

James E. Slaughter, Inspector-General of the Army of Tennessee.

John McCausland, Cavalry Leader in the Shenandoah Valley.

William H. Payne, Leader of the Black Horse Cavalry.

Alexander W. Reynolds Led a Brigade in the Army of Tennessee.